MISSISSIPPI POLITICS

MISSISSIPPI POLITICS

The Struggle for Power, 1976–2006

JERE NASH AND ANDY TAGGART

FOREWORD BY JOHN GRISHAM

UNIVERSITY PRESS OF MISSISSIPPI

JACKSON

www.upress.state.ms.us

The University Press of Mississippi is a member of the
Association of American University Presses.

First edition 2006

∞

Library of Congress Cataloging-in-Publication Data

Nash, Jere.
   Mississippi politics : the struggle for power, 1976–2006 / Jere Nash and
Andy Taggart ; foreword by John Grisham. — 1st ed.
      p. cm.
   Includes bibliographical references and index.
   ISBN-13: 978-1-57806-907-1 (cloth : alk. paper)
   ISBN-10: 1-57806-907-6 (cloth : alk. paper) 1. Mississippi—Politics and
government—1951– 2. Political parties—Mississippi—History. 3. Power
(Social sciences)—Mississippi—History. 4. Politicians—Mississippi—
Interviews. I. Taggart, Andy. II. Title.
F345.N37 2006
976.2'063—dc22   2006017300

British Library Cataloging-in-Publication Data available

For Holly and Oliver
FROM JERE

and

In memory of my dad, who taught me to think for myself
FROM ANDY

CONTENTS

FOREWORD

My career in Mississippi politics was practically over before it began, and you'd need to dust the state capitol for fingerprints to find anything I left behind. Once elected, in 1983 at the age of twenty-eight, I never warmed up to the job.

I ran for a seat in the legislature for two reasons. The first was very practical—I knew I could win. The gentleman who'd represented my corner of DeSoto County had served in the House of Representatives long enough, and I was confident I could take him out. I spent $5,000 and knocked on 3,000 doors and won easily. One of the first campaign contributions was mailed in by Jere Nash, then an operative with some semi-shadowy do-gooder outfit that was preaching responsible government and progressive policies. Jere's office was in the same Jackson building with the only known gay rights advocate in the state, and it wasn't long before my opponent linked things together. I was soon on the ropes, defending the $500 gift and wishing I could send it back.

The second reason, the only one of real substance, was frustration. I was upset because the legislature placed so little emphasis on education. Growing up in Mississippi, I was painfully aware that my state was the only one without a kindergarten system.

Moments after taking office in January of 1984, I lined up on the wrong side of House Speaker Buddie Newman. It was a symbolic fight by some young hotshots, and when the bloodletting was over I was lucky to have a parking space and a desk. I was three hours away from home, too far for a daily commute. I was stuck at the state capitol with little to do.

So I began writing my first novel. I also began taking notes. Some of the finest storytellers around were these seasoned politicians who arrived from every corner of the state, and, with plenty of time on their hands, polished their material. There were certain spots in the bowels of the capitol where they would congregate, usually around a coffee pot, and exchange outrageous and hilarious stories. As a harmless rookie, I was allowed to sit and listen. There were times when I laughed until I ached.

(The party ended for me when word leaked that I was writing something. After that, when I walked upon a group, things became very quiet.)

(About those notes. I still plan to write a big thick novel about Mississippi politics, complete with all of the stories and lies and tall tales I have stolen over the years, but, frankly, I'm waiting for some of the characters to pass on. I wouldn't want to embarrass anyone, nor do I want to get sued, again.)

Though not exactly a major force in the legislative process, I did, however, by virtue of the wisdom of the voters back in DeSoto County, have a ring-side seat. Things were changing in Mississippi. Slowly, as always. The state had finally approved a kindergarten system, and funding it and the rest of public education was a mammoth struggle. The Black Caucus was growing in number and gaining clout. So were the Republicans.

Reform was in the air. For decades the state had been controlled by a handful of cranky old mossbacks who frowned on education and industry and new ideas. They usually came from small towns in dry counties and the annual legislative sessions in the big city of Jackson were full of parties and all manner of socializing. This was more important than meaningful legislation.

Local governments were plagued by corruption and inefficiencies. Roads and highways were not being built. Colleges and universities were begging for money. Anyway, there were lots of problems, and few solutions. But there was an atmosphere of being fed up. How long would we be fiftieth in every category?

The young reformers took the capitol by storm in the 1987 elections. Ray Mabus, with a Harvard law degree, was elected governor, after serving four years as state auditor (every office is elected in Mississippi), a position that enabled him to terrorize the good-ole-boys who'd been plundering county coffers forever. Mike Moore was elected attorney general; Marshall Bennett as treasurer. Dick Molpus was the secretary of state. All were young and energetic and the future looked very promising.

At least for some. I picked the wrong guy for Speaker again in 1988, and was once again banished to the sidelines. I resumed my secret writing career, and in April of that year, while at the capitol, received the magical phone call from New York. My first novel was going to be published! I was suddenly tired of law and tired of politics, and it was time to move on. I finally resigned in 1990, after seven very unproductive years in the House. Someone else needed the job. I had finished two books and was racing off in a different direction.

Andy Taggart arrived on the scene about the time I was leaving, and we did not know each other. He was also on the other side of the street from Jere Nash and me, not that it mattered a great deal back then. Things were much more civilized and much less partisan. Their balanced collaboration has produced this wonderful history of the changing of Mississippi politics.

When I arrived at the capitol in January of 1984, the House and Senate had a few black members, a handful of Republicans, everyone else was a white Democrat, the governor (never a Republican) could not succeed himself and was constitutionally overshadowed by the legislature, the state's boards and commissions were stacked with cronies, horse racing was a hot issue but the Baptists killed it, a few radicals wanted a state lottery, and the notion of casino gambling was so farfetched that it was never discussed.

Mississippi has a rich history of colorful politics, but the changes in the past thirty years have been astounding. In the pages that follow, Jere Nash and Andy Taggart present a lively account of the fight for political power.

JOHN GRISHAM
May 21, 2006

PREFACE

In the winter of 2004, when we approached the University Press of Mississippi
with the idea for this book, our proposal was straightforward—document the
contemporary political history of our state, using interviews with participants
as our primary resource. It had been nearly thirty years since Mississippi last
voted for a Democratic presidential candidate—Jimmy Carter in 1976—hence
our decision to begin with that year. Democrats controlled state government
in 1976; now they are struggling to retain a modest amount of power. We proposed to explain that development as part of our overall chronicle of the events
and movements that define the politics of today.

By the time we delivered our manuscript to the Press two years later, we
had concluded that our original proposal had been too narrow. First, we realized our inquiry was ultimately about the acquisition and exercise of political power, not merely partisan transformation. The growth of the Republican
Party, at the expense of the Democratic Party, only partially explained the current political landscape in the state. The role of the legislature, the struggle for
power between the governor and the legislature, and the influence of voting
rights and reapportionment in empowering black Mississippians were equally
important topics.

Second, the more we tried to understand the events of 1976, the more we
found ourselves examining the years leading up to that pivotal year. As it
turned out, 1976 was not the start of something new, but instead a climax—
the fortunes of Democrats have been headed downhill ever since. To understand why, we worked our way back to discover the origins of the modern
Democratic and Republican parties in Mississippi. Much of what happened
in 1976 and in the years that followed had its genesis in the preceding

generation—a period stretching from the early civil rights initiatives of President Truman in 1948 through the Supreme Court's *Brown v. Board of Education* decision to the passage of the Civil Rights and Voting Rights acts and up to the school desegregation orders in the early 1970s. For these reasons, we open this book with two chapters that explore the beginnings of the political parties—and what they represent—as we know them today. In many ways, then, this book is an exploration of politics in Mississippi that followed the civil rights movement.

Finally, why write this book at all? History reminds us that the world in which we live is not of our own doing. Men and women in public life inherit a political terrain that was forged long before they walked onto the playing field. It has been our experience that those who recognize this tend to be the most successful.

Teddy Roosevelt summed up another reason why we wrote this book when he once honored individuals who chose to leave the sidelines and enter the fray: "The credit belongs to the man in the arena whose face is marred by dust and sweat and blood, who strives valiantly, who errs, and who comes up short again and again, who knows the great enthusiasms, the great devotions, and spends himself in a worthy cause. The man who at best knows the triumph of high achievement and who at worst, if he fails, fails while daring greatly." We undertook this endeavor to record the lives of those who have participated in the arena of Mississippi politics. We could have told the historical facts of the period we cover in fewer pages, but the ways in which individuals made that history would have been left untold. We hope the lives we depict will inspire younger generations to consider careers in public service.

In the end, though, power and politics are worthy subjects of study for the simple reason that the exercise of power and the practice of politics have real consequences for the 2.9 million Americans who call Mississippi their home. It matters when people ask and think about the kind of elementary, secondary, community college, and university education systems Mississippi will support; how many and what kinds of jobs will be created; what effort will be made to protect and conserve the environment; whether highways and bridges, so critical to a rural state, will be maintained and expanded; what kind of effort will be expended, and at what level of funding, to prosecute crime; and the extent to which the state will provide services to the nearly one-fifth of Mississippians at or below the poverty line. Politics is how we resolve those issues. The study of politics is how we understand them.

ACKNOWLEDGMENTS

The people who made this book possible are, of course, the people who made the history we have recorded. We interviewed 115 of them—some over the phone searching for a specific nugget of information, others for hours in person, letting them tell their life stories to us. Five of the people we interviewed died during the course of this three-year project, while six others passed away before we could arrange an interview. We read transcripts of interviews that others had conducted with another seventy men and women who participated in Mississippi's political history. The people we interviewed were all generous with their time, their memories, and their opinions. It is a rare privilege indeed to spend two or three hours with so many individuals and have the opportunity to record their life experiences. The list of the people we interviewed and the oral histories we read are included in the sources and notes. We are grateful that the University of Mississippi has agreed to archive the digital recordings and to Andy Mullins and Jennifer Ford for making this happen.

The largest collection of oral histories in Mississippi is at the Center for Oral History and Cultural Heritage at the University of Southern Mississippi and represents one of our state's historical treasures. More than 4,000 oral histories are on file at the center, pertinent to a wide range of historical inquiry. We are grateful for the help we received from the center's staff—Stephen Sloan, Curtis Austin, Sue Rodriguez, and Linda Vanzandt—in responding to our many questions and requests for copies of transcribed interviews.

For nearly the entire duration of this three-year project, David Warrington worked full-time with us, providing all manner of research assistance. His home was the Mississippi Department of Archives and History, where he spent most days reading and copying relevant articles from the collection of Mississippi daily and weekly newspapers the Archives maintains, many dating back to the early 1800s; sifting through their collection of oral histories; and obtaining copies of articles from the many journals they have on file. David, we thank you for your devotion to this project, and we join David in expressing our appreciation to the entire Archives staff for their generous cooperation, especially Clinton I. Bagley, Joyce Dixon-Lawson, Grady Howell Jr., De'Niecechsi Layton, and Anne Webster.

We spent countless hours at the Mississippi Law Library, where in addition to taking full advantage of its quiet spaces for writing, we relied on the legislative journals and records of court cases dating back to early statehood as well as full access to the library's rare book room, where we read books and pamphlets we would not have found anywhere else. The Law Library staff—Charlie Pearce, Liz Thompson, and Geraldine Bell—were always helpful and supportive.

We were fortunate that the three years we spent writing this book coincided with Kyle Kendall's tenure as a student at Millsaps College and Nancy Brown's sabbatical from her teaching position in Jackson. Every other week or so we would give Kyle and Nancy a list of graduate theses or dissertations, scholarly journal or law review articles, an elusive piece from some out-of-state newspaper, or books long out of print and ask for copies. The request was simple, the execution anything but. Kyle made good use of the holdings and the interlibrary loan program at the Millsaps College Library, while Nancy searched the Internet or the shelves and the microfilm collection of the Eudora Welty Library or had the document shipped to us through Welty's interlibrary loan program. Both Kyle and Nancy were unrelenting in fulfilling our requests, a determination that earned our admiration and gratitude.

The interviews we conducted generated over 275 hours of digital recordings, many of which were faithfully transcribed by Kay Barksdale, Lucian Dixon, Suzette Watts, and Terri Henderson and her staff at The Executive Level.

For reading portions of the manuscript and offering countless improvements to our early drafts, we thank Henry Barbour, Gil Carmichael, Danny Cupit, Wayne Edwards, Marcie Fyke, Todd Gee, Ray Mabus, Les McLemore, Dick Molpus, Billy Mounger, Luther Munford, Steve Patterson, Charles Pickering, Clarke Reed, Lance Stevens, Bennie Thompson, William Winter, and Wirt Yerger. Louisa Dixon and Charles Sallis read and critiqued the entire manuscript and were a constant source of encouragement and good advice.

Other friends we want to thank who provided help along the way include Libby Cajoleas, Paulette Collins, Bessie Grant, John Horhn, Pam Johnson, Peter Koury, Melody McAnally, Danny McDaniel, Tom Rhoden, Carol Joy and Tommy Sparkman, and John Waits.

The three years we spent on this work were underwritten by the Mississippi History Project, Inc., a nonprofit, tax-exempt organization established to preserve and record the state's history. Our family and friends who made very generous contributions of their time and their money to the fund and thus made this book possible were Paul Benton, Jaye Calhoun, George Casey, Danny Cupit, John A. Eaves Jr., Jerry Johnson, Joey Langston, Bill Liston, Mike McRee, Bill Mendenhall, Alan Moore, Lane Murray, Margie and Jere Nash, Joe Nash, Janet and Luther Ott, Hugh Parker, Crymes Pittman, Len Sanderson, Richard Scruggs, Jim Waide, Ginger Weaver, and Leila Wynn.

It was nearly three years ago when we first approached Seetha Srinivasan at the University Press of Mississippi about publishing this book. She liked the idea from the very start and told us to begin writing. To Seetha and her entire staff, we thank you for your confidence in us and your commitment to this project. Copyeditor Robert Burchfield's keen eye and attention to detail saved us from many embarrassing mistakes.

In one sense, this book is about origins: the beginning of the modern Democratic and Republican parties in Mississippi, the first reapportionment lawsuit, the source of legislative power, and the events that began to compromise it. While there have been hundreds of people who have influenced our political careers and who deserve recognition, we wanted to close these acknowledgments by recognizing and thanking those who got us started. For Jere Nash, it was Kathleen Stewart Richey, John Price, Bill Junkin, Joe Yoder, and Dick Schneider. For Andy Taggart, it was Tom Hewlett, Pat Presley, Billy Hicks, Oliver Houck, and Lanny Griffith. Each of them saw some promise in us, nurtured us, and gave us opportunities to grow. Our political journeys since then would not have been possible without them. We are forever grateful.

JERE NASH
Jackson, Mississippi

ANDY TAGGART
Madison, Mississippi

MISSISSIPPI POLITICS

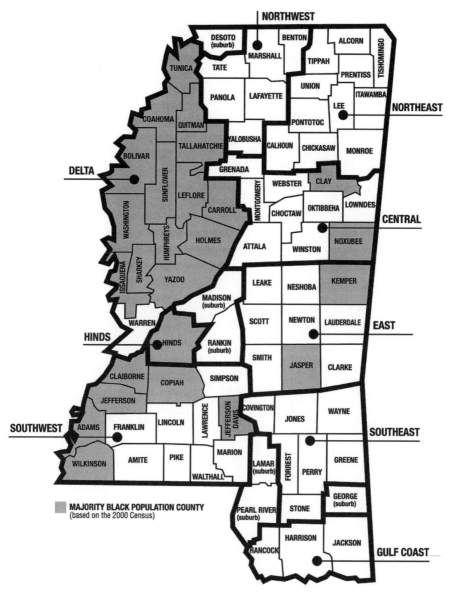

The geographical regions presented here were developed for the political campaign analyses referred to throughout the book.

INTRODUCTION

Power concedes nothing without a demand. It never did, and it never will.
  – FREDERICK DOUGLASS

This book is about political power—the quest for power and the use of power to govern Mississippi. In 1890, white Democrats consolidated their political power, and for more than seventy years, if you were not a white Democrat in Mississippi, you had no power. Two groups sought to change that equation: Republicans and African Americans.

In the decades following Reconstruction, Mississippi politics was characterized by the comment a young black girl once made to an aspiring candidate: "If you keep your foot on my neck and keep me in the ditch, you ain't going anywhere either."[1] White Democrats maintained political power by driving a psychological, legal, and economic wedge between white and black Mississippians. That strategy survived as long as it did because the state's political leaders knew instinctively what two scholars once observed about white Mississippians: "[Their] tendency to nurture traditions and to remember the past is but the natural inclination to look back to what was, and now seems to be, a brighter period. Their social heritage produces a fierce pride in their own history, customs, and institutions. . . . It also produces resentment against external criticism and resistance to outside reformers."[2] Elected officials created a political climate fueled by resentment and preserved by defiance. William Simmons, a leader of the Citizens' Council in the 1960s, once captured its spirit: "I was born in Mississippi . . . and I'm the product of my heredity and education and the society in which I was raised, and I have a vested interest in that society, and I along with a million other white Mississippians will do everything in our power to protect that vested interest.... It's primarily a struggle for power and I think we would be stupid indeed if we failed to see where the consequences of a supine surrender on our part would lead."³

Removing the government's foot off the collective neck of black men, women, and children was seen as nothing less than surrender, regardless of the consequences. As a result, the success of Mississippi politicians—and their reelection prospects—were "insured not by what they did for Mississippi, but by what they stopped."⁴ At the same time, any movement by Republicans was undermined by Democrats who conveniently blamed them for creating the problem in the first place. One early GOP candidate remembered vividly the response to his campaign: "[I received] telephone calls saying they were going to kidnap my children, burn my house, and that I should leave those damn Republicans alone. 'Hadn't your father ever told you about how it was during the depression?' they would ask. And that the Republicans were responsible for freeing the slaves?"⁵

Those politicians of a bygone era, all white and all Democrats, were incapable of change. And it cost them. And it cost the state. Their defiance led to federal intervention on a scale not seen since Reconstruction. Consequently, Republicans began to reacquire political power in Mississippi when large numbers of white voters abandoned a national Democratic Party they came to believe was sympathetic to the federal intervention. Barry Goldwater carried the state in 1964. Richard Nixon won it eight years later at the same time Thad Cochran and Trent Lott were first elected.

To stop the growth of Republicans, a coalition of Democrats formed in 1975 and 1976 that most thought was unbeatable. For those two campaigns, black voters joined with rural white voters first to elect Cliff Finch governor and then to carry Mississippi for Jimmy Carter. As 1976 came to a close, it appeared that a unified Democratic Party had found a way to maintain political power. The Democratic lineup included Governor Finch, Senators John Stennis and Jim Eastland, Congressmen Jamie Whitten and Sonny Montgomery, and all but five seats in the state legislature.

The honeymoon, however, was to be short-lived: 1976 was the last year Mississippi gave its electoral votes to a Democratic presidential candidate. Thirty years later, a Republican occupies the Governor's Mansion; four of the other seven statewide elected officials are Republicans; the seats once held by Stennis, Eastland, Whitten, and Montgomery are now filled by Republicans; and the GOP has 71 of the 174 members in the state legislature.

The civil rights revolution was the impetus for the nascent growth of the Republican Party. That transformation was predicted by Lyndon Johnson on the day he signed the Civil Rights Act of 1964 when he told an aide, "I think we just delivered the South to the Republican Party for a long time to come."[6] But as many white Mississippians were beginning to accept the changes wrought by the civil rights revolution, Republicans continued to attract white voters because of a cleansing process forced on the two national parties. In the decades leading up to the 1960 presidential election, the country's two major parties embraced the full range of political ideologies. The Republicans mixed the "northeastern liberalism" of Nelson Rockefeller with the middle-of-the-road image of Dwight Eisenhower and the more ideologically conservative Barry Goldwater. The Democrats maintained a "big tent" for southern Democrats like Jim Eastland, the middle-of-the-road Adlai Stevenson, and the more liberal Hubert Humphrey. Working in both parties, activists sought to sharpen and narrow the public policy positions of each party and purge those who disagreed. This process of definition, which began in 1960 and reached its apex in 1984 with the re-election of Ronald Reagan, is the key to the transformation of what used to be the one-party Democratic South. By 1984, Republicans would proudly proclaim themselves conservative while Democrats were stuck with the liberal label. While those words would take on different meanings with different people, they gradually began to signify where the two parties stood on a broad range of cultural issues. And for better or for worse, the overwhelming majority of white Mississippians are "conservative" on all of them.

The movement of whites to the Republican Party was sustained after the 1970s because the overall temperament and outlook of the average Mississippi white voter, insofar as he or she relates to politics, have been and continue to be almost exclusively influenced by the voter's cultural perspective, as opposed to economic considerations. For generations, race dominated the culture of the South. It was the exclusive criterion applied to the acceptability of public officials. Today, race has been absorbed into a broader panoply of cultural issues as religious leaders, women, homosexuals, and other activists have entered the world of politics with their own demands. To the average white Mississippian, school prayer, the Ten Commandments, abortion, gay marriage, and gun control have joined affirmative action, quotas, and school busing to form a juggernaut of cultural issues that can easily undermine a Democrat's quest for public office.

Three factors prevented the movement of whites from the Democratic Party to the Republican Party from happening overnight.

First was the nearly hundred-year old habit of voting Democrat. Talk with any Republican activist from the 1950s and 1960s, and he or she will echo what GOP activist Gil Carmichael once said: "Those first races were teaching people they wouldn't turn green when they voted Republican."[7]

Next was the reservoir of power incumbent Democrats had built up as a result of that voting habit. Republicans were not asking to join the Democratic Party; they were attempting its overthrow. Those in power quite naturally fought it, regardless of the labels appended to their names on the ballot.

Finally, there was seniority. Particularly in Congress and in the state legislature, voters were reluctant to give up the benefits that accrue to states and localities when their elected officials chair important committees or serve in leadership positions. Consequently, Republicans have largely made their gains over the years by winning open seats vacated by retiring Democrats or convincing incumbent Democrats to switch parties.

Black Mississippians journeyed an altogether different road to political power. They first had to regain the right to vote. For all practical purposes, African Americans in Mississippi did not enjoy that right until after the passage of the Voting Rights Act in 1965. White Democrats then used reapportionment—the drawing of district boundaries—to thwart that right until federal judges intervened nearly fifteen years later. Arranging the district lines of Mississippi's congressional delegation and of the 174 members of the state House and Senate had more to do with altering and rearranging the allocation of political power in the state than any other issue we will explore in this book and is why reapportionment was the most vexing and contentious issue the Mississippi legislature confronted over the last thirty years.

For Republicans and African Americans, winning elections was the means to achieving power. With power, they could determine public policy. And that brings us to the state capitol. Entering Mississippi's capitol building from the north side and walking up the stairs to emerge onto the third floor, the visitor would find that the governor's office lies directly across the rotunda; to the right is the chamber of the House of Representatives and to the left is the Senate chamber—the three centers of political power in Mississippi are all located within yards of one another. If there is a favorite observation of political pundits in the state, it is that Mississippi has a weak governor and a strong legislature. That is, most of the power to affect public policy ultimately resides with the legislature. As with any piece of conventional wisdom, political life in the capital city has never been that simple, though there is no question that the legislature has long enjoyed the upper hand. As a result, over the years, for both Republicans and African Americans, the focus of their quest for power was most often the legislature.

Two events occurred in 1982—an education reform movement headed by Governor William Winter and a lawsuit filed by Attorney General Bill Allain— that would signal a shift of power to the governor, a development fully realized after Republican Haley Barbour became governor and Republican Amy Tuck was reelected lieutenant governor in 2003. As the subsequent legislative sessions progressed, it became clear that the governor and the Senate were acting in concert, arrayed against a more populist House still in nominal control by Democrats. For the first time, a governor had split the legislature, not just on one issue but on most substantive issues. The institutional memory of the legislature was such that, previously, issues had always been decided on the basis of race or geography or economics or religion. With a lifelong Republican activist as governor and with the largest concentration of Republicans in the legislature since Reconstruction, party affiliation became a dominant factor in legislative votes: legislative issues were debated as Republican issues or Democratic issues, a shift in context unprecedented in contemporary Mississippi political history.

During the first two years of Barbour's term, on virtually all critical issues, the Senate became an extension of the governor's office, representing the Republican position on public policies, while the House, led by its Democratic Speaker, Billy McCoy, came to represent the Democratic position. The conflicts generating the widest coverage by the media were funding for the state's Medicaid program and for elementary and secondary education. By the end of the 2004 session, reporters were observing that "potentially disruptive partisanship is brewing at the Capitol."[8] While Hurricane Katrina has moderated the partisan approach to governing as this book is going to press, and the lieutenant governor and the Senate appear to be charting a course more independent of the governor's lead, the role of party will no doubt become more and more influential at the state capitol.

Because politics is ultimately about what men and women do with the power they gain after winning elections, we spend a significant portion of this book describing how the exercise of power at the legislature has changed over the last thirty to forty years. We do this chiefly by focusing on public policy issues that resulted in systemic changes in the way legislators engage in the business of politics and government. These include the 1982 Education Reform Act, the 1982–1984 litigation removing legislators from executive branch boards and commissions, the 1987 Four-Lane Highway program, the successful effort in 1989 and 1990 to legalize casino gaming, and the struggle over tort reform between trial lawyers, on one side, and business and health care interests, on the other, a struggle that consumed the legislature from January 2002 until May 2004.

The monumental education, highway, and gaming measures would not have been adopted without the changes imposed on the legislature by reapportionment. Those changes were twofold: more urban and more black members were elected, and legislators were elected from single-member districts, making it easier for voters to hold them accountable for their performance in office. The passage of tort reform legislation was made possible by the influx of Republican legislators.

In the history we document, we show that many of the political changes experienced in Mississippi came as a result of larger forces at work throughout the country. The breakdown of the Democratic "solid South" and the empowerment of black voters were national movements that Mississippi could not resist, though the state's white Democratic elected officials held out longer than most. In one sense, it is a story captured by historian Neil McMillen: "I've come to the conclusion in studying history that human agency, what we do as human beings, has to move with the grain of time, with the grain of history. This moving against the grain of history, these social movements [can't sustain themselves]. We don't hear about them. The movements that succeed are the movements where human agents are working with a changing, evolving, relatively welcoming historical structure."[9]

On the other hand, the historical movements identified by McMillen make possible the change, but don't guarantee it. It takes individuals of vision, courage, and ambition to recognize a "welcoming historical structure" on the horizon and then use it to advance political goals and political transformations. This phenomenon happened over and over again in Mississippi during the years about which we write. White Democrats reared in the 1950s and 1960s were forced to concede power, not because they wanted to, but because others used litigation, legislation, and campaign organizing to make demands that were too formidable to withstand.

CHAPTER 1

HISTORY OF MISSISSIPPI DEMOCRATS

1948–1975

The Black man, because of the tyranny of racism over the mind of the white South, has been able, without intention or knowledge, to dominate Southern political and governmental life. . . . Whites fell into the trap they had so cleverly and determinedly made for blacks: absolute dominion. . . . The Negro, like a fearsome ghost, has haunted and driven the white man.
—SAMUEL DUBOIS COOK[1]

We believe in the separation of races in all phases of our society.
—Resolution adopted by the Mississippi Democratic Party, 1964[2]

The second-most tumultuous period in Mississippi's history—1960 to 1965—occurred a hundred years after the first. It was in the summer of 1860 that the Mississippi delegation walked out of the national Democratic Convention.[3] The protest was sparked by the convention's failure to support slavery in the territories. Six months later, Mississippi seceded from the Union. The Civil War came to a close in the state in the spring of 1865 when General Richard Taylor surrendered what remained of Mississippi's troops.

The Reconstruction Acts of 1867 vested black males with the right to vote. Within a few years, 60,167 black men were registered to vote, compared to only 46,636 white men.[4] White Democrats soon realized that winning control of state government through the legitimate use of the ballot box was unlikely. Using force and intimidation in the elections of 1875, white Democrats seized power from the Republicans who had enforced Reconstruction and enfranchised the newly freed slaves. Historians James Loewen and Charles Sallis described a campaign where "undeclared war raged up and down the state." In Aberdeen on election day, a white militia company trained cannons on the polls, while at a precinct in Claiborne County, whites stacked guns near the polls and dug trenches. Armed white men "accidentally" fired shots near black voters, and in "some places graves were dug and Negroes told they would be put there if they voted Republican."[5] Another historian, Bradley Bond, concluded, "The Democratic policy of rule or ruin had successfully proven itself. So staggering had the violence been that even though a federal grand jury believed it could indict thousands of election law violators, it chose not to, fearing additional violence."[6] Not surprisingly, the Democrats carried the state. The successful use of illegal methods and brute force to win campaigns became known as the Mississippi Plan and was modeled by whites in other states to overthrow Republican rule.[7]

The following year, and for each of the succeeding seventeen presidential elections, the state of Mississippi gave its electoral votes to the Democratic nominee. That string of victories came to a halt in 1948.

THE DIXIECRATS AND MASSIVE RESISTANCE: 1948–1959

A candidate for reelection in 1948, President Harry Truman called on Congress to abolish poll taxes, make lynching a criminal offense, and ban segregation in interstate transportation. Truman then issued an executive order barring discrimination in the armed forces.[8] At the Democratic National Convention that summer, the delegates adopted a strongly worded platform in support of civil rights. It was too much for Mississippi's white Democrats. Reminiscent of 1860, Governor Fielding Wright led the way for the entire Mississippi delegation to walk out, along with half of the Alabama delegates. Advocates of "states' rights" then met in Birmingham and nominated South Carolina Governor Strom Thurmond for president and Wright for vice president.[9] The Dixiecrat Party of 1948 was born.

By the time Truman proposed his civil rights initiatives, the separation of black and white lives, and the near total subordination of blacks to whites, was the reality in Mississippi. For all practical purposes, blacks could not vote or serve on juries. Unless separate accommodations and entrances were provided, blacks were not allowed into public theaters, parks, circuses, restaurants, bowling alleys, roller rinks, swimming pools, tennis courts, hotels, motels, and barbershops. Cities maintained three restrooms in train stations: one for white men, one for white women, and one for "colored." Taxi drivers could not carry a black passenger and a white passenger at the same time. Blacks had to sit behind white passengers on buses. Railroad cars, railroad waiting rooms, and buses had separate accommodations for blacks and whites. Blacks in Mississippi went to separate schools, lived in separate neighborhoods, and were buried in separate cemeteries. Even in hospitals, black and white patients were treated in separate quarters and were prevented from using the same entrances. Anyone found guilty of publishing "arguments or suggestions in favor of social equality or intermarriage" could be imprisoned. The manifestation of the relationship between blacks and whites was found everyday in the signs that hung over entrances and exits, water fountains, waiting rooms, and ticket windows: "Whites Only" and "Colored."[10]

The essential nature of this environment for the Democratic Party was explained by Charles Sallis: "The mere presence of the politically impotent Negro, then, was the cause of the 'Solid South' and the continuance of the Democratic Party as the 'White Man's Party.' The identification of party with race was complete. The Democratic Party became a closed corporation, open to whites only. One was born into the party; to question the party which prevented Negro equality was to question the 'Southern Way of Life.' "[11]

This "way of life" is what the leaders of the Dixiecrat Party knew was at stake. If they could garner enough electoral votes to deny either President Truman or Thomas Dewey, the Republican nominee, a majority of the Electoral College, then the House of Representatives would decide the election, and the Dixiecrats would be in a strong position to influence the outcome, in return for pledges to abandon civil rights initiatives.[12]

Yet the Dixiecrats failed to grasp how the country had changed. Black men had served with white men in World War II. The economy was moving from one dominated by agriculture to one dominated by manufacturing and trade, and, consequently, racially diverse cities were growing and becoming more politically important, at the expense of rural areas. And a steady migration of blacks from the South to the North, where they could get decent jobs and vote, had transformed them into a growing force to be reckoned with at the polls, a situation that had not gone unnoticed by northern Democrats.[13]

While America was transforming itself, southern white Democrats ignored the political implications. The results of the 1948 election should have been a warning: only four states voted for the Thurmond-Wright ticket: South Carolina, Mississippi, Louisiana, and Alabama. Former Governor William

Winter, who watched the 1948 revolt as a newly elected state representative, later summed up the outcome: "Truman's upset victory over Dewey without the support of the Solid South thus nullified the elaborate efforts to throw the election into the House of Representatives. More importantly, it demonstrated that the Democratic Party no longer had to rely on Southern support to win."[14] Clark Clifford, an adviser to President Truman, remarked after the 1948 election: "The Negro vote in the crucial [northern] states will more than cancel out any votes the President may lose in the South."[15] Rather than turn the South into a force to be reckoned with, the Dixiecrats had instead converted the South into a force to be ignored.

The decade following the Dixiecrat movement was characterized by Mississippi politicians playing the race card during campaigns back home while holding their collective nose to work within the national Democratic Party structure. This ability to maintain credibility with the national party was due partly to the two governors Mississippi voters elected: Hugh White in 1951 and J. P. Coleman in 1955, who, while segregationists, did not allow race to define their entire outlook on public policy.[16] It was also due to the Democrats regaining control of both the U.S. Senate and House of Representatives in the 1948 elections, yielding the fruits of the seniority system to the state's congressional delegation, all Democrats. Governor White ushered the state back into the good graces of the national party in 1952 when Illinois Governor Adlai Stevenson was nominated for president. Stevenson helped mend fences with southern delegations by choosing Alabama Senator John Sparkman as his running mate and by encouraging the Democratic convention to adopt a civil rights plank Governor White could tolerate.[17]

Then came May 17, 1954. Mississippi Congressman John Bell Williams was the first to declare it "Black Monday."[18] The U.S. Supreme Court had issued its unanimous opinion in *Brown v. Board of Education*. With this one decision, the legal rationale for segregation was destroyed, upending the entire southern way of life.[19]

Considering the immense pressures faced by a white people who believed their entire way of life was threatened, the dramatic response to *Brown* is at least comprehensible. Neil McMillen once described the context:

[Many Southerners thought] they would have to leave the United States if black people were given human rights because it would be the end of the world. Our way of life, which had been ingrained in them, presupposed black degradation

[14]

and white supremacy and any change in that would destroy the world. . . .
They valued white skin and white supremacy more than the rule of law, more
than their own religious faith actually. . . . This state was bombarded with neo-
orthodox racial thinking from the pulpit rather like the 1850s in the march up
to the war. From the pulpit, from university lecterns, from newspapers, from
television stations, from every corner . . . the wagons were circled.[20]

Still, looking back on it more than fifty years later, what actually happened
in Mississippi is scarcely believable. The Speaker of the Mississippi House of
Representatives, Walter Sillers, asserted that "the only thing for the state to do
is to go out of the public education business."[21] In its famous front-page editorial, "Bloodstains on White Marble Steps," the *Jackson Daily News* sought to
legitimize violence as a response to *Brown*: "Human blood may stain Southern soil in many places because of this decision, but the dark red stains of
that blood will be on the marble steps of the United States Supreme Court
building."[22]

Despite the evidence that what worked in 1875 could not work eighty years
later, the public and private white leadership in Mississippi, with but few exceptions, waged an unrelenting war against the efforts of the federal government
and the increasingly organized and motivated black citizenry to repeal segregation. The consequence, as William Winter has noted, was that it "became
difficult to consider significant issues outside the context of this one overriding
concern. The result was that much of the energy of the people was consumed
in this struggle, and many other pressing needs were neglected or deferred."[23]

The day-to-day coverage by the national press of what happened during the
next ten years in Mississippi is both voluminous and remarkable. The books,
journal articles, and graduate dissertations that have been written after the fact
would fill a small library. The summary that follows here does not pretend to
capture the richness and poignancy of the available literature. The reasons
for all the national attention become obvious after reading even a portion of
the history of the period. There is an old observation that journalists love to
cover a conflict. Mississippi more than satisfied their appetite. The nation's
reactions to *Brown* and all the subsequent events of that day were at their most
outlandish, their most violent, and their most unrelenting in Mississippi. As
New York Times reporter Anthony Lewis explained: "The revolution that so
profoundly changed American race relations between 1954 and 1964 stopped
at the borders of Mississippi."[24]

No sooner had *Brown* been issued than Tom Brady, a state judge from Lincoln County, wrote and published *Black Monday*, which for many became the intellectual justification to oppose the decision. The subtitle reveals much about the prevailing state of mind at the time: "Segregation or Amalgamation . . .America Has Its Choice."[25] That summer, the first Citizens' Council was organized in Indianola to fight the "all-out war being waged against the white race." Within two years, more than 80,000 Mississippians had joined, and the councils were exercising significant political influence throughout the South. "Institutionalized bigotry in a more or less respectable setting"[26] is how one writer later characterized the group that by 1956 had established a national headquarters in Greenwood.[27]

In the fall of 1954, the state legislature approved and the voters ratified a constitutional amendment that would authorize the abolishment of the public school system, a provision the legislature never used.[28] Stone County Representative Joel Blass was one of the most vocal opponents of the 1954 constitutional amendment authorizing the legislature to abolish public schools. The Citizens' Council targeted him for defeat in 1955, and sent some of their members to "see an old man named Hester out in the western part of Blass's district." As Blass remembered:

> *Mr. Hester had a habit of holding his head way back and squinting. They watched him plow around till he got back up to the side of the road where they stopped the car. They got out and started to talk to Mr. Hester about what a bad man I was. And they talked and talked, and they wound up and said, "By the way, I don't hold it against him, but he's a Catholic." So, Mr. Hester chewed on his straw a minute and squinted and then spat chewing tobacco, and he said, "Well, I'll tell you, I don't give a damn if he's a priest. I'm going to vote for him. He don't let the bastards piss on him."[29]*

In August 1955, Emmett Till was lynched in Tallahatchie County, and Mississippi became a focal point for coverage of civil rights by national and international media. In a dramatic trial, Till's killers were acquitted in the "first great media event of the civil rights movement." But the verdict emboldened blacks in Mississippi and became a "frame of reference" for the activists who were beginning the movement.[30]

As 1955 came to a close, an event in Montgomery, Alabama, reverberated throughout the nation: Rosa Parks was arrested when she refused to surrender her seat on a bus to a white rider. That night black leaders organized a boycott of city buses. Numan Bartley describes what happened next: "The discipline and dignity of blacks, the nonviolent philosophy that Martin Luther King developed and articulated during the protest, and King's leadership captured the imagination of journalists and national liberals. The sometimes devious, sometimes bullying, and always inept white leadership in Montgomery lent contrast and drama." A year later, the Supreme Court outlawed segregated buses.[31]

The Mississippi legislature created the State Sovereignty Commission in 1956, and embarked on a public relations campaign on behalf of segregation. For the next ten years, the commission "spied on civil rights workers, acted as a clearinghouse for information on civil rights activities . . .[and] funneled funds to pro-segregation causes."[32] As the Sovereignty Commission was being created, the southern states' congressional delegation took action. Nineteen of the region's twenty-two senators and 82 of the 106 representatives signed the "Southern Manifesto," condemning the Supreme Court's "unwarranted exercise" of "naked judicial power" and applauding the "motives of those states which have declared the intention to resist forced integration by any lawful means."[33] Every member of Congress from Mississippi signed it.

In September 1957, Mississippians felt the threat worsen when Congress enacted the first civil rights legislation since Reconstruction.[34] Then the South's darkest nightmare became real: President Eisenhower ordered federal troops to Little Rock, Arkansas, to ensure the integration of Central High School. It was President Dwight Eisenhower versus Governor Orval Faubus. It was the federal government versus the state government. It was the authority of the federal courts to see their rulings enforced versus the authority of state politicians to defy those orders. Unlike 1875, the federal government would not ignore lawlessness; Eisenhower's bold play demonstrated the federal government's resolve to enforce judicial decrees.

By the time the 1959 elections in Mississippi came around, the pressure on the system had become too much. White voters chose a governor who would prove disastrous. In the Democratic primary that year, the candidates for governor were Lieutenant Governor Carroll Gartin, Jackson trial lawyer Ross Barnett, and Clarksdale District Attorney Charles Sullivan. Knowing that Gartin would be the frontrunner, the Citizens' Council and its followers sought a strong opponent. Not only was Gartin allied with outgoing Governor J. P. Coleman, branding him as a "moderate" on the race issue, but in 1954 he took the step that might have cost him the election in 1959: he ran against

Senator Jim Eastland.[35] Barnett thus became the candidate of choice, making his third try for the Governor's Mansion. Meanwhile, outgoing governor Coleman took the unusual step of running for the legislature, leading to rumors that his goal was to be Speaker. And once Hugh White endorsed Gartin, the opposition had a ready made issue: they demonized a "potential" White-Coleman-Gartin "dynasty." Barnett articulated the most strident positions on segregation and defeated Gartin in the runoff, with Eastland's help. Years later, a reporter captured an unrepentant Barnett in a 1983 interview: "'Oh yes, oh yes,' Barnett gleamed when asked if he had won any big lawsuits recently. 'Settled a big one not long ago . . . $125,000 for a 9-year-old Negro boy.' Then, as if to thumb his nose at 1983, he spelled it out: 'That's n-i-g-g-e-r.'"[36]

THE CIVIL RIGHTS MOVEMENT: 1960–1963

This long confluence of choices by white Mississippians then took the state on a dreadful course. In the Governor's Mansion was a man nourished by adulation, compelled to play to the crowds, dependent on the Citizens' Council and legislative leaders for political advice, and with neither the interest nor the backbone to challenge the status quo.[37]

Less than two weeks after Barnett's inauguration, black students at North Carolina Agricultural and Technical College took seats at a local Woolworth's lunch counter reserved for whites and refused to move until served. Bartley calls that event in February 1960, the day "the revolt against segregation began." Hundreds of students joined the protest, the national press gave the demonstration coverage, and soon students in other areas were engaged in their own lunch counter sit-ins. More than 50,000 people participated in protests in the spring of 1960. In October, the Student Nonviolent Coordinating Council (SNCC) was organized.[38]

Across the South, the pent-up frustrations of a hundred years of legalized segregation would not be turned back: change was coming. In Mississippi, though, "change" was not a word found in the white vocabulary.

In Biloxi, on the sunny afternoon of April 24, 1960, more than 125 black men, women, and children attempted to use the sandy beaches, which at the time were restricted to whites. They were assaulted by a large group of whites with pool sticks, clubs, chains, and lead pipes.[39] Meanwhile, the Citizens' Council moved front and center, enjoying "limitless access to the corridors of state power during the Barnett administration. Indeed, by forging political alliances and adroitly manipulating public opinion, it managed so thoroughly to obscure all distinction between public and private authority that by the early sixties the organization was the almost unchallenged arbiter of Mississippi politics."[40] Locked arm in arm with the Citizens' Council was the State Sovereignty Commission, which began to investigate virtually anyone suspected of being a "racial agitator."[41]

Into this volatile environment came the 1960 presidential election: Richard Nixon for the Republicans and John Kennedy for the Democrats. Ignoring the lesson of 1948, Barnett opted for the independent course, alone among southern states, and organized a slate of unpledged electors to oppose the major party nominees. At one level, his thinking was the same as Fielding Wright's twelve years earlier: if the election were close, Mississippi could use its electoral votes as leverage. But at a different level was naked defiance. Barnett told a meeting of his supporters: "whether this state has a say finally in the naming of the next president, Mississippians, when Kennedy or Nixon force integration on the south, can say to their children that 'We stood against it. . . . We did not put it on you.'"[42]

Unlike 1948, however, many top state Democratic officials carried out a strong campaign for Kennedy. By then Mississippi's congressional delegation had accumulated seniority, which could be at risk if they opposed the national ticket.[43] Barnett was unfazed: his "Unpledged" ticket carried the state.

The Freedom Riders arrived in Jackson in the spring of 1961. Choosing to confront the southern laws segregating bus transportation, a team of integrated bus riders set out to travel from Washington, D.C., to New Orleans. Attracting national media coverage, the buses met their first violence in Alabama, where mobs attacked the riders and firebombed the buses. Mississippi took a different approach. Once the riders crossed the Mississippi state line, a contingent of state troopers escorted them to Jackson, where police met them and herded them into jail cells.[44] Robert Moses arrived in McComb in the late summer to start a voter registration drive. A SNCC field organizer, Moses eventually became a leading SNCC worker in the state and the director of the 1964 "Freedom Summer" campaign.[45]

It was during this period that James Meredith began his journey to the University of Mississippi, in an attempt to become the first African American to enroll. He was not the first to try. In 1958, Clennon King attempted to register at Ole Miss. After Governor Coleman sealed off the campus and allowed King to appear at the registrar's office, King was then taken off campus and committed for two weeks to the state mental hospital.[46] The episode led Governor Coleman to observe that any black who would attempt to enter the all-white institution was, by definition, a "lunatic."[47]

Meredith, however, enjoyed the support of the U.S. government, though it required fourteen months of litigation by the National Association for the Advancement of Colored People (NAACP) and the Justice Department and ultimately the use of armed forces on campus to obtain his enrollment. At one point during the legal proceedings, the Fifth Circuit Court of Appeals could no longer contain its exasperation: "the [Meredith] case was tried below and argued here in the eerie atmosphere of never-never land."[48] On the night of September 13, 1962, after Governor Barnett had concluded a statewide television address calling on Mississippians to join him in opposing Meredith, a reporter asked state Representative Joe Wroten of Greenville, one of only two legislators who opposed Barnett, to comment. "In my opinion," Wroten remarked, "what [Barnett] has called for is anarchy and insurrection against the government of the United States of America. His so calling will lead to bloodshed and violence and rioting."[49]

By the time the state had run out of options, and Meredith's enrollment was imminent, state Senator E. K. Collins of Laurel was calling for victory, "regardless of the cost in money, regardless of the cost in prestige, and regardless of the cost in human life."[50] On the Saturday night before Meredith registered, and while Barnett was in the middle of negotiations with Attorney General Robert Kennedy, Ole Miss hosted Kentucky for a football game in Jackson. Barnett was there at Memorial Stadium. Historian Taylor Branch has described the scene:

> *The war fever of the political crisis boosted the normal emotions of the football rite to the heights of pandemonium, and by halftime the crowd was shouting 'We want Ross!' in a deafening roar. Barnett made his way to the fifty-yard line, where he raised a fist of defiance and cried out over the loudspeakers: "I love Mississippi!" The roar intensified, and Barnett, nearly overcome, rose above it to let loose another shout: "I love her people!" Then at the peak: "I love our customs!" These three short sentences were enough to ignite pre-battle ecstasy. People were ready to die.[51]*

Journalist Curtis Wilkie spoke for many of the people we interviewed who were there that night when he wrote: "I would not have traded my seat for a million dollars. I knew I was witnessing the final convulsions of the Civil War."[52]

President Kennedy believed Barnett's intransigence so outlandish that he spent Sunday night explaining to the American people on national television why the University of Mississippi must admit Meredith. By the time Kennedy had finished, riots had broken out across the campus, killing two and injuring more than 375. Meredith began classes the next day and graduated in 1963.[53]

With the passage of time, historians have obtained a variety of new sources about these events, including the recorded telephone conversations between Barnett and members of the Kennedy administration. While he was publicly urging defiance at every opportunity, Barnett was privately conferring with the president and the attorney general over the details of Meredith's enrollment.[54] What is now clear is that Barnett was so enraptured with the outpouring of support for his defiant stand that he was incapable of recognizing the catastrophic ramifications of his actions.[55] For Barnett, it was as if Little Rock had never happened.

The 1963 elections followed the tragic debacle at Ole Miss. While the campaign rhetoric of that year would fuel the fires of segregation in the state, it would also give the civil rights movement a potent issue. By this time, the "movement in Mississippi was desperate." The effort to register voters had "proven to be a dismal failure." Funding coming to Mississippi was being diverted to other states, where voter registration drives were more successful. White Mississippi was holding firm. To avoid these pitfalls, Bob Moses and others conceived the idea of a "Freedom Vote." Since blacks were denied the right to vote, why not ignore the regular polling places and create a separate set of mock polling locations and allow blacks to cast their votes there to demonstrate the injustice that would take place on election day when only whites would be voting? More than 80,000 blacks participated in the mock election. Many observers have argued that it represented a turning point for the movement, "crystallizing" the value of participation by blacks in the political process.[56]

While civil rights groups were organizing Freedom Vote, Paul Johnson Jr. and J. P. Coleman were opposing each other in the Democratic primary for governor. Johnson was lieutenant governor under Barnett and had confronted Meredith at Ole Miss. A news photographer caught Johnson greeting Meredith and federal marshal James McShane in Meredith's third try to enter the university. Johnson's campaign consultants altered the photo to make it appear as though Johnson was raising his arm to stop Meredith from entering the university.[57] They reproduced the doctored photo on thousands of flyers and advertisements and gave Johnson the slogan he needed: "Stand Tall With Paul." Coleman, on the other hand, came under attack for his 1960 endorsement of Kennedy. On a tour of the state in 1956, then Senator John Kennedy had spent the night at the Governor's Mansion at Governor Coleman's invitation. The Johnson team ran advertisements with a photo of a bed in the mansion with the caption: "Jack Kennedy slept here; make sure that Kennedy never sleeps here again, nor J. P. Coleman either." The campaign reached its ugly peak at a Johnson rally. Many of Johnson's supporters wore rubber ape masks, and at one point Johnson asked the crowd if they knew what NAACP stood for. When they cried "NO!" Johnson gave them the answer: "Niggers, Apes, Alligators, Coons and Possums." Johnson won with 57 percent of the vote.[58]

In the middle of the primary campaign and the Freedom Vote, Medgar Evers, the NAACP field secretary in Mississippi, was shot and killed by Byron de la Beckwith. Less than three weeks after Mississippi's general election, President John F. Kennedy was assassinated. Five days later, President Johnson addressed Congress and called for the passage of civil rights legislation.[59] Byron de la Beckwith was acquitted of the murder of Medgar Evers during two trials in the early 1960s, though after evidence was uncovered that the Sovereignty Commission attempted to influence the jury, he was retried and convicted in 1994. It was during the first trial, in January 1964, that a *New York Times* reporter recorded this exchange between Hinds County District Attorney Bill Waller and Judge Leon Hendrick:

> *Waller asked prospective juror W. E. Greer: Do you think it is a crime for a white man to kill a nigger in Mississippi?*
> *Judge Hendrick: What was his answer?*
> *Waller: He's thinking it over.*[60]

THE MISSISSIPPI FREEDOM DEMOCRATIC PARTY: 1964

The Democratic Party in Mississippi has historically served one purpose: acting as the connection between state elected officials and national politics. The party holds precinct, county, and state conventions every four years to elect delegates to the national convention. Prior to the 1970s, national conventions mattered because the delegates actually had a hand in choosing the party's nominee for president. Today, almost all states conduct presidential primary elections to determine the nominee, long before the convention meets. The other function many state parties customarily perform never materialized in Mississippi: that of a central campaign headquarters for Democratic candidates—recruiting candidates, raising money for candidates, and providing them with professional assistance. Individual candidates organized and managed their own campaigns, with little input from state party officials. Consequently, the state party had always been a bit player in the grand scheme of political maneuvering.

That all changed in 1964 when a number of civil rights leaders focused their attention on the state party. In 1964, the members of the party's governing body were white, as were all party officials. They stood in opposition to everything that civil rights organizations were trying to accomplish. The state party became a target: the validity of the delegation from Mississippi would be challenged at the national convention.

The idea of forcing the national party convention to choose among competing delegations from Mississippi was nothing new. Republicans from different factions in Mississippi had forced the Republican National Convention to choose among two different groups from 1928 until 1960. Even less remembered is that small groups of Mississippians opposed the seating of the Regular Mississippi delegations at the 1948, 1952, and 1956 Democratic National Conventions.[61] But the Mississippi Freedom Democratic Party (MFDP) confrontation at the 1964 Democratic National Convention is by far the most famous, and the most consequential.

The decision to organize a separate political party in 1964 grew out of profound disenchantment with the lack of progress being made in black voter registration. Challenging the state party at the high-profile national convention was one way to bring to Washington's attention the need for more direct federal involvement.[62] Establishing the MFDP was just one of the many initiatives of the coalition of civil rights groups that were organizing Freedom Summer. Freedom Summer involved a massive organizational undertaking that ultimately resulted in nearly 1,000 volunteers journeying to Mississippi in 1964 to teach in "Freedom Schools," help with voter registration efforts, and assist with litigation.[63]

It was in the early days of Freedom Summer that James Chaney, Michael Schwerner, and Andrew Goodman were murdered. Two days after their bodies were found in an earthen dam in rural Neshoba County, the MFDP held its state convention at the Masonic Temple in Jackson, where several thousand delegates and spectators assembled—the first time since Reconstruction that so many Mississippi blacks had gathered in one place to challenge the white power structure.[64] Forty-four delegates were elected to attend the national convention and vie for the seats assigned to Mississippi.

The state Democratic Party, known as the "Regulars," held its convention just a few weeks after President Johnson signed the Civil Rights Act of 1964. After condemning the newly passed legislation, Governor Johnson urged the delegates to withhold their endorsement of a presidential candidate until after the national convention.[65] If the national party adopted a strong civil rights program, then Mississippi Democrats could support the Republican nominee, Senator Barry Goldwater, one of only six Republicans who had opposed the act.

The decision about which delegation to seat at the national convention fell first to the Credentials Committee. The MFDP brief to the committee set out in great detail the failure of the Regulars to support the national party.[66] The testimony by MFDP members made the case for giving the seats to their new party organization. But the evidence and stories of personal heroism were no match for the will of President Lyndon Johnson. Having convinced himself that acceding to the MFDP challenge would ruin any chance he might have of carrying southern states in the general election, Johnson sought a compromise between the opposing delegations.[67] But Johnson did not anticipate Fannie Lou Hamer.

The Credentials Committee convened the Saturday before the start of the convention in Atlantic City, New Jersey. Having attracted national media attention in the weeks leading up to the convention, the committee's deliberations of the Mississippi challenge were broadcast live by the major television networks.[68] The Regulars went first, and their lead-off witness was Senator E. K. Collins, the same man who had inflamed passions before the 1962 Meredith fiasco, this time denying that there was discrimination in his home state. The other speakers did little better.[69] Next up were the MFDP representatives, including Aaron Henry, chairman of the delegation and head of the Mississippi NAACP; Rita Schwerner, wife of the slain civil rights worker; and Martin Luther King Jr. But the person who "captured the hearts and minds of the audience was not a product of Morehouse College and Boston University such as Dr. King, but a product of the Mississippi Delta's cotton fields and shanty towns, Mrs. Fannie Lou Hamer."[70]

In the hearing room packed with other challenge delegations, newsmen, television commentators, and cameramen, journalist Theodore White described what happened:

One gets the flavor best, not by considering the issues raised, but by considering and listening to a voice. On Saturday afternoon, as the committee moved to consider the situation. . . . Mrs. Fannie Lou Hamer rose to testify. . . . She proceeded to tell of her effort to register to vote, going back as far as 1962, and as her fine, mellow voice rose, it began to chant with the grief and the sobbing that are the source of all the blues in the world. The hot muggy room was electrified as she concluded her narrative of a Mississippi Negro's life when one attempts to register.[71]

By the age of seven, Hamer was working on a plantation near Ruleville, picking cotton as a field hand. She was forty-four years old when she attended her first civil rights meeting in 1962 and learned then, for the first time, that she had a right to vote. Hamer raised her hand when volunteers were recruited to spend the next day trying to register. Not surprisingly, her attempt was rebuffed at the courthouse. What happened next is what brought Hamer to the 1964 convention. After Hamer left the courthouse, the clerk called the owner of the plantation where she worked. By the time Hamer returned home, the owner was on his way over. If she persisted, he told her, she would no longer have a job. So, Hamer left. Bob Moses heard about her determination and recruited her to join the movement. The following summer, on her way home from a meeting, she and six coworkers were arrested in Winona for trying to eat lunch at the bus station. Her description of what happened in that jail transfixed the Credentials Committee members:

So they had me lay down on my face, and they beat with a thick leather thing that was wide. . . . They beat me and they beat me with the long flat blackjack. I screamed to God in pain. My dress worked itself up. I tried to pull it down. They beat my arms until I had no feeling in them. After a while the first man beating my arms grew numb from tiredness. The other man, who was holding me, was given the blackjack. Then he began beating me.[72]

By the time Hamer concluded her remarks with her famous—"I question America; is this America, the land of the free and the home of the brave where . . . our lives be threatened daily because we want to live as decent human beings?"—the Johnson campaign was in panic.[73] Within minutes the president called his own news conference, pulling the cameras away from the credential hearing.[74]

Needing time to overcome the Hamer testimony, Johnson forced the committee to postpone its decision, and he ordered Minnesota Senator Hubert Humphrey, who desperately wanted to be Johnson's vice presidential choice, to resolve the Mississippi crisis, or he would have "no future in the party."[75] Three days later, Humphrey had a proposal: (1) Regular delegates who submitted to a loyalty oath would be seated; (2) MFDP members would be recognized as honored guests; (3) two MFDP delegates, Aaron Henry and Ed King, would be named delegates-at-large; and (4) delegates to the 1968 convention would be chosen on a nondiscriminatory basis.[76] Having instructed the Federal Bureau of Investigation (FBI) to tap the phones of key MFDP leaders and engage in related surveillance activities, Johnson knew which Credentials Committee members the MFDP was recruiting to its cause. He used this information to lobby those same members to accept Humphrey's compromise.[77] Johnson won the committee vote; it was then take it or leave it time for both delegations.

While urged to accept the settlement by party liberals and movement leaders, the MFDP voted overwhelmingly against the compromise: they sought recognition as voting delegates, not as honored guests; if they were going to accept two at-large delegate positions, the MFDP would select their own representatives. They would not be told who could speak for them. For the MFDP, their cause was a moral crusade, and it "took precedent over politics."[78]

The Regular delegation likewise rejected the compromise and walked out, refusing to sign the loyalty oath. Its official statement ended with a refrain heard repeatedly since: "The Mississippi Democratic delegation did not leave the national Democratic Party; it left us."[79]

In the end, the MFDP initiative focused enormous attention on Mississippi, paved the way for a successful challenge to the Regular delegation in 1968, and unleashed "a national political reform movement [that] directly led to Democratic Party guidelines that provided an expanded national role for blacks, women and young people."[80] The white leaders of the Democratic Party in Mississippi either remained quiet during the 1964 campaign or, as in the case of Congressman John Bell Williams and Speaker of the House Walter Sillers, endorsed Goldwater.[81] Goldwater carried Mississippi with 87 percent of the vote, his best performance in the country.

Lyndon Johnson, on the other hand, carried all but six states and crushed Goldwater on his way to winning the presidency. Before he was appointed U.S. District Judge, Dan M. Russell Jr. was a lawyer in Hancock County and was asked by Senator Eastland to serve as one of the seven electors whose names would be on the ballot in support of Lyndon Johnson's presidential campaign. He agreed, and sometime later, a few of his friends began to give him a hard time about supporting LBJ. Motivated by their heckling, Russell made them a bet: Hancock County would lead Mississippi for Johnson on election day. Russell proceeded to contact everyone he knew in the county, telling them Goldwater was going to carry the state, saying that Goldwater didn't need Hancock's vote, and asking if they would vote for LBJ so he could win his bet. After the votes were tallied, Hancock County delivered 37.1 percent of its vote to LBJ, highest in the state. The seven counties that followed were all from north Mississippi.[82]

THE MODERN DEMOCRATIC PARTY: 1965–1968

One of the bitter ironies for those who foment political change is that often they are not the beneficiaries of that change. Such was the case with the MFDP. The mere fact of the challenge that the MFDP brought in 1964 was not unprecedented, but the extraordinary amount of attention it generated certainly was. The MFDP focused the nation on the pervasive racism in Mississippi and created a dilemma for national party leaders: if the Regulars failed to integrate their delegation, the 1968 convention would no doubt seat a challenge delegation. Still to be resolved over the next four years was who would fill the role of the challenge delegation.

The MFDP's decision to turn down the compromise at the 1964 convention surprised many and shocked more than a few national party leaders.[83] For these political professionals, compromise is the currency of the trade. Only ideologues and moral crusaders refuse a compromise, a tendency that makes them unwelcome at the table professional politicians use to conduct business. The MFDP, however, was sustained by their faith in the moral rightness of their cause.[84] To seek to overcome the virtually impregnable position created by Mississippi's white power structure, civil rights activists had no choice but to be strident, overbearing, and uncompromising. Without a faith in the moral rightness of their cause, engaging in that battle would have been impossible.

Nevertheless, when the professionals in charge of the national party realized that a challenge delegation was likely in 1968, they went looking for men and women who understood the value of compromise.[85] Efforts to create a new party in Mississippi began early in 1965. Several different approaches were tried, and the fight was cast between the MFDP—viewed as ideologues unwilling to compromise—and groups regarded as moderates. The question was which one would emerge as the alternative to the Regulars. Eight days after President Johnson signed the Voting Rights Act of 1965, the Young Democrats of Mississippi held their state convention and became that alternative.

On August 14, 1965, a Young Democrats chapter was organized in Mississippi when a group of whites sympathetic to the civil rights movement joined forces with a number of black leaders. At this statewide meeting, the battle lines were drawn. In the morning session, Hodding Carter III, the white editor of the *Greenville Delta-Democrat Times*, and Cleveland Donald, the second African American admitted to Ole Miss, were elected co-chairmen of the group. By the afternoon, however, MFDP members asserted their power, gained control of the meeting, and elected their own president and vice president. When that happened, the "moderates," led by Carter, walked out. The dispute then moved to the national Young Democrats organization. Which faction would they choose to represent Mississippi? Controlled by national party leaders, the national Young Democrats chose the "moderate" faction, leaving Carter's group with the authority to launch a campaign for the delegate seats at the 1968 convention.[86]

The 1967 elections were the first since 1890 in which candidates in Mississippi had to contend with black voters. The Voting Rights Act of 1965 had enfranchised several hundred thousand blacks, and as one scholar explained, "Its impact was almost incomprehensible to the politicians of the state. The assumptions and fiber of politics which had existed for a century were recast."[87] When Carroll Gartin died suddenly of a heart attack in late 1966, the field for governor narrowed to Congressman John Bell Williams and State Treasurer William Winter. A member of Congress for twenty-one years, Williams achieved martyr status in Mississippi when the Democratic leadership in Congress stripped him of his seniority and a committee chairmanship after he endorsed Barry Goldwater in 1964. Williams later told a crowd, "I told them you can take that committee and put it in a place where it would be physically uncomfortable."[88]

Williams made race an issue by denouncing federal desegregation guidelines, asking if Mississippi was "ready to surrender to the great society," and advertising that "William Winter's election will insure Negro domination in Mississippi elections for generations to come." In one campaign commercial Williams declared: "The Negro has demonstrated a sex attitude that has greatly alarmed white parents." Winter, on the other hand, called himself a "Jim Eastland, John Stennis Democrat," and, while claiming to favor segregation, he stressed that a cool-headed, pragmatic approach to the problem was needed. Williams defeated Winter, garnering 55 percent of the vote.[89]

On March 31, 1968, President Johnson stunned the nation when he announced he would not be a candidate for reelection. The war in Vietnam had ruined his presidency. Four days later, Martin Luther King Jr. was assassinated outside his hotel room in Memphis. By the end of the week, riots had taken place in more than a hundred cities across the country.[90] The world of presidential politics was turned upside down. In Mississippi, though, the 1968 presidential campaign was reduced to only one candidate: Alabama governor George Wallace, who ran as an independent. His campaign was the vehicle white voters used to express their anger and resentment at the civil rights movement and the role of the federal government in enforcing the changes to their culture wrought by the newly enacted civil rights laws. Wallace's campaign was also the way for the established Democratic leaders of the state to bid farewell to the national party, for it was in 1968 that the national convention refused to seat the Regulars, instead awarding Mississippi's seats to a newly formed "Loyalist" Democratic Party.

Soon after the 1967 elections in Mississippi, members of the Young Democrats, the NAACP, and other organizations with a "moderate" reputation formed a coalition and began developing a challenge to the Regulars at the 1968 convention. At the same time, the MFDP was pursuing its own challenge. National party leaders, recognizing that a confrontation could not be avoided, gave their support to the moderates.[91]

In April, Vice President Hubert Humphrey spoke at Ole Miss, and with a number of leading state Democrats present, he called on the Regulars to send an integrated delegation to the 1968 convention. Governor Williams refused to attend and vetoed a move to have Humphrey address a joint session of the legislature.[92] At a meeting of the Regulars' executive committee, a resolution placing the committee on record as having "no objection" to blacks entering the state party died when Williams objected.[93] By May, it became apparent to the MFDP that the only way to defeat the Regulars was to join the coalition, which they did at the urging of MFDP chairman Lawrence Guyot. On June

21, 1968, the unified group was formally organized as the Loyalist Democratic Party of Mississippi.[94] The Loyalists elected Hodding Carter III and Aaron Henry as temporary co-chairmen. It was the end of July, and the Loyalists had a few short weeks before the Credentials Committee of the national convention would meet in Chicago. During that time, the Loyalists conducted precinct and county conventions in seventy-three counties, held district conventions in early August, and hosted a state convention on August 11. The Loyalist state convention welcomed more than 3,000 delegates and spectators. After a memorial service for Robert Kennedy, who had been assassinated only a month earlier, representatives of the three national candidates for president addressed the convention, all of whom sought the Loyalists' support. Charles Evers was elected national committeeman, and Patt Derian was elected national committeewoman.[95] On the eve of the national convention, the *Jackson Clarion-Ledger* spoke for many of the Regular Democrats when it wrote: "Hodding gave the signal; Aaron rang the bell; Evers shouted All aboard; And the party went to. . ."[96]

By the time the delegates assembled in Chicago, the Vietnam War had pushed the civil rights movement backstage. The lead stories from the convention were the brutal way in which Mayor Richard J. Daley's police handled the Vietnam protestors and the ugly nomination fight in which Vice President Hubert Humphrey defeated Minnesota Senator Eugene McCarthy. The Regulars had little good they could say for themselves in front of the Credentials Committee, especially after state Senator Bill Burgin, representing the Regulars, exclaimed that the committee was willing to "cast bona fide Democrats to the wind" in order to earn black votes in other parts of the country.[97] The Loyalists, with the backing of all major candidates for president, were handed the delegate seats, the first time in history an entire delegation had been replaced.[98]

The response among the Regulars was disbelief. Leon Bramlett, chairman of the Regulars, expressed amazement at the "minority psychosis that seems to have paralyzed this country."[99] Worried about losing white southern votes, Humphrey met with Aaron Henry, Charles Evers, Patt Derian, and other Loyalists to persuade them to reach a compromise with the Regulars. As they were negotiating, a waiter entered the room with a sandwich and drink, but for Humphrey only. What happened next Derian remembered as one of "life's glorious moments." Soon after Humphrey started eating "in front of us, Aaron reached over the table, grabbed half of Humphrey's sandwich, and announced, 'Hubert, I'm hungry.'"[100] The Regulars refused any entreaty and instead endorsed George Wallace, who got more votes out of Mississippi than any other state but his native Alabama.[101]

BLACK VOTERS REDEFINE THE DEMOCRATIC PARTY: 1969–1975

Voting and campaign politics took a backseat in 1969 and 1970 to school deseg-regation. Sixteen years after the *Brown* decision, federal courts finally required Mississippi to abolish its dual system of public education and unify its black and white schools. By the end of the 1970 school year, more than 50,000 white students and 1,000 white teachers had abandoned the public schools, effec-tively doubling the number of private schools in the state. Governor Williams took to statewide television to complain bitterly about the judicial decrees, but his words were empty of effect. Mississippi's public schools were integrated. Nonetheless, in almost all the majority black school districts, a new dual sys-tem soon existed: most white students went to private academies while black students attended the public schools.[102]

By the spring of 1970, the Vietnam War was consuming the nation. President Nixon's announcement of the Cambodian invasion in April triggered protests throughout the country's college campuses. On May 4, four students were killed when Ohio national guardsmen opened fire on students demonstrating on the campus of Kent State University. Ten days later, more than seventy-five highway patrolmen and city police fired on a demonstration unrelated to the war by black students at Jackson State University. Two students were killed and twelve others wounded. The FBI later counted more than 300 bullet holes in the front of the women's dormitory where the demonstration took place. No officer was ever charged.[103]

The 1971 campaign for governor is widely portrayed as the first in which the major candidates avoided blatant racial appeals to the voters. The top candi-dates were former Hinds County District Attorney Bill Waller and Lieutenant Governor Charles Sullivan. While Waller and Sullivan refrained from direct racial appeals, a third candidate, Jimmy Swan, more than made up for them. He liked to say, "The time has come to quit pussyfooting around. Integra-tion is here. . . . I will never accept it!"[104] The campaign is more memorable, however, for Waller's coining the term "Capitol Street Gang"—referring to the downtown street in Jackson that was home to banks, utilities, law firms, and

[31]

other "establishment" leaders. Once Sullivan opted to portray himself as the "dignified, silver haired statesman who would restore Mississippi's reputation and image nationally," he set himself up for attack as the "establishment's" representative. Waller attributed Mississippi's underdevelopment to the proposition that "while we change the name of the governor the same old political machine remains in power." He promised to take the governor's office away from the Capitol Street Gang and return it to the "people." The race issue was also revealed in the way the candidates talked about education. Waller promised, for example, to "defend to the hilt the right of private schools." Ross Barnett openly endorsed Waller, as did Eastland. Waller won with 54 percent of the vote.[105]

While Waller tried in early 1972 to unify the Regulars and Loyalists, neither side was willing to make significant concessions, and Mississippi sent two delegations to the Democratic National Convention. The convention stuck with the Loyalists and rebuffed the Regulars. As Waller's term progressed, representatives from both factions continued to negotiate and work toward an agreement for the 1976 campaign.[106]

The gubernatorial campaign of 1975 presaged the way in which Democrats could win a statewide race within the new political dynamic in Mississippi: black voters were fully aligned with the Democratic Party, while a growing number of white voters in the cities and the suburbs were moving to the Republican Party. Neither party, however, could produce enough votes to win a statewide election solely on the basis of these constituencies. Therefore, the target for both parties—a topic we will revisit throughout this book—became the rural white voter.

In 1975, the Democratic candidates for governor were former District Attorney Cliff Finch from Batesville, Lieutenant Governor William Winter, and former District Attorney Maurice Dantin from Columbia. Finch instinctively knew the target and became the "working man's" candidate. He devoted one day each week to "working" at blue-collar and farming jobs—driving a bulldozer in Jackson, operating a drag line in Greenwood, or plowing a field near his hometown of Batesville. These stunts attracted press coverage and were made a part of Finch's television ads. The same reservoir tapped by Waller in 1971 with his attacks on the Capitol Street Gang served to sustain Finch's campaign. Winter, on the other hand, hurt his cause when he declared: "I am convinced that the people do not want a clown or stuntman leading them for the next four years." Finch's response was directed at the rural white voter: "If they call them rednecks, clown or whatever, then I'm proud to be one." All of a sudden, Winter represented the establishment and Finch became the outsider. The outcome was preordained. Finch won with 58 percent of the vote.[107] Finch's appeal to the "working man" carried over into the general election. Against a well-funded Republican candidate, Gil Carmichael, Finch prevailed by bringing black voters and rural white voters together—a coalition that has become known as the "Blacknecks and the Rednecks."[108] The question for Democrats then became: how long could they keep that coalition intact?

POSTSCRIPT

Deep into election night 1975, long after the polls had closed, the Democratic nominee Cliff Finch was waiting for election returns at his campaign office when his secretary let him know that Oliver Eaton, Finch's Prentiss County coordinator, was on the phone. Finch winked at the crowd, put Eaton on the speaker, and said: "Oliver, how's it going?" The crowd in the office heard Eaton's reply: "Cliff, now I'm going to tell you. This is serious. You've got a 2,000-vote lead here in Prentiss. If you're gonna need more than that, you're gonna have to tell me now. I need to know now!"[109]

CHAPTER 2

HISTORY OF MISSISSIPPI REPUBLICANS

1955–1975

*Let it be said by way of fuller identification or introduction of Wirt Yerger,
Jr., that he's a nice, soft-spoken young man and comes from one of the finest
families in Mississippi. But what he doesn't know about that rough-and-
tumble American game called politics would fill any good-sized library in
the nation. Wirt Yerger, Jr. has gone far from the faith of his fathers.*
—FRED SULLENS, *Jackson Daily News*, October 20, 1957

In the spring of 1865, soon after Mississippi had surrendered its troops,
Governor Charles Clark sent William L. Sharkey and William Yerger
to Washington to meet with President Andrew Johnson to make plans
for Mississippi to rejoin the Union. Ninety years later, William Yerger's great-
great-nephew would begin the modern-day Republican Party in Mississippi.
The temerity of Wirt Yerger Jr. to sully the family legacy and scandalize an
entire state's culture by organizing a Republican Party is no doubt what provoked Fred Sullens, the blunt *Jackson Daily News* editor.

For Yerger and others to nurture a Republican Party in Mississippi, however,
generations had to come and go in order for the events of June 15, 1868, and
those that followed, to become part of the distant past. On that June day, the
Republican president of the United States dispatched federal troops to Jackson,
forcibly removed Governor Benjamin Humphreys from the state capitol "at
the point of bayonets" and installed General Adelbert Ames head of a military government. Radical Reconstruction had begun.[1] For the next seven years,
Republicans controlled state government.

The 1870 legislature convened with 110 Republicans, 35 of whom were
black. After ratifying the Fourteenth and Fifteenth amendments to the U.S.

Constitution, legislators moved to fill U.S. Senate seats left vacant from seces-
sion. One went to Hiram R. Revels, the first African American ever to serve in
the U.S. Senate—the same seat held by Jefferson Davis before he resigned to
become president of the Confederacy.[2]

Four years later, the legislature appointed the second black to serve in the
U.S. Senate: Blanche K. Bruce. Until 1966, when Edward Brooke was elected
from Massachusetts, Mississippi was the only state in the nation to have had
African Americans represent it in the Senate. John R. Lynch became the first
black Speaker of the state House of Representatives and then the first black
Mississippi congressman. Over the course of these seven years, blacks were
elected lieutenant governor, secretary of state, and superintendent of education. The 1874 legislature boasted sixty-four black members, a black Speaker
of the House, and a black president of the Senate, all Republicans.[3]

It was more than white Democrats could stomach. In chronicling
Mississippi's history in 1908, Department of Archives Director Dunbar Rowland surely captured their feelings when he wrote how the state was "sickened
at an orgy of negro and 'carpet-bag' control that reads like the record of some
unhappy planet. Then the scene shifted and retribution came."[4] Retribution
came during the campaign of 1875, when violence and lawlessness provoked
Governor Ames to plead with President Grant for federal forces. In the November elections, white Democrats, using tactics both legal and illegal, elected a
majority to the legislature. The first order of business when they assembled in
early 1876 was to remove from office the Republican governor, lieutenant governor, and superintendent of education. Rowland exalted at the culmination:
"Thus ended the last remnant of an unspeakable regime."[5]

The memories would be long lasting—eighty-eight years would pass before
Mississippi gave its electoral votes to a Republican nominee for president and
116 years before a Republican moved back into the Governor's Mansion.

THE BIRTH OF THE MODERN GOP: 1955–1960

The Republican Party we know today in Mississippi was conceived in the fall of
1955, though for nearly thirty years two groups had been at war for ownership
of the state GOP. The successor to the party that managed state government
during Reconstruction was known as the Black and Tan Republican Party. In
1924, Perry Howard assumed control. A black lawyer from Holmes County and

the son of former slaves, Howard lived most of his life in Washington, D.C., and returned to Mississippi infrequently to conduct party affairs. He ultimately represented Mississippi on the Republican National Committee for thirty-six years, the longest period of service for any member yet recorded. Howard's nemesis was George Sheldon, a former Nebraska governor who moved to Mississippi in 1909. Sheldon organized the Lily-White Republican Party in 1927, served one term in the legislature in the 1920s, and ran for governor in 1947. Given that Democrats wielded all the political power in the state, the fight between the Black and Tans and Lily-Whites was reduced to which faction the national Republican Party would recognize as the official state party. The Black and Tan delegation was inevitably seated at every national convention.[6]

Republicans in Mississippi during this time rarely fielded candidates for office, spending more time fighting among themselves than recruiting candidates for public office. The phenomenon was described by Alexander Heard, a leading political scientist in the 1950s: "The most signal characteristic of the party's southern leadership" was its "lack of interest in winning elections." His prescriptions were simple: "To a greater or lesser degree in every southern state, there must be changes in the high command if the party is to grow," and "the greatest stimulus to party growth lies in a continuous stream of serious candidates—the contest for office is the backbone of party politics."[7]

In 1952, the GOP gave Mississippi and other southern states a Republican candidate for president around whom white voters could rally: World War II hero General Dwight D. Eisenhower. Writing in 1992, political scholars Earl Black and Merle Black thought the choice pivotal: "The net result of Eisenhower's southern invasion was the disappearance of the Solid Democratic South in the electoral college."[8] Not wanting to associate himself with the warring party factions in Mississippi, Eisenhower formed a separate campaign organization—Citizens for Eisenhower. E. O. Spencer, manager of the Walthall Hotel in Jackson, was chosen its leader. With Eisenhower at the top of the ticket, with some amount of peace between the two Republicans factions in the state, and with the help of a newly formed "Democrats for Eisenhower" organization, the GOP polled almost 40 percent in the November election, the highest showing in Mississippi for a Republican since 1884.[9]

The implications were readily apparent: "For the first time since Reconstruction significant [Democratic] political leadership openly campaigned for the Republican ticket. . . . The degree to which loyalty to the Democratic Party had been little more than a vehicle for maintaining white supremacy became suddenly and starkly apparent. And the genie of party loyalty once loosed from the bottle was never again replaced."[10]

With the election of Eisenhower as president in 1952, the issue of who ran the state Republican Party machinery suddenly meant something. In those days, the state party controlled patronage, a practice not limited to federal judicial nominations. The president appointed, for example, the postmasters for each local post office, all on recommendation of the state party leadership. The postmasters hired all the clerks and mail carriers and contracted with local businesses, oftentimes on recommendations from the party. It took two years of internecine party warfare before E. O. Spencer was given the authority to supervise this party-building machine.[11]

About the same time, Wirt Yerger Jr. returned to Jackson after graduating from college and spending two years in the military. Yerger's family operated an insurance agency in Jackson, and he joined his father to work in the business. In the fall of 1955, Yerger was in New York attending an insurance school. Practicing law in New York at the time was Charles McWhorter, the national chairman of the Young Republican Federation. Yerger had concluded that Mississippi needed the benefit of a competitive two-party system and that Republicans needed the benefit of a new party organization, free of the infighting and personality conflicts that characterized the other GOP groups. It turned out that a good friend of Yerger's, Tom Crockett, attended Harvard Law School with Roger Moore, who knew Charles McWhorter. A couple of letters and phone calls later, and Yerger had an appointment with McWhorter.

McWhorter told Yerger that if he could get the names of thirty-five people on a petition and "come to our meeting in Des Moines [Iowa] in February, we will present you the charter for the Mississippi Young Republican Federation." After "persuading and cajoling" enough of his friends and family members to sign the petition, Yerger traveled to Iowa in February 1956, where McWhorter presented the charter "with a lot of hoopla" because, as Yerger remembers, "I was kind of an oddity, a Republican in Mississippi."[12]

By the time the 1956 presidential election year rolled around, three factions were poised to vie for power: the Black and Tans headed by Perry Howard; the Lily-Whites now headed by George Sheldon's son, Anson; and Citizens for Eisenhower, chaired by E. O. Spencer. Into this mix came the newly formed Young Republicans. As it happened, Yerger had grown up in the same neighborhood as Spencer's family and had played with their sons throughout childhood. On returning from Iowa, Yerger knew just the connection he needed to make in order to contest the party leadership in Mississippi—the father of his boyhood friends. They met and agreed to join forces.[13]

The scene of the leadership battle was the Mississippi Republican Party state convention held on March 22, 1956, in the Hinds County courthouse. While the stakes would ultimately prove to be very high, it must have seemed like a small social gathering to the forty-one delegates who participated. Since the Black and Tans refused to recognize either the Lily-Whites or the Eisenhower group, this convention would determine which faction would represent the Mississippi Republican Party in the battle for recognition against the Black and Tans at the convention. With the help of Spencer, the Young Republicans recruited enough people to attend the convention to elect a majority of its members to the State Executive Committee, which chose the party chairman. The *Jackson Clarion-Ledger*, always eager to undermine Republicans, made a point of reporting that the convention failed to take up a resolution favoring segregation when Yerger objected that it might prevent the delegation from gaining recognition. The only item of business left was to elect the party chairman, a decision that would be made at the State Executive Committee meeting that followed. Anson Sheldon and Yerger vied for the position. With Spencer's backing, Yerger was elected by a margin of one vote, eight to seven. The Young Republicans and the disaffected Democrats who had formed Citizens for Eisenhower had defeated the Lily-Whites and assumed control of one of the factions of the Republican Party in Mississippi.[14] Now, it was on to the national convention in San Francisco and the struggle with the Black and Tans.

By the time the Republicans convened, Perry Howard was seventy-nine years old, though he had one last fight left in him. He used it to thwart the new Yerger organization. Howard threatened to campaign against Eisenhower with northern black voters if his group was not once again recognized. Unwilling to take that risk, the Eisenhower organization forced a compromise between the competing delegations: Howard's group was given eight of Mississippi's fifteen delegates, while Yerger's group drew the remaining seven. Howard would remain as national committeeman, but Yerger's faction would be officially recognized at the 1960 convention as the sole Republican Party for Mississippi. The compromise was drafted, and all the principals signed it except Yerger, who condemned it as a "dirty deal." For Yerger, the full victory would have to wait for four years. But in the interim his group would operate the party in Mississippi, dispense patronage, and serve as the official state contact for the national party.[15]

The 1956 election was a repeat of 1952. Stevenson got about the same vote in Mississippi, carrying the state. Eisenhower won reelection though, and a new Mississippi Republican Party was united and could finally begin the serious work of party building.

Then came Little Rock. On September 2, 1957, Arkansas Governor Faubus ordered National Guard troops to surround Central High School to prevent court-ordered desegregation. Two weeks passed while Faubus continued to ignore court directives. On September 20, the federal court lost its patience and ordered Faubus to permit the black students to enroll. A few hours later, the governor pulled his troops. Events began to spiral out of control when mobs assembled at the school. On September 24, Eisenhower dispatched soldiers to Little Rock to enforce the court order. In a scene that would be repeated at Ole Miss almost five years later to the day, the president held a televised news conference, informing the nation he was forced to use federal troops because "demagogic extremists had placed in peril the cornerstone of American liberties."[16]

The reaction in Mississippi was predictable. The *Meridian Star* asked: "Has Our Freedom Ended?" The *Laurel Leader-Call* reminded readers that "federal troops are in a southern city, as they have not been since the days of Reconstruction." The *Jackson Daily News* put it more bluntly: "Perhaps it is not polite to make inquiry at this crucial moment but it would be interesting to know just how the so-called Democrats for Eisenhower in Mississippi feel about the way the President is using Federal bayonets to ram integration down the throats of the Southern people. If there was a time for political repentance in sack cloth and ashes this is it."[17]

The state Republican Party, which had spent the previous year quietly building its base, had scheduled an organizational conference in Jackson for October 2. But the original purpose of the meeting was all but thrown aside by a Republican president sending federal troops to a southern city to enforce school integration. Charles McWhorter, the guest speaker, arrived in Jackson to a situation so tense that, out of concern for his safety, he stayed with B. B. McClendon Jr., the state party's legal counsel, rather than at a hotel.[18] The most profound crisis in the growth of the Republican Party in Mississippi had been triggered by a Republican president. Would the leadership desert their president? Would the party get stuck, once again, with the stigma of Reconstruction it had worked for seventy years to overcome? On October 2, Spencer wired the president: "Your unwarranted act in ordering military force has completely destroyed our Eisenhower organization and everything accomplished in Mississippi during the past five years. Therefore, I have no alternative except to resign." Other party officials and activists joined Spencer in abandoning the party, an exodus described by a gleeful *Jackson Daily News*: "The followers of Eisenhower in Mississippi have departed faster than the Israelites out of Egypt."[19]

Yerger wrote to party leaders arguing that resignation was the easy course and urging party loyalists to "stick together." Yerger replaced Spencer as head of patronage, the uproar began to die down, and later that year the first Mississippi Young Republican Convention was convened. In summing up the shock of Little Rock, a scholar observed: "The hard core of the party faithful had been isolated, and they became the nucleus of the present day party."[20] That nucleus spent much of the next two years recovering from Little Rock and preparing for the 1960 national convention, for it was there that Yerger and company planned to hold the party leaders to their 1956 promise. On January 9, 1960, Yerger received the registration materials for the July convention in Chicago. While a copy was sent to Perry Howard, he was in failing health and made no effort to organize opposition. For the first time since 1928, Mississippi would be sending one unified party to the convention.

THE REPUBLICANS GAIN A FOOTHOLD: 1960–1965

For those in Mississippi who birthed the modern Republican Party, their strongest contempt was reserved for the "northeastern liberals" who controlled the party in the days before 1960. These Mississippians were convinced that both national parties took the South for granted—or, more precisely, wrote it off. They sought to reverse that political calculus. They wanted a South involved in the highest reaches of government, and in the case of the Republican Party, they sought to change the orientation from one based on the northeastern brand of Republican liberalism to one based on the conservatism rooted in the South and West. Seeking to redefine the national Republican Party, they started with presidential campaigns.[21] They knew instinctively what Earl Black and Merle Black once observed: "Presidential politics is the great engine of the American political system."[22]

At the 1960 GOP convention in Chicago, Richard Nixon, Eisenhower's vice president for eight years and the leading contender for the nomination, faced a dilemma: the philosophical direction of the party versus his need to lock up the nomination. Theodore H. White described the opportunity:

> *For twelve years now this problem of Negro vote and Negro rights has roweled the Democratic Party. Northern Democrats . . . agreed that in the area of civil rights the federal government should supercede state authority and intervene in state affairs. But Southern whites wish to deal with their race problem on their own; and the support of Northern Democrats for federal intervention in Southern race problems has shaken, perhaps permanently, the Democratic grip on its old Southern base. Concurrently has come the phenomenal growth of the Republican Party in the South, resting in large part on the recognition of grow-ing millions of Southerners that the Regular Republicans, who seek to curb the powers of the federal government in general, are their natural allies in preserv-ing state sovereignty in race relations too. The prospect for the Republican high command is thus tantalizing in the extreme. If they adopt a civil rights program only moderately more restrained than the Democrats', the South can be theirs for the asking.*[23]

The leaders of the 1960 Mississippi delegation assumed Nixon would indeed seize this opportunity. They certainly never anticipated that he would strike a deal with the devil himself—New York Governor Nelson Rockefeller, the leader of the liberal wing of the GOP.[24] In Chicago, though, the Mississippi delegates came face to face with both the civil rights issue and the role of northeastern lib-eral Republicans when Nixon "exploded a bomb at a Monday afternoon press conference" and declared he would fight for strong civil rights language in the Republican platform.[25] Everyone in Chicago knew that Nixon had arrived at this decision as part of a compromise with Rockefeller to unify the party behind Nixon's nomination.

Tuesday and Wednesday saw Mississippians threatening to abandon Nixon to demonstrate their displeasure at both the stronger civil rights position and the behind-the-scenes deal. To keep the delegation on board, Nixon spoke before the group, and, while he refused to back down, he argued that the GOP platform was weaker than that adopted by the Democrats. More important, he committed to campaign in Mississippi. The delegation stuck with Nixon for the sake of party unity.[26] Nixon kept his promise and campaigned in Mississippi on September 24, 1960, the first time a presidential candidate had appeared in the state in more than a century.[27] Nixon spoke to a crowd of over 8,000 in front of the Governor's Mansion, telling them that "what we Republicans stand for is closer to what you stand for."[28]

Kennedy took the White House, and Governor Ross Barnett's "Unpledged" slate took Mississippi, winning a plurality with 39 percent of the vote. While the Republicans could only muster 25 percent of the vote in 1960, they increased the number of people voting the GOP ticket by 21 percent over 1956. Party leaders in Mississippi then turned their attention to the 1963 state elections, to the 1964 presidential campaign, and to the process of defining the Republican Party.

THE SOUTHERN STRATEGY: 1960–1968

"Southern strategy" is a term many use to explain how Republicans took over the South by the way they defined themselves. There are as many characterizations of the strategy, and as many accounts of when it began and how it was exploited, as there are books and articles that have been written about it. Jack Bass and Walter DeVries wrote that the "origin of what became the Republican 'southern strategy' was a speech in 1961 by Barry Goldwater in Atlanta. 'We're not going to get the Negro vote as a bloc in 1964 and 1968, so we ought to go hunting where the ducks are,' he declared. Goldwater then spelled it out, saying that school integration was the 'responsibility of the states. I would not like to see my party assume it is the role of the federal government to enforce integration in the schools.'"[29] Reg Murphy and Hal Gulliver, on the other hand, give Nixon credit for creating the "southern strategy" in 1968, when he made a deal with South Carolina Senator Strom Thurmond to "ease up on the federal pressures forcing school desegregation" in return for Thurmond's support in Nixon's second try at the presidency.[30]

Conservatives defend the "southern strategy" by arguing it was a way to achieve the "principal aim" of the party, which was "the preservation of individual freedom . . . that liberal domestic policies lead to a national welfare state in which workers lose their freedom through heavy taxation and the recipients . . . lose their personal liberty through bureaucratic regulation."[31] Liberals, on the other hand, view the "southern strategy" as nothing more than "a cynical strategy, catering in subtle ways to the segregationist leanings of white Southern voters."[32] They are both right. The conservatives who rallied around Goldwater after the 1960 campaign believed Communism was the greatest international threat to the country and that a burgeoning federal bureaucracy, financed with higher taxes, was the greatest domestic threat. To obtain an electoral majority, they saw a chance to pick up southern white voters disaffected with the national Democratic initiative on civil rights.

This new conservative message was all that Yerger and his allies needed to form the basis for an organizing strategy. The Goldwater campaign was their ticket to define and grow a new Republican Party in Mississippi. Yerger and his finance chairman, Buddy Klumb, were part of the "draft Goldwater" movement, a national crusade officially launched in early 1963. Yerger had been elected chairman of the group of southern Republican Party leaders in 1961, which formed the early base for the Goldwater movement. For Mississippi, the draft Goldwater campaign reached a boiling point when he attended a Jackson fund-raiser on November 29, 1962. More than 1,500 enthusiasts heard the Arizona senator attribute the rise of the Republican Party in the South to "the invasion of states' rights by the New Deal, the Fair Deal, and the New Frontier."[33]

Knowing that the best way to build a party was to develop the organizational skills necessary to run competitive campaigns, Yerger and his colleagues recruited a number of candidates for state and local offices in 1963. Among them was Klumb, who went to the Copiah County courthouse to qualify for the state Senate. When he was given the form to qualify as a Republican, he noticed it was preprinted with the word "Democrat" in the blank space preceding "Primary Election." Then the clerk warned him, "Young man, you know what happened to the last two Republicans in Copiah County? One got shot right out here on the courthouse lawn and the other barely got out of town that night with his life. I'm not so sure I would do this if I were you."[34] Nevertheless, Klumb qualified. Though he lost his campaign, he is still alive and well today.

Another recruit was Rubel Phillips, a lifelong Democrat from Alcorn County, who switched parties to run for governor. Paul Johnson Jr., fresh from winning the Democratic primary with his segregationist "Stand Tall With Paul" slogan, became the first Democrat in the twentieth century to face a well-funded general election opponent. Phillips decided to go toe to toe with Johnson on the race issue. He claimed to be the only candidate with no ties to the Kennedys, and in fact his slogan became "K.O. the Kennedys." Proclaiming the GOP to be the only truly conservative party, he called himself a staunch segregationist and argued that a strong two-party system would actually "undermine the Negro" because "Negroes are all Democrats." In short,

Phillips claimed that because he was the only candidate not associated with the national Democratic Party, he was the candidate most able to defend Mississippi's "way of life."

The Democrats were outraged. At a rally toward the end of the campaign, outgoing Governor Ross Barnett invoked the events of 1876 when he reminded the crowd that Democrats "had gathered the courage to send the Republicans where they belong [that year]; once again we are calling on Mississippi Democrats to push out this Republican threat." The day before the election the *Clarion-Ledger* editorialized: "By attempting to set up a two-party system in Mississippi, the GOP is actually campaigning for minority control of the state by splitting the white, conservative majority." This appeal worked, as did the realization of local officials that a successful two-party system might one day mean opponents for them. In the end, the Mississippi Democratic Party, voters were assured, "is entirely independent and is free from any national party"—a refrain still heard in Mississippi.[35] Nevertheless, Phillips earned almost 40 percent of the vote—and garnered more actual votes than Nixon received in 1960. Phillips carried seven counties and came close to winning half a dozen more. Johnson sought revenge in the legislature that followed.

When Yerger was once asked to describe his greatest satisfaction as party chairman, he said, "That's easy to answer." He went on to explain his party's successful opposition to the attempt by Governor Johnson in the 1964 legislature to "end this Republican upstart movement once and for all."[36] Johnson's revenge was a package of twenty-two bills considered by the legislature that year, all of which would have imposed severe restrictions on the ability of the Republican Party to organize and field candidates. The most cunning proposal would have required the GOP to hold a primary election at the party's own expense, and, for the results to be legally valid, at least 10 percent of all voters would have had to participate in the primary—a practical impossibility in the early 1960s.[37] Yerger organized local Republicans against the legislation, and then captured the attention of some national reporters who covered the issue in a way that ridiculed the state.[38] The uproar led the House to mutiny against its leadership and vote down the bills. When asked to explain the defeat, an exasperated House member told reporters, "If you want the answer, see Republican Chairman Wirt Yerger. He seems to be in control of the House."[39]

The Mississippi GOP was on a roll. At the party's state convention in May, delegates came from all but three of Mississippi's eighty-two counties. Later at the national convention, Mississippi delegates helped nominate Goldwater for president and joined the cheering when Goldwater ended his acceptance speech "with the final, unforgettable thrust at the Party moderates: 'Extremism in the defense of liberty is no vice! ... Moderation in the pursuit of justice is no virtue!'"[40] As the gathering was drawing to a close, Frank Magee of NBC-TV turned on the camera for a live interview with the Mississippi chairman. Magee opened with some softball questions leading up to, as Yerger remembers, "the one question that was the reason he wanted the interview in the first place."

Magee asked, "Mr. Yerger, are Negroes welcome in the Mississippi Republican Party?" Buddy Klumb was standing right next to Yerger and remembers Yerger's exact comeback: "If they're conservative, they are."[41]

Later in the campaign, the Mississippi GOP held a fund-raising dinner at the Coliseum with South Carolina Senator Strom Thurmond as the keynote speaker.[42] The former head of the Dixiecrat Party, who had just switched to the Republican Party, attracted more than 2,300 people. Congressman John Bell Williams, whose endorsement of Goldwater at this rally would later cost him his seniority in Congress, knew his politics. As Republican activist W. D. "Billy" Mounger pointed out, "Yerger showed John Bell a poll that had over eighty percent of the people going for Goldwater, and John Bell couldn't stand not being on that side."[43] It was during the Goldwater election that Yerger recruited Mounger to the cause of the Republican Party. Over the last forty years, Mounger has become one of the most significant contributors to the rise of the GOP in Mississippi.

In the middle of the campaign, on July 2, 1964, President Johnson signed the watershed Civil Rights Act of 1964. Only twelve days earlier, Goldwater had been one of the six Republican senators to oppose the bill's final passage. On what it meant for the Republican Party, historians Charles Whalen and Barbara Whalen wrote: "The public's perception of a party's ideology ... is usually formed not by an individual senator's or congressman's philosophy or by the sum total of their views; rather, it is predicated upon the more widely heralded statements of the party's presidential candidates."[44] Mississippi voters proved the value of that observation on election day 1964. The results were stunning. Goldwater received more than 87 percent of the vote in Mississippi, winning every county, his best showing in the country. His coattails helped an unknown Republican candidate for Congress in Mississippi's Third District, Prentiss Walker, defeat the twenty-two-year Democratic incumbent Arthur Winstead. The *Clarion-Ledger* said it all: "Goldwater scored a smashing victory in

Mississippi. . . . The first Republican to carry the state since Grant won it with the aid of reconstruction bayonets. Goldwater . . . won the gratitude of many Mississippians for his vote against the 1964 Civil Rights Act."[45]

Ironically, the 1964 landslide forms the basis for what almost all state GOP leaders view as their single greatest strategic mistake—failing to recruit candidates against the other members of Congress or against Senator John Stennis. What could have happened in Mississippi did in fact happen next door in Alabama: five Republicans were elected to Congress on the coattails of Goldwater. Three of the Alabama candidates defeated incumbent Democrats, while the other two won open seats. In Mississippi, though, the party was divided over whether to recruit opposition candidates; some did not want to rock the boat and risk alienating possible Goldwater voters by opposing Stennis and the congressional incumbents.[46] But in the end, Republicans today agree with Mounger's assessment of their failure to field a full complement of candidates: "it was naive and stupid."[47]

Goldwater's loss to Lyndon Johnson set the stage for the resurgence of the GOP nationally. Journalists Thomas Edsall and Mary Edsall concluded: "The Goldwater campaign served as the vehicle for an ideological revolution within the Republican Party. This intra-party revolution ended the domination of the pro-civil rights, northeastern wing . . . and thus placed the GOP in position to capitalize on the white reaction that, in the second half of the 1960s, materialized in the North as well as the South."[48]

While Mississippi Republican leaders were at their national convention in 1964, Governor Johnson was able to achieve at least a modicum of retribution for the 1963 Rubel Phillips showing. Toward the end of a summer special session, Representative Buddie Newman proposed to amend the law establishing election commissioners. In Mississippi today, election commissioners are the five citizens elected in each of the state's counties charged with conducting general elections. Prior to 1968, however, each county had only three election commissioners, appointed by a state board composed of the governor, attorney general, and secretary of state, all of whom were Democrats. As a consequence, every election commissioner was a Democrat.

Leading up to the 1963 election, the state GOP began to invoke a little-known provision in state law that stipulated that the commissioners "shall not all be of the same political party." The Democrats were stacking the deck against the GOP throughout the counties, and the pesky Republicans were demanding the letter of the law be enforced. While the Phillips vote put a scare into the

Democrats, it was the incessant complaining about the unfair appointments that drove the legislature to give the upstart GOP a lesson in hardball politics. Newman's bill made only one change to the law: it removed the eight offending words, "shall not be of the same political party." The bill passed the House on July 9, but it got bogged down in the Senate eight days later, where it almost died until Senator Bill Hilbun reminded his colleagues that in addition to the Democratic and Republican parties in the state, there was "another party known as the freedom democratic party and it's just a bunch of Negroes." Hilbun warned that unless the law was changed, each county election commission faced the possibility of having one Democrat, one Republican, and "a Negro." The prospect overwhelmed the Senate, which immediately passed the bill.[49]

By 1966, Yerger had been chairman of the state Republican Party for ten years, and he was ready to relinquish the title. The state party enjoyed a permanent office, a full-time staff, a stable source of funding, and a growing membership. Buddy Klumb, the state finance chairman, was in line to succeed Yerger. Personal reasons prevented Klumb from accepting the position, however, so Clarke Reed, a member of the State Executive Committee from Greenville, agreed to take on the role.[50] In their 1976 book on southern politics, Jack Bass and Walter DeVries would write of Reed that his "political influence [would become] unequaled by any other nonofficeholder in the south."[51] At Reed's request, Mounger became state finance chairman, a job he once characterized as a "thankless, miserable job, the one that nobody else" wanted. For the next ten years, the two of them nurtured the party and became the best of friends—until 1976.[52]

All the while he was planning for a successor, Yerger was also drumming up support for someone to oppose the legendary Jim Eastland in his Senate reelection bid of 1966. There had actually been some talk in party circles that Yerger might run, and Yerger admits to having given it serious consideration. Unbeknownst to everyone, newly elected Congressman Prentiss Walker also had Eastland in his sights. Looking back on it, Yerger believes that Walker got wind of a news conference that Yerger had called to announce his resignation as party chair. Apparently, Walker thought Yerger was about to announce for Eastland's seat. So on the same day that Yerger held his farewell press conference, Walker announced for the U.S. Senate, without informing anyone. According to Mounger, Walker "saw a burning bush that read, 'United States Senator.'"[53]

Without a presidential candidate's coattails, Walker could muster only 29 percent of the vote. At the same time, a little-known Democratic state legislator, G. V. "Sonny" Montgomery, was elected to Walker's seat in Congress. Net score for 1966: Mississippi Republicans were humiliated in their race against Eastland and lost their only seat in Congress. Most of the leadership agreed with Yerger's assessment: Walker's decision to run and the colossal margin of his loss "set the party back in the state by about ten years ... because he literally shattered the morale that we had going up to that time."[54]

John Bell Williams was the Democratic candidate for governor in 1967. The disgraced member of Congress had become a hero in Mississippi. To maintain the momentum of the Republican Party organization, Mounger and Reed convinced Rubel Phillips to run again.[55]

The 1967 general election campaign is noteworthy for the strategy Phillips adopted: knowing that Williams was unassailable on his right, the GOP decided to run to his left. In speeches and advertisements, Phillips made his case: "As long as they remain Mississippians, the Negro and the white are bound together, even though they may live separate lives in separate communities. They are bound together so closely that neither can rise significantly without lifting the other. They are bound so tightly to one another that neither can keep the other down without paying the awesome penalty of restricting his own advancement."[56] In a television commercial where he looked into the camera and talked directly to the voters, Phillips laid it on the line against the "old guard establishment" who were nothing more than a group of "self-perpetuating politicians, selfish money grubbers, contract seekers, influence peddlers, thought control artists and miscellaneous hangers on and they are all held together by an interlocking pattern of financial and political self interest." He called them the "undemocratic establishment" who were opposed to change. Phillips made the case that this "establishment" was responsible for keeping Mississippi at the bottom. They were bound together not to help the people but to sustain their own power.[57] Conversely, Williams, the Democratic nominee, knew only one message in response to the massive registration of black voters that had taken place since the enactment of the 1965 Voting Rights Act: "If you don't vote ... you know who will!"[58] Turnout increased 23 percent over the 1963 election, with almost all of that increase coming in majority black counties. Phillips's percentage of the vote dropped from 38 percent in 1963 to 30 percent in 1967, though his absolute vote total decreased by only 5,136. Phillips lost many of the white voters he had earned in the 1963 race, but he picked up the overwhelming majority of new black votes.

REPUBLICANS EXPAND THEIR FOOTHOLD: 1968–1975

While the 1968 independent presidential campaign of George Wallace overwhelmed the Democratic and Republican candidates in Mississippi, it nonetheless created an opportunity. Clarke Reed explained how years later: "The southern strategy was just pure election politics . . . look at the math. The south was going for Wallace and Nixon could get it next time."[59] In the same way Yerger had used Goldwater, Reed used the Nixon presidency to define the party in the state. At the 1968 Republican National Convention in Miami, the Mississippi delegation teamed up with the delegations from South Carolina and Florida to deliver more than seventy votes to Richard Nixon, enabling him to win the nomination on the first ballot, defeating their old rival Nelson Rockefeller.[60] In 1969, Nixon endeared himself to Mississippians when he toured the ruins of the Gulf Coast in the aftermath of Hurricane Camille, in the process becoming the first sitting president since 1937 to set foot on Mississippi soil.[61] And in 1971, the U.S. Supreme Court handed Nixon the perfect "southern strategy" issue when it approved the forced busing of students to achieve school integration. As Thomas Edsall and Mary Edsall concluded, "While busing served as a mobilizing issue for the Republican Party, it fell like an axe through the Democratic party."[62]

The political landscape therefore gave state Republican leaders hope that 1972 had the possibility of turning into a 1964-like landslide. At about the same time that they set out to recruit candidates, three Democratic incumbent congressmen in Mississippi announced their retirements: Charles Griffin in the Fourth District, Thomas Abernethy in the Second, and William Colmer in the Fifth. The state GOP had been handed the gift of three open seats.

Mounger assumed responsibility for recruiting a candidate in Griffin's open seat. One day in early 1972, he received a call from Mike Allred, a Jackson lawyer active in the party. Allred had talked with Thad Cochran, who had expressed an interest in the post. After meeting with Mounger and being urged to consider running as a Republican, Cochran raised the possibility with his law partners. To his pleasant surprise, they encouraged him to say yes. With the backing of his law firm and with Mounger's commitment to make fund-raising "his top priority," Cochran qualified. In 1972, the thirty-four-year-old Cochran was having a hard time convincing himself early on that he would win, especially when he came home after his first meeting with Mounger and asked his wife, "Rose, how would you like to be married to a congressman?" Her reply: "Which one?"

Cochran soon realized, however, that the numbers could turn his way: he was in a general election campaign against Ellis Bodron, a Democrat with twenty-four years of service in the legislature and the embodiment of the "old guard" political establishment, and Eddie McBride, a black independent who had been recruited into the race by Fayette Mayor Charles Evers and other Loyalist Democrats.[63]

In 1972, the Fourth Congressional District, with a 30 percent black population, occupied the southwest corner of the state, including all of Hinds County. The outcome would hinge on black voters: would they stick with the Democrat or would they cast their lot with the black independent? Evers had only one complaint against Bodron. As mayor of Fayette, Evers had wanted to build a nursing home there. In Mississippi, nursing home locations are effectively determined by the legislature. Bodron, as an influential member of the state Senate, and a nursing home owner himself, blocked Evers's initiative. The 1972 campaign was payback, and with Evers campaigning actively for McBride, the final vote was preordained. With Nixon's coattails and Evers's help, Cochran won with a plurality of 48 percent of the vote. McBride pulled enough black voters off Bodron to make the difference.

In the Second Congressional District, which included the heart of the Delta, there were more black voters and no black independent. Republican candidate Carl Butler, a Columbus high school teacher, couldn't overcome the demographics of the district, losing to the Democratic nominee, David Bowen, by nearly 30 percentage points.

It was in the southeastern and Gulf Coast counties, home to the Fifth District, where the Nixon coattails would prove most helpful. Only three years had passed since thousands had greeted President Nixon in the aftermath of Hurricane Camille. For four years, Trent Lott had served as assistant to Democratic Congressman William Colmer, who was retiring after forty years in office. A number of local GOP activists appealed to Lott to campaign as a Republican. Unable to get a firm answer, they invited Lott to Dewey Lane's house in Jackson County, where they were going to commit time and money to his campaign if he qualified as a Republican. Lane remembers that Lott "walked in the door, saw the crowd, and said, 'I've got good news for you. I'm going to run as a Republican.' He had made his decision en route. . . . He would rather be defeated than become a mouthpiece for something he didn't believe in." As Lott remarked years later, "I just felt more comfortable with the Republicans."[64] With Nixon's help and Colmer's endorsement,

Lott carried ten of the twelve counties in the district, winning 55 percent of the vote.

Then there was Jim Eastland, also on the ballot, standing for reelection to his sixth consecutive term in the U.S. Senate. Before the qualifying deadline, James Meredith showed up at the secretary of state's office and signed up to oppose Eastland, as a Republican.

Meredith's filing took the state GOP leadership by surprise; they knew that someone other than Meredith needed to carry the GOP banner against the most powerful figure in Mississippi politics. Remembering his reaction at the time, Meridian businessman and Republican activist Gil Carmichael stated: "James Meredith came back down here and announced as a Republican candidate. I got a feeling Jim Eastland would love to run against Meredith. And Meredith would have loved to run against him. That would have been fun. But those of us that are trying to build a party didn't care for our party to be used as a darn vehicle for two people loving to fight each other."[65]

A small committee was organized to recruit another Republican candidate willing to oppose Eastland. At one meeting, the participants turned to Carmichael and asked him to qualify. In response to Carmichael's protests that he had no money, the group promised to raise the funds. When Carmichael argued he had a business to run and couldn't be on the road all day, Reed promised to "buy him an airplane." The "hotbox" worked.[66]

After Eastland and Carmichael won their primaries, Carmichael was to learn a painful lesson about politics: President Richard Nixon, a Republican, supported Senator Jim Eastland, a Democrat, against Carmichael. Nixon not only needed Eastland to confirm his judicial appointments, but depended on him to pass other legislation as well. Soon after the primary, Carmichael was visited by an emissary of John Mitchell, Nixon's campaign chairman: there was an ambassadorship waiting for Carmichael if he would withdraw from the race. Carmichael responded that he was in to stay. Jesse Brent, a Greenville businessman, was appointed head of Nixon's reelection effort in the state. No one in Mississippi was closer to Jim Eastland than Jesse Brent. At one point Nixon's attorney general, Richard Kleindienst, gave a speech in the Delta town of Cleveland and declared that if he lived in Mississippi, he'd be voting for Eastland.[67]

But the worst was yet to come. Toward the end of the campaign, Vice President Spiro Agnew traveled to Mississippi for an old-fashioned campaign rally. The Nixon campaign allowed Agnew to keynote the rally, with one stipulation: Gil Carmichael would not be invited. Mounger remembers it as "horrible, it was sickening to me, truthfully, and it was just [a] miserable experience to tell Gil Carmichael.... Wayne Weidie was manager of the Carmichael campaign ... and he really hit the ceiling.... I thought he and Clarke [Reed] were almost going to come to blows on the thing." According to Mounger, the Nixon campaign told Agnew, "If you go down there and we find out that you did something public with Carmichael, which we will know, that's fine, but when you come back, the only thing that you are going to get to do as vice president of the United States is what the Constitution says you can do."[68]

The Agnew stunt backfired. All of a sudden, Carmichael became the underdog. As he recalls the situation: "It hurt bad because he had great imagery down here. But then we sat down and said, 'How in the hell do you turn this thing around?'"[69] The press learned of the deal and went out of their way to give Carmichael free publicity.[70] In the end, Carmichael did better than anyone expected, polling nearly 39 percent of the vote. At one point, it was much closer. Carmichael remembers "running into Woods Eastland, the senator's son, at an event several years later who said 'You scared my daddy to death.... Our poll showed that on October 1 you had us beat'... and that's when they poured the money in." Eastland later complained, "That son of a bitch [Carmichael] cost my friends a half million dollars" in October.[71]

Mississippi was Nixon's best state in 1972, giving him 78.2 percent of the statewide vote. And with the election of Thad Cochran and Trent Lott to Congress, Mississippi's journey to the GOP was back in gear. Carmichael offered a final assessment of the 1972 campaign: "What was so lost in Mississippi history is that probably one of the best contributions that James Meredith [made in the state], besides the integration of Ole Miss, [was] really helping the Republican leadership in the state learn how to put on a primary."[72] When asked in a 1974 interview if there would have been any GOP opposition to Eastland if Meredith had not entered the race, he responded, "Frankly, probably not."[73] Mounger's final assessment on what the Nixon campaign did to Carmichael: "It shows you how little the people were that were running the committee [to reelect Nixon].... It's that kind of thinking that brought on Watergate."[74]

In 1972, the Republican candidates began a theme they have used to their advantage in Mississippi ever since: Butler, Cochran, Lott and Carmichael all publicly supported their party's nominee for President and their party's platform. The Democratic candidates, on the other hand, rarely mentioned, and in most cases disavowed, their party's nominee, George McGovern, and his platform.

In early 1973, a young law student became executive director of the state Republican Party—Yazoo City native Haley Barbour. Carmichael remembered that something else happened that year: "After the 1972 race, Agnew was feeling real bad about what had happened to me. He called me to Washington and I sat down with him, and said, 'We'd like to give you some reward for not backing and supporting you.'" Carmichael was appointed to the federal Highway Safety Advisory Commission.[75]

In 1974, the Watergate debacle caught up with Richard Nixon, and he was forced to resign the presidency that summer. Then came the 1975 governor's race. Gil Carmichael returned, this time against Cliff Finch. Much of the bad blood that materialized between the Gerald Ford and Ronald Reagan campaigns in Mississippi in the year to come had its genesis in this election. The reason: many believe the 1975 campaign for governor is a race the Republicans should have won. And they believe Carmichael lost it. They blame him for public policy positions he advocated in the campaign that were both unnecessary and unpopular—and, worst of all for the party faithful, liberal.

Over the course of the general election, Carmichael called for a new state constitution and ratification of the Equal Rights Amendment to the U.S. Constitution, and supported federal aid for a nearly bankrupt New York City government.[76] A story from Mounger captures one event in particular, a meeting of potential financial contributors to Carmichael's campaign: "Boy, we're just going to get a lot of money out of this group," Mounger recalls, "Well, Gil gets in there and, as a total shot out of the blue, he says that he had just taken a position for handgun registration. Boy! You talk about putting a blue funk on everything! I sat there and my gut just said, 'Ooph!' I started choking. I said to myself, 'Don't tell me he said that!'"[77]

In the end, Carmichael got a stunning 45 percent of the vote, providing fodder for disgruntled supporters who believe he would have been elected governor but for the positions he took during the campaign. Others argue that by drawing a clear contrast between himself and Finch, he helped to create the base the Republican Party now enjoys throughout urban and suburban Mississippi. One poll taken after the election found, for example, that "two-thirds of Carmichael's votes came from people who had never before voted for a Republican candidate."[78] A young Tim Carpenter, who would later manage a number of GOP campaigns in the state in the 1980s, offers a more personal example: "The look between Gil Carmichael and Cliff Finch, was to me night and day, and you know here was somebody who wanted to move the state forward ... and that solidified the fact that I know I'm in the right party."[79]

When asked about the campaign years later, Carmichael admitted the gun issue had been a mistake but observed, "I am perceived by a lot of ultra-conservatives...as a liberal. . . . Now, I understand their worry or concern about that, because many times my answers to questions are not even in the area where the common thought is at that time."[80]

POSTSCRIPT

When Wirt Yerger Jr. was seriously considering a campaign for public office, his good friend and colleague Billy Mounger warned him: "Wirt, there is only one person in the world that you would be totally pleased to support and help elect to office. That would be yourself. And five minutes after you were elected, you'd hate yourself."[81]

CHAPTER 3

THE BEGINNING OF THE END

1976

My name's Jimmy Carter. I'm a born again believer saved by the blood of
Jesus Christ, and I'm governor of Georgia and with your help, I'm gonna be
president of the United States.
—JIMMY CARTER, Jackson, Mississippi, Fall 1975[1]

O nly once in the fifty years since the 1956 presidential election has Mississippi given its electoral votes to the Democratic nominee for president—in 1976, to Jimmy Carter. In 1976, America celebrated its bicentennial. Gerald Ford was president, having assumed the office two years earlier owing to an unprecedented series of events in American history. A member of Congress from Michigan for nearly twenty-five years, Ford was chosen by President Richard Nixon to succeed Spiro Agnew, who resigned the vice presidency on October 10, 1973, because of criminal investigations into his conduct as Maryland's governor. Then, on August 8, 1974, after evidence was produced that he had participated in the cover-up of the Watergate break-in, Nixon addressed a national television audience and announced his resignation. Ford was sworn in as president the next day.

What follows is the story of Mississippi politics in 1976—the Democratic Party of Mississippi would finally unite its warring factions; the Mississippi Republican Party would nearly disintegrate during the course of sending the single most pivotal delegation to the Republican National Convention; and the state itself would become a battleground in the general election campaign to determine the country's next president.

ELECTION DAY

We begin our chronicle in the early morning following election day 1976. Two hours past midnight, Jimmy Carter had 265 electoral votes, 5 short of victory. Of the states not reporting final results, only Illinois, Ohio, California, and Mississippi possessed enough votes in the Electoral College to make the difference. Carter needed only one; Gerald Ford needed them all.

The phone lines between Carter's Atlanta headquarters and his Mississippi office in downtown Jackson were without rest. The race had been close all night. Danny Cupit, Carter's campaign codirector in Mississippi along with Fred Banks, had been on the phone all night, giving his contact at the Carter headquarters in Atlanta, Phil Wise, the vote returns as they came in. Wise begged for some final results. Cupit just couldn't say: key precincts were still reporting. Near the end, Wise let his exasperation overflow with Cupit, "This is getting down to where Mississippi is going to make the determination whether this guy gets elected president of the United States, so could you give me a little bit more feedback!"[2]

As the minutes ticked by, Carter's anxiousness got the best of him, and he started calling Governor Cliff Finch. "Well, Finch was the eternal optimist so when Carter would call, Finch would say, 'You've got it in the bag, you've won,' so Carter would go back and tell Wise," who would then call Cupit, who had no choice but to say, "Phil, that's not true!" During the middle of all this back and forth between Jackson and Atlanta, Cupit decided to leave the office and ride down the street to the "victory party" to rally the hundreds of supporters, waiting like everyone else for the final returns. As Cupit was gone, Wise called wanting yet another update and was informed that "Cupit's gone to the victory party." "What victory party?" Wise exploded. "The networks haven't given Mississippi to Carter! Why didn't someone call and tell us the news?" Narrowly averting a complete campaign meltdown, Cupit got back in time to return Wise's call and clear things up.[3]

At one point, Mark Hazard, a staffer on loan to the Mississippi campaign from Jim Eastland's office, got a call from a supporter in Alcorn County, wanting to know why the Mississippi vote had not been reported by the television networks. Hazard gave him the numbers—still too close to call. Whereupon Hazard was told: "Hell, just tell 'em Mississippi went for Carter, and we'll find the votes up here in the morning!"[4]

At 2:30 A.M., Finch put in another call to Carter to tell him that it looked like Mississippi was going Democratic. At the same time an aide handed the phone to Carter, NBC gave Mississippi and thus the presidency to Carter. "Cliff," Carter said over the sounds of rebel yells in his suite, "Mississippi just put me over the top. I love every one of you!"[5]

THE DEMOCRATIC PRIMARY

Jimmy Carter put the Iowa caucuses on the political map and transformed them into the heavyweight they represent today in the world of presidential nomination campaigns. A relatively obscure one-term governor of Georgia, Carter was looking for a way to surprise the media and gain attention before the New Hampshire primary. So, for over a year, Carter traveled across Iowa, meeting voters, making speeches, and impressing small town editors. By the time the other candidates realized what had happened, it was too late for them to respond. On January 19, 1976, Carter won the caucuses, beating his closest rival two to one, and overnight became the leading contender.[6]

The next caucus state was Mississippi. George Wallace was making his third try for the presidency, and the question posed by the national press was this: what would this southern state do in choosing between two southerners?[7]

The caucuses in Mississippi were historic, however, for a more important reason. At ten o'clock in the morning of Saturday, January 24, when Democrats throughout the state traveled to their precincts to choose among the Democratic candidates for president, black and white Democrats participated in the same caucuses—the Loyalist faction of the party had united with the Regular faction to form a unified Democratic Party in the state for the first time since the dawning of the civil rights era.[8] While newspapers reported some instances of discord between Regulars and Loyalists, most of the caucuses went smoothly. In a show of party solidarity, Tom Riddell, the state chairman of the Regulars, withdrew his name as a delegate from his precinct and asked that a black teacher replace him. Riddell stated: "It was my duty to resign and let him go ahead" because the precinct had not selected a black delegate.[9] By the time county and district conventions were held over the remainder of February, the two factions had completed their merger, and Wallace had won almost half the delegates, with Carter coming in second.[10]

On February 29, a unified Democratic Party held its state convention, and for the first time, a black man was elected to share the state party's leadership. Aaron Henry, head of the NAACP and chairman of the Loyalist faction, and Tom Riddell, a Canton businessman and head of the Regular faction, were elected by the 800 delegates as co-chairmen. The Regulars had wanted a single chairman since they knew they had the votes to elect someone who was white. The deal that "clinched the merger" was a compromise stipulating the co-chairmen arrangement until the 1980 state convention, when the party would revert to a single chairman. As one Regular conceded: "I'll put up with it for four years."[11] So, for nearly ten hours that day, blacks and whites, liberals and conservatives, farmers, businessmen, and laborers worked together to overcome their differences to knit their party together.[12]

Governor Finch is given much of the credit for making the merger of the two factions a reality. He campaigned on the issue and after taking office encouraged his supporters to unify the party. While Mississippi's congressional delegation favored the merger to protect their seniority positions in Congress, and while it helped that Jimmy Carter was a southerner, the magnet that attracted the bulk of the Regulars to the unified caucuses was George Wallace. When the Alabama governor made his first campaign for the White House in 1968, he competed as an Independent. Eight years later, he returned as a Democrat. Thus, the only way George Wallace could garner Mississippi's delegate votes was for his followers to participate in the primary caucuses. By 1976, it was more important for his white supporters in Mississippi to elect Wallace than it was to boycott the unified caucuses.[13]

Throughout the rest of May and into June, as Carter closed in on the nomination, the target for his Mississippi campaign was the conversion of Wallace delegates to Carter delegates. That effort ended on June 9 when Wallace officially endorsed his fellow southerner for the nomination. As one reporter observed: "George Wallace's nod to Carter may fill whatever cracks have been left in the merger of the once rivaling factions of the Democratic Party."[14] For nearly twelve years, a core group of activists, operating under the Loyalist banner, had worked to join the state Democratic Party to the national party. In 1976, they had a governor committed to the unity effort and two presidential candidates whose campaigns facilitated the unity effort. All in all, the proponents of a unified party were able to take advantage of opportunities in 1976 that had theretofore been unavailable. As with most seminal events in our state's political history, it happened through a combination of perseverance and timing.

The Democratic National Convention convened on July 12, and for the first time in more than thirty years, the delegation from Mississippi was united and in support of the party's nominee. Since Carter's nomination was a foregone conclusion, the unified delegation from Mississippi became one of the news events of the convention.[15] Following his acceptance speech, Carter was joined on the rostrum in a final celebration by Democratic politicians from all parts of the country, one of whom in particular would soon play a pivotal role in Carter's victory in Mississippi—George Wallace.

THE REPUBLICAN CONVENTION

As the 1976 Republican National Convention was winding down, Billy Mounger crawled into a car to head back to his hotel and "just burst out in tears. . . . I've never been that upset. . . . I've never, honestly, as a grown man or a young man, ever cried as profusely as I did at that time."[16] Ronald Reagan, Mounger's candidate, would not be the Republican nominee for president. And if any one state was credited for that decision, that state was Mississippi.

As 1976 unfolded, however, no one anticipated that Mississippi Republicans would come to dominate the political news in the weeks leading up to the convention. Clarke Reed had earlier announced his resignation as state chairman, saying it was "time to step down" after ten years.[17] A young state senator from Laurel, Charles Pickering, was chosen to head the state GOP, though it was agreed Reed would lead the delegation to the national convention. All were allied in the cause of Ronald Reagan and his pursuit of the presidency against Gerald Ford.[18]

At the April state GOP convention, the delegates made two critical decisions that would ultimately break apart friendships, steer the state party on a more conservative course, and provoke grown men to cry. First, the delegates adopted the "unit rule"—Mississippi's thirty votes at the national convention would be cast as a bloc for one candidate, based on a majority vote of the delegates. Second, the delegation would remain uncommitted until the national convention in order to maximize its influence.[19]

About the same time, the Ford campaign drafted Harry Dent, a former Nixon White House political aide from South Carolina, to help with recruiting southern delegates. One of the first activists to contact Dent was John Davis, a volunteer for Gil Carmichael in his 1975 run for governor. While Republicans across the country were assuming that Mississippi was solidly for Reagan, Davis told Dent that "there's gold to be mined in that Mississippi delegation. . . . We can turn the Reagan tide in Mississippi around and win all 30 votes under [the] unit rule."[20] Davis knew the delegates, had worked with them on behalf of Carmichael, and was convinced many of them were not wed to Reagan. By this time, Carmichael and Jackson City Commissioner Doug Shanks had been appointed co-chairs of the Ford campaign in Mississippi. Davis joined with Carmichael and Shanks and started calling the delegates, while Dent began working on his old friend from the Nixon days, Clarke Reed.

By early summer, with the primary elections over, the contest for the nomination between Ford and Reagan remained too close to call. Neither candidate had a majority of the delegates. The hunt for votes shifted to the uncommitted delegates. When Reagan came to Biloxi in June, his support appeared strong in the state as he declared he would reform welfare, give more federal power to the states, and "get Washington out of the classroom and get God back in."[21] It was during this trip, however, that the ominous sounds of party discord surfaced in the press, when Doug Shanks, a Jackson city commissioner and a delegate to the convention, announced he would break the unit rule and vote for Ford. Shanks, Davis, and Carmichael were slowly recruiting delegates to back the president.[22] Even Reed was admitting Reagan was slipping: "I would say today that Reagan is ahead but there are enough uncommitted delegates that a majority could vote either way."[23] With just one month left before the national convention convened in Kansas City, Mississippi had the largest bloc of uncommitted delegates in the country, thanks to the unit rule.[24] The national press had begun to frame the battle: the candidate who gets Mississippi gets the nomination.[25]

The lobbying of the Mississippi delegates became so intense that the *Jackson Clarion-Ledger* was reporting that "First Lady Betty Ford and her husband's opponent, former California governor Ronald Reagan, had joined cabinet officials and congressional leaders in telephone efforts to round up Mississippi support at the Republican National Convention."[26] Haley Barbour, then state GOP executive director, remembers many of the delegates were on a first-name basis with Betty Ford.[27] It was then that Carmichael conceived the idea of getting delegates to commit to Ford by sending telegrams directly to the White House.[28] They began to report these commitments to the press and demonstrate movement to Ford. The Reagan campaign was convinced Carmichael was inflating his numbers, but the tactic worked.[29]

In an effort to counter the telegram ploy, Reed called a meeting of the delegation on Sunday, July 25.[30] Unbeknownst to Reed, the Reagan campaign had concluded that something drastic was needed to overcome the slippage that was occurring among delegates who had previously committed and those who remained uncommitted, most notably in Mississippi.[31] Across the country, the one-on-one lobbying of delegates by the White House was too intense to ignore. Barbour had predicted it several months earlier: "We felt like either Reagan would beat Ford in the primaries or Ford would win the nomination. . . . Reagan cannot compete with the White House."[32] Reagan's solution, virtually unprecedented, was to name his choice for vice president in advance of the convention: force Ford's hand, put pressure on him to name his choice, and try and break apart his fragile coalition of delegates. Since Reagan believed he had a firm hold on delegates from the South and West, his campaign looked to the Northeast for someone to share the ticket.[33]

Back in Jackson, at Reed's Sunday meeting, Reagan's southern director, David Keene, joined Dent and Dick Cheney, Ford's White House chief of staff, along with throngs of reporters waiting "for some glimmer about how the delegation might vote." Emerging from their closed-door meeting, the delegates announced that both the unit rule and their uncommitted position remained intact. It was clear to everyone, though, that the delegation was no longer solidly for Reagan.[34] After the gathering, however, Keene pulled Reed aside and told him a secret. The rest of the world would learn about it the next day: Reagan would name Richard Schweiker, a liberal Republican senator from Pennsylvania, as his vice presidential running mate.[35]

Dent heard the announcement the next day and called Reed immediately, urging him to switch to Ford. Dent knew that for Reed, one of the "unforgivable" acts for a Republican candidate was to attempt to "balance" a conservative ticket with a liberal. At a June meeting of the Mississippi delegation, Reagan was specifically asked if would pick a philosophically compatible running mate or one who was different to broaden the base. Barbour remembers Reagan's response: "He didn't believe in picking somebody different. He thought it was a sham. He would pick his philosophical twin so that if something happened to him, the guy that became president would be just like him." This was not the first time Reagan had disparaged a "balanced" ticket, and Reed has long argued that it was a chief reason he backed Reagan.[36]

After making it through the day while his phone "wouldn't stop ringing," Mounger called a meeting at his house that evening to discuss Schweiker.

Among those present were Reed, Pickering, Barbour, Tommy Giordano (a Reagan volunteer coordinator), and Swan Yerger (a Reagan delegate to the convention). Reed stunned the group when he admitted he was considering a move to Ford. The national press, in the state to cover Sunday's caucus, stayed over after the Schweiker announcement: the reaction in Mississippi was critical. By the time the meeting was over, it was near midnight, and more than fifty reporters and television crews were camped out in Mounger's front yard. From then on, "no one got any peace."[37]

Tuesday morning, Reed called Keene and Dent and told them he was close to endorsing Ford. Dent called Cheney and told him to "play the big card"—the president should call Reed. In the meantime, "virtually every political reporter in America" was calling Reed and every other delegate. Tuesday night, Reed called Keene to say he was backing Ford. Keene's response: "I told [Clarke] he couldn't do it because he had given his word" to support Reagan. When Reed said he had made promises to others as a result of the Schweiker announcement, Keene pleaded, "Well, screw them, not me!"[38] Keene asked Reed to wait twenty-four hours, which he agreed to do. That same night, Reagan called Mounger, the first time the two had spoken since the Schweiker announcement. Mounger remembered his exact words to Reagan: "You have just given me yesterday the worst dose of castor oil I've ever had in my life. . . . You got every part of my insides. . . . I am a hollow shell."[39] But Mounger had decided to stick with Reagan.

Wednesday was D-Day. The Pennsylvania delegation, which Schweiker was trying to convert to Reagan, was coming to the White House the next day for a face-to-face meeting with the president. Ford needed to tell them that Reagan had lost Clarke Reed.[40] Mississippians woke up that morning to the *Clarion-Ledger*'s analysis: "Schweiker Damaging Reagan Bid—A *Clarion-Ledger* poll indicated Ronald Reagan's choice of Sen. Richard Schweiker as a potential running mate has cost him the edge he once held among Mississippi delegates."[41] By the time the paper hit the newsstands, Mounger and his team were trying to salvage Reagan's support and secure Reed. As Mounger once described his reaction to Schweiker: "I jumped straight up in the air and out of my shoes but I landed back in them. The only man in the United States that didn't end up back where he started was Clarke."[42] Wirt Yerger Jr. summed up the feelings of many when he observed, "While I thought it was a mistake to pick Schweiker, that was no reason to leave Reagan. People do make mistakes and I think he made one, a big one. . . . You just hope that a heart attack doesn't happen."[43]

Reed, however, was distraught. He called Dent late that afternoon and read his statement. Anxious to get the news out to the television networks, Dent pushed him to release it through the state party. Dent's newest problem was that the party's executive director, Haley Barbour, was a Reagan supporter and was stalling. At 8:00 P.M., Barbour released the statement, though Dent had already leaked it to CBS's Walter Cronkite.[44] Dent rejoiced the next day: "Pennsylvania held, and the South appeared to be cracking."[45]

For Mounger, Reed broke his word to support Reagan.

For Reed, Reagan betrayed conservative principles Reed had supported all his life when he tried to balance the ticket.

For Mounger, Reed capitulated to the pressure because he wanted to be on the winning side and was looking for an excuse to switch.

For Reed, his decision was an act of conscience.[46]

To this day, the two men don't speak to each other.

Reagan had lost momentum—delegates from around the country assumed that if Reagan couldn't hold Mississippi, he was a loser.[47] Thursday morning's *Clarion-Ledger* gave the Reagan campaign the bad news: "Just as Reagan appeared to be recovering from the wounds created by his choice of running mate, the announcement by Reed presented a serious, possibly mortal blow."[48]

As the Reed statement was being distributed, Tommy Giordano received a call from Thad Cochran, telling him he would be flying down the next day with President Ford. Giordano asked Cochran about Schweiker. His reply: "He is the most liberal kook on Capitol Hill, and it scares me to death to think that he could be a heartbeat away from being president." Having focused more on the politics of the choice, rather than the public policy implications, Giordano admitted he had never thought about it like that. He publicly switched to Ford the next day.[49]

President Ford traveled to Jackson on Friday to court the delegation. A headline in the *Clarion-Ledger* captured the drama: "Reed—Eyes of the Nation Upon Him." A separate article described the scene: "Ford's arrival climaxes a frantic week of delegate chasing by both sides in Mississippi, which now holds the greatest number of technically uncommitted delegates in the country."[50] The Ford visit boosted the work of his team in Mississippi and netted public endorsements from Congressmen Thad Cochran and Trent Lott.[51]

Five days later, Reagan and Schweiker flew to Jackson to lobby the delegation directly. "Today could be judgment day for former California Gov. Ronald Reagan," was the *Clarion-Ledger's* analysis. Dent made yet another trip to Jackson to attend the meeting, calling Cheney afterward to say that Schweiker "just didn't do well with the delegates."[52] The *Clarion-Ledger* summed up the Schweiker performance:

> *The Republican senator from Pennsylvania tried to shed his liberal voting image before Mississippi's delegation to the Republican National Convention. Schweiker attempted to justify his liberal voting record to the conservative delegation by explaining he represents a liberal Pennsylvania constituency when he votes in the Senate. Ronald Reagan came to Jackson Wednesday hoping to bolster his support among Mississippi Republicans, but left with his position apparently somewhat weakened.*

Shanks believed Ford had the delegation when Giordano stood up at the meeting and said, "You know, you told us there would be no ideological split on the ticket and you betrayed us, and I ain't supporting you."[53] Mounger, however, was not giving up.

Barbour captured the performance of the two candidates. It was a plus for Ford, and Reagan "would have done much better to have left Schweiker at home."[54] With less than a week to go before the opening of the convention, the phone calls and letters were continuing to inundate the embattled Mississippi delegation. A newspaper poll showed Ford with twenty-eight delegates and Reagan with twenty-two.[55]

Dewey Lane, a delegate from Pascagoula, once described the scene as the drama moved to the convention in Kansas City: "The media just encamped. They had us outnumbered about three to one in our motel. . . . They were just swarming all over, constantly pulling each one aside, trying to pick our brains and see what we knew."[56] Mounger remembered: "You couldn't escape. The TV cameras were everywhere. I mean you can't eat. You can't breathe, for the reporters. Everybody is wanting a story, every second. . . . You almost feel like you can't go in and take a shower, that there's going to be a TV camera on you."[57] Mike Retzer, a delegate from Greenville, recalled driving up to his hotel and "seeing this 125-foot microwave tower in front of the building. If anything symbolized the stature of the Mississippi delegation, [it] was its own direct link to the TV networks."[58]

Saddled with a campaign that was losing momentum, Reagan tried one last maneuver to shake some votes his way: change the convention rules to force Ford to name his vice presidential candidate early. For the rules vote to succeed, the Reagan campaign would need the entire thirty votes from Mississippi. By this time, as Shanks remembered, "Mississippi had been blown completely out of proportion. I mean I was being interviewed at least twice a day on national television. One of our Ford delegates had a crush on singer Pat Boone. The Reagan camp found out about it and the next day Pat Boone showed up to take her to dinner. Another delegate who prayed constantly for Reagan told me right after it was all over that we were all going to hell." In an interview years later, Shanks told of Bill Dease, a delegate who worked at Jackson State and who got stuck in Kansas City traffic. Dease called the Ford campaign and said "'I'm a Mississippi delegate,' and they sent a limousine after him. I mean it was just a completely unreal situation."[59]

On Tuesday, the delegation was lobbied by Treasury Secretary William Simon, Texas Senator John Tower, former Texas Governor John Connally, assorted Hollywood stars, and Reagan himself. "Their efforts—such as a speech by actor Efrem Zimbalist Jr. that brought tears to his eyes—looked at times more like a spiritual revival than a political confrontation." During all of this, Mounger remembers David Keene coming over to the delegation sometime before the vote on the rule change: "He asked me, 'What's your count on [the rule change]?' I said, 'Hell, David, I don't know.' He said, 'You don't know! Well, we've got to know.' I said, 'Damn, how can I tell you. . . . I've got several people on the fence. . . . I can't tell you how they're going to vote for Ford and Reagan, how in the hell am I going to tell you how they are going to vote on [the rule change]. . . . It is going to fall out damn near thirty-thirty . . . it can be either way.'" Keene knew then they were in trouble.[60]

The delegation finally voted: thirty against the rule change, twenty-eight for Reagan's position, with one absent. The unit rule yielded all thirty Mississippi votes for Ford.[61] Dent described it as the "shoot-out at the O.K. Corral. It was the crucial vote in the convention."[62]

At one point before the state-by-state roll call on the rule change, tensions were running high, with the Ford people—Giordano, Shanks, and others—getting into a loud argument with Reed, Mounger, and Pickering. Barbour ushered them off to the side underneath a stairway, trying to shield the group from a press captivated by any excitement in the Mississippi delegation. At one point, the argument got so loud that Barbour, in an effort to distract the press and provide cover for the group, began to shout the eighty-two Mississippi counties in alphabetical order. Barbour remembers that everybody got into the act, and "when I got through all eighty-two, someone said, 'Now, let's hear you do them backwards.' Everybody just roared! And I did it—I did them backwards! People were just in hysterics." Mission accomplished: the press had forgotten about the upheaval underneath the stairway.[63]

All eyes were on Mississippi when the roll call began to decide the fate of the proposed rule change. The Reagan people asked for a delay at the last minute to check their votes.[64] Mounger and others were pressuring Reed to pass when called upon to announce the Mississippi vote. Shanks and Giordano were "yelling in his face" to give the vote. By this time an "enormous crush [had] developed around the delegation ... and the hall [grew] quiet" as the time came for Mississippi's decision.[65] To the outrage of the Ford supporters, Reed acceded to Mounger and passed, and there was the "biggest moaning in that [convention]. It was just like 'My Lord! Here's that Mississippi delegation that has been at the top of the news and everything and they pass!' "[66] On the second round, the delegation cast its thirty votes against the rule change, joining a majority of the convention to oppose the last attempt by the Reagan campaign to win the nomination.

The vote on Wednesday night for president was anticlimactic. The Mississippi delegation broke the unit rule and cast sixteen votes for Ford and fourteen for Reagan, contributing to Ford's winning margin for the party's nomination. The article in the next day's *Clarion-Ledger* said it all:

> *Can Leaders Salve GOP Wounds?—As Mississippi Republicans return from the site of their bloodiest confrontation over a presidential nomination, the healing of wounds of that fight and the resolution of a division in party ranks may lie with new state GOP leadership. No doubt, much of the struggle here merely showed the state party was, as Mounger said, "going through growing pains. It isn't the old college fraternity it used to be when we could all meet and agree on everything."[67]*

When Shanks and Giordano arrived at the convention for the Thursday night acceptance speeches, two Secret Service agents were waiting for them: "Will you please come to the president's box? Mr. Dent is waiting on you." Shanks remembered what happened next:

> *There was the entire cabinet and their wives and Harry's holding court with a NBC reporter Doug Kiker. Dent introduced us: "Doug, here are the boys from Mississippi. I couldn't have done it without them." Harry said, "Let's have a*

drink of the president's whiskey." One of the cabinet member's wives came over
and got real snotty with us and Dent wheeled around and said, "Madam, will
you kindly move your ass. The reason your husband has a job is because of these
two boys."[68]

Looking back on it some thirty years later, the Reagan people have argued they needed a dramatic move to overcome the successful White House lobbying of uncommitted delegates and to offset the pronouncements of prominent GOP leaders like Clarke Reed, who were beginning to argue publicly that Reagan couldn't win. Naming the vice presidential candidate ahead of the convention was the option Reagan and his strategists chose. If Mississippi was critical, as the Reagan insiders have since maintained, they never talked directly with Clarke Reed or Billy Mounger or Haley Barbour to ask them what it would take to salvage the delegation for Reagan. They never consulted with their team in Mississippi before naming Schweiker. What is clear is that Shanks, Carmichael, Davis, and others were in constant communication with the national Ford campaign, working hand in hand with them to win over the delegation. The Reagan campaign never employed a similar two-way exchange of information and strategy options with their supporters in Mississippi.

Two years after the convention, Haley Barbour had this to say about Clarke Reed: "In the 1976 convention, he along with some other people went through some things that not ten people a century go through. People perceive . . . that he had the national nomination for president for the Republican Party in his hands. People really and truly thought that Reed could control this delegation and that this delegation was going to decide if Reagan or Ford was going to be the nominee."[69] If that was indeed the case, though Reed argues it was not because of the determination of Shanks and others to break the unit rule, then the Reagan campaign made one of the classic campaign mistakes: a small group of consultants and staff, closeted in a faraway office, thought they could impose their decision on activists all over the country.

One journalist who covered the convention observed later that "it will never be entirely clear whether [Reagan] could have won with Mississippi."[70] But today, when you talk with Mississippians who were Reagan supporters in 1976, their bitterness stems from the belief that Reagan was the only candidate who could have defeated Carter, that Ford was too closely linked with Nixon to survive a general election campaign. As one Reagan supporter said later, "[We] would a whole lot rather have Reagan with Schweiker, than to have Jimmy

Carter. And most of us perceived Reagan as the only person who could beat Jimmy Carter."[71] Haley Barbour quantified the belief: "Gerald Ford is a safe 47 percent, but he can't win. Reagan may get forty, but he may get fifty."[72]

Four days later after the convention, Clark Reed licked his wounds and was elected one of the national party's eight vice chairmen by a twenty-five to twelve vote of the southern Republican National Committee members.[73]

THE GENERAL ELECTION

For the first time since African Americans regained the right to vote, the Democratic Party had nominated a candidate for president who could capture a good share of the white vote, combine it with a solid black turnout, and take Mississippi. To realize this possibility, the Carter campaign identified two targets in the state: mobilize its base of black voters and win over a significant portion of rural white voters. To counter this possibility, the Ford campaign isolated its own two targets: mobilize its base of urban-suburban white voters and win over a significant portion of rural white voters.

When it came to attracting rural white voters, the 1976 Carter campaign in Mississippi brought to the task two heavyweights Ford couldn't match: Jim Eastland and George Wallace. Meanwhile, the Democrats enjoyed three other advantages: their candidate was a southerner, their state party was unified behind its candidate, and their candidate was a Southern Baptist who would share his religion without embarrassment. On the other hand, the Ford campaign was forced to rely on a state GOP that was badly split, emotionally spent, and less than fully enthusiastic about its candidate who called Michigan his home.

A Carter visit to the state on September 17 kicked off the general election campaign in Mississippi. Accompanied by Senators Eastland and Stennis, the Carter entourage campaigned on the Gulf Coast for state Representative Gerald Blessey, who was opposing Congressman Trent Lott. Carter told the crowd that the civil rights movement was "the best thing that happened to the South in my lifetime," while Eastland told the press: "I'm for him all the way."[74]

With their polls showing a close race in Mississippi, the Ford campaign rented the steamboat *Natchez* and journeyed down the Mississippi River, telling riverside crowds that "Carter better get down here and do some repair work." On the boat with Ford were former Congressmen William Colmer,

Prentiss Walker, and John Bell Williams.[75] The ever-present Harry Dent told the press that Carter was dropping in the polls because "the man really is a liberal—a born again liberal."[76] Off the boat, Ford took a day to travel along U.S. Highway 90, speaking to thousands in Bay St. Louis, Gulfport, Biloxi, and Pascagoula.[77]

Jimmy Carter then did something that created havoc for a campaign that had targeted rural white voters: an interview with him was published in *Playboy* magazine. As Jules Witcover points out in *Marathon*, his book about the 1976 campaign, the most fascinating part of the interview focused on Carter's views about his religious convictions and their intersection with public policy. A Southern Baptist, Carter was never hesitant to talk about his Christian faith. Carter explained what it meant to be a Baptist:

Committing adultery, according to the Bible which I believe in, is a sin. For us to hate one another, for us to have sexual intercourse outside marriage, for us to engage in homosexual activities, for us to steal, for us to lie, all these are sins. But Jesus teaches us not to judge other people. We don't assume the role of judge. . . . All Christians, all of us, acknowledge that we are sinful, and the judgment comes from God, not from another human being. . . . What Christ taught about most was pride, that one person should never think he was any better than anybody else.

Then Carter, perhaps carried away with making his point, remarked:

I try not to commit a deliberate sin. I recognize that I'm going to do it anyhow, because I'm human and I'm tempted. . . . Christ said, 'I tell you that anyone who looks on a woman with lust has in his heart already committed adultery.' I've looked on a lot of women with lust. I've committed adultery in my heart many times. This is something that God recognizes I will do . . . and God forgives me for it.[78]

The reaction was immediate. Many religious leaders condemned the use of a forum like *Playboy* for Carter to air his views. To overcome the repercussions in Mississippi, the Carter staff recruited Owen Cooper, a prominent Yazoo City businessman and a former president of the Southern Baptist Convention, to endorse Carter.[79] Hodding Carter III, who by this time had moved to Atlanta to work for Jimmy Carter in his national campaign office, remembers a different reaction to his candidate's emphasis on religion. Sent by the campaign to California to convince liberals in the Democratic Party there to stick with the former Georgia governor, Hodding Carter was at a meeting where a white liberal stood up and asked indignantly, "You're asking us to support some damn Georgia redneck," at which point a black delegate rose and said, "I'll take a born-again Baptist Georgian who now says he's got religion on race before I'll take you boys who are a bunch of hypocritical sons of bitches!"[80]

Meanwhile, the Ford campaign began to make its own mistakes. The president sought to cut funding for the Tennessee-Tombigbee Waterway in northeast Mississippi, provoking Governor Finch to publicly rebuke Ford.[81] Then, in his second debate with Carter, Ford made the most serious blunder of his campaign when he claimed that the countries in Eastern Europe were not controlled by the Soviet Union.[82] By the middle of October, newspapers were calling the race in Mississippi "too close to call."[83] In a speech to a local civic organization, Clarke Reed said, "I can tell you from authoritative polls, we're not safe in either camp." Reed expressed satisfaction, however, that for "the first time in anybody's lifetime we have had a contest. Both sides are not taking Mississippi for granted."[84]

"Under the radar screen" is a term often used to describe an activity that goes largely unnoticed by the press or the general public. Such was the case with the phone call that Carter campaign codirector Danny Cupit made every other morning to Senator Jim Eastland. Eastland would give Cupit a few of his supporters to contact. The next time they talked, Cupit would report on the calls and discuss any necessary follow-up. Eastland would then give him a few more to call. This give-and-take lasted for most of the fall campaign. Cupit remembers one call he made to a rural mail carrier who "went all over the county delivering mail and knew every soul in the county." Almost all of the calls resembled the one Cupit made to a state legislator in Oktibbeha County: "You tell [Eastland] that if he's for Carter, I'm for Carter and I'll do everything I can to help." Cupit once described the implications of this calling program: "It was the first time I saw graphically the influence that Jim Eastland had on Mississippi politics; it gave Carter instant credibility with the white power structure of the state."[85]

In the closing weeks of the campaign, George Wallace presented Jimmy Carter with a gift. In Jackson for a routine meeting with Governor Finch, the Alabama governor responded to a prearranged question about Carter at a press conference by endorsing his candidacy. What happened next may have made the difference in Mississippi on election day. Wayne Edwards, a Carter campaign staffer, secured a tape of Wallace's endorsement—"if Jimmy Carter loses this election, it will be the last opportunity for someone in the South to win the White House"—added a version of "Dixie" in the background, and all of a sudden had a powerful radio advertisement. Edwards bought ads on radio stations targeted to white audiences, especially in northeast Mississippi, and Steve Guyton, another campaign worker, spent the next several days with "a briefcase full of tapes and campaign checks" traveling to the radio stations delivering the ads. "We saturated country radio with that ad until election day," Edwards remembered years later.[86]

The national election was the closest since 1916: Carter polled 50.1 percent of the national vote. In Mississippi, Carter carried the state with a plurality of 49.6 percent—a mere 14,464 votes made the difference.

THE VOTE

When rural white voters are targeted in a statewide campaign in Mississippi, the eleven-county region in the northeast corner of the state instantly becomes the battleground for one simple reason: it contains the highest density of rural white voters in the state. In 1972, these voters gave the Democratic presidential nominee—George McGovern—a mere 11.9 percent of the vote; four years later, they gave Carter 61.6 percent, the largest movement of any region in the state. Overall, Carter earned his highest returns in northeast Mississippi, more than any other region, including the predominantly black Delta. While African American counties increased their aggregate Democratic vote total by 109 percent over 1972, northeast Mississippi produced the largest increase in actual Democratic votes: a 584 percent increase over 1972.

A postelection analysis of the national turnout by then Republican strategist Kevin Phillips found the same trend:

In the case of Jimmy Carter's narrow victory, group after group claims to have provided the critical margin. Different yardsticks will yield different results of course; in raw percentages, blacks did best by Carter. But in terms of 1972 electoral group shifts . . . affluent suburbanites and upper-middle-income professionals in many areas did almost as well by Ford [in 1976] as by Nixon in 1972. The real key lay in the working class and lower middle class constituencies, routinely ignored by Gerald Ford type Establishment Republicanism.[87]

In Mississippi, those voters are found throughout the state, but they overwhelmingly define the northeast region. Haley Barbour characterized the election day outcome more succinctly: "The thing that hurt us most is that a lot of people voted their geography rather than their philosophy." It was not a lesson the GOP would forget in 1980, nor one Barbour would personally forget some twenty-seven years later in his own race for governor.[88]

LOOKING AHEAD

Back in Atlanta the day after the election, Hamilton Jordan, Jimmy Carter's national campaign manager, hosted the team's last staff meeting and offered the real reason for his candidate's win: "I've got an announcement to make. So all of you know the secret weapon. You all know that Mississippi put us over the top last night. And how did we get Mississippi? We got Hodding [Carter] the hell out of Mississippi."[89]

On December 1, Billy Mounger sent a letter to a friend recounting the events of 1976: "The state now has the dubious distinction of sabotaging Reagan and clinching for Carter. What infamy!"[90] The Democrats couldn't agree more as 1976 came to a close. The future looked promising indeed. As Mississippians were preparing for the Christmas holidays, however, an ominous article appeared in the *Clarion-Ledger*, noting that former Governor Bill Waller might oppose Jim Eastland in 1978, "whether or not Sen. Eastland decides to seek re-election."[91] Hodding Carter summed up what happened next: "I was really naïve. I thought we could keep it stitched together."[92]

POSTSCRIPT

Reaping the spoils of winning the presidency in 1976, the Democrats in Mississippi sought to have Mark Hazard appointed by the president as head of the Farmers Home Administration in the state. The bureaucracy at the Department of Agriculture was being less than cooperative, postponing the decision for months, which eventually led to a meeting in Washington between Danny Cupit and Eastland to discuss the appointment. While Cupit was explaining to the senator how the appointment was being held up, Eastland asked his secretary to get the president on the phone. A few minutes later, Carter's chief of staff, Hamilton Jordan, returned the call, asking if he could help. Eastland explained his interest in having Hazard appointed: "Mr. Jordan, are you going to make me waste the president's time to get this boy appointed?" A few minutes later, Eastland's secretary rang in to say that Secretary of Agriculture Bob Bergland was on the line: "Put him through," says Eastland. "Senator," Bergland told him, "I just want you to know I am approving the press release that will be issued in a few minutes naming Mark Hazard director of the Farmer's Home Administration in Mississippi."[93]

THE CAMPAIGN TO SUCCEED JIM EASTLAND

1977–1978

In 1978, his last year in office, Jim Eastland asked Senator Ted Kennedy to deliver the commencement address at the University of Mississippi. In his opening, Kennedy reported to the crowd that he had asked Eastland, "How can you invite a Kennedy to be graduation speaker at Ole Miss?" Eastland responded, "Because I'm not running for re-election."
—*JACKSON DAILY NEWS*, May 15, 1978

For the past sixty years, only four men have served Mississippi in the U.S. Senate: Jim Eastland, John Stennis, Thad Cochran, and Trent Lott. The most colorful, transparent, racially inflammatory, and overtly political of these has been Jim Eastland.

JIM EASTLAND

Known for the trademark cigar in the corner of his mouth and his love of good whiskey, Eastland served for nearly thirty-six years in the Senate, and along the way became Mississippi's premier political power broker.[1] He arrived in the Senate before Pearl Harbor; outlasted seven presidents; urged defiance of *Brown v. Board of Education* in the harshest terms imaginable; counted the Kennedy family among his friends; approved the appointment of every federal judge after 1956, when he ascended to the chairmanship of the Senate Judiciary Committee; and has been called everything from "a great man" to "common as pig tracks."[2] At the height of his power he commanded a cadre of loyal followers throughout the state who helped to elect four governors in a row, starting with Ross Barnett and ending with Bill Waller; won reelection in 1972 with the help of President Nixon, who repudiated the Republican Party's nominee in that campaign; and proved crucial to Jimmy Carter's 1976 victory in Mississippi.

Some have speculated that Eastland would have run again in 1978 if he had drawn no opposition, that it was the prospect of a competitive and expensive election that made him think twice, if for no other reason than he disliked campaigning. Others have made the case that by the time he had to make a decision, there was so much bickering among his closest supporters that he just threw in the towel. Still others have argued that Mrs. Eastland was ready for him to come home. Perhaps he instinctively realized campaigns had changed and knew he wanted no part of the television-driven, candidate-packaged approach to winning elections. As one Eastland friend observed: "Back then, you could do [campaigns] with field men and organizations and making stump speeches and working the phones. One of the things that Eastland would do is he would come to a town and gather up three or four [of his] closest friends who happened to be the most influential people in town, and they'd get in the back seat of the car and have a drink of whiskey, and he'd be on to the next stop."[3]

Eastland was a master of a political world that is unrecognizable today. Personal relationships formed the basis for political success when Eastland started his political career. When he left, a politician's future was determined in large part by how well he or she could deliver a short, concise, quotable sentence or two in front of a television camera. Reaching large numbers of voters through press conferences, television, direct mail, and phone banks were techniques foreign to Eastland, as once recorded by a journalist who covered one of his rare press conferences:

There he was, Big Jim, the inscrutable one, the master politician holding only his second known press conference anywhere in Mississippi in the last 25 years. Mostly the answers were grunts signifying yes or no, interspersed with a few declarative sentences of a dozen words or so. But Big Jim had come back to his home grounds ... and painfully allowed himself to be interrogated. ... Eastland emerged unscathed, although it took him two big black cigars to get through the ordeal.[4]

Jim Eastland assumed power in Washington in 1956 when he became chairman of the Senate Judiciary Committee. For almost a quarter of a century, every person nominated for the federal judiciary and every piece of civil rights legislation had to first pass through his committee. Pick up anything to read about how the 1957 Civil Rights Act or the 1964 Civil Rights Act or the 1965 Voting Rights Act was passed, and a significant section will be devoted to how the legislation became law in spite of the opposition mounted by Eastland. That reputation made him a hero in Mississippi. *Time* magazine presented the contrasting opinion when it put Eastland on the cover of one of its issues in the 1950s, calling him "a symbol of racism in America."[5]

The writer who decides to chronicle Eastland's life in a biography will have the unenviable task of placing into context some of the harshest and most indefensible oratory made by any political leader during the civil rights era. Eastland's influence during the years following *Brown* is undeniable, as captured by historian Numan Bartley: Eastland was "a relentless crusader who was never far from where decisions were being made. And he was probably the most influential individual in shaping the [opposition to *Brown*]."[6] The speech Eastland gave on August 12, 1955, to a cheering audience in Senatobia was typical of his response to the *Brown* decision: "On May 17, 1954, the Constitution of the United States was destroyed because the Supreme Court disregarded the law and decided that integration was right. You are not required to obey any court which passes out such a ruling. In fact, you are obligated to defy it."[7] If there was a low point in Eastland's career, it had to have occurred on a February evening in Montgomery, Alabama, in 1956. Eastland was the featured speaker at a Citizens' Council rally, described by the local newspaper as the largest pro-segregation rally in history. More than 12,000 people packed the Montgomery Coliseum to hear Eastland proclaim: "In every stage of the bus boycott we have been oppressed and degraded because of black, slimy, juicy, unbearably stinking niggers ... African flesh-eaters. When in the course of human events it becomes necessary to abolish the Negro race, proper methods should be used.... All whites are created equal with certain rights, among these are life, liberty, and the pursuit of dead niggers."[8]

Eight years later, on the afternoon of June 23, 1964, Eastland came up short when he telephoned President Johnson about James Chaney, Michael Schwerner, and Andrew Goodman, the civil rights workers who had been missing for two days in Neshoba County. J. Edgar Hoover, the FBI director, had called President Johnson earlier in the afternoon to report that his agents had found the burning remains of the car the three men were last seen driving. While Johnson was waiting for Hoover to call back and let him know if bodies were inside the car, Eastland called Johnson "to suggest that the disappearance was a hoax. . . . The president listened to Eastland's assurances that Governor Paul Johnson fully expected the men to turn up. . . . 'Okay, now here's the problem, Jim,' the president responded, 'Hoover just called me one minute ago' with news of the burned out car."[9]

Eastland survived the civil rights revolution and maintained his power in the Senate because of his personal relationships with individual senators. What comes across time after time in interviews with people who knew and who worked with Eastland is that, for Eastland, his positions on the public issues of the day were never personal. He was as good a friend with the liberal members of the Senate as he was with the conservatives. He never broke his word once he had made a commitment, and he never held grudges, as explained by one of his fellow senators: "No matter how much power he has in the Senate, I have never seen Jim Eastland invoke a reprisal against an adversary."[10] The relationship that epitomizes his approach to senatorial life was his friendship with the Kennedy family. Introducing Kennedy at the Ole Miss commencement in 1978, Eastland said, he's "a man of his word, a hard worker, a tenacious fighter for what he believes is right. . . . He and I don't always agree but in disagreeing I have never found him to be disagreeable."[11] When he was serving as attorney general, Robert Kennedy made good use of his family's relationship with Eastland to obtain confirmation of his choice of Burke Marshall for assistant attorney general for civil rights, though Kennedy remembered the senator didn't make it easy when he brought Marshall over for a meeting with Eastland: "I have Mr. Marshall outside who is going to be head of our Civil Rights Division. I thought you'd like to meet him. He's going to put Negroes in your white schools in Mississippi." As Kennedy recorded the conversation in his journal, "Eastland snorted and said, 'I don't want to see him.' I said, 'Come on, see him for a minute.' So, I brought Marshall in. They looked at each other in the eye and exchanged some words. Afterward Eastland said he wouldn't hold Marshall's appointment up, but he wanted it understood that he was going to vote against him. As he put it, 'I'd vote against Jesus Christ if he was nominated for that position.' "[12]

Eastland recognized that retaining his power meant respecting his fellow senators, understanding their local politics, and dealing with them truthfully and candidly. A classic example can be found in a book Jack Bass wrote several years ago about the role of the Fifth Circuit Court of Appeals in enforcing the civil rights laws in the South. Several paragraphs were devoted to the selection by Eastland of his friend Charles Clark, a Jackson lawyer, for a position on the Fifth Circuit. Bass wrote:

> As one of the state's leading legal strategists to hold down desegregation, Ross Barnett's lawyer in the Ole Miss crisis, and legal counsel to the challenged Democratic Regulars from Mississippi at the 1968 DNC, Clark anticipated opposition from Senate liberals. With the nomination sitting in a Judiciary subcommittee, Eastland bided his time until Moratorium Day in May 1969, when most of the liberals on the Judiciary Committee were away from Washington making antiwar speeches on college campuses. Eastland called up Clark's nomination before the full committee, which reported it out with almost no debate, then sent it immediately to the Senate floor, where without delay it was routinely confirmed.

Contrary to the impression that Eastland tricked his committee colleagues, waiting for a time when they would be gone, Clark made clear in an interview years later that Eastland had notified all the committee members of his interest in having Clark serve on the Fifth Circuit. After they had privately given Eastland their support for Clark, some of the "liberal" members of the committee asked Eastland to bring the nomination up for a vote when they would be out of town.[13]

As he lost the legislative battles over civil rights and as black Mississippians became voting Mississippians, Eastland began to adjust to a new southern "way of life." After Nicholas Katzenbach became Lyndon Johnson's attorney general, he once remembered getting an angry call from Eastland, complaining about civil rights workers who were threatening to register black field hands who lived on his Sunflower County plantation. "That's private property, and you keep them out of there," Eastland ordered. Katzenbach explained he had no authority to tell civil rights workers where they could or couldn't go, then advised Eastland that he could solve the problem by getting everyone on his place registered. "They'll vote for you, anyway," Katzenbach said. Eastland thought a moment and said, "I'll do it today."[14]

In 1977, when Eastland was publicly contemplating a reelection campaign, he visited with state NAACP chairman Aaron Henry and asked Henry to help him. Henry "kind of stammered and said, 'Wait a minute, Senator, you know, there's some things that have got to happen before we can do any good, before we can help you.' [Eastland] said, 'What are those things?'" On Henry's list was a black staff person. Several months later, Ed Cole, the manager of Charles

Evers's 1971 campaign for governor, became the first black person ever hired by Eastland. Soon thereafter, Henry endorsed Eastland.[15] A year or so later, Curtis Wilkie covered Ted Kennedy's Ole Miss commencement speech for the *Boston Globe*: "We toured the campus where John F. Kennedy's army had suppressed a revolt; sixteen years after that unpleasantness, his brother was treated as an honored guest. After his speech, everyone attended a reception at the Oxford Country Club. Aaron [Henry] was here. . . . When he spotted Eastland, Aaron rushed to embrace him and planted an affectionate kiss on his cheek." Returning to Washington that night, Kennedy told Wilkie, "There are two things I would like to have from that reception . . . a picture of Aaron Henry kissing Jim Eastland . . . and a picture of Jim Eastland, when he realized someone had a picture of Aaron kissing him."[16]

THE CAMPAIGN TO SUCCEED EASTLAND

The Democratic Primary

On March 10, 1978, former Governor Bill Waller held an extraordinary press conference. Not only did he announce that he "expected" to be a candidate against Jim Eastland, but he went on to publicly criticize Eastland, saying he had been "somewhat shocked" when Eastland announced his intention to seek a seventh Senate term: "There are so many problems in our country. I happen to believe that a young man who has some stamina and vigor is needed."[17] Ten days later, Waller officially announced, making Eastland the center of his campaign: "We need a 60 hour a week man in Washington, not a six hour a week man," adding that Mississippi needs "a fighter who can represent our state in a dynamic manner. . . . We don't need to relate to tradition."[18]

The next day, Eastland, seventy-three years old at the time, announced he was withdrawing as candidate for reelection.[19] The fallout was instantaneous: "Almost every candidate who'd won or lost in the last 10 years seemed to be rethinking his 1978 political plans."[20] By the end of the month, Governor Cliff Finch, former Marion County District Attorney Maurice Dantin, and former Lieutenant Governor Charlie Sullivan had joined Waller in the Democratic primary, Congressman Thad Cochran and state Senator Charles Pickering had qualified in the Republican primary, and Fayette Mayor Charles Evers had announced as an Independent.

For the Democrats, the outcome would hinge on two factors: who would Eastland support, and who would make the least unfavorable impression among the voters? The decision for Eastland was easy: Waller, whom Eastland had helped to elect in 1971, had committed the unforgivable political sin of betraying a loyalty; Sullivan had crossed Eastland years earlier and had never attempted to make amends; Finch's tenure as governor was quickly becoming a dismal failure. That led to a meeting at the Eastland plantation in Sunflower County between Dantin and Eastland and then a meeting between Dantin and a group of Eastland supporters and campaign staff. Dantin agreed to run, and they agreed to work for him.[21]

The voters knew less about Dantin than Waller, Sullivan, or Finch. Waller had served as governor and Sullivan as lieutenant governor. Finch was the incumbent. Dantin was the relative unknown in the field and thus attracted voters who had complaints with the other candidates.

The only spark of controversy in the entire primary occurred on May 17 when the *Jackson Clarion-Ledger* ran a front-page article detailing the role of the Finch administration's commissioner of banking, Jimmy Means, in raising money from bankers for Finch's campaign. Means admitted contacting bankers he regulated, both from the Finch campaign office as well as his state office, and admitted asking for political contributions. Means's innocent response: "As long as they run a good bank, they'll have no problem with Jimmy Means."[22]

Dantin stunned the pundits by leading the primary. Finch made it into the runoff. Sullivan came in third, and Waller, viewed by many as thoroughly ungrateful, came in fourth among the major candidates. Toward the end of the runoff, Finch, ignoring Waller's lesson, made Eastland the campaign's centerpiece with a television ad that became "the talk of the town." The narrator in the ad spoke ominously of "meetings being held in smoke-filled rooms in a desperate effort to handpick a successor to the U.S. Senate seat" while showing an "unidentified" man smoking a cigar and making phone calls with a bottle of scotch.[23] On election day, Dantin carried 73 of the 82 counties, defeating the incumbent governor with 65 percent of the vote. Jim Eastland could take comfort in one last political triumph.

The Republican Primary

Soon after he was reelected in 1976, Congressman Thad Cochran walked over to Eastland's office in Washington for a visit. Having decided to run for the

Senate in two years, Cochran wanted to travel around the state and begin to make a name for himself outside his congressional district. Cochran also wanted to let Eastland know of his intentions and assure him that he would only be a candidate should Eastland choose to retire. Cochran remembers that "after I gave my speech about my plans, Eastland told me a secret, 'Well, I'm not going to run.'" More than a little taken aback, Cochran could only summon, "Really?" After assuring the senator that he would keep this revelation in complete confidence, Eastland then volunteered his reasoning: "I'll be too old." Cochran recalled, "I got into high gear. I started running right then. But I told no one."[24]

A year or so later, Eastland still had not revealed his decision to anyone else. In the meantime, state GOP chairman Charles Pickering commissioned a poll to test Eastland's popularity and convened a meeting with Thad Cochran, Trent Lott, Gil Carmichael, and Haley Barbour to discuss future campaign opportunities. The subject: who would run for the Senate in 1978, and who would run for governor in 1979? Carmichael told the group he was in the race for governor; Lott said he preferred to stay in the House; and while Cochran expressed an interest in the Senate seat, he said he would not oppose Eastland. That left Pickering, who believed the Republicans needed to field a candidate in the Senate race, regardless. With poll results showing that Eastland was vulnerable, Pickering began to travel around the state, meeting with key Republicans and making tentative campaign plans. A few weeks later, Eastland made his public announcement, and after Pickering reconvened the group to digest the news, they decided to have a primary: Pickering was in, but so was Cochran.[25]

As with many elections in Mississippi, the outcome was determined by geography. If Cochran ran a mistake-free campaign, he had it won.[26] Pickering represented a small Senate district of 50,000 people in Jones County. Cochran represented the twelve-county Fourth Congressional District, or about 500,000 people. On election day, Pickering kept the race close with Cochran in the other four congressional districts, but then Cochran's congressional district reported its vote totals: Pickering received 1,812 votes versus Cochran's 27,940. The primary election was over.

The General Election

Thus it was that the general election match-up in Mississippi's first U.S. Senate election in three decades without an incumbent was populated by Democrat

Maurice Dantin, Republican Thad Cochran, and Independent Charles Evers. As he had six years earlier in his first race for Congress, Cochran would win with less than a majority, and once again he owed his victory to Charles Evers.

Born in 1922 in Newton County, Charles Evers has lived a life that novelists spend years trying to portray. After serving his country in World War II and coming home to discover that Jim Crow didn't make exceptions for black veterans, Evers left Mississippi in 1955 for Chicago, where he prospered as a nightclub owner and racketeer, "a complex blend of capitalist and Christian," as one writer described him. Evers returned to Mississippi when his brother, Medgar, was assassinated in 1963; became a leader in the NAACP; organized marches and boycotts throughout southwest Mississippi; helped found the Loyalist faction of the state Democratic Party; ran a courageous campaign for Congress in 1968; was elected mayor of Fayette in 1969; and waged a statewide campaign for governor in 1971, as he once explained, "to demonstrate to other blacks that they could run and not get shot." After helping Thad Cochran win his campaign for Congress in 1972, Evers began to drift away from the Democratic Party, complaining Democrats were "wishy-washy," were "phony," and took "blacks for granted." His harshest criticism was reserved for welfare: "Democrats in particular thrive off of social programs. They live off of poor folks. And the whole system is to keep them poor and dependent on the government and we can control them." He refused to support Carter in 1976 and by 1978 was fully aligned with the GOP.[27]

Evers remains to this day unashamed of his career in Chicago, his work in the civil rights movement, and his transformation to a Republican. Long-time civil rights activist Harry Bowie captured Evers in one debate he had with Evers:

> *Charles stole my thunder. He [told the crowd]: "People talk about me, how I'm this and I'm that. They say I like money. Well, you're a fool if you don't like money. Yes, I like money. I like every bit of money I can get. And they say that I like power. What's this flack about? It's about power. If you don't want power, you shouldn't be out here doing this. They said I like women. Lord, have mercy. Any woman who wants me, I'm available." And every time he said one of those things the crowd would go "Yea, yea, yea." So there wasn't anything for me to say.*[28]

Throughout the campaign, Evers's appeal for votes was simple: "You need somebody that looks like you and talks like you and has suffered like you."[29]

Wayne Edwards, Dantin's campaign manager, knew the election was lost when Muhammad Ali hosted a parade for Evers through Jackson, attracting a crowd of more than 40,000. Then he was joined by Kris Kristofferson to lead a motorcade through the Delta, where "black children followed World Heavyweight Boxing Champion Muhammad Ali as if he were the pied piper of their dreams," while "white women flocked to movie actor and country-western singer Kris Kristofferson, seeking his autograph and screaming in delight at his kisses." Evers had known Ali for several years, and Ali and Kristofferson just happened to be in Natchez in the fall of 1978 making a film. After agreeing to the campaign travel, Ali appeared in a television commercial for Evers: "If you don't vote for Charles Evers, I'm going to bop you!"[30]

Cochran became senator in the same way he first became a congressman: winning with more votes than his opponents, but with less than a majority. Cochran received 45 percent of the votes, Dantin 32 percent, and Evers 23 percent. Evers carried ten of the state's majority black counties and drained votes from Dantin throughout the state. Evers's relative strength led one Democratic college professor to offer this tongue-in-cheek remark to a colleague, "If we could have just gotten Dantin out of the race, we could have elected Evers!"[31]

Years later, when asked about the 1978 campaign, Evers said: "Well, I didn't like [Dantin] and I liked Cochran. . . . I knew that all we needed to help not get Dantin elected was for me to run. . . . Nobody else could help get enough black votes so that Cochran could win and that's why I ran. . . . I was bent on me being senator or Thad Cochran."[32]

The significance of Cochran's victory to the growth of the Republican Party in the state was underscored by an observation Gil Carmichael once made: "The Senate seat will establish a two party system in Mississippi." Winning the governor's office wasn't what was needed because the governor couldn't succeed himself indefinitely, like a senator. "The Governor comes and goes. . . . He makes a dent and then you lose the governorship, and the dent disappears. . . . But once you get one of your senators . . . it will just drive a peg in the ground so deep so nobody will ever take it out again. The two party system will be here."[33]

THE RISE OF JON HINSON

In the general election to fill Thad Cochran's congressional seat, Jon Hinson, the Republican, faced John Hampton Stennis, the Democrat. Hinson was thirty-six years old, and had worked for nine years in Washington for Congressman Thad Cochran and his predecessor, Charles Griffin. Stennis, forty-three at the time, had served in the state House of Representatives since 1969. Hinson was from Tylertown; Stennis was from Jackson. Hinson's father was a Walthall County supervisor and his mother a librarian. Stennis's father was, well, "the Senator."

There is only one piece of information the student of political history needs to know about what used to be the Fourth Congressional District in Mississippi: geography determined the winner. Until it was dissolved in 2001, the Fourth Congressional District occupied the southwest corner of the state, with Jackson and Hinds County serving as the northern anchor. After Thad Cochran vacated this seat in 1978 to run for the Senate, the winner in an open election came from the southern and rural part of the district, regardless of party affiliation. A candidate coming from Hinds County bore the kiss of death. In the open elections of 1978, 1981, 1988, and 1998, the winners came from Walthall County, Pike County, Lincoln County, and Jefferson Davis County, respectively, all in the southern part of the district. Their opponents were from Hinds County: a Jackson lawyer in 1978, a Jackson businessman in 1981, a former Viet Nam–era prisoner of war (POW) from Hinds County in 1988, and a Jackson lawyer in 1998. In 1978, Hinson's family roots were in the southern part of the district; John Hampton Stennis's home was Hinds County. Hinson won the election with 52 percent of the vote.

Handling the television advertising for Hinson was a young Jacksonian named Stuart Stevens, who over the next thirty years would become one of the premier Republican media consultants in the country. Stevens would end up back in Mississippi in 2003 to coordinate all of the advertising for Haley Barbour's gubernatorial campaign.

Tucked away on page sixteen of a long story in the *Jackson Clarion-Ledger* about Hinson's victory was this notice, added almost as an afterthought: "Hinson, a bachelor . . . is engaged to the secretary of Georgia congressman Bo Ginn."[34] Within less than two years, however, questions about his sexual preferences would force Hinson to hold an extraordinary news conference.

POSTSCRIPT

On March 4, 1977, Governor Cliff Finch approved legislation abolishing the State Sovereignty Commission. Ten days later, Fannie Lou Hamer, one of

Mississippi's civil rights pioneers, died at the age of sixty. She once said: "We in the South can bring this nation out to human decency and humane respect, but to do that people must realize that whether he's white as a sheet or black as a skillet, out of one blood God made all nations." And "Cause you see, if we are free people as Negroes, if we are free, then I don't think you're supposed to tell me how much of my freedom I'm supposed to have."[35] More than 1,500 persons attended her memorial service at Ruleville Central High School and heard Andrew Young, President Carter's newly appointed ambassador to the United Nations and the first African American to represent the United States in that capacity: "When she stood up to injustice, it never dawned on me that I would run for Congress, much less be an ambassador. Many of us would not be what we are now if Mrs. Hamer hadn't stood up then."[36]

On page six of the Indianola newspaper that covered Hamer's funeral, there is a photo of Andrew Young standing with Aaron Henry and a few others outside the school. The photo is so evocative because it depicts a scene so apparently normal, unless you knew that less than twelve years earlier, blacks had no political power in Mississippi. Now a black man, who had organized civil rights activities in Mississippi in the early 1960s, was representing his country at the United Nations.[37]

CHAPTER 5

DEMOCRATS WIN ONE
AND REPUBLICANS LOSE ONE

1979

*Winning public office is often a combination of luck, timing, and shrewd
campaign techniques . . . [but for] William Winter, it seems to have been a
matter of patience, waiting for the day when Mississippi would be ready
for him.*

—BETHANY LAMAR BASKIN, "The Rise of William Forrest Winter"[1]

As this book goes to press, William Winter is eighty-three years old.
His public career will celebrate its sixtieth anniversary in 2007, for it
was in 1947 that Winter was first elected to the state House of Representatives from Grenada County, the same year Fielding Wright was elected
governor and John Stennis was first elected to the U.S. Senate.

In 1956, Winter did something no one had done since 1928 and that no one
would attempt again until 1992: he took a campaign against a sitting Speaker
of the state House of Representatives all the way to a recorded vote on the floor
of the House. Walter Sillers, first elected to the House from Bolivar County in
1916 and chosen Speaker by his colleagues in 1944, was by 1956 the most powerful individual in state government. In the House, it was Walter's way or no
way, and Walter's way was to protect the status quo and take whatever steps
were necessary to enforce segregation. Sillers once summed up his approach
to public policy: "As long as men live some will be in want, and all shall live
in some sort of fear. To attempt to provide otherwise will meet with about
as much success as an attempt to change the laws of gravitation. It is against
nature and cannot be done."[2] Winter and a number of his contemporaries

in the House believed Mississippi could do better. In the fall of 1955, Winter announced for Speaker, initially encouraged by his friend J.P. Coleman, who was elected governor that year.

One day after the 1955 statewide elections, Coleman remembered getting a phone call:

> I was in Ackerman. . . . Mr. Sillers called and wanted to come see me at my office in Ackerman. He said he preferred to see me there to Jackson. I said, "That's fine, when can you come?" He said, "This afternoon." He came. He said, "Now I want to tell you that if you do not oppose me [in the Speaker's race], I have the votes at the moment. I'm not vainglorious enough to think that you might not take them away from me if you set your head to it." But, he said, "if you will just leave the race alone. . . . I'll guarantee you I'll see that your program is passed, every bit of it, is passed."[3]

Coleman made the decision to abandon Winter in favor of the Speaker's request with the hope of passing his legislation. After Coleman urged Winter to withdraw, Winter and his supporters caucused the night before the vote at the King Edward Hotel in downtown Jackson. Without Coleman's support, they were doomed to lose. Everyone in the room knew if they forced a roll call vote, Sillers would relegate them to insignificant committees and refuse them any meaningful legislative work. Winter told the group, "If you want to make this race, we'll make it." The unanimous response was, "Let's go to the floor."[4] The next day the vote was ninety-four for Sillers and forty in favor of Winter.[5]

Three months later, on the last day of the legislative session, Mrs. Tom Bailey, the state tax collector, unexpectedly died.[6] A few hours later, Winter was sitting at his desk on the House floor when he was asked to come to the governor's office. Governor Coleman told him: "I couldn't support you for Speaker, but I can appoint you State Tax Collector"—a statewide elected position they both knew paid extremely well but could also serve as a platform for Winter to gain statewide recognition and launch a campaign for another office.[7] As Coleman remembered years later, "That was one of my motivations for my appointing him state tax collector. . . . He had not asked for it, but I wanted to do something on the permanent record and make amends for my inability to help on the Speaker's race."[8] In making the appointment public two days later, Coleman said, "Today, those who said that I would accept the help of a friend, then desert him, can take a look."[9]

Over the next twenty-three years, Winter would be elected state tax collector, state treasurer, and lieutenant governor and lose two campaigns for governor. After suffering defeat against Finch in 1975, he had convinced himself his career was over.[10]

THE 1979 CAMPAIGN FOR GOVERNOR

If there was an opportunity for the Republicans to take the Governor's Mansion, 1979 was the year. Cliff Finch had proven to be a miserable governor. By the end of his third year in office, the voters had had enough of Finch's scandals and mismanagement. Polls taken during his 1978 Senate race confirmed his low favorable rating; if anything, his standing with the voters had deteriorated over the ensuing months.[11]

A Democratic administration rocked by scandal matched with a united Republican Party coming off a stunning win in a Senate race—what more could Mississippi's GOP ask for as statewide elections loomed? What happened that year confirmed an immutable rule in the new two-party Mississippi: in a contested race between a Republican and a Democrat for a high-profile office, the party that is not united will lose against a party that is. In the 1976 presidential race, the state GOP was badly demoralized after its national convention; the Democrats were solidly behind Jimmy Carter. The Democrat won. In the 1972 Fourth Congressional District race and the 1978 Senate race, Charles Evers split the base of the Democratic Party. The Republican won. The rule would hold for 1979.

The Republicans

For Republicans, Gil Carmichael made it known early in the season that he was in the race: he wanted a rematch, not against Finch, but against Finch's record. Carmichael believed he was in a position to gently remind the voters that if they had chosen the candidate who had engaged in a serious and intelligent discussion of the issues and who had offered a record of achievement in lieu of campaign gimmicks, Mississippi would be far better off. That vision was thwarted by a fratricidal Republican primary and by the Democrats, who nominated a candidate recognized for the same qualities of character and competence as Carmichael claimed for himself.

For many of the conservative leaders of the Republican Party, the lost opportunity of the 1975 campaign for governor and the 1976 Reagan-Ford fiasco were still fresh memories. Carmichael was, in a word, unacceptable. In the opinion of Billy Mounger, it was "better to lose to a Democrat than win with Carmichael, and have the Republican Party associated with his administration."[12] Wirt Yerger Jr., Mounger, and others began putting the word out among the party faithful they were "looking for a candidate." Mounger remembers getting a call one day from his friend John Bell Williams. Williams had a suggestion: what about Leon Bramlett, a Delta farmer who served as chairman of the Democratic Party during Williams's tenure as governor?[13] One conversation led to another, and before long, the word was out. The *Clarion-Ledger* wrote that Bramlett was meeting with Yerger and Mounger, and in his characteristic bluntness, Mounger admitted that "it's publicly known that I'm not pro-Carmichael."[14] On the last day to qualify, Bramlett announced as the "conservative alternative" for Republicans, telling Yerger, his new campaign manager, that what finally convinced him to do it was the recognition that "Gil could not win in November."[15]

Carmichael enjoyed name recognition and volunteers among the Republican faithful from his two previous campaigns. Bramlett had the financial backing and volunteer support of most of the Reagan activists. The outcome was close and the campaign brutal. In the end, Carmichael won with 17,216 votes compared to Bramlett's 15,236. While Yerger and Mounger were able to deliver a 2,000-vote margin to Bramlett in Hinds County, they couldn't make up for the name identification that Carmichael had built up in the other urban areas of the state. Years later, Carmichael summed up his reaction: "Bramlett was put up against me because they were scared to death of me. You see, I represent a threat to the old status quo, and I do. I came out of [the primary] very scarred. . . . It was bloody, and it was the most excruciating experience that I have ever gone through in my life."[16]

The Democrats

For the Democratic primary, the only mystery as the deadline for qualification drew near was whether William Winter would join the race. Former Madison County District Attorney Jim Herring had announced, promising a crackdown on corruption, taking advantage of the scandals of the Finch administration.[17] Lieutenant Governor Gandy was in, as were Jackson lawyer John Arthur Eaves and Charlie Deaton, a state representative from Greenwood.

As he was leaving his office one afternoon in January, Winter bumped into Bill Cole, a former staff member, who was helping a candidate for lieutenant governor that year and who indicated to Winter they were doing a poll and asked permission to add Winter's name to the survey for governor. Winter agreed, and soon Cole was calling to tell him he could be elected governor.[18] After spending the next several months talking with friends and supporters, Winter entered the race, "amid great skepticism on the part of almost everybody," while making the centerpiece of his announcement "the corruption and mismanagement" of the Finch administration and linking Gandy, as lieutenant governor, to Finch.[19] While Gandy was the frontrunner, her campaign was saddled with two weighty political disadvantages. First, she had served as lieutenant governor while Cliff Finch was governor—guilt by association. And second, she was, well, a "she."

For the first time in Winter's career, his reputation as a moderate, as an experienced politician who had served in a number of other public offices, and as a public official who presented an articulate and professional image would work to his advantage—a contrast to the disastrous and reckless performance of Finch. And for the first time he had the backing of people who had supported Finch and "who were so totally disillusioned with his performance that they wanted to make it up to me, what they did to me in 1975."[20]

The Winter team knew from early polling that their candidate's best shot at winning the Democratic primary was to end up in the runoff with Gandy. The polls showed the state just wasn't ready to elect a woman. What followed is now part of Mississippi political folklore. The goal of Winter's campaign became one of definition: draw a picture for the voters of the job of governor in a way that would convince voters Winter was the right candidate. Because of Gandy's candidacy, "toughness" became part of the overall image they wanted to convey. Then, as today, the easiest way to get to "tough" is through the military and law enforcement. Winter had served in World War II and as governor would command the National Guard. Two commercials were produced to evoke the "toughness" theme. One showed Winter standing in front of moving tanks at Camp Shelby, a background for Winter to promise he would remove politics from the Guard. A second ad showed Winter firing a handgun at a Highway Patrol weapons range. Winter told a reporter the ad meant to show his concern for law enforcement, but also included a "secondary aspect . . . to show the wide range of responsibilities of the governor." The underlying message, though, was only a little less subtle and reinforced perceptions that many voters held, wrongly or rightly, about how a woman might perform as governor. The commercials were so effective against Gandy in the primary that polling done by Winter's campaign indicated it was conceivable she might not make the runoff. They hurriedly pulled the ads and waited to use them again in the runoff.[21]

As Winter had hoped, Gandy made the runoff election with him. The outcome then was never in doubt: Winter defeated Gandy, getting nearly 57 percent of the vote and carrying all but fourteen counties. Thanks to Finch, all of the characteristics that defined Winter—"articulate, historically oriented, thoughtful"—characteristics that had worked against him in earlier campaigns, now propelled him into the general election and one campaign away from the Governor's Mansion and "one of the greatest comebacks in Mississippi political history."[22]

The Outcome

Years later, Carmichael remembered that Winter was the only Democratic candidate he didn't want to face in the general election—their approach to campaigning, their positions on public policies, and their reputations as moderates were virtually identical in the minds of the voters. Given that, the voters, Carmichael feared, would opt for someone with experience.[23]

The divisive Republican primary likewise did nothing to help: "By the end of the primary [our polling showed] I was . . . twenty to thirty points . . . behind Winter," Carmichael recalled, "So I had to fight to climb back up and it was almost hopeless."[24] Winter won by 149,568 votes, with 61 percent. Carmichael carried only three counties—Rankin, Harrison, and Jackson. Billy Mounger once boasted that it was the only general election in which he ever voted for a Democrat.[25] In an oral history years later, Winter offered this assessment: "It was the right time. Which says a lot about one's political career. You can do everything right and still lose. In 1979, spending less money . . . not being as well organized, it was the easiest race I ever made."[26]

In the department of "you never know who may be supporting you," Winter recalled this vignette from his 1979 campaign: "But the last campaign I made for Governor, one of the most gracious and hospitable experiences that I had was being entertained by Mrs. Sillers at her home in Rosedale, where she and other members of her family had a lunch for me, pledged their full support in my race for governor."[27]

THE CAMPAIGN FOR ATTORNEY GENERAL

Wayne Edwards first made a name for himself as a DJ on a local radio station in Jackson while attending Millsaps College. He later engineered the George Wallace radio ad for Jimmy Carter in 1976. It happened that radio was destined to play yet one more song in Edwards's political career in Mississippi. Edwards was communications director for Bill Allain's campaign for attorney general in 1979. Allain's Republican opponent was Charles Pickering, who over the course of the fall campaign had turned the race into "his to lose"—Pickering's opinion polls showed him winning in the closing weeks of the campaign.

On the Sunday morning before the Tuesday general election, Edwards walked into his advertising agency and a staff member remarked: "I never thought Bill [Allain] would be a racist." Edwards stopped dead in his tracks and asked her what she was talking about. Listening to a radio station with a predominantly black audience, she had heard this ad: "Do you realize that a man who has worked against blacks for years wants to be your attorney general," the announcer asked rhetorically. "That's right," the ad continued, "Bill Allain has fought against civil rights his entire career. As assistant attorney general, he tried to block the integration of public schools. Bill Allain is a former member of the Citizens' Council. Remember, you can keep Bill Allain out of government by voting for Charles Pickering."[28]

Edwards called the station, got a friend to make a copy of the ad, picked it up, transcribed it, and then called Allain: "Bill, do you want to be attorney general?" Edwards asked his candidate. The Allain campaign had been handed a gift.

By that afternoon, Edwards and his team had developed a strategy. Allain drafted a statement for release to the press, calling the advertisements "gutter tactics" and "a disgrace to all Mississippians, both black and white." Edwards made copies of the ads and began contacting every political reporter in the state. By this time in the campaign, it was obvious that Winter was going to easily win the governor's race, so reporters were looking for some last-minute election controversy to cover. Edwards gave them a hot one. Later that Sunday afternoon, Edwards, no doubt remembering the value of his Wallace radio ad for Carter, rushed to get Pickering's commercial on "every country radio station in the state." As Edwards recalled the event years later, "I'm sure it elicited the response among some rural white voters, 'You mean Pickering was not a member of the Citizens' Council?'"[29]

A "fly-around" is a standard campaign activity that requires the candidate to fly to each city in the state with a local television station (Jackson, Greenville, Tupelo, Columbus, Meridian, Hattiesburg, and Biloxi). Due to Mississippi's relative small size and few media markets, a fly-around can be completed in one day and is a way for a candidate to ensure maximum coverage on the evening news in all the state's media markets. Both the Allain and Pickering campaigns had scheduled fly-arounds for the day before the election. Edwards rearranged Allain's schedule so Allain's stops would precede Pickering's. The time had come to put Pickering on the defensive.

Pickering's press conference in Jackson that Monday morning was at a local motel. So, Edwards scheduled Allain's right before, at the same hotel, and in the same room Pickering had reserved. Edwards then retained a professional lighting crew to light the room. As Edwards said, "We wanted [Allain] to look fresh for all the television cameras and when they saw we had it lit, the news crews didn't unpack their lights." Allain opened with: "Mr. Pickering has attempted to turn Mississippi politics back 20 years with gutter politics based on gimmicks and lies. . . . My opponent has lied to the people of Mississippi. He says one thing to the black community and another to the whites."[30] "But the key thing was the lighting, which was crucial, and as soon as Bill finished, we pulled down our lights. Pickering was coming in right behind us, and the stations had to go with their camera-top mounted lights," which emit a fraction of the light as the professional setup and "which made Pickering look like he had black eyes from the shadows, and . . . so visually he looked gaunt and defeated in that press conference. I wish I could say we thought all of that through in advance, but we weren't thinking about the impact it had on Pickering as much as we wanted to make Bill look like a winner."[31]

Pickering's memory of that Jackson press conference was just as vivid, though more succinct: "The press ate my lunch."[32] Pickering was "deluged with questions" from reporters energized over a controversy. Pickering said he had failed to listen to the ads and would not have approved them.[33] Pickering admitted that his aides had been told that Allain had once belonged to the Citizens' Council, but he acknowledged the campaign had no proof. Asked why he pulled the spots, Pickering replied, "I would not have used them for the reason we are ahead."[34]

The next day Gil Carmichael lost his race for governor by 149,568 votes, while only 21,271 votes—out of 610,391 cast—separated Pickering from Allain. Carmichael carried only three counties; Pickering won twenty-one in his losing bid. Late on election night, in a solemn speech to his supporters, Pickering claimed that his lead in the race had been diminished by the ads on black radio and that running the ads had been a mistake, yet he accepted "full responsibility" for them. "I couldn't have gotten more ink over one mistake if I had assassinated a presidential candidate."[35] At the time, Pickering said, "I feel very strongly and very firmly that without [the radio spots] we would have won."[36]

Two days after the election, the *Clarion-Ledger* published a revealing analysis of the debacle:

> *The ad man for Pickering said Thursday he should have prevented the airing of two campaign commercials that Pickering says cost him the election. "I should have stopped them," Stuart Stevens said in a telephone interview from Washington. Stevens said he had written the ads in consultation with Robert Wright, of Wright-McNeal and Associates, a black advertising firm in Washington that handles black oriented political advertising for the [national Republican party]. Stevens said that although he had the authority to keep the spots off the radio, airing them had been a collective decision involving himself, Wright, GOP staff member Richard McBride, and Jackson lawyer Grady Jolly. "I think I could have vetoed the spots. But any of us could have. That's just the way the campaign was run." The Saturday before the election, he said, the Pickering staff realized that Carmichael was going to lose the election by a landslide. "In all our polling, if Carmichael went down by 60–40 there was no way we expected to win. So the group decision to run the ads was made." Stevens credited the ads with a stronger than expected Pickering showing in black areas. Stevens agreed that Pickering had not reviewed the ads before they were aired.[37]*

Remembering the campaign years later, Pickering said a poll they had done the week before the election showed him far ahead of Allain, which is why he remains convinced he would have won the election but for the ads.[38]

POSTSCRIPT

As 1979 was drawing to a close, two events took place that would come to define the 1980 presidential election year. On November 4, Iranian militants seized the U.S. embassy in Tehran, taking sixty-three Americans hostage. Six weeks later, the Soviet Union invaded Afghanistan. Jimmy Carter's response to these foreign policy crises would ultimately be the undoing of his presidency.

CHAPTER 6

THE ORIGINS OF REAPPORTIONMENT

1890–1979

Boy! What's your name? Goddamned nigger twenty years old, ain't old enough to register himself, come down here to get other niggers to register. If you stay down here long enough, you gonna make a mistake. . . . Boy, if you feel so . . . sorry for these black sons of bitches, why don't you take them up North with you? Before you . . . black communist sonofabitches started coming down here, everything was all right. Niggers down here don't need to vote . . . ain't supposed to vote.

—**Spoken to a Civil Rights Worker in 1963 by a Jackson Police Officer**[1]

T
he vote is the source of power in a free society. Incumbent office-holders who wield political power know this. The Jackson police officer knew it. While the Voting Rights Act of 1965 swept away virtually all the legal obstacles that had prevented blacks from voting, white politicians used a little understood procedure called "reapportionment" to deny blacks the right to cast a vote that mattered. Long after lunch counters were integrated, long after buses were integrated, and long after schools were integrated, African Americans in Mississippi were still fighting for their vote to mean something. That barrier was finally overcome in 1979 for elections to the state legislature and in 1982 for congressional elections.

Central to any analysis of the role of reapportionment is an understanding of the history of the right to vote in Mississippi—a right withheld from black Mississippians by the 1890 state constitution and restored by the Voting Rights Act of 1965. Both the 1890 constitution and the 1965 act remain in effect today.

THE RIGHT TO VOTE

In the years following the 1875 takeover of state government by white Democrats, the role of African Americans in Mississippi politics became more and more tenuous. Some whites considered blacks to be unworthy of participating in American democracy, citing the white supremacy argument: "The Negro is not a white man with a black skin. He is a different race. He is barbarian, and barbarians cannot rule civilized people."[2]

Still, as long as blacks were able to participate in the process, politicians quite naturally sought their votes. Over time, winning the black vote meant buying the black vote, or as one delegate to the 1890 constitutional convention explained, "it is no secret that there has not been a . . . fair count in Mississippi since 1875."[3] Charles Sallis joins other historians who maintain that "only after the Negro threatened to become the decisive balance of power in [elections] did the movement for legal disfranchisement seriously gain momentum." A consensus soon developed among white leaders that the solution was simply to remove the black voter from the equation. Strip blacks of their right to vote, as one official disingenuously urged, "to prevent the Democratic election officials from stealing their votes."[4]

The need to resolve the issue gained urgency in early 1890 when Congress began consideration of the "Force Bill," which would have authorized the federal government to oversee state elections. With the memory of Reconstruction and "Negro Rule" fresh in their minds, white Democrats in Mississippi knew they needed to act and act quickly. A constitutional convention was called for August of that year to address the issue of the black voter once and for all. As one delegate remembered years later: "All understood and desired that some scheme would be evolved which would effectually remove from the sphere of politics in the State the ignorant and unpatriotic Negro." At the time of the 1890 convention, more than 57 percent of Mississippi's 1.3 million citizens were African Americans. Of the 134 delegates to the convention, 130 were Democrats, and all, save one, were white.[5]

When the convention approved the new constitution, Mississippi became the first state to legally disfranchise black voters. Known as the "Mississippi solution" or the "Second Mississippi Plan," its essential elements were copied by almost all of the southern states over the next ten to twenty years.[6] The approach required creativity, however, since the delegates had to contend with the Fifteenth Amendment, which prevented states from denying the right to vote based on color or race. In remembering the convention some years later, one delegate patted himself on the back for the display of ingenuity: "[There was] scarcely a conceivable scheme having the least tendency to eliminate the Negro vote that was not duly considered by the . . . Convention. It is regrettable that all the suggestions . . . were not recorded; had they been preserved, the record would be a monument to the resourcefulness of the human mind."[7]

The constitution imposed a $2 poll tax for anyone wanting to vote, payable two years in advance of the election. A residency requirement of two years in the state and one year in the precinct was imposed. And in lieu of specifying an educational requirement, the framers created a unique literacy test, requiring any potential voter to be able to read any section of the state constitution and, if required by the registrar, to explain it.[8] Fearful that the constitution might fail in a referendum, the convention simply declared it to be in effect. The "people" never voted to ratify the document.[9] Summing up the prevailing mood among the delegates and the press, the *Winona Times* wrote: "its submission means its defeat."[10]

The impact was immediate. The first voter registration under the new constitution took place in 1892. Of the 120,611 potential white male voters, 68,127 were registered, roughly the same as the 1867 count. Of the 150,409 potential black male voters, 8,615 were registered: 6 percent of those eligible, compared to 67 percent in 1867. An analysis of election turnout is even more revealing: for the 1876 presidential campaign, when the franchise was fully available to white and black men, 164,776 votes were cast. In the 1892 presidential campaign, a mere two years after the constitution was adopted, only 52,519 voters cast a ballot. It was not until 1940 that more Mississippians voted in a presidential election than voted in 1876.[11]

The 1892 Mississippi Supreme Court affirmed the decision not to submit the new constitution to the voters.[12] In 1898, the U.S. Supreme Court upheld the suffrage restrictions, concluding that they "do not on their face discriminate between the races, and it has not been shown that their actual administration was evil, only that evil was possible under them."[13]

For white Democrats, however, a few thousand black voters represented a future horror: over time, as their education and income increased, more African Americans would overcome the poll tax and literacy hurdles and qualify to vote. How to solve that nagging problem? In 1902, the legislature authorized a political party's state executive committee to exclude any person it chose from participation in its primary. The Democratic Party in Mississippi soon restricted its primaries to whites only. Since nomination by the Democratic Party at the time was synonymous with winning the general election, exclusion from the primary represented the complete elimination of blacks from electoral politics.[14] When the "white primary" was legally challenged, southern states argued that party organizations were "private associations" and should be free to exclude whomever they wanted. In a series of decisions in the first half of the twentieth century, the U.S. Supreme Court accepted this argument. It was not until 1944, when it had become clear that the Democratic primary served as the equivalent of the general election in Mississippi and throughout most of the Deep South, that the Supreme Court ruled the white primary unconstitutional.[15]

In spite of that 1944 ruling, Mississippi's restrictions on voting were so well executed that even six years later, only 19,367 of the 497,354 potential black voters in the state were registered. Fourteen counties, including several with a majority black population such as Carroll, Jefferson, and Tallahatchie, had no black registered voters.[16] Even as late as 1965, white Mississippi was holding firm. In spite of four years of intensive civil rights activities in the state, black voters had not increased their number by any appreciable amount: only 28,500 were registered out of an eligible population of 422,000.[17]

Statistics merely summarize the effect. They fail, however, to answer the question: How did they do it? The registration procedure required by the state is one answer:

> The applicant must complete the form perfectly without any assistance. Questions 1–17 request such information as the applicant's name, age, occupation, residence, citizenship and criminal record. Question 18 requires him to copy a section of the Mississippi Constitution selected by the registrar. Question 19 requires him to write an interpretation of the section he has copied. Question 20 calls for a description of the duties of citizenship under a constitutional form of government.[18]

In rural Clarke County, African Americans never saw the registration form. The registrar once testified in a trial that when blacks came to register: "I just suggested to them that they go back home and consider this matter and think it over."[19]

Herbert Lee was a black farmer and a leader in voter registration efforts in southwest Mississippi. One fall morning in 1961, while standing beside his pickup, he was gunned down. Soon after identifying the killer as state Representative E. H. Hurst, a witness was killed in his front yard by three shotgun blasts.[20]

How the registration procedure was employed by the Issaquena County registrar provides another answer. The registrar there made good use of the provision requiring applicants to interpret a section of the constitution. One white hopeful, for example, was asked to interpret Section 35 ("The Senate shall consist of members chosen every four years") and was approved with his answer: "equible wrights." A black applicant was typically given the 142-word section on corporate tax exemptions to interpret and then routinely failed, no matter how eloquent the reply. By October 1964, in this small Delta county, 100 percent of the eligible white population was registered. Not one black citizen's name was on the rolls.[21]

THE VOTING RIGHTS ACT OF 1965

In response to these acts of defiance, and hundreds like them across the South, Congress began consideration of the Voting Rights Act in 1965. Two events soon took place that left Congress with no option but to pass it.

The first event is well known and the more decisive. In Selma, Alabama, on the afternoon of Sunday, March 7, 1965, state troopers and sheriff's deputies attacked some 500 people marching for stronger federal voting laws. The clash occurred as the protestors were crossing the Edmund Pettus Bridge. White spectators cheered as the marchers were beaten with clubs and whips and then tear gassed. The bloody attack was broadcast that night by television networks and was front-page news the next morning. Seven days later, President Johnson addressed a joint session of Congress on national television, declaring: "At times, history and fate meet at a single place to shape a turning point in man's unending search for freedom. . . . So it was last week in Selma, Alabama. . . . Rarely, in any time does an issue lay bare the heart of America itself. . . . This time, on this issue, there must be no delay, or no hesitation, and no compromise with our purpose. . . . We have already waited a hundred years and more for the time for waiting is gone."[22]

The second event is much less well known, even in Mississippi. As part of its campaign to bring national attention to racial discrimination, the Mississippi Freedom Democratic Party (MFDP) ran candidates against the incumbent members of Congress in the 1964 elections. Because blacks were not allowed to vote, the MFDP challenged the right of the entire Mississippi congressional delegation to be seated. More than 150 lawyers from around the country volunteered legal assistance in early 1965 on behalf of the MFDP, many of them traveling to Mississippi to take depositions of more than 400 witnesses, documenting the ways in which white officials had prevented blacks from voting. The record of these depositions, in three volumes totaling more than 3,000 pages, was made public while Congress was debating the Voting Rights Act and offered overwhelming evidence that nothing short of drastic federal intervention would ensure that African Americans had the right to vote.[23]

Signed by President Johnson on August 6, the Voting Rights Act of 1965 enacted sweeping changes, but three in particular brought immediate relief to African Americans in Mississippi.[24] The first abolished the lengthy residency requirements and prohibited the use of any test to qualify voters.[25] The second authorized the use of federal officials to work in local courthouses to register voters and to observe voting at polling places during elections.[26] By the end of 1965, federal examiners were assisting voters in nineteen Mississippi counties, more than in any other southern state.[27]

The third provision, called "preclearance," was then, and remains today, the most controversial. It requires states to seek approval from the Department of Justice to "preclear" any change in any law related to elections before it can take effect. The preclearance provisions applied to any state that utilized a test as a prerequisite to register to vote and had less than 50 percent of its voting-age population either registered or voting in the 1964 presidential election. When the standards were applied in the summer of 1965, jurisdictions covered by the preclearance provision included Mississippi, five other southern states, and parts of five other states.[28]

The day after the Voting Rights Act became law, the *Jackson Daily News* complained that "the rape of the South continues. What else is new?"[29] In the meantime, Mississippi officials continued to circle the wagons. Mississippi and four other southern states joined with South Carolina to challenge the constitutionality of the act. On the one-year anniversary of the Selma attack, the U.S. Supreme Court affirmed Congress's actions: the "unremitting and ingenious defiance of the Constitution" in the South required the extraordinary measures contained in the Voting Rights Act.[30] Mississippi's attorney general filed lawsuits in state courts to prohibit local registrars from acknowledging any voters registered by federal examiners, a move that was subsequently overturned by federal judges.[31] When the legislature came to Jackson for its regular session in early 1966, defiance remained the official policy. By the time they adjourned, legislators had passed thirteen bills to undermine the intent of the Voting Rights Act. One group of bills, for example, turned many elective school superintendents into appointive positions.[32] Civil rights groups promptly filed suit, arguing that the state had failed to submit any of these changes to the Justice Department for approval. The Mississippi lawsuits were consolidated with a similar case from Virginia, and on March 3, 1969, the U.S. Supreme Court struck down the state legislation and, more important, ruled that the preclearance provisions applied to virtually any election law change enacted by the legislature or any political subdivision.[33] The decision has been called "the *Brown v. Board of Education* of voting rights."[34] By 1967, Mississippi's black registration had jumped from 7 percent to 60 percent.[35]

REAPPORTIONMENT

After passage of the 1965 Voting Rights Act, politicians in Mississippi came face to face with the prospect of blacks voting for the first time in seventy-five years. In many parts of the state, white legislators represented districts populated by more black voters than white voters. Virtually overnight, a sizable number of white incumbents faced the likelihood of losing the next election. What to do? The answer was reapportionment.

With the exception of statewide offices like U.S. senator and governor, other state officials are elected from districts of varying sizes, the boundaries of which are adjusted at least every ten years following the U.S. Census to account for population changes among the districts.[36] To an elected official, nothing is more essential for electoral success than determining which voters will and will not be in his or her district. Where the boundary lines are drawn can literally determine an election's outcome before the first vote is cast.

The redrawing of districts in southwest Mississippi on the heels of the Voting Rights Act illustrates the legislature's solution. The majority black county of Jefferson has Claiborne County as a neighbor to the north and Lincoln County as a neighbor to the east. Claiborne is majority black and Lincoln is majority white. Prior to 1966, when blacks were not allowed to vote, Jefferson and Claiborne each had its own representative, elected countywide, while Lincoln was allocated two representatives. Thanks to the Voting Rights Act,

Jefferson and Claiborne were each poised to elect an African American representative in the 1967 elections. To prevent that outcome, the legislature made use of multimember districts for the first time in the state's history. It combined Jefferson with Lincoln to create one House district with a combined population that was majority white and that was allocated two representatives. Claiborne was combined with its majority white neighbor to the north—Warren County—to create a combined white majority district that was assigned three representatives.[37] The reapportionment plan enacted by the 1966 legislature, which made use of similar multimember districts throughout the state, was so successful that in the 1967 elections only one African American was elected to the 174-member legislature that served a state with a 42 percent black population.

Civil rights organizations were left with no choice but to turn to the courts. To understand the litigation journey they undertook, we return to the 1890 constitution.

The delegates to the 1890 constitutional convention took the extraordinary step of writing into the constitution the boundaries for the state House and Senate districts, which remained unchanged until 1963.[38] For seventy-two years, Noxubee County and Hinds County each sent three members to the House of Representatives. But by 1963, Noxubee's population had stabilized at 16,826 while Hinds's had grown to 187,045, a population imbalance of nearly twelve to one. Harrison County offered a more striking example. With a population of 119,489, it was allocated one representative, just like Issaquena County, with 3,576 people.[39]

Similar disparities between urban and rural areas were widespread throughout the country. But incumbent politicians, almost all from rural areas, loathe to give up any power, had refused to redraw district lines to account for the population shifts. Doing so would have meant putting their own elections at risk. For the first half of the twentieth century, the U.S. Supreme Court declined to consider reapportionment disputes, asserting the issue was a "political thicket" and not a subject for judicial review.[40] By the beginning of the 1960s, however, the inequitable representation had become too great for the Court to ignore. One scholar noted that in at least fourteen states, districts with less than 20 percent of the people could form a majority in either one house or the other.[41]

When the Supreme Court announced its decision in *Baker v. Carr* on March 26, 1962, the course of American politics was changed forever. The justices ruled

that reapportionment cases were subject to judicial scrutiny.[42] The case origi-
nated in Tennessee, where the legislature had refused to reapportion itself for
nearly sixty years. The population disparities among the rural and urban areas
resembled those in Mississippi, and the Court found the variances resulted in a
violation of the equal protection guarantees of the Fourteenth Amendment. In
a series of cases that followed, the Supreme Court developed its famous "one-
person, one-vote" rule: "We hold that, construed in its historical context, the
command of Article I, Section 2, that Representatives shall be chosen by the
People of the several States, means that as nearly as is practicable one man's
vote ... is to be worth as much as another's."[43] Later that year, in a case from
Alabama, Chief Justice Earl Warren coined his memorable line: "Legislatures
represent people, not trees or acres. Legislators are elected by voters, not farms
or cities or economic interests. . . . Weighting the votes of citizens differently . . .
merely because of where they happen to reside, hardly seems justifiable."[44]

In the wake of these decisions, the Mississippi legislature was confronted
with two groups who demanded fair representation: people who lived in the
rapidly growing urban areas of the state and African Americans. The incumbent legislative leadership, all from rural counties, ignored the pleas of the
large cities and opposed the overtures from African Americans. The courts,
then, were the only recourse.

UPTON SISSON

The first reapportionment lawsuit filed in Mississippi had nothing to do with
black representation, nor was it filed by civil rights lawyers. On October 18,
1960, a group of six businessmen from the Gulf Coast sued the legislature. The
apparent instigator and lawyer for the effort was Upton Sisson.[45] The businessmen brought to the court's attention the dramatic imbalances in population
among the districts.

The case, which predated *Baker v. Carr*, was filed in state court, not federal court. In a remarkable show of independence and courage, the state judge
refused to dismiss the suit. During the course of the litigation, the decision
in *Baker v. Carr* was issued and gave new impetus to the Gulf Coast proceedings.[46] Sisson declared that "if one were to look at apportionment today, one
might think seats [in the legislature] were distributed on the basis of acres of
cotton and boll weevils and not population."[47] On June 7, 1962, Hinds County

Judge W. T. Horton agreed with Sisson and ordered the legislature to redistribute its seats on an equal population basis. Horton ruled the makeup of the legislature was "so inequitable, insidious, and disparaging that it is repugnant to and in violation of the Constitution." Horton's boldness didn't stop there: he gave the legislature until November 24 to draw their own lines, and should they fail, he would do it for them. Sisson declared the decision would "alter the entire political and economic life of Mississippi for the next 100 years."[48]

Governor Ross Barnett called the legislature into special session on September 16 to respond to Horton's declaration. Only in Mississippi could such a momentous power shift be overshadowed by another event: Barnett's special session coincided with James Meredith's enrollment at Ole Miss. By the time the legislature had left town, the collective mood must have been pretty sour: Ole Miss had a black student, and the rural areas of the state had lost significant legislative power.

While the House grudgingly adopted a plan that adjusted district lines for its members to account for population imbalances, the Senate proved unwilling to jeopardize the reelection of any of its incumbents. It simply increased the number of senators from fifty-two to eighty-two, one for each county. Since legislative apportionment was embedded in the 1890 constitution, the changes had to be submitted for voter approval. Sisson asked Judge Horton to nullify the plan. He refused, saying the people had a right to vote, but in an uncharacteristic declaration by a Mississippi judge, he threatened to nullify the plan if voters didn't: "The people have a right to vote on this, but what the people say on their ballots is not necessarily constitutional."[49] With the Coast rallying opposition to the plan, it lost by a sizable margin. Under pressure from the judge, Governor Barnett called the legislators back to the capitol. Three days before Christmas, the legislature satisfied the Coast and the judge, concluded its business, and went home for the holidays. The revised plan was approved by the voters early the next year. Harrison County would now be sending six representatives to the state capital, instead of one. Two and a half years later, the fight became even more bitter, because hundreds of thousands of blacks could finally vote.

CONNOR V. JOHNSON

Reenter the Mississippi Freedom Democratic Party (MFDP). It had challenged the Mississippi Democratic Party at the national convention, it had challenged the legitimacy of the Mississippi congressional delegation, and now it would challenge the Mississippi legislature. The mission would take fourteen years and eight trips to the U.S. Supreme Court before victory was achieved, but in the end, this litigation fashioned a policy of creating districts in which black voters had a fair chance to elect one of their own—the vote of black citizens would finally mean something.

The lawyers who nursed the litigation through a decade and a half of roadblocks achieved something quite remarkable. When they began, the U.S. Supreme Court was focused exclusively on making sure districts had roughly the same number of people. By the time the lawsuit was concluded in 1979, courts were concerned with not only *how many*, but *which* voters compose a district. Along the way, the Court eliminated the use of multimember districts, or those from which two or more candidates were elected, requiring instead the exclusive use of single-member districts, smaller districts from which only one representative or one senator could be elected.

A group of legal experts once commented on Mississippi's contribution to this legal evolution: "Federal courts entering Mississippi's political thicket were confronted with a complexity of issues far surpassing those addressed in prior cases. The Mississippi apportionment dilemma thus precipitated one of the most complex and enduring struggles faced by any state."[50] Another lawyer was more succinct: "Mississippi became a crucible in which modern federal voting rights law was largely forged."[51]

On Sunday afternoon, October 3, 1965, Peggy Connor walked down to the front of Jackson's Masonic Temple to the cheers of hundreds who were watching. She joined seven other MFDP members who signed the documents necessary for the lawyers to file their historic lawsuit against the legislature, when it became known as *Peggy J. Connor, et al. v. Paul B. Johnson, Governor, et al.*, or as the years went by, simply *Connor v. Johnson*.[52] A Hattiesburg native, Connor joined the MFDP movement in 1963 after hearing a Fannie Lou Hamer speech. Before becoming the lead plaintiff in *Connor v. Johnson*, she had been jailed twice for picketing and had been an MFDP delegate to the 1964 national convention. When once asked if she minded spending time in jail, she said, "Oh no, I thought I was getting freedom." One day many years later, she was called to jury duty. On the form for prospective jurors was the question, "Have you ever sued anyone?" Connor wrote: "I filed suit against the state of Mississippi."[53]

The special three-judge federal court that would hear the case for its fourteen-year duration would prove to be as formidable an obstacle as the legislature. Headed by J. P. Coleman, who by this time had been appointed a federal judge, he was joined by Judges Harold Cox and Dan Russell, white Mississippians unyielding in their opposition to creating opportunities for blacks to serve in the legislature.

By 1965, population equity among districts was accepted law, leaving the Coleman court with no choice but to follow that mandate. The legal fight then turned on the refusal of the court to create districts from which black candidates had legitimate prospects of being elected. There was only one way to accomplish that goal: districts would have to be subdivided into small, single-member districts, using precinct boundaries as the building blocks. Never before in the history of the state had anything smaller than a county been used to define a legislative district. The MFDP lawyers were urging the Coleman court to break counties apart, and combine parts of counties with parts of other counties to create districts from which black candidates had a reasonable chance to get elected. It was more than Coleman, Cox, and Russell could fathom.

On July 22, 1966, the judges ordered the legislature to redraw its districts to comply with one-person, one-vote in advance of the 1967 elections.[54] In the years since the 1962 Sisson litigation, the U.S. Supreme Court had imposed more stringent one-person, one-vote guidelines, leading the Coleman panel to set a December 1 deadline for the legislature to approve a new plan after finding that a majority of the House could be elected by 40 percent of the state's population and that a majority of Senate could be elected by 37 percent of the state. "It cannot be rationally explained," wrote the court, "why representatives and senators from Washington County should represent 19,660 people while the representatives and senators from Claiborne and Jefferson Counties should represent 6,996 people."[55]

The legislature adopted a plan before the deadline, but because drawing district lines to equalize population among the districts would have jeopardized incumbents, legislators failed to meet the new one-person, one-vote tests. In this plan, the legislature first created the multimember districts to thwart black representation, such as the districts in southwest Mississippi described earlier. While the court made a few changes to the legislature's plan to conform it to the one-person, one-vote mandate, it ignored the pleas of Connor's lawyers to create fair districts for blacks.[56] But deep in the Delta, where black majority counties were surrounded by other black majority counties, there was little that could be done to forestall the inevitable: Robert Clark was elected from Holmes County to become the first black House member in the twentieth century.

After the 1967 elections, both sides waited for the 1970 federal census, preparing for the 1971 elections and the next legal battle. The legislature came to Jackson in early 1971 and, using the newly released census data, attempted to craft a plan to equalize the population among districts. Once again, legislators just couldn't bring themselves to undermine the status quo: many of the districts exceeded the population guidelines, and all the multimember districts were retained.[57] Civil rights lawyers dusted off the *Connor* litigation and appealed to the same three-judge federal court. On May 18, 1971, the Coleman court rejected the legislature's plan, and the judges formulated their own. Once more, they substantially adopted the legislature's districts: keeping county boundaries intact and retaining multimember districts.[58] By this time, Hinds County, which had a 40 percent black population, was sending eleven members to the House and five to the Senate—all white.[59] Yet the court rebuffed the petition of Connor's lawyers and allowed all the members to continue to run countywide. If divided into single-member districts drawn fairly within the county, at least four of the representatives and two of the senators could have been black.[60]

The civil rights lawyers representing Connor appealed the federal court's failure to create single-member districts. On June 3, 1971, the U.S. Supreme Court ruled that "when district courts are forced to fashion apportionment plans, single-member districts are preferable to large multimember districts as a general matter." The Supreme Court instructed the district court "absent insurmountable difficulties," to "devise and put into effect" a single-member district plan for Hinds County. In the world of reapportionment jurisprudence, this ruling was the beginning of the end for discriminatory multimember districts. Throughout the 1960s, the Supreme Court had rejected a series of challenges to multimember districts; *Connor* was the first case in which the Supreme Court ruled against multimember districts, and it never looked back.[61]

By this time, it was clear that Coleman, Cox, and Russell were going to be as stubborn as the legislature. Thirteen days after the Supreme Court issued its decision, Coleman announced that the "difficulties" in crafting a plan for Hinds County were indeed "insurmountable"—its original plan was kept intact, which called for 89 percent of the House members and 62 percent of the Senate members to run in multimember districts.[62] The judges did, however, promise to appoint an expert to assist them in devising single-member districts for the larger populated counties in time for the 1975 elections.[63]

The promise of the appointment of an expert remained unfilled in 1972, 1973, and 1974. Not until May 7, 1975, a few weeks before the qualifying deadline for elections that year, did the court reconvene to consider the issue. By that time, the legislature had adopted a new reapportionment plan, retaining multimember districts protecting the white incumbents, in spite of warnings that the move was not legal.[64] On May 19, the Coleman court approved the legislative plan in its entirety. The plaintiffs quickly filed an appeal to the U.S. Supreme Court, which just as quickly reversed the Coleman decision.[65]

Ten years into the litigation, the Coleman court capitulated with regard to the most populous counties—Hinds, Harrison, and Jackson—and crafted single-member districts for each of them. The districts for the remainder of the state remained intact.[66] Three newly elected black representatives from Hinds County joined Robert Clark when the House convened in January 1976.

By this time, Mississippi's attorney general, A. F. Summer, was complaining that Connor's lawyers were trying to draw districts to "guarantee" the election of black legislators.[67] The irony, of course, is that Sumner was defending laws that had guaranteed the election of white legislators for more than eighty-six years.

After the election, Connor's lawyers pressed the Coleman court to revisit the issue of single-member districts in anticipation of the 1979 elections. When Coleman postponed the hearings, the lawyers had had enough. They filed yet one more appeal to the Supreme Court, and on May 19, 1976, the Court agreed with the plaintiffs and ordered Coleman to hold hearings within thirty days and produce a "constitutionally acceptable" plan for the legislature.[68] Coleman's public response—"there will be no reluctance, no foot dragging and no hanging back"—belied his talent at obstructionism.[69] It would take Connor's lawyers three more years and two more trips to the Supreme Court to make Coleman hold true to those words.

In August, Coleman capitulated with regard to single-member districts, ordering the abolishment of all multimember districts for the 1979 elections, though he was clearly not happy:

In constructing a system of single member legislative districts, this court is compelled to ignore the requirements of the Mississippi Constitution that each county shall have one representative. We are compelled to abandon two 159 year old state policies: (1) multi-member legislative districts and (2) never fracturing county boundaries in the composition of legislative districts. In short, by the erection of single member legislative districts, we have revolutionized Mississippi's system of legislative elections.[70]

Buried deep in the decision, however, Connor's lawyers discovered that Coleman's distaste for districts from which black candidates could get elected was unabated. The court had fashioned many of the district lines in such a way as to favor the election of white legislators. In southwest Mississippi, for example, Coleman combined the majority black county of Claiborne with the majority white county of Lincoln, to create a majority white district, when he could just as easily—and perhaps more logically—have combined Claiborne with Jefferson County, its majority black neighbor to the south, to create a senate district composed of a majority of voters who were black. Less than a year after the Supreme Court had ordered Coleman to craft a "constitutionally acceptable" plan, it was forced to confront its intractable district court in Mississippi once again when the *Connor* lawyers appealed.

On May 31, 1977, the Supreme Court invalidated the Coleman plan and called his hand: "In view of the serious questions raised concerning the purpose and effect of the present [plan's] unusually shaped legislative districts in areas with concentrations of Negro population, the District Court ... should ... draw legislative districts that are reasonably contiguous and compact, so as to put to rest suspicions that Negro voting strength is being impermissibly diluted."[71] By this time, Coleman was backed into a corner. He ordered the state legislature and the plaintiffs' lawyers to draw plans within ninety days and prepare for a trial.[72] When the court convened in February 1978, it found that the legislature had failed to adopt a plan, provoking Coleman to remark that he was "about to be convinced there are insurmountable obstacles" to reapportionment. "I'm tempted to issue an order to that effect," Coleman said sarcastically, "and see what the Supreme Court says to that."[73] Coleman sent the legislature back to the drawing board, finally concluding that he and Cox and Russell had "had enough."[74] The legislature, realizing, like Coleman, that it had run out of maneuvering room, finally approved a plan that was acceptable to the courts.[75]

At the conclusion of the 1979 election, with the new districts in place, seventeen African Americans would take the oath of office as members of the state legislature, including Aaron Henry, state president of the NAACP, and Henry Kirksey, one of the original 1965 plaintiffs in the *Connor* lawsuit. The imposition of small, single-member legislative districts and the presence of a significant number of blacks in the legislature would transform the way power was exercised at the state capitol.

J. P. COLEMAN

For the full fourteen years of its life, the special three-judge panel that adjudicated the *Connor* litigation was headed by J. P. Coleman, native of Choctaw County, former circuit judge, former attorney general, former governor, and former state representative. Appointed to the Fifth Circuit Court of Appeals in 1965, he served until his retirement in 1981.

Coleman became governor in 1956 on the heels of such momentous events as the Supreme Court's *Brown v. Board of Education* decision, the mobilization of the Citizens' Council, and the lynching of Emmett Till. For the four years of his administration, he is generally credited with pursuing as moderate an approach to the issue of integration as was allowable under the circumstances then prevalent in Mississippi. Coleman achieved notoriety when he publicly referred to the legislature's passage of a bill calling for the "nullification" of the *Brown* decision as "legal poppycock,"[76] and when he vetoed a bill requiring the NAACP to publicly disclose its members.[77]

The establishment of a Veterans Administration (VA) hospital in Jackson, next to what is now the University of Mississippi Medical Center, represents a lasting example of Coleman's defiance of the legislature. Until the federal government announced its intention to build a VA facility in Jackson, veterans in the state had to travel away from Mississippi for treatment. The legislature initially supported the construction of a VA hospital, giving the governor the authority to sign the deed transferring the state-owned land to the VA. That was before they discovered the federal government required VA facilities to be integrated. All of a sudden, public pressure mounted on Coleman to prevent the construction of the hospital. Coleman remembered what happened next: "[The legislature] just in effect . . . dared me to sign the deed. Well, driving by there one afternoon on the way to Ackerman, I told my wife, 'I'm going to sign that deed. I'm not going to pass on this question in the light of today. I know what will happen ten years from today, people will pass this vacant lot and say if we hadn't had a damned fool for Governor there would be a hundred million dollar hospital sitting up there now.' So I announced that I was going to sign the deed."[78] The legislature backed off.[79]

Trying to square that moderate record with Coleman's performance as chief judge in *Connor v. Johnson* represents a mystery we were unable to solve in the course of writing this book. Coleman failed to mention the *Connor* litigation in any of his four lengthy oral histories that are publicly available. None of his former law clerks we interviewed had any recollection of Coleman discussing the case with them; he apparently did his own work. Dan Russell, who served with Coleman on the three-judge panel, described in his memoir how Coleman and he would "work out a jigsaw puzzle of districts for hours and hours," though he failed to mention why the court continued to ignore the directives of the Supreme Court.[80]

Perhaps Coleman inadvertently described his approach when he informed the crowd at the 1963 Neshoba County Fair: "[States' rights] can be maintained peacefully. But not by knocking over the paramount rules of the United States. You just have to learn how to plow around them."[81] Or perhaps a civil rights worker was more observant. "Coleman is a very good historian, one of the best political historians in the state. It's just that his view of what happened is distorted. . . . J. P. Coleman was not invented last year. How he feels about [the *Connor*] case is part of his life."[82] What is clear is that Coleman did everything he could to avoid creating legislative districts from which African Americans had a fair chance of electing legislators of their race. He single-handedly postponed the inevitable.[83]

HAROLD COX

Judge Harold Cox, on the other hand, was transparent with his feelings. Cox was appointed to the federal district court in Mississippi by President Kennedy in 1961 at the urging of Cox's close friend and chairman of the Senate Judiciary Committee, Jim Eastland. Virtually anything written about southern judges contains one or more anecdotes about Judge Cox and his efforts to undermine implementation of civil rights laws. Then Attorney General Robert Kennedy was so worried about Eastland's support of Cox that he invited Cox to Washington for an interview, the only time Kennedy remembers having a personal meeting with a prospective judge: "We sat on the couch in my office . . . and I said the great reservation that I had was whether he'd enforce the law. . . . He assured me that he would."[84]

As it turned out, no judge was reversed more regularly thereafter on civil rights cases than Harold Cox.[85] In 1964, when the federal government was litigating a voter registration case in Judge Cox's courtroom, Cox told the Justice Department attorney that he was "not interested in whether the registrar is going to give a registration test to a bunch of niggers on a voter drive." Later that day, Cox complained that the African American plaintiffs were "acting like a bunch of chimpanzees."[86]

In a case in Forrest County, the Justice Department produced statistics showing that of the 7,495 blacks of voting age, only 25 were registered. Cox's response: "I think that the Court could take judicial notice of the illiteracy that is prevalent among the colored people, and I do know that of my own knowledge, and the intelligence of the colored people don't compare ratio-wise to white people."[87]

A lawyer with the Justice Department, John Doar, once pushed Cox a little too far, and in a famous response to Doar, Cox wrote: "I spend most of my time fooling with lousy cases brought before me by your department in the Civil Rights field, and I do not intend to turn my docket over to your department for your political advancement.... You are completely stupid.... I do not intend to be hurried or harassed by you or any of your underlings."[88]

Greenville attorney Victor McTeer had two strikes against him when he appeared before Judge Cox in a civil rights case during the early 1970s: he was black and he was not from Mississippi. Having moved to Mississippi from Maryland to practice law on behalf of civil rights plaintiffs, McTeer was ill-prepared for the Cox treatment. As McTeer was preparing to make his argument, Cox said, "I guess this is another one of those nigra versus white folks cases." Taken aback, McTeer found himself responding to Cox: "What the hell did you say?" The courtroom fell completely silent until Bill Allain, representing the state as an assistant attorney general, came to McTeer's defense: "Don't worry about it Judge, he ain't from here."[89]

In the end, though, civil rights lawyers came to view Harold Cox as their best friend, as one of them later observed: "If the Fifth Circuit saw Cox's name on an opinion from Mississippi, they would reverse it without hardly looking at it."[90]

George P. Taylor was the lead attorney on behalf of the *Connor* plaintiffs in the early 1970s. Over the course of his stay in Mississippi, Taylor worked to befriend Cox; even though they agreed on virtually nothing, he tried to maintain a cordial relationship. Getting ready to leave the state to take a position with the University of Alabama in the early 1970s, Taylor went by Judge Cox's office to say good-bye. Taylor remembers Cox being gracious and cordial at the parting, and as Taylor was leaving, Cox pulled him aside and confided, "People think I'm a racist. I may be a bigot, but I'm not a racist."[91]

HARTMAN TURNBOW

Hartman Turnbow was a legendary civil rights activist in Mississippi and was among the first black residents of Holmes County to register to vote. When he and thirteen other activists lined up at the courthouse to register one day in early 1963, the deputy sheriff said, "Okay, who's gonna be the first." As the story goes, Turnbow stepped forward and said, "Me, Hartman Turnbow. I came here to die to vote. I'm the first." Turnbow's independence and courage were legendary throughout the movement, as was his arsenal of weapons. The first time civil rights activist Lawrence Guyot met him, Turnbow said, "Now I'm with y'all, but I ain't about none of that nonviolence."[92]

POSTSCRIPT

It was election day 1967, and Les McLemore was twenty-two years old. His grandfather woke him up early, saying they were going to vote. The Voting Rights Act had given McLemore's grandfather and hundreds of other blacks in DeSoto County and thousands throughout the state the right to vote for the first time in their lives. Remembering the day years later, McLemore said, "He was dressed to the nines and he told me 'We're going to vote today. I want you to dress like you're going to church. This is important.'" McLemore's grandfather had read newspapers and discussed issues of the day with his grandson all his life. McLemore remembers that first election day as

one of his proudest days . . . because I had been talking politics all these years with my grandfather and . . . this was like a culmination, I mean for him, he talked about it. . . . He kept his Sunday clothes on all day. . . . It was the culmination for him of his civic duty and responsibility. I remember it was like my cousins and neighbors and friends, older people, people my age, and it was like we were at the polls for hours, I mean, we voted, right, and we just stood around . . . celebrating. After we voted, everybody who came through, we were there greeting them, and the amazing thing is that my grandfather was not the only person who said "this is such a special day I'm going to dress up." I mean, you probably had the best-dressed black voters in the country in that precinct that morning. It was like a community celebration, like a holiday, that whole day. People were excited about having voted and they were just talking about it. It was like a church service when they're serving dinner on the grounds, you know, and people just wouldn't leave, they sort of kept coming, migrating in and out.[93]

Today, Les McLemore is serving his fourth term as a member of the Jackson City Council.

Driving to Wesson, Mississippi, one afternoon in early 2004 with Congressman Bennie Thompson, one of the authors was asked how the book was coming. The interview with McLemore having occurred only a few days previously, the election day story was told to the congressman. At the conclusion, Thompson leaned over and said, "You know, my father died before he ever had the chance to vote."[94]

CHAPTER 7

RONALD REAGAN AND JON HINSON

1980–1981

Had I identified myself more with the rural folks, I'd have beat Finch,
because I beat him in every city in the state.
—GIL CARMICHAEL[1]

Gil Carmichael lost the Governor's Mansion to Cliff Finch in 1975, a loss largely due to public policy positions Carmichael adopted in the campaign that cost him white voters in rural Mississippi. It was a problem Ronald Reagan sought to overcome in 1980.

RONALD REAGAN AND THE PURSUIT OF THE RURAL WHITE VOTER

As 1980 began, domestic and international events were jeopardizing the reelection of President Carter. On the home front, inflation reached double digits, interest rates approached 20 percent, and the price of a gallon of gas was breaking records. In October, Ford and General Motors announced the two worst quarterly losses in American industrial history. Joblessness was spreading, and investors were nervous. Crime was rising to a level that saw New York City recording more than 2,000 homicides a year. Carter's foreign policy was also going nowhere. Western European nations were expressing doubt about the will and ability of the United States to shore up the North Atlantic Treaty Organization (NATO) alliance. The militants who had seized the U.S. embassy in Iran the previous year continued to hold fifty-two Americans hostages, and the Soviet Union, ignoring American protests, was actively engaged in military action in Afghanistan.[2]

THE DEMOCRATS IN MISSISSIPPI

The compromise that unified Mississippi Democrats in 1976 required the use of co-chairmen—one white and one black. Tom Riddell, a Canton business-man, and Aaron Henry, president of the NAACP in Mississippi, were selected. The concession was palatable to many whites because it specified that the co-chairmanship would expire at the end of 1979. Unless reenacted, the party would revert to a lone chairman in 1980.[3]

Soon after his election, Governor Winter began to argue the time had come to abandon the dual chairmanship. Predictably, a number of black activists opposed Winter's position.[4] When Democrats held their state convention in April, Winter endorsed Danny Cupit, a white Jackson lawyer and co-chair-man of Carter's 1976 campaign, as his choice for party leader. Neither side was budging from its position, however, so the delegates created a special com-mittee to resolve the dispute. Aaron Henry and Jack Harper, the white veteran Sunflower County chancery clerk, were chosen to select the committee mem-bers. Winter pleaded for party harmony at the convention: "We've got enough trouble battling the Republicans, we don't need to be battling one another."[5] Winter then proceeded to create his own trouble.

When the party's executive committee met on May 10 to choose a chairman, the special committee had completed its task: all sides had agreed to a single chairman, with Cupit as the nominee. Winter opened the meeting with a brief pep talk, and all was going well until the end of his speech, when Winter made the case for a single chairman and concluded, "I think at this time what we need to lead this party is a white chairman."[6] Steve Patterson, an aide to Win-ter, couldn't believe it: "The reaction was awful." A black participant spoke for many when he remarked, "I tuned out when William Winter made that state-ment." The thirty-five black delegates refused to participate in the remainder of the meeting, and many walked out. Whether they would stay with the party was not clear.[7] Soon after hearing about the debacle, national Democratic officials summoned state party leaders to Washington. With the memories of the 1964 and 1968 convention fights still lingering, and with the 1980 conven-tion a few months away, John White, the chairman of the national Democratic

Party, arranged to meet with Cupit, Patterson, and others. What transpired at the meeting Patterson recalls as "political maneuvering at its absolute best."[8]

The Mississippi delegation arrived for the meeting and was ushered into White's conference room. After a long wait, White came in, engaged in perfunctory handshakes, offered no "small talk," and immediately launched off with:

Let me give you boys some advice. Y'all done kicked Aaron Henry in the face, and for the rest of your life you gonna be known as racists. Now, if I was y'all, I'd get back on that state airplane of yours and go back home and do whatever it takes to fix this. . . . Why the stupidest thing I've ever heard of is the Democratic governor getting involved in internal Democratic politics. Now I'm gonna tell you right now. You ain't gonna get any support out of this national party, WHATSOEVER. DO YOU UNDERSTAND ME?[9]

White left, meeting adjourned. Patterson remembers leaving Washington on the long trip home with all of them thinking they had no choice but to approach Henry and resolve the dispute.

The next day Patterson met Aaron Henry for breakfast and noticed a dramatic change in his attitude: Henry likewise was ready to work something out. After a few weeks, they agreed to create the position of executive vice chair, with that appointee to be of the opposite race as the chairman. The other piece of the compromise stipulated that Henry would become national committeeman. The state executive committee met, adopted the agreement, and elected Cupit as chairman. The Democrats were back together, ready to fight for Jimmy Carter one more time.

Several months later, Patterson was having breakfast with Henry and toward the end of their conversation said, "Aaron, let me tell you about our conference with John White." As he told the story, Henry's eyes came to life. "Why that sonofabitch," Henry exclaimed. "You know what? White had me come to Washington and told me the exact same thing!"[10]

THE REPUBLICANS

While the Democrats were trying to keep their black-white coalition together, the Republicans were working to heal the conservative-moderate divisions created by the 1976 fiasco and the 1979 Bramlett-Carmichael bloodbath. Early on,

Congressman Trent Lott was appointed chairman of Reagan's 1980 presidential bid, and in a show of party unity, more than 1,200 supporters attended a GOP fund-raising dinner in February, with Gerald Ford as the keynote speaker.[11]

The conservatives, however, were to make one last run at Clarke Reed. Meeting in Jackson on the same day as the Democrats, the state GOP held its convention to choose delegates to the national convention and, more important, decide whether Reed would remain as national committeeman. For weeks, a number of Reagan conservatives, remembering Reed's 1976 decision, had waged a campaign to unseat him for that party post. "The emotion of the seven-hour day ... heightened when Reed entered the crowded convention hall just before the vote for national committeeman. Reed, who was recuperating from an airplane crash that left him in a body cast, was wheeled to the front of the room on a portable stretcher. When the vote was over, Reed had won 134 votes to defeat" three other candidates. As the convention began to hear reports of the walkout by blacks at the Democratic convention down the road, black Republicans "began pushing their fellow delegates to make a good faith effort to recruit other blacks. In response, the convention elected three black alternate delegates to the national convention."[12]

Over the course of the Republican primaries that followed around the country, Ronald Reagan overcame one opponent after another. By the time Reagan acknowledged the moderate wing of the party by naming George Bush as his running mate, Mississippi Republicans were fully behind his candidacy.

THE GENERAL ELECTION

In covering the 1980 campaign, journalist Jeff Greenfield summed up the situation facing Carter: "During the Carter years, the central claim of the post-New Deal Democratic Party—that it could manage the economy and produce sustained growth—collapsed under the combined weight of inflation, escalating oil prices, unemployment, high interest rates, and industrial stagnation."[13] And when Carter's foreign policy team could not bring home the American hostages or curtail the Soviet Union's invasion of Afghanistan, the voters had had enough.

When an incumbent is faced with a record as dismal as Carter's, the campaign has but one choice: convince the voters that his opponent would be much worse. While this makes for an ugly, personal campaign, about which journalists will bitterly complain, the incumbent's only available strategy is to attack, which is what Carter did, relentlessly claiming that Reagan was inexperienced and dangerous. Four years earlier, Carter had carried every southern state except Virginia. For Reagan to win, he had to turn this geographic juggernaut around. His campaign strategy was the same as Ford's in 1976—mobilize the urban-suburban base and win over the rural white vote. Mississippi offered the perfect vehicle to focus on rural whites—the Neshoba County Fair. By 1980, the fair had been opening its gates in the rural eastern part of the state every August for ninety-one years, and while it still offered the kinds of activities once associated with county fairs all over the state, it was primarily known for the public-speaking opportunities it offered politicians.

Lanny Griffith was state GOP director in 1980 and knew instinctively the fair was the perfect match: "It was not a mistake that Reagan went to the Neshoba County Fair, rather than Jackson. This was sort of heresy, going out in these rural areas . . . [but] I know from my standpoint in 1980, we were just obsessed with how you turn around these rural counties and get them started voting with us."[14] The connection was made. Reagan traveled to Philadelphia, Mississippi, on an early August Sunday afternoon, becoming the first presidential candidate in the history of the Neshoba County Fair to speak. More than 15,000 people jammed the fairgrounds to hear Reagan kick off his fall campaign in the state. Reagan's speech was a classic: attack Carter, but do it with humor; appeal to southern patriotic values by focusing on Carter's record of cutting defense spending and engaging in a naive foreign policy that made America look weak; and applaud individual initiative by criticizing government social programs.

Reagan on Carter: "People have been telling me Jimmy Carter is doing his best. That's our problem."

Reagan on America's standing in the world: "This was once a proud country. . . . Today our friends don't know whether they can trust us and certain enemies have no respect for us."

Reagan on the federal government: "[I read] all about [the fair] in *National Geographic*. How did you ever accomplish this without a federal program?"

In the middle of his speech, Reagan made his trademark contrast between government bureaucracy and the individual:

I think even more important . . . is to bring back to this country what is so evident here: bring back the recognition that the people of this country can solve

the problems. . . . In more recent years with the best of intentions, they have cre-
ated a vast bureaucracy . . . to try and solve all the problems. . . . I believe that
there are problems like [welfare], education and others that should be turned
back to the states and the local communities with the tax sources to fund them.
I believe in states' rights and people doing as much as they can for themselves.[15]

Reagan's use of the term "states' rights"—in the county where three civil rights workers were murdered in 1964—was interpreted by Democrats as Reagan's way of appealing to whites by embracing the famous "code word" used by white politicians in the 1950s and 1960s to defend segregation. Reagan denied the charge, claiming it was meant to indicate his support for returning to the states government spending programs. To this day, neither side in the debate has given an inch.

Reagan capitalized on two key events leading up to his 1980 campaign that allowed him to broaden his base to include rural whites. The first is known simply as "Proposition 13." In 1978, California voters overwhelmingly approved a constitutional amendment—Proposition 13 on the ballot—that would dramatically curtail property taxes in that state. The adoption of the amendment represented the culmination of a grassroots citizens' campaign fed up with taxes they believed too high. The national media covered the campaign extensively, and the two-to-one margin of victory ignited "tax revolts" in many other states and provided evidence Reagan needed to support his position that government had become too expensive.[16] Mississippi joined the revolt in 1979 when the legislature easily passed an $83 million tax cut.[17] Linking Democrats with failed and expensive government programs financed with high taxes was Reagan's specialty in the campaign: "Carter has blamed OPEC, he has blamed the Federal Reserve, he has blamed the lack of productivity on the American people; he has accused the people of living too well . . . that we must sacrifice and get used to doing with less. We don't have inflation because the people are living too well. We have inflation because the government is living too well."[18]

The second event actually had its origins in Mississippi and has been called the "spark that ignited the religious right's involvement in real politics." In 1969, civil rights lawyers in Mississippi filed suit against the Internal Revenue Service (IRS), arguing that tax-exempt status should not be granted to private schools formed in response to school desegregation. After winning their case in 1971, the lawyers were forced to resume their legal action in 1976 when the IRS failed to ensure that private schools adopted nondiscriminatory policies. Jerome

Kurtz was appointed IRS commissioner by President Carter and on August 22, 1978, changed course and issued tough new restrictions on the ability of private schools, many of them sponsored by churches, to claim tax-exempt status. "It kicked the sleeping dog," said one conservative activist. The Moral Majority was soon organized, and in 1979 its first executive director remarked that "Jerome Kurtz has done more to bring Christians together than any man since the Apostle Paul."[19]

By 1980, Lanny Griffith was witnessing the fallout:

I was looking at this from a very pragmatic and disciplined analytical stand-point, which was somehow we gotta move [rural white voters] to start voting our way . . . and if you look at it now you see the way Reagan mobilized con-servative Christians. . . . All of a sudden you saw people who were conservative in their religious doctrine were now moving from Democrats. Reagan did an amazing job transforming that, which was a great irony in view of the way Carter had originally positioned himself as Southern Baptist.[20]

A week before the election, Reagan and Carter held their one and only debate. In his closing statement, Reagan articulated the standard by which incumbents are now judged: "Are you better off than you were four years ago? Is it easier for you to go and buy things in stores than it was four years ago? Is there more or less unemployment in the country than there was four years ago? Is America as respected throughout the world as it was?"[21]

Ten days before election day, Reagan visited the Mississippi Sheriffs Boys Ranch in rural Lowndes County. Five days before election day, First Lady Rosalyn Carter campaigned at the Tennessee-Tombigbee Waterway site at Columbus.[22] And four days before election day, President Carter flew to Jackson to give a last-minute campaign pep rally to more than 5,000 in front of the Governor's Mansion: "I consider myself to be a true Southerner representing the ideals and commitment that have made us proud of the ideals of our region and land." Cupit met up with Carter in Memphis and traveled to Jackson with the campaign entourage. He remembers Carter's staff getting the latest poll results on the flight down to Jackson and, with them, the bad news projecting Carter's likely defeat.[23]

The election was an Electoral College landslide for Reagan, who won all but six states. The popular vote was closer, but still decisive—Reagan won 51 percent while Carter received 41 percent, with independent candidates gathering the rest. The South flipped on Carter. In 1976, Carter carried every southern state except for Virginia. Four years later, he could only manage to carry his home state of Georgia. As for Mississippi, the vote was again a squeaker. Carter carried the state by 14,463 votes in 1976 and lost it four years later by just 11,808 votes.

In executing a campaign strategy for Mississippi, Reagan succeeded where Ford failed—voters in the urban and suburban areas turned out in record numbers, and the proportion of rural white voters supporting the Democrat was reduced. In the three urbanized Gulf Coast counties, for example, Carter got 32,957 votes in 1976 and 32,088 in 1980. Reagan, however, received 52,761 compared with the 40,149 who voted for Ford. In DeSoto County, the fast-growing Mississippi suburb south of Memphis, Reagan increased the Republican vote by 55 percent. As for rural white voters, Reagan started the process of winning them over. In the ten-county area of northeast Mississippi, Reagan cut Carter's 1976 margin of 62 percent by nearly 6 percentage points.[24]

Across the country, Republicans gained control of the U.S. Senate in 1980, for the first time since 1952. Republicans won twelve seats from Democrats, including the defeat of nine incumbents.[25]

THE TRAGEDY OF JON HINSON

The 1980 general election was shaping up to be an easy reelection for Congressman Jon Hinson. The Democratic nominee, Britt Singletary, was a relatively unknown Jackson lawyer. Even more critical was the independent candidacy of Les McLemore, a Jackson State University political science professor who had roots in the civil rights movement reaching as far back as the 1964 Mississippi Freedom Democratic Party. When asked years later why he ran for Congress, McLemore said: "I got involved through the displeasure of the black community with the elimination of the co-chair of the Democratic party. And when William Winter said there was no need for that, a lot of the black leaders felt very strongly that Aaron [Henry] should be continued as a co-chair. We wanted to show them that blacks could not be taken for granted."[26]

Then Stuart Stevens got a phone call from his client Jon Hinson. Stevens had produced Hinson's television commercials in the 1978 campaign and was set to help him again in 1980. Hinson began: "Stuart, there's something I didn't tell you back in the '78 campaign." Stevens thought to himself: "When a political consultant gets a call from a candidate who says 'there's something I didn't tell you,' you know he's not calling to tell you good news."[27] On Friday, August 8, 1980, Hinson divulged publicly what he had confided to Stevens—in September 1976, he had been arrested in Arlington, Virginia, while committing an obscene act. He had settled the matter by paying a $100 fine. Thirteen months later, he was at an X-rated movie theater in Washington when a fire destroyed the building, killing nine people. Hinson was one of four survivors, and in early June he had given a deposition to lawyers handling civil suits filed by families of victims of the fire. Hinson's startling admission: both of these sites were "frequented by homosexuals."[28]

After hearing the news, Billy Mounger, one of Hinson's earliest supporters, immediately called the congressman and arranged for a meeting. Mounger asked him point blank: "Are you a homosexual?" Hinson denied he was gay, said his minister was backing him, and convinced the conservative Republicans that it was all part of a troubled past. The meeting broke up with his candidacy intact. Wirt Yerger Jr., another early backer, told the press: "These things took place at a time when he was caught up in emotional problems, before I ever heard of the guy. He had solved the problems and put them behind him by 1978, and he's done an outstanding job since then."[29] A week later at another press conference, Hinson, with his wife at his side, explained his reasoning behind the disclosures: he was "sick and tired of worrying they would become public. . . . I was reasonably certain that others had the information, but I didn't know when it would come out." And Hinson was compelled to declare flatly: "I am not, never have been, and never will be a homosexual."[30]

Reporters then began the process they do best: digging and peeling back the layers. Bit by bit they found information Hinson had withheld. The *Jackson Clarion-Ledger* soon disclosed the theater that burned was more than an X-rated movie house for homosexual films. It was also a club with more than 22,000 members where a "full range of sexual activities [were] conducted in empty rooms adjacent to the viewing area."[31] A couple of weeks later, the *Clarion-Ledger* devoted a front-page story to the revelation that Hinson had been to the theater on numerous other occasions. Even more damning: Hinson had delayed the deposition until June 6, three days after the Republican primary.[32]

Then, the *Jackson Daily News* broke the most detailed report yet of Hinson's 1976 arrest. The "obscene act"—which took place at the Iwo Jima Memorial in Arlington, Virginia, a gathering place for homosexuals—occurred when Hinson exposed himself to an undercover detective. Hinson was immediately arrested. He was photographed and fingerprinted at a local jail and released. A court date was set for September 23, 1976, at which Hinson failed to show. The judge issued a summons for him to appear on October 7, a date he ignored. A third court hearing was set for October 21, and once again there was no Hinson. The judge issued a warrant for his arrest, and only then did Hinson respond. On October 28, he pleaded guilty to a reduced charge of creating a public nuisance and was fined $100.[33]

In a campaign, when potentially damaging but truthful information becomes public, the goal becomes simple: discredit the source of the information. To the Hinson campaign and his GOP supporters, the newspaper reports were roundly criticized as "junk journalism" and "journalism of hysteria."[34] The reluctance of the Republican leaders to give serious consideration to the disclosures may have been explained by Mounger:

> You'd think that a man who had acknowledged frequenting a homosexual theater would have been run out of Mississippi. But he's got a great voting record. He's been with us conservatives on every issue right down the line. There are folks that think we would rather have a queer conservative than a macho, all-man liberal, and they may be right, but he says he is not and was not a homosexual, and never performed a homosexual act, and I believe him.[35]

On election day, Hinson received only 39 percent of the vote, but it was enough to win with a plurality. McLemore came in second with 30 percent, leading Singletary by 656 votes, who finished third. A relieved Hinson told his supporters on election night: "It's been a hard three months. The worst three months I've spent in my life. I felt like Lazarus, returned from the dead."[36]

The End

All was well in the Hinson world until the morning of February 4, 1981. Jon Hinson left his office by a private door, walked over to an adjacent congressional office building, to an isolated restroom, and met Harold Moore, a twenty-nine-year-old Library of Congress clerk. Unbeknownst to Hinson, the Capitol Police were watching the restroom through a peephole, following a tip that homosexuals gathered there. A few minutes later, Hinson and Moore were arrested on felony charges of committing oral sodomy. Hinson posted a $2,000 bond and was released from jail at 4:25 P.M. Jackson time.[37] The word, however, had already reached Mississippi. The legislature was still in session, and within five minutes of the news hitting the capitol, the Jon Hinson jokes were making the rounds. His career was over.

There was no forgiveness this time. Party Chairman Mike Retzer announced: "I'm calling for his resignation." Billy Mounger was distraught: Hinson "is sick. . . . We trusted him and he just didn't play the game straight with us. I think he should resign."[38] That afternoon, the *Jackson Daily News* editorialized, "Jon Hinson has pushed his own self-destruct button."[39] That evening, ABC News carried the story to the nation: "The voters of the district may have believed Hinson enough to reelect him, but today Hinson's Democratic opponent was saying I told you so."[40]

By the next day, Hinson was in a psychiatric hospital, ignoring the demands back home for his resignation. The *Clarion-Ledger* was reporting on its front page that the Hinson arrest was the "talk of Washington."[41] It took Hinson nearly a month to officially resign from office.[42] Hinson's minister defended the wait: "I don't think people realize that an emotional and mental sickness is just like any other sickness. Your mind can't do some things when you have an emotional sickness. . . . People kept asking him to do something [resign] that he just wasn't capable of doing."[43] Several months later, Hinson pleaded no contest to the charge and received a one-year probation.[44]

The Republican transformation in Mississippi was perhaps best captured by a shopper in Hinson's hometown of Tylertown, the day after his 1981 arrest, who said "he had figured all along that Hinson was gay, but had voted for him just the same because a gay was better than a Democrat."[45]

The Aftermath

One reason Hinson gave for making public the extraordinary disclosures was the fear that his Democratic opponent—Britt Singletary—knew about them and would use them in the campaign. Hinson alleged that his 1978 Democratic opponent—John Hampton Stennis—had learned about the incidents and had perhaps passed the damaging information along to his law partner, John Holloman, who was serving as Singletary's campaign manager. The first that Holloman heard about the arrest and fire was from Hinson's press conference.[46]

At the time of Hinson's 1976 arrest, he was a member of then Congressman Thad Cochran's staff. In response to questions about what he knew, Cochran told the *Clarion-Ledger* that he was campaigning for reelection in, ironically, Hinson's hometown of Tylertown when Capitol Police called to notify him that a warrant had been issued for Hinson's arrest: "I knew that it was alleged to have occurred at the Iwo Jima Memorial and that had to create suspicions in my mind, but he told me that it was a mix-up and frankly I gave him the benefit of the doubt." Cochran said he did not know the original charge was for "an indecent and immoral act," only that Hinson told him it was for disturbing the peace and that he had been under a lot of emotional strain and pressure. Both Cochran and Hinson were in Tylertown on October 21 for a campaign event, the day of the scheduled third court date.[47]

On New Year's Day, 1984, Clifton and Lyndell Hinson—Jon Hinson's parents—were killed in a fire that swept through their house in the early morning hours. Clifton Hinson had recently been reelected to his fourth term as a Walthall County supervisor. Lyndell Hinson was assistant librarian at the Walthall County Library.[48]

Jon Hinson died at the age of fifty-three at his home in Silver Spring, Maryland, on July 21, 1995, from respiratory failure associated with AIDS.[49] In a 1993 article he wrote for the *Roll Call* newspaper in Washington, Hinson said of the 1980 campaign: "I was not yet emotionally ready to confront what on some deeper level I knew I'd eventually have to face—specifically that my sexual orientation is homosexual." In early 1994, he returned to Mississippi to speak at a fund-raising benefit for a gay community center in Biloxi.[50]

THE CAMPAIGN TO SUCCEED HINSON

In Mississippi, there are no party primaries in a special election to fill a vacancy. All candidates qualify in one election, and unless one of them gets a majority, the top two vote-getters run three weeks later in a runoff election. The special election was set for June 23, 1981.[51] Given that election scenario, and the possibility that a large group of Republican candidates in a field with a large group of Democratic candidates could split the GOP vote and prevent any Republican from getting into the runoff, the state GOP decided to hold a "convention" and "nominate" one candidate, although there was no legal requirement that other Republicans could be forced out of the race by means of this process.[52] Chosen was forty-five-year-old Liles Williams, a vice president with the Stuart C. Irby Company in Jackson.[53]

The Democrats, unaccustomed to that kind of discipline, opted to let any-one qualify.[54] The major candidates were all white: Wayne Dowdy, thirty-seven years old and mayor of McComb, a town in the southern part of the district; Ed Ellington, forty, a state senator from Jackson; and Britt Singletary, thirty, a Jackson lawyer and the party's 1980 nominee. The campaign was noteworthy for one event: Wayne Dowdy endorsed the extension of the 1965 Voting Rights Act, the only major candidate to take that bold step.[55] Enacted in 1965 with a five-year life span, the act was reauthorized by Congress in 1970 for five years and again in 1975 for seven years. Unless reenacted in 1982, key provisions of the act would disappear from federal law. Knowing this, civil rights groups across the country made extending the law their number one priority.

On election day, Williams led the ticket, as the Republicans had hoped, with 44 percent. Dowdy, relying on support from the southern part of the district, came in second with 27 percent. Singletary and Ellington were a distant third and fourth. In the runoff, it was a head-to-head Democratic-Republican con-test, and the stakes became high indeed as the election—the only race for a congressional seat in the entire nation since Reagan's election seven months previously—was seen as a referendum on both Reagan's policies and the popularity of extending the Voting Rights Act. "For the Republicans," said one observer, "they fear it will be seen as a grassroots rejection of Reagan's budget program, in a state the president narrowly won last November."[56]

Dowdy attacked many of Reagan's policies, while Williams attached himself firmly to the newly inaugurated president.[57] In a district that at the time had a black voting-age population in excess of 39 percent, Dowdy's support of the Voting Rights Act became a major issue. In the end, though, the Republicans suffered under the geographical burden described earlier: their candidate was from Jackson. In spite of being outspent, Dowdy carried every county in the southern part of the district except for Lincoln, losing it by less than 100 votes. Williams won Hinds and Warren, the two counties that formed the northern boundary of the district. Dowdy prevailed by 912 votes in a district that Reagan had carried just seven months earlier by more than 6,200 votes.

The Dowdy win took on larger-than-life proportions in Washington. The *Washington Post* reported that "worried Republicans yesterday began study-ing the implications of their loss of a house seat in a conservative Mississippi district, while Democrats welcomed their upset winner, Wayne Dowdy, as a harbinger of the end of President Reagan's honeymoon."[58]

POSTSCRIPT

For a few brief weeks in early 1980, Governor Finch was a candidate for the presidency. He left Mississippi in a red and white pickup truck telling reporters, "I'm in this race until we take office."[59] His campaign reached its pinnacle when a photograph of Finch relaxing in a heart-shaped bathtub in Tucson, Arizona, appeared on the front page of the *Clarion-Ledger* with the caption "Nothing to Hide: Former Gov. Cliff Finch, hoping to make a clean sweep of the presidential primaries, takes a breather on the campaign trail."[60]

CHAPTER 8

EDUCATION TRANSFORMS
THE LEGISLATURE

1982

It's boat-rocking time in Mississippi.
—GOVERNOR WILLIAM WINTER, January 1982[1]

Fans of late-night television back in 1982 might remember watching David Letterman debut his late show on NBC. Parents of young children might recall being dragged to the movie *E.T.: The Extra-Terrestrial* later that summer. Others might remember mourning the deaths of Thelonious Monk, John Belushi, Ayn Rand, Satchel Paige, or Glenn Gould.

Few national events however made as great an impression on Mississippians as did political changes in the state, for 1982 was the year the existence of the Mississippi legislature broke out of the confines of the closed world of politicians, lobbyists, and reporters and roared into the collective consciousness of the average voter. Before 1982, the legislature was "the bunch in Jackson" that few Mississippians knew or cared anything about. After 1982, the Mississippi legislature was as well known as the local sheriff, and not nearly as popular. One event and one man triggered the transformation.

THE MISSISSIPPI LEGISLATURE

Outside the 174 legislators and their immediate families, lobbyists, reporters, and assorted political activists, how does one begin to explain the legislature to the remaining 2.9 million Mississippians? While the standard textbook explanation is a good start—the branch of state government that sets taxes and appropriates the proceeds to fund programs; issues bonds to pay for highways, buildings, and equipment; establishes the laws by which every local and state governmental entity operates; and creates the agencies that regulate activities ranging from air and water pollution to the practice of cosmetology—it is hardly sufficient.

In large measure, Mississippi's future will be determined by a resolution of critical public policy issues—education; public safety; economic development initiatives; construction of highways, airports, and ports to facilitate commerce; management of our natural resources; health care; and other services for residents who otherwise could not afford them. Those issues will be resolved by our legislature. When assembled under the roof of the New State Capitol, the men and women elected to the legislature today closely reflect the political mindset and demographics of the state. Such was not always the case.

Reapportionment

Until Upton Sisson's lawsuit was resolved in 1963, legislative seats were filled almost exclusively by white men elected from rural Mississippi. While Sisson's litigation addressed some of the urban-rural imbalance in the legislature, it was not until the *Connor* litigation was settled in 1979 that the racial makeup of the legislature began to more closely mirror the state's population. Reapportionment not only created a more urban and a more African American legislature, it created a more responsive legislature.

The vehicle for that transformation was the single-member district—a small geographical area, composed of a relatively compact population, limited to one representative. Before *Connor*, most legislators were elected from multimember districts—large geographical areas with a larger number of voters electing two or more legislators—a more confusing arrangement for the average voter. Advocates of the single-member district embrace its inherent accountability—the smaller area focused on just one legislator makes it easy for voters to know their legislator and thereby influence their legislator. Opponents charge this enhanced accountability fails to give the elected official any freedom to act in a way that he or she might think is best for the state, versus the narrow interest of his or her district.

Jim Simpson Sr., a state representative from Harrison County for many years, summed up the case for the status quo: "Single-member districts make for a more responsive [legislator] to that district. It makes, too, a less responsible state lawmaker." Simpson explained that before *Connor*, when he was elected from the entire county,

> *if I did something even if it was right that was against the special interests of the tourism business, then I had the manufacturing community . . . the sea-food community . . . the education community . . . that I could balance it off. In single-member districts, you go to single-issue politics. . . . It makes for a more responsive government, but it doesn't make a politician, unless he's highly unusual, make every decision based on what is good for the community. . . . Rather, he says, "How will this politically affect the district in which I live?"*[2]

Simpson raises the age-old question: should an elected official vote the way his or her constituents would vote, or should an elected official digest all the available information on an issue, weigh the evidence, and then do what he or she thinks is "right." While single-member districts don't resolve that question one way or the other, the politics of such districts require that an elected official take the time to interact with constituents before an important vote and explain his or her rationale for the vote. Legislators can still make the "right" votes; they just must be prepared to defend those votes to constituents.

It was a legislature with more urban members and more black members, as well as with that newly established connection between the legislator and the voter, that Governor William Winter exploited in 1982.

LEADERSHIP AND COMMITTEES

The Mississippi legislature is what management consultants label a "top-down" organization—power is held by a few members who hold key leadership positions. At the top are the presiding officer of the House of Representatives—the Speaker—and the presiding officer of the Senate—the president. In Mississippi, the Speaker is elected by the House membership; the lieutenant governor, elected statewide, serves as the Senate president.

In 1982, the Speaker was C. B. Newman, though those few who didn't call him "Mr. Speaker" called him "Buddie." First elected to the House from Issaquena County in 1951, Newman had served continuously ever since, becoming Speaker Pro Tempore in 1974 and Speaker in 1976. Newman was mentored by Walter Sillers and was Ross Barnett's floor leader in the House.

Brad Dye, lieutenant governor in 1982, was elected to the House in 1959 and the state Senate in 1963, and in 1967 he took a post in John Bell Williams's administration. Chosen state treasurer in 1971, he lost a bid for lieutenant governor in 1975, but came back four years later to win. He was a protégé of Jim Eastland.

The presiding officers refer all bills to committees, appoint all committee members, and appoint all committee chairmen. They control the flow of legislation on the floor of their respective houses by ruling on parliamentary matters and choosing whom to recognize—or not—for the offering of motions or other floor procedures. By rule, by custom, and by force of their personalities, Mississippi's Speaker and lieutenant governor can defeat virtually any piece of legislation they do not like, and can ensure passage in their respective chambers of almost any legislation they favor.

The bulk of the legislature's work is done by committees. The committees receive bills introduced by the members and recommend bills for consideration by the full House or Senate. Once appointed, committee chairmen have near total authority over the work product of their respective committees. A committee chairman is under no obligation to allow his or her committee to consider a bill that is referred to it. During debates, a chairman is under no obligation to recognize a member of his or her committee to speak on a bill or to make a motion. Committee chairmen keep no minutes of committee meetings, few recorded votes, and no tape recordings of deliberations. In describing the power of committee chairmen, one legislator observed: "If he doesn't want to meet, you don't meet. If the committee has 100 bills and he decides that only two should be considered that's all you consider. . . . If you're not a member of a committee and that committee has your bill, you're at the complete mercy of the chairman."[3]

It was to this institution that William Winter brought the issue of education reform. And it was the issue of education that began to change the institution.

THE SAGA OF EDUCATION REFORM

As legislators convened in January 1982 for their ninety-day regular session, public education had been on Winter's agenda for two years.[4] In 1980, at Winter's request, the legislature had created a special education study commission. Chaired by Tupelo businessman Jack Reed, the commission spent the remainder of the year documenting that Mississippi was the last state without a mandatory public kindergarten system and the last state without a compulsory school attendance law; that it paid its teachers at a level at or near the bottom on national salary scales; that it had no way of measuring the performance of its schools; and that the system was too politicized—the state superintendent of education was elected statewide, and the State Board of Education consisted of the attorney general, the secretary of state, and the state superintendent.[5]

When the 1981 legislature ignored the reforms recommended by the Reed commission, Winter's staff spent the remainder of that year organizing community, business, and education groups to lobby legislators on behalf of education.[6] At the beginning of 1982, Winter continued his campaign for education reform. This time, in a speech to the legislature, he got personal:

> We are here to put the most creative thoughts we have into the solution to problems that are not going to go away and that cry out for this legislature to address. We keep looking for easy answers. . . . We keep trying not to rock anybody's boat. Well, I want to tell you it's boat-rocking time in Mississippi. It's time to get off our backsides and decide we aren't going to let anything or anybody or any set of circumstances keep us from making this state more competitive. And if we are not willing to take that approach, then we haven't got any business being here.[7]

By 1982, the rallying cry for advocates of reform had been narrowed to one word: kindergartens. Getting young children ready for school and joining the other states that required public kindergartens became the focus. To cover the price tag for kindergartens, Winter proposed increasing the oil and gas severance tax, a move fiercely opposed by the state's oil and gas industry. Representative Simpson, a proponent of Winter's plan, once identified the opponents of kindergartens: those opposed to increasing the severance tax, those opposed to any tax increase, and a group of about 20 opposed on racial grounds. Simpson described the reasoning of the third group as, "I'm not building any damn babysitting service for blacks."[8] Winter believed he could overcome the reluctance to raise taxes if he could sell the importance of education reforms to a majority of the legislature.[9] In the meantime, he received an unexpected gift.

THE EVENT AND THE MAN

On February 3, 1982, Winter's public pressure campaign showed signs of having some influence. House Bill 936, legislation authorizing kindergartens in public schools, passed the Education and Appropriations Committees, and was placed on the House calendar, ready for debate, the first time the issue had survived that far into the process.[10]

The Mississippi legislature conducts its business according to deadlines. A House bill must pass the House committee to which it was referred by a certain date, and then it must pass the full House by a certain date. Deadlines then exist for House bills sent to the Senate. A similar system is imposed on bills introduced in the Senate.

The kindergarten bill faced a House floor deadline of February 11. If the bill did not pass the House by that date, it would automatically die. On February 10, Representatives Robert Clark and Tommy Walman, chairman and vice chairman of the House Education Committee, respectively, told Newman privately they planned to request recognition for a procedural motion to allow the House to debate the bill that day. That day was critical, for everyone knew the rules required a special two-thirds vote to authorize debate of bills on a deadline day. While Clark and Walman believed a majority of the House might support kindergartens, they knew two-thirds would not. Newman said he would recognize neither of them.[11]

As the day was winding down, and the kindergarten bill remained on the calendar, Clark stood:

> The Speaker: For what purpose does the gentleman from Holmes County [Mr. Clark] seek recognition?
>
> Clark: For a motion, Mr. Speaker.
>
> The Speaker: State your motion.
>
> Clark: To advance House Bill 936 to the top of the calendar for immediate consideration.
>
> The Speaker: The gentleman is not recognized.
>
> [Walman rose immediately]
>
> The Speaker: For what purpose does the gentleman from Pike County [Mr. Walman] seek recognition?
>
> Walman: For a motion, Mr. Speaker.
>
> The Speaker: State your motion.
>
> Walman: To advance House Bill 936 to the top of the calendar for immediate consideration.
>
> The Speaker: The gentleman is not recognized.

[While other House members began to object, Representative Simpson stood.]
The Speaker: For what purpose does the gentleman from Harrison County
    [Mr. Simpson] seek recognition?
Simpson: For a motion, Mr. Speaker.
The Speaker: State your motion.
Simpson: I move the House stand adjourned until ten o'clock tomorrow.

The Speaker put the motion to the House: "All those in favor of the motion say aye"—at which point members favoring adjournment yelled "aye."

"All those opposed to the motion say nay"—at which point those members wishing to stay and take up the kindergarten bill yelled "nay," a collective nay that was clearly louder than the ayes.

It was 5:35 P.M. as Newman rapped his gavel on the podium and proclaimed, "The ayes have it. The House stands adjourned." He then turned and walked off the dais.[12]

And he kept walking; he ignored calls and shouts from the floor demanding a roll call vote. If at least twelve members stand after a voice vote, the rules require a roll call vote, and more than twelve members had jumped up seeking recognition.[13]

By this time, House members were in an uproar, not fully comprehending what had just happened, but also not believing what had just happened.[14] With that one act, the issue of education reform became associated with the abuse of power in the legislature.

Sonny Merideth, a representative from Greenville and a Newman floor leader, had canvassed the members that afternoon, asking them when they wanted to adjourn. He remembers a majority wanted to adjourn early, well before the House would get to kindergartens. He gave that information to the Speaker and to Simpson, who was recognized each day for the motion to adjourn. Merideth contends that Newman believed a majority wanted to adjourn, they just didn't yell as loudly as those who wanted to stay. To this day, Merideth believes the House would have adjourned with a roll call: "I had walked the floor and it wasn't close. The majority was ready to adjourn. But they didn't holler as loud for adjournment as those who were opposed. The Speaker just thought those for it didn't holler as loud."[15] Simpson agreed, once speculating that a majority of the House had been to Newman and said, "I don't want to vote on this. If it comes to a vote, I've got too many blacks and too many educators in my area. I'm going to have to vote 'yes', but I don't want to vote on this."[16]

In an interview years later, Newman gave his version of the events:

Now, the Speaker of the House, a lot of people don't understand, is something like a chaplain. You know, if you're in trouble in the Army, you seek out the chaplain. The speaker of the House to me is like a mother hen, protect your brood, protect your members, and I like to be strong, I like it. I'd rather be strong than weak any day. I'd rather be strong and wrong than weak and right, to be frank with you. I saw the chairman and vice chairman of the Education Committee standing up. I knew what they wanted. I knew exactly what they wanted. I knew what the members wanted. I knew that the members did not want to vote on that piece of trash. I knew that. They came to me in droves. "We don't need to get to that bill."... Jim Simpson got up for recognition and I recognized Jim. And he said, "I move we adjourn"... and I rapped the gavel and said, "motion prevails" and walked off the podium like I've done many, many times, no different. I didn't pay any attention to it.[17]

Whether inadvertent or not, the move by Newman set in motion a series of events that would ultimately transform the legislature and pass education reform.

THE OUTCRY

The next morning, Representatives Fred Banks of Jackson and Leslie King of Greenville addressed the full House, criticizing Newman for his refusal to honor the House rules by not calling for a recorded vote on the motion to adjourn. Later that day, Clark was allowed to make his motion for immediate consideration of House Bill 936, but since it was deadline day, the motion needed a two-thirds vote. The margin was 70-48, nine shy of two-thirds.[18] The vote, however, became a symbol: a majority had voted for kindergartens, but the will of that large majority had been thwarted by one man.

By the weekend, the press had identified a villain: "With a single action, the 60-year-old Newman changed the odds and stacked the deck against public kindergartens in Mississippi."[19] Slowly over the next few months, Buddie

Newman became the target for all that was wrong in Mississippi; he was standing in the way of progress and using arcane rules to keep it that way.

At one point, Charles Bannerman, a leader of Winter's education programs in Greenville, called Winter's staff to say a close friend of his was a producer with ABC in New York and they might be interested in the Newman story.[20] One thing led to another, and on Thursday night, August 26, the ABC show *20/20* aired a feature called "A Case Study in Political Wheeling and Dealing—With Children's Futures at Stake." The program informed "the nation that Mississippi is alone among the states in not having state supported public kindergartens. The question it asked was why." Buddie Newman was the answer. Newman called the piece a "hatchet job," but the Pascagoula newspaper editorialized that the *20/20* report "told the nation what Mississippians have known all along. The public interest is in the hands of a few power brokers."[21]

THE *CLARION-LEDGER*

On April 1, 1982, the Gannett Corporation acquired the *Jackson Clarion-Ledger*, the *Jackson Daily News*, and other newspapers owned by Jackson's Hederman family.[22] Three months later, the *Clarion-Ledger* and *Jackson Daily News* had a new editor, Charles Overby. A Jackson native, Overby had served as a Washington correspondent for the *Jackson Daily News* out of college, then went to work for Gannett, and later became an editor of a Gannett newspaper in Florida. He later joined Governor Lamar Alexander's staff in Tennessee and ultimately became chairman of the Tennessee Republican Party.[23]

The reporting of Winter's education initiative by Overby would prove pivotal. For eight days in late November, the paper produced a comprehensive series of articles about the problems facing public education. It was the coverage of the December special session, however, that set a new standard for journalism in the state. The newspaper flooded the capitol with reporters, publishing two or three articles a day, identifying how individual legislators voted in committee, and writing caustic editorials. Its most famous editorial followed a House floor vote and "inducted" the members who had opposed kindergartens into a "Hall of Shame."[24] Overby helped connect the legislators to their constituents: "The high water mark of our reporting was the putting of faces with committee action which helped the average reader understand who was doing what."[25]

On April 18, 1983, the *Clarion-Ledger* was awarded the Pulitzer Prize for Distinguished Public Service for its coverage of education reform in 1982.

THE WINTER ORGANIZATION

The one unchecked power wielded by a Mississippi governor is the ability to require legislators to attend a special session, at the time of the governor's choosing, and limited specifically to the issues of the governor's choosing. There is no better way to focus attention on a public policy issue than to call a special session. At a news conference on April 6, Winter first raised that possibility.[26] After watching legislators ignore his pleas for education reform during three regular sessions, Winter contemplated drastic action. "I realized that if we were going to pass any sort of meaningful education reform, it would not be done in a regular session, because there are too many stumps you can hide behind. I had to command the agenda."[27]

Simply calling a special session would not be sufficient. And more lobbying by Winter and his staff would not pass a bill. It was time to take advantage of the psychology of single-member districts and the immutable fact of the calendar: 1983 was an election year. David Crews, a Tupelo native and Winter's press secretary, put it simply: "What made [the plan] work was that legislators could say 'no' to staff members and to William Winter. . . . The person they can't say 'no' to is that constituent."[28]

The Winter administration proceeded to organize a political campaign, but this time the goal was not to elect a candidate, but to pass a bill. The first step in a campaign is to educate the voters. For the rest of the spring and into the summer and early fall, the education effort was accomplished primarily through speeches to any group, large or small, that would have Winter or a member of his staff come talk about education. Over the next six months, more than 800 speeches were delivered. In addition to informing voters about the issue, the speeches served another purpose. At the end of each speech, anyone interested in joining the campaign filled out a volunteer card. By the end of November, the names, addresses, and phone numbers of more than 40,000 education supporters from all eighty-two counties were on file in the governor's office.[29]

A political campaign is not a campaign without a rally. In Winter's education campaign, they were called "education forums," and they were scheduled for the fall in Oxford, Vicksburg, Columbus, Greenville, Jackson, Laurel,

McComb, Meridian, and the Gulf Coast. The plan was for Winter to keynote each forum, followed by smaller sessions with the participants to discuss specifics of education. Getting business and community leaders together with educators to organize for action in such a public way was a first in Mississippi. The risk, of course, was that no one would show up.

The first forum was scheduled for Oxford High School on September 7. The advance team prepared handouts for 500 people, though they hoped a "respectable" 300 would show. By 6:00 P.M., the lines into the high school started forming. Buses started to arrive. Dick Molpus, a native of Philadelphia and a staff member, re-created the scene he saw as he and Winter flew into Oxford: "As we started circling coming into the airport, I tapped Winter's shoulder and pointed down at the school. As far as you could see there were cars, there were buses coming in off the highways, traffic was backed up." More than 2,000 people filled the auditorium, packed the school cafeteria, and emptied out into the hallways.[30]

Over 9,000 people attended the forums in September and October. One legislator complained the forums had created "real, almost panic level hysteria. . . . It was a well-dressed, well-perfumed hysteria, but it was hysteria. . . . That hysteria translated itself into a lot of political pressure."[31]

"GO" OR "NO GO"

On the election day 1982 ballot was a constitutional amendment to create a new state board of education, replacing the secretary of state, attorney general, and superintendent of education with educators, parents, and business leaders. The amendment would also abolish the elected superintendent of education and require the new board to appoint someone with education credentials. Winter invited his staff over that night to watch the election returns. He had thought to himself that if the voters approved the amendment—signaling an interest in reforming the state's educational system—he would call a special session. While close, the amendment passed 219,973 to 203,005. The margin was sufficient to proceed.[32] Two weeks later, Winter made it official: the legislature would be required to attend a special session on December 6.[33]

The outcry was predictable. Legislators argued the issue should be considered in the regular session. Sonny Merideth, chairman of the House Ways and

Means Committee, specifically complained that more time was needed to consider such a comprehensive proposal. Prior to the session, Winter met with the two committee chairmen who would make or break the legislation—Merideth and Senator Ellis Bodron, a thirty-four-year veteran lawmaker from Vicksburg and chairman of the Senate Finance Committee. At this meeting, Winter made a concession that caught their attention. For the previous two years, Winter had focused his entire lobbying effort on raising the oil and gas severance tax to pay for the reforms. The legislative leadership refused to support an expensive new program without a specific funding source, and the oil and gas lobby had proved too formidable an opponent. Winter's concession: if they chose a revenue source other than oil and gas severance taxes, that would be okay with him.[34]

The next day, the legislative leadership met behind closed doors to discuss Winter's proposals. After the meeting, Dye and Newman spoke to the press. When asked if Merideth's proposal to adjourn early was discussed, Dye said: "To tell you the truth that was not discussed because we weren't thinking in those terms." Merideth then scheduled a meeting of his committee that weekend to begin work.[35] The *Clarion-Ledger*, however, expressed skepticism: "Through public forums, countless public statements, and now a special session on education, [Winter] has brought the problems of the state's public education system to the fore. But as he makes a last push to force the legislature to address those problems, it remains to be seen if the attention he has gained can be translated into actual support."[36]

Days before the special session convened, Winter wrote a letter to the more than 40,000 people who had signed up to help: "There are very few moments in the history of our state or in our lifetime when we can act to control our destiny and the destiny of our children. This is one of those moments."[37]

THE CHRISTMAS SPECIAL SESSION

Legislators began arriving at the state capitol on Monday morning, December 6, the first time legislators had used the building since it was closed for a comprehensive renovation in 1979. "It has become a tradition," the *Clarion-Ledger* wrote, "the governor issues a report calling for changes in the state's public school system, and the legislature ignores it. Every governor since Paul B. Johnson, Jr. has issued such a report, and every legislature since 1964 has refused to act."[38] Later that day, Senator Bodron told a reporter his committee would not consider any tax legislation during the special session.[39]

At 12:30 P.M., Winter was escorted to the rostrum in the magnificently restored House chamber to address a joint session of the legislature, where he joined Speaker Newman and Lieutenant Governor Dye. The three men shared much history. In the early 1930s, their fathers had served together in the legislature. Newman and Winter were House colleagues in the early 1950s. Dye had managed John Bell Williams's campaign for governor in 1967, defeating Winter in the runoff. Winter and Dye were from the same hometown. As teenagers, first Winter and then Dye had driven Jim Eastland around the state in his early Senate campaigns. These men had been called to political careers as early as they could remember. Now, as 1982 was coming to a close, these three men were at the peak of their careers—they were exactly where they wanted to be—and the question the special session would answer was this: how would they use their power?

Winter greeted both of them, turned to face a House chamber in which he had once served, and spoke of the occasion:

> The needs of education and the relationship of those needs to our future growth and progress cannot be put aside any longer. . . . Per capita income is tied directly, unequivocally, and irrefutably to education. Unless we take some very specific actions to improve our educational system, it will never be adequate to move our state out of last place in per capita income. It's time to act now. . . . I hope that we will seize the opportunity to do the most significant thing that you or I may have the privilege of doing.[40]

The next day, two things happened—one, fully expected, the other, totally unexpected. A Senate committee refused to approve kindergartens. That move was expected. From the other side of the capitol came the unexpected: Representatives Robert Clark and Sonny Merideth came to an agreement: whatever Clark's Education Committee approved, Merideth's Ways and Means Committee would fund.[41]

Merideth explained why it happened years later: "Yes, I was very much in favor of adjourning. I thought William had walked us into a box where we were going to have to take what he put out there because we were coming up on Christmas. . . . I thought we were going to produce a flawed product because we didn't have time. Well, the staff . . . worked overtime and compensated for that." Merideth remembered that he was "stomping to adjourn" and the Speaker told him, "Sonny, this House isn't going to adjourn," and Merideth thought to himself, "If we're not going to adjourn, we're going to have to do our business. . . . We'd better make the best we can, not just punt, but I'm talking about really get in the trenches and make some quality legislation . . . [because] when you get your ass whipped on adjourning and you're the chairman of the [funding] committee, you've got to wake up and roll."[42]

Momentum was waking up. And by Friday, Merideth was on a roll. Clark's committee had produced a comprehensive education reform bill, designated House Bill 4: public kindergartens, compulsory school attendance, and teacher pay raises. Merideth's committee provided the funding and sent the bill to the full House.[43]

The House convened at noon on Saturday. After a lengthy presentation of the bill, representatives began offering amendments—sixteen different amendments. Some improved the bill, and were adopted; others sought to weaken it, and were killed. Along the way, members began to complain that even if the House were to pass such a historic bill, the Senate would remove kindergartens, to which Representative Walman responded: "This body has never charted its course by what happened down the hall, and by God I hope it doesn't start now. I want, for one time, for the Senate to have kindergartens on the floor for a vote."[44]

As the afternoon turned into evening, people in the capitol began to sense that something special was happening. After eight hours of debate, Representative Clark made the motion to approve the bill. The Speaker called for the vote and ordered the clerk to open the voting machine. Beside each member's name on the huge electronic board at the front of the chamber is a green light for "yes" and a red one for "no," and on each member's desk is a small box with corresponding green and red buttons. The Mississippi Constitution requires a three-fifths vote to pass a tax increase, and while people on both sides of the issue were holding their breaths, green lights and red lights popped up on the board.

As he had done a thousand times before, the Speaker intoned, "Has everyone voted, has everyone voted, has everyone voted? Close the machine, Mr. Clerk." The machine tabulated the vote and flashed the results on a small screen in front of the Speaker. Newman's next words surprised even the staunchest backers of the bill: "By a vote of 80 yeas and 38 nays, the bill passes." The vote was overwhelming. A collective expression of relief, joy, shock, and exhaustion was let loose at one time. Representative Hainon Miller from

Greenville could hardly believe what had happened: "I've been waiting for this moment for 15 years."[45] A new day in education was on its way to the Senate. On Monday, Dye referred the bill to the Education Committee and to the committee charged with approving the revenue to fund the programs: Finance.[46]

By early Tuesday, the Senate Education Committee, chaired by Chickasaw County Senator Jack Gordon, had signed off on the bill in full and sent it to Finance. All eyes were on its chairman, Ellis Bodron. The Finance Committee debated the bill until late Tuesday evening, and unexpectedly adjourned without taking action.[47] The bill appeared to be in trouble. David Crews, Winter's press secretary, called Charles Overby that night and told him the grim news. It was late, and the next day's edition of the paper was already on its way to the printer. Overby stopped the presses and rewrote the headline for the morning paper.[48] Wednesday morning the *Clarion-Ledger* informed its readers: "Gov. William Winter's education reform package faces its toughest test yet in the Senate Finance Committee this morning. . . . After sailing along for almost two days, the bill was becalmed overnight in the Finance Committee."[49]

What David Crews, Charles Overby, and most others didn't know was that Dye had intervened. The night the bill passed the House, Dye called Bodron. "Ellis," he said, "what you do with your politics is fine, but in running your mouth, you've hurt my politics. Your politics is now my politics. I want to add some Senate things to the House bill." Bodron's response: "If I understand you correctly, we are not only going to call, we're going to raise." Dye: "That's correct. Now Ellis, I want a commitment out of you right now—that this bill is going to come out of Finance Committee and you'll support it. If you're not, this is going to be the first time the Education Committee has ever raised taxes in this state." Dye got his assurances.[50]

The next day, the Finance Committee stripped kindergartens from the bill by a vote of 11-9. Then one of the opponents made a motion to "table the bill." This was it. A vote to table was a vote to kill the bill. In committees, there are no roll call votes: it's done the old-fashioned way—members raise their hands, and the chairman counts. As chairman of the committee, Bodron asked for the members in support of the motion to raise their hands. He counted ten. He then asked the members who opposed the motion to raise their hands. He counted ten again. Bodron keep his commitment to Dye and voted "no." The bill remained alive. That didn't keep Bodron from making "impassioned speeches" against the press, the governor, kindergarten supporters, and teacher organizations. At one point, he criticized Winter's staff for "stirring up a tremendous amount of emotion," and then derogatorily referred to the young staffers as the "Boys of Spring." For David Crews, Bill Gartin, John Henegan, Ray Mabus, Dick Molpus, and Andy Mullins, Bodron's intended criticism became a badge of honor—to this day, Henegan displays on the wall of his law office a photograph of Winter's team bearing signatures of each of the key staffers over the caption, "The Boys of Spring." Bodron's committee finally approved the legislation and sent it to the full Senate. Victory. Kindergartens could be fought out on the floor.[51]

At 10:08 Thursday morning, Senator Gordon called up House Bill 4 for consideration and began explaining the bill. After lunch, Tupelo Senator Perrin Purvis offered the amendment to restore kindergartens. In the Senate, there is no electronic voting machine; a clerk calls aloud the name of each senator. With all fifty-two senators voting, Purvis's amendment needed twenty-seven votes to pass. Supporters and opponents had lobbied members all day, keeping their own counts; the vote appeared very close. When the roll call began on Purvis's amendment, everyone had their lists in hand, ready to compare their tallies with the actual vote. The gallery was packed, and one by one, the names were called, and one by one, the members shouted their votes. Months of hard work, thousands of hours on the road, and countless speeches were riding on this one vote. It was the symbol. At the end of the roll call, while everyone was waiting and watching, the clerk counted the vote, and handed it to Dye, who announced the result: "By a vote of 26 ayes and 25 nays, the amendment is adopted." Later that afternoon, Gordon moved adoption of the bill; by that time, the vote wasn't even close: 43-9. Senator Bill Minor of Holly Springs offered the best assessment of the procedural moves that had led to such an overwhelming final vote: "We're making some gut votes here today."[52]

For the next three days, a conference committee composed of Representatives Sonny Merideth, Robert Clark, and Mike Nipper and Senators Ellis Bodron, Jack Gordon, and John Fraiser worked to resolve the differences between the House and Senate versions of the bill. Conference committee meetings are closed to the public, so for the first time in the session, everyone stood around in the halls for hours on end, waiting. On Saturday, the mood was hopeful when Clark told a reporter: "The truth is I've never been in a conference committee in the 16 years I've been here where the mood is more relaxed than it is in there."[53] By the next day, however, the committee was deadlocked over when to start the kindergarten program and how to pay for the new programs.[54]

Then, late Sunday, the conferees finished their work and sent a completed bill to both houses. When the members got to their desks Monday morning, they found a conference report that mandated statewide kindergartens, created a new reading aide program by placing teaching assistants in the first three grades of elementary schools, enacted a compulsory attendance law, provided teacher pay raises, created the initial accreditation system for public schools, established powers and responsibilities of the new board of education, created a training program for school administrators, and paid for it all with more than $110 million in increased sales and income taxes. Would momentum continue to power a bill that represented a complete victory for Winter? Robert Clark once observed: "When I began to weigh the value and benefits of the Education Reform Act against a sales tax increase, I realized the people I was trying to protect, the poor people of the state, were going to be helped more by a tax increase than anybody else because they're the ones that needed [education reform] the most."[55] The House voted first, approving it 96-25; about an hour later, the Senate passed the bill 37-13. Years later, when asked about the bill's passage, Merideth said, "The thing had kind of had a life of its own, and all you can do is teach it to walk and talk, you couldn't kill it."[56] Jack Gordon agreed: "You could have repealed the Ten Commandments in that bill and I think it still would have passed."[57]

Four days before Christmas, a relieved and jubilant William Winter signed the bill. He walked down the hall of the capitol, first to the Senate, and then to House, to thank them: "At no other time in the history of Mississippi . . . has a Legislature come into a special session in a two-week period of time [and] enacted so sweeping a series of measures as has this Legislature."[58] In 1954, while a young member of the House of Representatives, William Winter had watched while the legislature and then the voters had passed a constitutional amendment authorizing the legislature to abolish public schools. Now, some twenty-eight years later, he had mobilized the citizenry and motivated the legislature to adopt a landmark education bill. The role of the legislature likewise was forever changed. The editorial writer for the *Clarion-Ledger*, David Hardin, explained the new power of accountability inherent in single-member districts: "The Legislature was often publicly viewed as a faceless, anonymous entity which made it difficult to get any leverage against or arouse any meaningful opposition. We wanted to give the Mississippi Legislature a face."[59]

It was left to Winter to offer the most candid assessment:

> As I have found in my own political career, there seems to be an element of timing. I think it was just that we were fortuitous enough to be able to have all the forces coming together at the right time, having built up almost by accident. There was certainly no overall master strategy developed from the beginning behind it all, but over the course of almost three years of having this emphasis on improved education building to a kind of crescendo that the legislature responded to. . . . You set a goal without having a clear map. It's a matter of persistence as much as anything else, just plain old persistence and using the lessons learned in earlier unsuccessful efforts.[60]

THE AFTERMATH

There were, of course, many factors associated with the passage of the 1982 Education Reform Act. Buddie Newman was responsible for three of the most important.

First, Newman's appointment of a supporter of education reform to chair the House Education Committee made the entire successful course of the legislation possible. In 1977, Robert Clark was vice chairman of the committee when the chairman, George Rogers, resigned his House seat to take a job with the Carter administration. Clark, if appointed, would become the first black committee chairman in the twentieth century. Would Buddie Newman, protégé of Walter Sillers, Ross Barnett's floor leader, appoint a black man to such a high profile position? Three years earlier, Newman was campaigning to become Speaker Pro Tempore, and his supporters were rallying support by getting members to sign a petition. Newman remembered: "I will never forget that the man who made it a majority on those petitions was Robert Clark. I was in the Ways and Means Committee when that happened, and they called me in the next room, and Sonny Merideth handed me the pen that Robert used to sign that petition."[61]

Second, the bill that Newman gaveled to death in February 1982 was a simple piece of legislation that merely authorized local school districts to operate kindergartens. It contained no mandate and no funding, no compulsory school attendance, no reading aides, no teacher pay raise, and no accountability provisions. Newman's role in single-handedly killing that legislation led to the rise of public sentiment and the passage of a much more comprehensive set of reforms.

Third, after the close of the 1982 regular session, Newman had appointed a special House committee to draft comprehensive education legislation. Almost all of the former House members we interviewed for this book gave much credit to the work of that committee in helping to focus on the need for education reform in the state.

Brad Dye and Buddie Newman were leaving a meeting with Winter at the Governor's Mansion one day when Newman turned to Dye and said, "This is the last time I'm going to do what I know I ought not do 'cause William Winter wants me to do it." Dye turned to his friend Newman and said, "Buddie, you realize this is the ninth time you have told me that."[62]

Almost three years earlier, William Winter had ended his inaugural address by quoting from a man he admired greatly, former Governor Martin S. Conner: "And if in this hour we shall set the public welfare as the only goal of our ambition, if we shall make it the supreme object of our effort, and dedicate to its achievement the best endowment of our lives, we need not fear for the results of our labors, nor for the future of the state."[63] That standard had been satisfied by the 1982 special session of the Mississippi legislature.

THE CAMPAIGN FOR THE SENATE

In 1982, U.S. Senator John C. Stennis was up for reelection. Though many would argue with the characterization, Stennis had regardless become one of the few Mississippi politicians accorded the status of "statesman" by state and national media. First elected in 1947 to fill the vacant seat created by the death of Theodore Bilbo, Stennis had never faced a competitive opponent in his five succeeding reelection campaigns. Haley Barbour decided that run of good luck should end. Barbour was thirty-four years old when he announced; Stennis would turn eighty-one during the course of the campaign. That contrast led to Barbour's campaign slogan: "A Senator for the 80s." Typical of Barbour's comments were: "Senator Stennis has put it as well and as succinctly as anybody could. The question of age is something for the people to decide," and "People are concerned about leadership for the future and want to make sure our state has effective, positive representation in the Senate for the next six years."[64]

One of the two noteworthy events of the campaign centered on the same issue that defined the 1981 congressional campaign between Wayne Dowdy and Liles Williams—reauthorization of the Voting Rights Act. By June, the legislation to retain the law was ready for a final congressional vote; Stennis had to make a decision. Would he change years of opposition to civil rights as well as votes he had cast against the law in 1965, 1970, and 1975? On May 25, he told reporters he would back the extension, saying, "We don't need to go back to the old days about voting."[65] Barbour, however, was "not going to forfeit the black vote to Stennis," arguing "I have confidence in the black voters of Mississippi. . . . They can see the record for the last 35 years the same as I can. They know that Stennis may have voted for the Voting Rights Act [this year], but they know how he voted in 1965, 1970 and 1975."[66]

The other event worthy of note was a replay of the 1972 decision by Richard Nixon to help Jim Eastland. On June 24, Barbour was in Washington and told a reporter after leaving the White House that "the support I am getting from the White House is full and total."[67] Three months later, the *Clarion-Ledger* disclosed that Stennis had met with Reagan and had secured his commitment to stay out of Mississippi during the campaign.[68] Lanny Griffith, Barbour's campaign manager, remembers the impact of Reagan's decision: "The wheels came apart when Stennis went to the president . . . and when the president agreed . . . it was pretty much what ended [the campaign]. . . . We had a lot of momentum, it was going good, the polling was looking good, we raised a lot of money, responses good, but man, it just came undone. I'll never forget the day."[69]

The one episode of that campaign that is still talked about today happened at the Neshoba County Fair. Stennis was scheduled to speak Thursday at the fair, and early that morning Barbour supporters decorated the grounds with signs congratulating Stennis on his eighty-first birthday, and Barbour volunteers then tried to present Stennis "with a birthday cake that looked like a raging forest fire—their paid cameras rolling without pause."[70]

The award for the cleverest line in the campaign went to Stennis when he turned the age issue on its head. Stennis told audiences that being a United States senator was "not a boy's job," and he asked rhetorically, "Should Mississippi send a boy to Washington to do a man's job?"[71] In the end, the campaign dynamics never changed from an initial survey that Stennis's pollster, Peter Hart, had presented to him early in 1982. After examining the poll results, Hart told

Stennis one day that he had "good news" and "bad news". The "bad news"—voters in Mississippi thought Stennis was too old for the job. The "good news"—they preferred him over any other candidate in the race.[72] Stennis won with 64 percent of the vote, carrying all but two counties.[73] Stennis told supporters on election night: "It's a long way from the south port of Jackson County to the northern tip of Alcorn County, back and forth, back and forth, but I made it on one aspirin tablet."[74]

It was in 1972 that Republican candidates in Mississippi first sought to link their opponents with the national Democratic Party. They were successful that year in causing heartburn among Democratic candidates because George McGovern, the presidential nominee, had adopted a very liberal party platform. By 1978, the contrast was so sharp that Maurice Dantin specifically asked President Carter to stay away from Mississippi. The 1982 John Stennis campaign was the last time Republicans had to contend with a Democrat who could trace his heritage back to the time long before the national parties began to identify themselves so completely with the "conservative" label or the "liberal" label. John Stennis had too much history with Mississippi voters for Barbour to cast the election in terms of a national Democratic versus Republican contest. To try and associate Stennis with a liberal, out-of-touch national Democratic Party just didn't hold water with Mississippi voters.

Even though Barbour lost, his campaign accomplished a larger purpose: it gave Republican volunteers and campaign operatives additional valuable experience at running major campaigns, and it continued to build a farm club of committed activists throughout the state who learned "what to do" and "what not to do" the next time a Republican candidate ran.

The day after the election, Senator Thad Cochran nominated Haley Barbour's cousin and Yazoo City law partner, William Barbour Jr., to replace retiring federal judge Harold Cox. Several months later, when the Senate Judiciary Committee held a hearing to consider William Barbour Jr.'s confirmation, John Stennis testified on his behalf.[75]

By 1982, Newton County native Joe Blount was a Democratic member of the state legislature when he agreed to manage Stennis's reelection campaign. After Haley Barbour was elected governor, he named Blount chairman of the State Tax Commission, one of the most prestigious appointments available to a governor.[76] It turns out Barbour and Blount had been "good friends" since attending the University of Mississippi together.

POSTSCRIPT

In the spring of 1982, Mike Retzer resigned as chairman of the state GOP. Mentioned in passing by the reporter who wrote about Ebbie Spivey, a Canton school teacher, becoming the new chairman, was the election of Vicksburg businessman Kirk Fordice as party secretary.[77] Fordice's behind-the-scenes work on behalf of the party over the next nine years would form the basis for the shock he would deliver to the political establishment in 1991.

CHAPTER 9

THE ALLAIN/BRAMLETT CAMPAIGN AND WILLIAM WINTER'S LEGACY

1983

I mean if you sat down to write a TV "Ripley's: Believe It or Not," this is what you'd write. You know, and it was fiction. You sit down and write fiction and add all these elements in as bizarre things. It was a lot stranger than fiction.
—CHARLES OVERBY, *Jackson Clarion-Ledger* Editor[1]

On October 23, 1983, a truck carrying more than 10,000 pounds of explosives rammed into a building in Beirut, killing 241 U.S. servicemen who were sleeping inside. They were part of a contingent of American servicemen in Lebanon helping to preserve a truce in that country. Four days later, the United States invaded the Caribbean island nation of Grenada. President Reagan claimed the move was necessary to protect nearly 1,000 Americans who were threatened by a new radical government.[2] These two events served as bookends for the most notorious campaign press conference ever held in Mississippi.

THE 1983 CAMPAIGN FOR GOVERNOR

By 1983, Republicans in Mississippi had elected a U.S. senator, won congressional races with four different candidates, and carried the state for three Republican presidential nominees. White Mississippi voters were becoming accustomed to supporting the GOP ticket in federal campaigns. State elections were a different story. Republicans knew they had to install someone in the Governor's Mansion, and they had to win a significant share of the seats in the legislature, if they were to have any hope of influencing public policy and building a long-term party structure. In running a candidate for governor, the Republicans had a problem. To use a baseball analogy, they had a weak bench. Only four men had waged competitive state campaigns as Republicans: Rubel Phillips, Gil Carmichael, Charles Pickering, and Leon Bramlett. Phillips, Carmichael, and Pickering had each been defeated twice. That left Leon Bramlett, the candidate of the conservatives in 1979 for governor. Reluctantly, once again, Bramlett agreed to run.[3]

While the lieutenant governor, attorney general, secretary of state, state treasurer, and state auditor each performs substantive duties, for a political party, these "down-ballot" offices also constitute the "bench." The positions provide their officeholders with a statewide platform to generate name identification, and they give candidates experience in running a statewide campaign.

In 1979, the Republicans had attacked Bill Allain in the final week of the campaign for attorney general, creating an opportunity for him to overtake his GOP opponent. In the intervening three years, Allain had become as well known as the governor, leading well-publicized fights against public utility companies for their excessive rate hikes, against legislators for violating provisions of the state constitution, and against local officials who ignored the state's open meetings law, a profile that allowed him to win the Democratic primary for governor against two well-funded candidates.

THE INVESTIGATION OF ALLAIN

Billy Mounger was walking through his office building in downtown Jackson one day soon after the primary elections when he ran into his good friend and fellow businessman Neal Clement, who asked him if he had heard the rumors about Allain. Mounger confirmed that he had. Clement's response: "Billy, golly, we're hearing so much, that guy sounds so bad that we ought to find out what the story is."[4] Mounger and Clement could barely believe the rumors: it was claimed that Allain regularly had sexual relations with black male transvestite prostitutes. Over lunch with their mutual friend Victor Smith, the three decided to investigate the validity of the rumors, basing their actions on the belief that "this stuff is really bad that we are hearing, and if it's as bad as they say, he shouldn't be governor, either Democrat or Republican, and somebody needs to do something about it. Well you know how these things work, we all looked at each other and said, well, that somebody is us."[5]

After obtaining a copy of Allain's divorce decree—Allain was married in 1964 and divorced six years later—the trio had it reviewed by a lawyer who reported: "You know what, I thought you guys were crazy, but when I read this divorce proceeding, I can't read anything into it other than she is accusing him of being essentially homosexual because in there was one phrase that said 'he would absent himself at night over long periods of time and failed to perform his husbandly duties.'"

They enlisted Bill Spell, a local attorney whom Mounger knew from Spell's tenure with the Mid Continent Oil and Gas Association, to coordinate the continuing investigation. Spell in turn retained the Pendleton Detective Agency on September 27, 1983, to do much of the legwork.[6] At the same time Spell was hiring Pendleton detectives, Bramlett was in the middle of reorganizing his campaign, having just fired many of his professional staff members and consultants. In the end, he and his campaign would become bystanders during the last two weeks of the campaign.[7]

A week or so later, at midnight, detective Robert Pendleton found himself walking into a house on Bratton Street, in an African American neighborhood not far from downtown Jackson. Pendleton remembers what happened next: We "knocked on the door. The door opened. There were no lights on inside.... So we couldn't see who was inside." The door closed, lights were turned on, and present before them were several black male prostitutes in drag. They began to tell Pendleton about Allain picking up transvestites. Pendleton soon arranged for several of the prostitutes who had been with Allain to take lie detector tests and to give sworn statements. Spell, in the meantime, had interviewed repair technicians at Allain's apartment building who claimed to have found homosexual pornographic materials in Allain's apartment while on an unannounced service call. Finally, Spell interviewed a Jackson police officer who told him about Allain "cruising" the area where black transvestite prostitutes solicited business.[8] Spell found three transvestites who signed sworn statements of having sex with Allain: David Holliday, Grady Arrington ("Nicole Toy"), and Donald Johnson ("Donna"); had them take lie detector tests; and then sequestered them in motel rooms in Mississippi and Louisiana during the course of the investigation.[9]

The Bramlett campaign, unaware of the Spell investigation, on its own began to raise the issue of Allain's divorce. In one speech, Bramlett's wife stated, "I'm running for first lady and I'm unopposed." The Allain campaign called the move "desperation."[10] Within a few weeks of being on the job, Pendleton and Spell had convinced Mounger that "this thing is just getting worse and worse."[11] It was time to try and get the press involved. On Friday, October 14, Spell gave the information to Charles Overby, editor of the *Clarion-Ledger*, whom Spell had known when they had both worked for Senator John Stennis. Three days later, Overby informed Spell he would not break the story, though he did assign two reporters to investigate the allegations.[12]

By this time, the word was out. *Clarion-Ledger* reporters started asking questions. Crymes Pittman, a Jackson lawyer who eventually represented Allain during the course of the investigation, was given information about the depositions by a friend who had access to them. Pittman forwarded them to the Allain campaign, and in the meantime, Mounger, Smith, and Spell began to inform Bramlett supporters of their findings.[13] On October 15, Allain released a poll that showed him 20 percentage points ahead, a spread that most people believed accurately reflected the state of the campaigns.[14]

Two meetings then took place that determined the outcome of the election. The first was with Leon Bramlett. Driving into Jackson from a campaign swing through Vicksburg, it was close to midnight when Bramlett and members of his staff met with Spell, Pendleton, Mounger, Smith, and Clement. Spell's group pushed for Bramlett to embrace the findings and go after Allain. Bramlett refused. They persisted. Bramlett was adamant. According to Mounger, "it got him, he was a good Christian, and he thought it was so gross . . . so gross that it just wasn't believable, and that was the problem."[15] Without the Bramlett campaign's endorsement of the allegations, Mounger, Smith, and Spell were left without an official entry into the campaign.

The second meeting was with Governor Winter. Mounger and his allies first met with David New, a Natchez oilman and Allain supporter. Mounger had known New for years and decided to give him the whole story so he could "bail out" of Allain's campaign.[16] New left his meeting with Mounger and went immediately to find Steve Patterson and other Allain supporters. While the reaction was "to hell with them, let 'em go," Patterson decided they needed to inform Winter of the allegations. They walked over to the Governor's Mansion to brief an astonished Winter. Joe Zucarro, an Allain supporter in Natchez, called that meeting "a turning point." Winter didn't believe the men would go through with publicizing the allegations, but if they did, the Democrats would rally behind Allain and "beat the hell out of them."[17] There would be no abandoning Allain if the attacks came, and come they would. Patterson called it "the high water mark of the Democratic Party in my lifetime."[18]

Mounger, Smith, and Clement met the next morning facing the fundamental question: Do we proceed or let it die? Mounger remembered the group thinking, "We've come this far, we're absolutely convinced and know the story is true, if we stop now, are we not doing everybody else a disservice? We're sitting on something that's horrible, and if we don't do something, we're guilty."[19]

THE PRESS CONFERENCE

Curtis Wilkie, a reporter for the *Boston Globe*, happened to be in Jackson on Tuesday, October 25, and wrote later that "in twenty years in journalism, I had never seen anything quite like it."[20] At 3:15 that afternoon, exactly two weeks before the general election, Bill Spell held a press conference and announced that "an investigation has developed clear and convincing evidence that establishes beyond a reasonable doubt that Attorney General Bill Allain, over a period of years, frequently has engaged in homosexual acts with male prostitutes." Even more shocking was Spell's disclosure that the male prostitutes were black transvestites. Spell disclosed Mounger, Clement, and Smith as the backers and Pendleton Detectives as the investigators. After revealing the black transvestites were receiving compensation for "lost wages" because he had them sequestered in out-of-state motels, Spell told how they had passed lie detector tests.[21]

During the course of the hour-and-a-half news conference, Norma Fields, a reporter with the Tupelo newspaper, had this exchange with Spell:

> *Fields: Are you attempting to ruin the man? Are you trying to defeat him? Are you trying to get him to withdraw? What are you doing?*
> *Spell: We simply seek the truth, which I thought was a common objective that we had with the media.*
> *Fields: Well, that's what I'm seeking from you.*
> *Spell: Believe me, what I've told you is the truth.*[22]

THE FALLOUT

Allain was at the Bank of Faulkner when Patterson caught up with him Tuesday afternoon. They had known the attack was coming; now it was for real. While he decided to go forward with a previously scheduled rally in New Albany that night, Allain told Patterson to call the other statewide Democratic candidates, some of whom were scheduled to attend the rally with Allain, and tell them about the allegations. "There's no reason for this to overflow and do damage to the rest of the ticket," Patterson remembers Allain telling him what to say, "I will understand if any other candidate has reservations about attending." Patterson called them all. Only one candidate expressed concern: Ed Pittman, the nominee for attorney general.[23]

Allain returned to Jackson that night to a meeting that would determine the campaign's course for the next two weeks. Dick Morris was Allain's pollster, and Bob Goodman was producing the television commercials. Together with Allain and his staff, they made use of a technique that has become known as the "counterpunch"—wait for your opposition to attack and then respond. In the collective mind of the voters, the opponent develops the reputation for engaging in a negative campaign, while even though fighting back, the responding candidate is perceived as simply defending himself or herself.[24]

The next day, in the wake of front-page news stories all over the state, Goodman filmed two new commercials: one featuring Allain's former wife, offering support to Allain. Another one showed a poster of Allain with an old farmer throwing a clump of mud at the poster. Allain's campaign announced that Pittman was making plans to file a defamation lawsuit. Danny Cupit, chairman of the Democratic Party, led the charge against Spell, telling one television reporter that while he realized attorneys could not solicit business, he wanted the opportunity to sue "because I'd like to collect substantial money and damages from Billy Mounger and his crowd." Finally, and just as important, Allain went on with his campaign.[25]

By this time, the Spell group was on the defensive. In today's campaign world, attacks on candidates by independent groups unrelated to any campaign are commonplace. In 1983, the practice was unheard of. Television and radio stations, as well as newspapers, were not accustomed to commercials unconnected to a candidate's campaign. Consequently, when the Spell group sought to buy advertisements to present its side of the investigation, almost all the state's television and radio stations and newspapers turned down the request.[26] As a result, Spell had no way to rebut the countercharges made by

Allain. With a monopoly on advertising, Allain controlled the dialogue. Years later, Mounger remembered the outcome:

> We were running daily polling [before the press conference], and to tell the truth Bramlett was just doing lousy, he was getting 29 percent or something and Allain was getting like, uh, high 50s or 60s or something. . . . So when this thing kicked up, Allain came all the way down from and Bramlett went up to about, they were right at even, about 36, 37 themselves. But when nothing could come forward to enhance the story, he was able to come in uncontested.[27]

Spell had to try something else: he demanded that Allain take a lie detector test. After Allain said he would take the test, Spell stipulated that an impartial person conduct the test. Allain said his campaign would make the arrangements. Spell declared that was unacceptable, but Allain ignored him. With no paid advertising available to him, Spell was left hanging. Then, on Thursday, Allain held a press conference to denounce the allegations. He described the criminal backgrounds of the prostitutes and complained they were bribed to lie about him. He labeled the transvestites as so insane that "even though they're men, they think they're women."[28]

Confronted with a solid Democratic Party behind Allain and no reliable method to inform the voters about the allegations, Spell's group was losing momentum. They had no alternative but to hold another press conference and embark on a series of meetings throughout the state. At the press conference, Spell released statements from three Jackson police officers who claimed to have seen Allain cruising in the area of Jackson known for prostitutes. Two of the sworn affidavits indicated they had witnessed Allain talking with prostitutes.[29]

While the statements were reported the next day, they got lost in other news. Feeling left out and ignored, the Bramlett campaign made its own startling announcement: if Allain could pass three independent lie detector tests, Bramlett would withdraw from the governor's race. That same day, an independent group of businessmen called on both Allain and Spell to submit to lie detector tests.[30]

Unbeknownst to the Spell group or the Bramlett campaign, Allain was in New Orleans that day submitting to a lie detector test administered by John Phillips, the chairman of the Louisiana Polygraph Association.[31] Thursday and Friday the Allain campaign shut down the Spell initiative and put an end to the Bramlett campaign. On Thursday, Allain and his attorney, Crymes Pittman, held a news conference to make two disclosures: Allain passed a lie detector test, and the parents of one of the prostitutes released affidavits describing their son as a thief, habitual liar, and drug addict, and totally unstable. While both Spell and the Bramlett campaign complained about the nature of Allain's polygraph, the test was enough to resolve doubts in the minds of most voters.[32]

On Friday afternoon, the Allain campaign held another news conference in which the former New Orleans police chief who had arranged Allain's test explained the procedure and testified to Allain's truthfulness. Patterson explained the strategy behind the back-to-back press conferences: "Let's do this in stages, and that builds credibility. Let's give the results, then let's put the expert on to prove the results. In other words, let's make our opening statement and then let's put our expert witness on."[33] That Friday evening, more than 300 Democrats attended a rally in support of Allain, with Kentucky Governor John Brown as the keynote speaker. Cupit welcomed Brown to the "mud and dirt capital of the world."[34]

ELECTION DAY

By the time voters went to the polls, the election had nothing to do with issues or party affiliations. The choice for the voters was summed by a *Memphis Commercial Appeal* editorial: "Instead of being asked to choose a governor on the basis of the issues, Mississippi voters are being asked to choose on the basis of which candidate is telling the truth about a scandalous charge that in all likelihood will never be resolved to anyone's satisfaction. That's the nature of dirty politics. It raises unanswerable questions at the expense of important issues."[35]

For many voters it came down to one question: Are the accusations credible? For others, it represented a chance to vote against negative campaigns. For the last two weeks of the campaign, Bramlett became almost a spectator. Even the Allain campaign paid little attention to him.[36] Mounger agreed: "It really got beyond Leon Bramlett."[37]

On election day, Allain won with 55 percent of the vote, carrying all but eight counties. What few remember is that more people voted in 1983 than in the 1979 gubernatorial campaign, and Bramlett received more votes than

Gil Carmichael received against William Winter four years previously. It was not the nature of the allegations that won the election for Allain; it was how the Allain campaign responded, it was how the Democratic Party leadership responded, and it was the inability of the Spell group to participate in the dialogue through paid advertising.

The 1983 campaign also had nothing to do with Democrats versus Republicans; that fight likewise got lost in the mud. The political party realignment that was in progress in Mississippi was given a holiday by this surreal episode in political campaigning.

THE AFTERMATH

Toward the end of 1983, Pittman secured the retractions of the three male prostitutes, who claimed they had been bribed to lie about Allain. These revelations were made public by the *Clarion-Ledger* on January 15, 1984, five days after Allain's inauguration. Pittman told the paper he considered the matter closed, and the campaign had made the decision not to file a lawsuit. Later that day, Spell held a press conference to deny the accusations that anyone had been bribed and revealed that he had testimony of more gay men who claimed to have had sex with Allain as well as statements from more Jackson police officers. To this day, Spell maintains Allain chose not to file a lawsuit because it would have given Spell's attorneys the right to obtain whatever documents and other discovery they needed to defend their case.[38]

On April 12, 1984, the ABC News show *20/20* made another appearance in Mississippi, in the form of Geraldo Rivera reporting on the 1983 campaign scandal. Rivera's take on the Spell disclosures can be summed up by the title of the program: "Anatomy of a Smear Campaign: Low Down and Dirty." Rivera portrayed Allain as a victim of the "dirtiest campaign in the history of Mississippi," while Spell described the segment as "a double-bladed axe job" on his group's investigation.[39]

CLOSING THE CHAPTER

In an interview years after the campaign, Danny Cupit summed up the position of the Democrats: "I think he suffered more than any human being has had to suffer in my lifetime simply to run for political office. And I wish there was something somebody could to do erase that because . . . it will go with him to his grave."[40]

To this day, Mounger and Spell are unrepentant. They believe Allain was guilty and that they had an obligation to present the facts. When asked in an interview for this book if their campaign proved futile because Allain won so handily, Mounger said, "It made a good governor out of Allain because he stayed in the Governor's Mansion and didn't do anything and didn't cause any problems."[41]

The day after the 1983 election, the *Clarksdale Press Register*, Bramlett's hometown newspaper, complained bitterly about Allain's victory: "He will be completely beholden to the Democratic party hacks who stood by him, to the black electorate who endorsed him solidly and worst of all to the self-seeking power brokers of the Mississippi legislature."[42] Within four months of taking office, Allain would show that editorial writer just how wrong he was.

WILLIAM WINTER'S LEGACY

While there is no doubt that some politicians have sought political power just to wield it, for most men and women who campaign for public office, power is a means to an end. How a person uses the power inherent in public office to accomplish change is surely a measure of that official's effectiveness. The ultimate test of effectiveness, however, cannot be measured until a politician leaves office. Is he or she succeeded by someone who will continue and build upon important public policy successes? Are capable people inspired to seek public office to effect similar changes in public policy? For those involved in the campaign of 1983, it is widely recognized that, as governor, Winter played a key role in holding the party together so that a Democrat could succeed him. Winter's legacy, however, was more far reaching.

In 1982, William Winter had harnessed the power of the governor's office in new ways to effect long-lasting changes in Mississippi's educational policy. But filling the down-ballot offices with like-minded candidates in subsequent elections is a part of Winter's legacy that is unmatched by any other governor. Five people who worked on William Winter's staff were later elected to state-wide office: Ray Mabus was elected state auditor in 1983 and governor in 1987; Dick Molpus was elected secretary of state in 1983 and reelected in 1987 and

1991; Bill Cole was elected state treasurer in 1983; Marshall Bennett was elected state treasurer in 1987 and reelected in 1991, 1995, and 1999; and Steve Patterson was elected state auditor in 1991 and reelected in 1995. Patterson also served as chairman of the Democratic Party from 1984 to 1987. Winter's direct influence on state policy and politics continued for another ten years after he left office; his indirect influence has yet to be fully measured.

William Winter's education reform initiative focused the public's attention on the legislature, and the legislature's reaction and Winter's persistence provoked a number of candidates to enter the 1983 legislative elections. Ellis Bodron, the chairman of the Senate Finance Committee and the most public opponent of education reform, was defeated. Other longtime incumbents who didn't survive the 1983 elections were Stone Barefield of Hattiesburg, Son Rhodes of Pascagoula, Kenneth Williams of Clarksdale, Bob Ferguson and Jim Neal of Jackson, and Algie Davis and Tommy Horne of Meridian. It was also in 1983 that a little-known lawyer in DeSoto County, inspired by the events surrounding the passage of the education reform legislation and embarrassed by the portrayal of the state by the national media, qualified to oppose the incumbent representative.[43] When the election was over, John Grisham was a new member of the Mississippi legislature.

POSTSCRIPT

William Alexander Percy once described Theodore Bilbo as "a pert little monster, glib and shameless, with that sort of cunning common to criminals that passes for intelligence. The people loved him."[44] First elected to the state Senate in 1908, Bilbo was chosen governor twice and U.S. senator three times. His 1985 biographer, Chester M. Morgan, said of Bilbo, "It is ironic that one whose [early] career had for so long been remarkably devoid of racist rhetoric should be remembered as the nation's vilest purveyor of white-supremacy twaddle. But the reputation is justified. From about 1942 until his death in 1947, Bilbo waged a relentless and often vicious battle against the incipient crusade for black equality in America. . . . His infamy as the 'archangel of white supremacy' was richly deserved."[45]

For more than twenty-six years, a statue of Theodore Bilbo had resided in the center of the first-floor rotunda of the state capitol. The Bilbo statue once provoked Holmes County Representative Robert Clark, the first African American elected to the legislature in the twentieth century, to recall his trip to the state capitol in 1968, soon after his election.

> *When I was first elected and came in, they told me to come in the south entrance. I don't know who told me to come in the south entrance, but somebody told me. Why they told me that was because Senator Bilbo's statue faces the south, and they said that Jim Eastland had told them to have me come in that way, that Bilbo was going to stop me. And after he didn't stop me, I understand Jim Eastland got on the phone and called Bilbo and asked him why he didn't stop me and what was all this about. Bilbo told Jim, said "Jim, when I [died and] left Mississippi I left it in your hands, best hands I thought I could find. I'm surprised that you're letting that nigger come in there." And Jim Eastland told Bilbo, said, "Well, Bilbo when you left here we didn't have all these damn civil rights laws and long hairs and everything. We got them here now and there isn't a damn thing I can do about it." And Bilbo said, "Yeah, Jim we got some damn nigger firemen down here, and there isn't anything I can do about it either."[46]*

As governor, William Winter made plans to quietly move the statue during the massive renovation of the building that began in early 1979 and ended days before the Christmas 1982 special legislative session. Bilbo wouldn't hear of it.[47] Even though Winter had made plans for the statue to be placed in a separate room away from the public area once the capitol was reopened, as he was making one last walk through the renovated building before its official opening, he discovered the Bilbo statue was right where it had always been. Winter couldn't believe it. The statue now had to be moved at the last minute, turning what Winter had hoped would be a quiet change into newspaper headlines and a very public story that lasted several days.[48] Relocating Bilbo's statue was just one more way William Winter changed the public face of Mississippi.

THE EROSION OF LEGISLATIVE POWER

1984

As attorney general, you get up in the morning and you drink coffee and have breakfast and you go and get your staff together and you say, "Who we going to give hell to today?" As governor, you get up and do the same thing but you say, "Who's giving us hell today?"

—BILL ALLAIN, Former Attorney General and Governor[1]

O n the same day in November 1982 that Governor William Winter announced the special session on education, a trial was concluding in a Hinds County courtroom. These two events would come to share equal billing for breaking the lock on power enjoyed for so long by the Mississippi legislature.

ALLAIN VERSUS THE LEGISLATURE

The U.S. Constitution established three separate branches of government—the executive, legislative, and judicial—in part to combat the abuse of power that flows from the accumulation of power. Governmental power was curtailed by spreading it among three distinct branches and by authorizing each branch to act as a "check" on the actions of the others. Mississippi has similar "separation of powers" provisions in Article 1 of its state constitution:

Section 1. The powers of the government of the state of Mississippi shall be divided into three distinct departments . . . legislative . . . judicial . . . and executive.

Section 2. No person or collection of persons, being one or belonging to one of these departments, shall exercise any power properly belonging to either of the others.

Over the years, though, enforcement of these provisions had fallen victim to the attitude reflected in the story told about a young Mississippi legislator, newly elected, who notices a piece of legislation that apparently violates the state constitution. He dutifully approaches the Speaker, bringing the matter to his attention. As the story goes, the Speaker puts his arm around his youthful colleague and says, "Now son, around here, we try and get as close to the constitution as we can."

By the early 1980s, legislators were not even close to the requirements of Article 1—thirty-six legislators served on boards that directly governed nine state agencies.[2] These thirty-six men, serving as legislators, passed laws that created these agencies and the appropriation bills that funded these agencies. Then, serving as board members, they participated in the implementation and administration of the programs of the agencies. But the legislative influence in the executive branch was far more pervasive because of the particular agencies involved.

While the opening sentence of Article 5 of the Mississippi Constitution declares that "the chief executive power of this state shall be vested in a Governor," executive branch agency heads had little allegiance to the governor before 1984. Their budget requests were submitted to the Commission on Budget and Accounting. Decisions related to the hiring of employees had to be approved by the State Personnel Board. Acquisitions of computer or telecommunications equipment had to be cleared by the Central Data Processing Authority; all other major procurements had to gain the consent of the Commission on Budget and Accounting. The Capitol Commission determined where an agency's office was to be located. All of these executive branch oversight agencies were governed by boards dominated by legislators. Consequently, the incentive to respond to the legislature rather than the governor was overwhelming for most agency heads. Other specific executive branch agencies, such as those with responsibilities for economic development, corrections, Medicaid, and retirement, were all governed by boards with legislative members.

Consider the Personnel Board system. Agency directors in Mississippi have limited authority over the organization of their staff, whom to hire for most positions and the titles to give to those positions, what to pay employees, and when to give salary raises. All of these decisions require approval of the

Personnel Board. Prior to 1984, the board was composed of four legislators and four laypersons appointed by the governor. Because of their inherent authority, legislators enjoyed a significant voice on the board and thus a significant voice in critical personnel decisions. When he was secretary of state, Ed Pittman testified about one of the many ways legislators endeared themselves to executive branch officials: John Waldrop, a member of the board and also a state senator, suggested to Pittman that he bring any personnel requests to him first to "smooth the way."[3]

About two years into his term as attorney general, Bill Allain decided it was time to give the legislature "some hell." In December 1981, Allain notified the thirty-six legislators serving on executive branch boards that they were in violation of the constitution.[4] After the legislature failed to address Allain's concerns during the 1982 session, the attorney general announced he would initiate legal action to remove the legislators.[5] When some last-minute negotiations with legislators collapsed on April 6, Allain made plans to resolve the matter in the courts.[6] The next day, in a move that caught many by surprise, the legislators sued Allain directly, asking a Hinds County judge to "rule that Allain was wrong when he asked the legislators to remove themselves from boards and commissions." Hours later, Allain walked over to the courthouse and filed his own lawsuit.[7]

What may have been a surprise to some was actually part of Allain's legal strategy. Allain was worried that in bringing suit against thirty-six individual legislators in Hinds County, the seat of state government, a judge could force Allain to litigate the dispute in the individual hometowns of each of the legislators, a legal nightmare: thirty-six separate trials and thirty-six separate judges instead of one trial and one judge. So, Allain paid a visit to his old friend Ed Brunini, the Jackson attorney representing the legislators, and made his pitch: "Mr. Ed, this is what I think we ought to do. I think it will be good if y'all bring suit right here in Hinds County and put it all here. And I'll let you file first, make you look good to the public, like y'all want this resolved. I'll give you a copy of my complaint. Then I'll file the next day."[8] The tactic worked. When the legislators brought their lawsuit in Hinds County, Allain's worries were over.

For three days in November 1982, Hinds County Judge Charles Barber heard testimony from both sides. He heard Brunini declare, "There is no such thing as the schoolboy notion of a complete separation of powers" among the executive, legislative, and judicial branches. "Each case has to be looked at in its own situation." Allain responded: "They're not even denying that these are executive boards. They just keep talking about this blending, this melding of responsibilities. Their idea of cooperation is that there should be a member of the legislature sitting right up there with you [pointing to the judge]. . . . When do you start this blending. . . . Where are you going to stop?"[9] Three months later, Judge Barber not only declared the practice an unconstitutional violation of separation of powers, he invoked a provision stipulating that a legislator who assumed a position in another branch automatically vacated his or her position in the legislature. Under Judge Barber's order, at the end of the year, the thirty-six legislators would lose their privilege to serve.

The legislators quite naturally appealed the verdict to the state supreme court, though they were unprepared for the high court's decision. On November 28, 1983, a few weeks after Attorney General Bill Allain had been elected governor, all nine justices joined in a unanimous opinion, upholding the decision of the lower court. Chief Justice Neville Patterson raised the critical question in the opening paragraphs of his opinion: "In broad terms the issue presented is whether Article 1. . . should be interpreted faithfully to accord with its language or whether it should be interpreted loosely so that efficiency in government through permissive overlapping of departmental functions becomes paramount to the written word."[10] Nearly 200 years after the framers of the U.S. Constitution resolved they were willing to sacrifice efficiency to prevent an accumulation of power, and almost 100 years after the authors of the Mississippi Constitution came to same conclusion, the state supreme court declared in clear and unyielding language: "If the system be found efficient and nevertheless in violation of the constitution, our duty is clear." The court gave the legislature seven months to remove its members from the boards in the executive branch. "I don't think anybody knows just how far-reaching the effects [of this decision] are" was the apt reaction of one state senator.[11]

Rewriting so much of the state's statutory framework took nearly four months of the 1984 legislative session. At one point, tensions between Allain and the legislature caused one legislator to remark, "War is coming. It looks like everybody's going to the wall."[12] Finally, though, on May 8, the legislature approved a 350-page bill removing legislators from all executive branch boards, consolidating a number of agencies under the governor's office, and, in the process, completing the "most massive reorganization in the history of the state."[13] After approving the bill, thirty-five representatives signed a public statement that summed up the feelings of many of their colleagues: "We voted in favor of this bill because we feel that it is our duty to respond to the official dictate of the highest court of our state; however, we are of the firm conviction that this massive and forced change is not in the best interest of the state of Mississippi and its citizens."[14]

In the end, the legislature argued state government was delivering efficient government in Mississippi, so why disturb it? Or as the group of thirty-five representatives so cogently put it: "Believing in the old admonition that 'if it's not broke, don't fix it', we are reluctant to change the present system, which has performed well, to a new system with no record." And, of course, the system did work well, if you were a member of the legislature. Allain's position was simple: the practice violated the state constitution. In creating three branches of government, separating the power, and creating checks among the branches, the framers were not interested in creating a government that was efficient; they were interested in creating a government that did not abuse the power inherent in any form of government. The framers were not trying to make it easy for government to pass laws and regulate the activities of the people. They wanted to make it hard. Allain also realized that enforcing the constitution would naturally increase the power of the governor, at the expense of the legislature. He had long believed the balance of power had favored the legislature for too long; now he had the chance to level the playing field.[15]

On May 9, 1984, Governor Allain signed into law the bill that not only removed legislators from all executive branch boards but that also dramatically increased the power of the governor.[16] It had been almost two and half years since then Attorney General Allain first notified legislators of his intentions. There would be more successful moves to curtail the power of the legislature and restructure state government in the years ahead, but few with the profound effect on the balance of political power that resulted from Allain's lawsuit.

THE CAMPAIGNS OF 1984

Reagan Consolidates Mississippi

Four years after Ronald Reagan kicked off his general election campaign in Mississippi, Walter Mondale began his own drive for the presidency at an August 1 rally on Capitol Street in downtown Jackson, "symbolizing the ticket's commitment to pursue Southern votes."[17] The problem for Mondale in the South was threefold.

First, the economic recovery of the previous two years was still in high gear, coming out of the bitter 1981 and 1982 recession. One of Reagan's ads captured the spirit he hoped voters would share about the economic boom the country was experiencing: "Americans are working again. So is America. . . . We are in the midst of a springtime of hope for America."[18]

Mondale's second southern problem was Jesse Jackson. For the first time in the country's political history, a black candidate ran a credible, very public, reasonably well financed, national campaign for the presidency.[19] While Jackson's campaign began as a vehicle to mobilize African American voters, it ended at the Democratic National Convention where Jackson bargained with white party leaders for specific policy positions, most notably affirmative action and quotas.[20]

Mondale's third, and perhaps insurmountable, problem came in the form of his own nomination acceptance speech, in which he promised to raise taxes to balance the budget. "By the end of my first term, I will cut the deficit by two-thirds. Let's tell the truth. Mr. Reagan will raise taxes, and so will I. He won't tell you. I just did." The reaction of Lee Atwater, Reagan's chief southern strategist, said it all: "Coming from my region [the South], I knew a tax increase is just outlandish. . . . I thought I had literally fallen asleep and was dreaming."[21]

When Reagan campaigned on the Gulf Coast in early October, he knew instinctively how to characterize Mondale's pledge for the average Mississippian: "I think the word shrimp means something different to our [Democratic] opponents than it does to Gulfport. To you, it's a livelihood; to them, it's your paycheck after they get their hands on it."[22] While Reagan was driving home the connection between Democrats and higher taxes, voters in Tupelo were raising the other issue that would come to haunt Democrats even to the present day. Mondale hosted a forum in the heart of northeast Mississippi, where he had to listen to an audience member describe the Democratic platform as "pro-abortion, pro-gay rights and anti-religion" and then ask: "Please tell us how you can be a good Christian and represent such perversions as this?"[23]

The ways in which the two national parties had come to define themselves during the campaign was captured by Washington writers Tom Edsall and Mary Edsall:

The presidential election of 1984 produced the consolidation of the often chaotic forces that had produced the conservative revolution of 1980. The Democratic

Party had come increasingly to represent . . . a liberal agenda that imposed costs on the majority for the benefit of those seeking special preference. . . . Meanwhile, the Republican Party . . . had fashioned strategies to combine a populist appeal with free-market economics, strategies highlighting sustained opposition to raising taxes, and continued antagonism to government regulation.

The Republicans had fashioned an

ideology that focused on conservative egalitarianism, an ideology revolved around "equal opportunity" rather than "equal outcomes"; around the idea that market mechanisms functioned most effectively to allocate scarce resources; and around the linkage of merit and status, and of reward and effort. It was an ideology that used opposition to federal tax burdens to unite the rich with the working class, as opposed to the use of federal spending to unite the poor with the middle class.[24]

In Mississippi, William Winter would suffer the consequences.

William Winter versus Thad Cochran

Thad Cochran was finishing his first Senate term and was up for reelection in 1984. By any reasonable standard, he should have been vulnerable. He had yet to win a majority in a competitive campaign. An outgoing Democratic governor had passed a landmark education bill, and an incoming Democratic governor had just won an overwhelming election in spite of a vicious Republican attack on his character. Consequently, national Democrats approached William Winter about taking on Cochran.[25]

That summer, Ole Miss Chancellor Porter Fortune announced his retirement, and it wasn't long before Winter was rumored to be a candidate for that post. For the rest of the year, the state College Board, charged with choosing Fortune's successor, and Winter engaged in a very public process of deciding if the two wanted each other. Finally, on December 14, the College Board offered Winter the position, which he immediately accepted. Five days later, he stunned the state by changing his mind and declining the offer.[26] For the next two months, Winter engaged in the same kind of public indecisiveness about whether to oppose Cochran, and on the day that Winter held a press conference to announce his decision, no one knew what to expect. When a reporter called Danny Cupit, the state Democratic Party chairman, to tell him that Winter would be a candidate, he said, "You're kidding."[27]

If Walter Mondale and Jesse Jackson and the back and forth with Ole Miss weren't enough for Winter to overcome, Johnnie Walls, a black lawyer from Greenville, spent August and early September contemplating an independent candidacy for the Senate. The media covered his bid extensively, especially when Walls and his supporters made a series of "demands" on the state party.[28] Walls's chief complaint was simple: black candidates "do not receive the same support we give whites."[29] The most celebrated example that year came when John Stennis endorsed William Winter's candidacy but refused to support Robert Clark, a black legislator and the Democratic Party's nominee against Republican incumbent Webb Franklin in the majority black Second Congressional District.[30]

Walls began to have second thoughts, however, when Ray Tribble, an influential white county supervisor from Greenwood, paid Walls a visit at his home in Greenville, "guaranteeing money, cars, and campaign funds" for his campaign. When Walls asked for the source of the largesse, Tribble wouldn't say.[31] Then, on the last day for independent candidates to qualify, Steve Patterson, then chairman of the state party, flew Walls to a rally in Columbia, South Carolina, where Jesse Jackson was one of the featured speakers. At Patterson's request, Jackson had agreed to meet with Walls, who remembers the conversation:[32]

> Jackson: Walls, what you doing?
> Walls: Thinking about running for the Senate.
> Jackson: Are you sure you want to do that?
> Walls: I'm thinking about it.
> Jackson: I want you to do a lot of thinking about it.

On the flight home, Walls knew he had to make a decision; it was the deadline to qualify. He had come to realize that his group had started too late, yielding too few supporters and not enough time to organize. Ultimately, though, Walls knew he didn't want to become the new Charles Evers. So, he decided to wait for another day.[33] But Johnnie Walls's complaint was simple: "White people have to look themselves in the mirror and ask why it's all right for them to represent them and us, but it's not all right for us to represent us and them."[34]

The inability of the white leadership of the state Democratic Party to address Walls's complaint would ultimately form the basis for a dramatic change of strategy for black leaders during the 2001–2002 legislative reapportionment process. Whether that strategy was good for the party is still debated today.

Nevertheless, once Walls decided against qualifying, Winter had to contend with the new reality in the U.S. Senate. For the first time since 1954, electing a Democrat in Mississippi meant little in terms of exercising real power, since the GOP now controlled the Senate. It was Cochran who was in the position to argue that his reelection would aid his climb up the seniority ladder toward a committee chairmanship and the source of real power in Washington.[35]

The 581,477 votes that Reagan received in Mississippi on election day 1984, representing 62 percent of all votes cast, reflected a landslide not exceeded by a Republican candidate for governor or president in the state until George W. Bush's reelection win in 2004. "Mississippi's love affair with Ronald Reagan is something to behold," was how one journalist described the phenomenon.[36] Cochran himself enjoyed a 61 percent victory.

In remembering the race years later, Winter said: "There was a reasonable expectation that the Democrats could pick up four or five seats and regain control of the United States Senate, which would have made Stennis chairman of the Appropriations Committee . . . which I thought was an advantage and almost a justification for making the effort to reclaim the Senate. As it turned out, it was a terrible year for a Democrat to be running."[37]

POSTSCRIPT

While in the state for the August campaign kickoff in 1984, Mondale's vice presidential running mate, Geraldine Ferraro, visited a farm outside Jackson for a meeting and press event. She was joined by Jim Buck Ross, Mississippi's commissioner of agriculture. At one point during their conversation, Ross mentioned that blueberries represented an expanding crop for the state:

Ferraro: Now I grow those.
Ross: You grow 'em? Can you bake a blueberry muffin?
Ferraro: I sure can. Can you?
Ross: Down here in Mississippi, the men don't cook.[38]

As it happened, Ross's drawl was so thick that national news networks resorted to showing subtitles of the conversation when tapes of the exchange were televised. The graphic image of the printed words beneath the visual images seemed only to underscore the vast cultural differences between the party of Minnesota's Walter Mondale and New York's Geraldine Ferraro, on the one hand, and of Pelahatchie's Jim Buck Ross and rural Mississippi voters, on the other.

CHAPTER 11

THE RISE OF MIKE ESPY

1985–1986

*Election Day 1986—at about one o'clock in the morning, Mike Espy
was driving to Vicksburg after speaking at his last campaign rally. On a
rural stretch of Highway 61, the car ran out of gas. Espy was wondering
to himself whether this was an omen when "lo and behold, here comes a
highway patrolman, lights flashing. We had a campaign bumper sticker
on, it was obviously a campaign car, and I thought I'm bound to get beat
up when a white highway patrolman gets out of the car. He comes to the
driver's side, and he looks at the driver, and then his eye catches me,
and he brightens up and says, "Good evening, Congressman." I said,
"I'm not yet." And he says, "You will be." And he helped us get gas,
and we went on our way. That night I won.*

—MIKE ESPY[1]

For nearly eighty-four years, the congressional districts of Mississippi tracked the traditional geographic regions of the state, including a district defined by the Mississippi Delta. On at least three occasions over that period, when the state lost congressional districts because of national population shifts, the legislature had to reconfigure the boundary lines. The traditional geographic regions were always respected in the realignment, specifically with respect to the Delta district.[2]

That all changed when the Voting Rights Act of 1965 transformed black Mississippi citizens into black Mississippi voters. Overnight, the Second Congressional District, comprised of the counties in the heart of the Delta, became a district with more African American voters than white voters.[3] Not only was the future of the white incumbent threatened in the 1966 elections, but the prospect of Mississippi electing its first black congressman in the twentieth century looked promising. What was the all-white legislature to do?

In the same way the 1966 legislature redrew the state legislative district lines to thwart the election of black legislators—combining majority black counties with majority white counties to yield districts that were majority white—the same legislature employed the same strategy to reconfigure the boundaries of the congressional districts. Their solution: divide the majority black Delta region among three congressional districts, combining majority black Delta counties with majority white counties outside the Delta to produce three districts, each with a majority white population.

The counties of the Mississippi Delta, most of which have large black majority populations, are situated in a north-south swath of land running parallel to the Mississippi River from Memphis, Tennessee, in the north to Vicksburg in the south. But after the 1966 redistricting transformation, the new district boundary lines ran east-west across the state. Tishomingo County residents, in the far northeastern corner of the state, found themselves represented by the same congressman as the voters in Coahoma County on the Mississippi River. In another district, the city of Meridian, on the Alabama state line, was drawn into the same district as Issaquena County, another county bordering on the Mississippi River. The rationale for these dramatic changes was explained by a legislator at the time: "We all know the Negro situation was the main factor."[4] In 1967, the U.S. Supreme Court upheld this scheme, and the east-west running boundary lines remained in place until 1982.[5]

THE DELTA CONGRESSIONAL DISTRICT RETURNS

The 1980 federal census revealed substantial shifts in the population among Mississippi's five congressional districts. Since the districts were consequently no longer in compliance with the one-person, one-vote requirement, the legislature created a special committee to develop new district boundaries. That committee held hearings throughout the state and received testimony on a variety of plans, but ultimately was forced to choose between two competing proposals. The "least-change plan" would maintain the east-west district lines relatively intact while making the minimal adjustments necessary to achieve one-person, one-vote parity. The "Simpson plan" was proposed by Gulf Coast Representative Jim Simpson, the centerpiece of which would create a Delta congressional district with a majority black population.

The committee deliberated throughout the summer of 1981 in a large room in the old Jackson Central High School that was serving as the temporary state capitol. During these sessions, the interests of white Democratic Party leaders diverged from the interests of black Democratic Party leaders. Black leaders argued for a congressional district from which a black candidate could get elected. With African Americans accounting for 35 percent of the state's population, black leaders believed one of the state's five congressional seats should be occupied by a black man or woman. Simpson's proposed Delta district was the likeliest way to achieve that end, as the largest proportion of black voters lived in that area. For black leaders, the solution was simple: return to the configuration that had existed for more than eight decades prior to the enactment of the Voting Rights Act.

From the vantage point of white Democrats, however, creating a district populated with enough black voters to elect a black candidate meant draining black voters from surrounding districts, leaving those districts with substantially higher numbers of white voters. In the minds of most white Democratic Party officials, more white voters translated into more Republican voters. More Republican voters in a district would ultimately elect more Republican candidates. Therefore, maintaining districts with a substantial percentage of black population, but less than a majority, was necessary to yield districts more likely to elect Democratic candidates. That was the theory of the least-change plan. And that was the rub for blacks: Democrats elected from any district drawn in a "least-change" configuration would be white. Even party officials conceded that racially polarized voting would prevent white voters from supporting black candidates. Blacks concluded they wanted to elect "one of their own," even if it jeopardized the ability of voters in the surrounding districts to elect Democrats.

During the deliberations of the special legislative committee, all of these issues and interests came into play. Led by Tommy Campbell, a white state representative from Yazoo City, the committee rejected the Simpson plan and adopted the least-change plan.[6] The full legislature subsequently confirmed the committee's recommendation in an August 1981 special session. Pursuant to the preclearance provisions of the Voting Rights Act, the plan was submitted to the Justice Department.[7] Campbell spoke for many white Democratic leaders when he argued it was virtually impossible to create a district with a substantial black voting majority without "robbing" white districts of so many black voters that the incumbent Democratic congressmen at the time—Jamie Whitten, David Bowen, Sonny Montgomery, and Wayne Dowdy—would become vulnerable to Republican challengers. Campbell asserted that black voters would be better served by having a substantial number of blacks in as many districts as possible, rather than combining them into one district simply to elect "a black face. . . . It's a choice between visibility and impact."[8] Campbell had concluded that a lawmaker with a constituency that was at least 40 percent African American was more sensitive to minority concerns. He argued blacks would lose political clout in the state's remaining four congressional districts if a Delta district were created. Emphasizing this position also served Campbell's other chief goal: protecting incumbents.[9] Other white Democrats like Claude Ramsay, president of the state AFL-CIO, echoed Campbell: "I don't blame blacks for feeling the way they do because they've been screwed pretty bad down here. . . . But with a [majority black] district we could wind up with one black congressman and four damn Republicans."[10]

Black leaders, on the other hand, had worked year after year to elect white Democrats, only to see those Democrats, once in public office, vote against the wishes of their black constituents. As one black scholar remarked: "Only the rhetoric of white politicians has changed since 1950."[11] Black leaders had lived through the previous twenty years in which white officials had opposed every attempt to dismantle segregation. Now that the barriers were largely gone, blacks were being asked to let white officials continue to represent them, as if those white officials knew what was best for their black constituents. That proposal revealed a benign paternalism that was more than most blacks could tolerate. Campbell remained unmoved: "The crux of this whole thing is whether or not visibility is more important than impact. What you want today may not be what you want tomorrow."[12]

On March 30, 1982, the Department of Justice weighed in on the debate when it refused to approve the least-change plan, declaring that the district lines "have been drawn horizontally [east to west] across the majority-black Delta area in such a manner as to dismember the black population concentration and effectively dilute its voting strength."[13] Campbell accused the Justice Department of "legal calisthenics" and promised to appeal the decision.[14] The political fears of white Democrats seemed well placed when the chairman of the state Republican Party admitted to urging the Justice Department to disapprove the legislature's plan.[15]

The competing forces in Mississippi politics now turned to the courts. The legislative committee voted to initiate litigation.[16] White Democratic leaders joined with the white Democratic incumbents to argue in support of preserving the existing congressional districts.

Civil rights lawyers and black leaders filed their own lawsuits in federal court, asking the court to approve a plan containing a Delta district. This reapportionment lawsuit was assigned to a new three-judge federal panel, and this court would prove to be dramatically different from the Coleman court the *Connor* plaintiffs faced for fourteen years.

Fifth Circuit Court of Appeals Judge Charles Clark was named as the circuit judge member of the special three-judge panel. During the James Meredith ordeal, Clark had been the attorney representing the College Board, and at the 1968 Democratic National Convention, he had testified for the Regulars. Clark was joined by District Court Judges William Keady and Lester Senter. In less than two months, however, the judges had determined the Simpson plan "accords with racial fairness by including a majority black district" and ordered congressional elections to be held under that plan.[17] Years later, Clark was asked about the dramatic contrast to the fourteen-year *Connor* saga. Soft spoken and choosing his words carefully, he explained: "We were of the opinion that the law required the creation of a district with a comfortable black voting majority."[18]

THE 1982 CAMPAIGN

For the chance to represent this new district, Robert Clark was the Democratic nominee, and Webb Franklin was the Republican nominee. When Holmes County voters elected Clark to the state House in 1967, he had become the first black legislator in the twentieth century. From those early days when he was first assigned a seat on the House floor at a two-person desk—and no one would sit next to him—to working his way up the seniority ladder to become chairman of the House Education Committee, Clark had developed a reputation as a conscientious representative. Webb Franklin, a lawyer from Greenwood, resigned his position as a state court judge and switched to the Republican Party to campaign for Congress.[19]

The John Stennis–Haley Barbour Senate contest was at the top of the election ballot that year, but without a presidential campaign to automatically guarantee a turnout, each candidate had to focus on getting his core voters to the polls. As Franklin would tell crowds, "If we sit on our behinds and if we don't stimulate people to go vote, then I think you know what is going to happen, because those who supported Robert Clark in the past have demonstrated an ability to get their favorable vote."[20] Similarly, black leaders feared that Clark would fail to receive the support of many white Democratic voters. A black preacher active with Clark's campaign best captured this expectation: "Most whites won't vote for a black, even if he was Jesus come down from the heavens. Even then, they'd be the first to say, 'That can't be Jesus. Everybody knows Jesus is white.'"[21]

To generate excitement among his core voters, Franklin spoke to the voters in a television commercial with a Confederate monument in the background: "There's something about Mississippi that outsiders will never, ever understand: the way we feel about our family and God, and the traditions we have. . . . We cannot forget about a heritage that has been sacred through the generations."[22] Franklin also circulated an insert in local newspapers that featured a large photo of Clark next to his own. Above both photos was a headline in red letters: "The Choice Is Yours For Congress." The caption under Franklin's photo: "In 1972, Webb Franklin began serving our community in the District Attorney's office, fighting crime, and working to preserve traditional conservative Mississippi values." The caption under Clark's photo reinforced the Republican strategy—link "Democrat" with "liberal": "In 1972, Robert Clark was working to elect liberal candidate George McGovern for president."[23]

On election day, Clark received 48.4 percent of the vote, losing to Franklin by fewer than 3,000 votes. In the same district, John Stennis defeated his Republican opponent by 61.5 percent to 38.5 percent, a margin of more than 32,000 votes. The suspicions of black leaders had been realized.

BACK TO COURT

During the 1982 campaign, Congress reauthorized the Voting Rights Act for another twenty-five years, and in the process, amended the law to make it easier for plaintiffs to prove discrimination in reapportionment lawsuits.[24] On May 16, the U.S. Supreme Court responded to this congressional action by ordering the three-judge panel in Mississippi to reconsider the district boundaries it created in 1982.[25] Seven months later, same three-judge panel redrew the lines and increased the black population in the Second District from 53.8 percent to 57.8 percent. The court found that "from all the evidence, we conclude that blacks consistently lose elections in Mississippi because the majority of voters choose their preferred candidates on the basis of race." Ironically, the Webb Franklin television ad with the Confederate memorial was among the factors cited by the Court as evidence that "Mississippi voters are urged to cast their ballots according to race."[26]

At this point, no one was happy. The lawyers for the black plaintiffs wanted a district with an even higher black population. The lawyers for the legislature—representing the viewpoint of white Democrats—were concerned about draining yet more black voters from surrounding districts. The Republicans, worried that the additional black voters could jeopardize the reelection prospect of their newest member of Congress, also opposed the decision. All the parties appealed to the U.S. Supreme Court. On November 13, 1984, the Court chose the middle course and backed the decision of the district court.[27] "It affirmed the progress that we've made so far, but refused to give us any more," explained the lawyer for the black plaintiffs.[28]

In the 1984 election held in the intervening months, however, Robert Clark had lost a rematch against Webb Franklin. The Reagan coattails and the Mondale drag had proven too much to overcome, even with the additional black voters. The margin was again about 3,000 votes in favor of Franklin.

THE MIKE ESPY CAMPAIGN

By the time politicians began thinking about 1986 elections, the prospect of defeating Republican Webb Franklin in the majority black Second Congressional District had led a number of the state's black leaders to give up hope, resigning themselves to waiting until the 1990 federal census and another opportunity to configure the district lines.[29] Among white Democrats, though, two heirs to famous Mississippi political families decided to vie for the nomination: Hiram Eastland, a cousin of former senator James Eastland, and Pete Johnson, grandson of former governor Paul Johnson and nephew of former governor Paul Johnson Jr. About the same time, a relatively unknown black lawyer began making the rounds, talking with activists, and testing the waters. Mike Espy had left his hometown of Yazoo City in 1971 to attend Howard University, followed by Santa Clara Law School. After earning his law degree, Espy returned to Mississippi in 1978 to help with the family business and practice law. He later joined Central Mississippi Legal Services, then took a job with Secretary of State Ed Pittman. Espy subsequently helped Pittman campaign for attorney general in 1983, and was hired as assistant attorney general after Pittman's victory.

In the meantime, Espy had "caught the campaign fever," though he sat back and waited. When it looked like the field was open in late 1985—Robert Clark decided against a third try, as did other prominent officeholders and leaders in the black community—Espy quietly resigned from the attorney general's office, withdrew all of his money from his state pension to cover his living expenses, and began his campaign.

Mike Espy brought to the campaign a family legacy few knew about. By 1986, the Espy family owned the largest black business in Mississippi, Century Funeral Home. Century was a chain of funeral homes throughout the Delta founded years earlier by the family patriarch, Thomas Jefferson Huddleston, known as "Cousin Tom." The funeral homes grew out of a hospital he founded in Yazoo City in the early 1900s, one of the first black hospitals in the state, built because Huddleston was "tired of seeing our women having babies in the cotton field." Cousin Tom not only left a family legacy in the Delta, but many of his children and relatives had made Chicago their home. One in particular was Uncle Leon, who by 1986 had become a millionaire owner of a chain of barbecue restaurants. Until he was thirteen years old, Espy had worked every summer in Uncle Leon's restaurants. Later, in 1986, Uncle Leon hosted several fund-raisers for Espy and became one of his largest contributors.[30]

The Espy campaign strategy for the primary was simple, but took many observers by surprise: build an organization in as many majority black precincts as possible, put one person in charge of each precinct, knit them together into the larger campaign organization, supplement it with radio ads programmed on black-oriented radio stations, stay off television, and keep a low profile. As far as "anyone could tell," Espy explained, "it was low-key, but below the surface, there was frenzy." The overriding goal for Espy was to avoid a runoff; he had just enough money to finance one campaign and just enough energy and enthusiasm among his supporters to get the vote out to the polls one time. Getting into a runoff with either Johnson or Eastland was a losing proposition, Espy believed.[31] On the night of the election, however, it looked as if a runoff was a reality. Espy woke up the next morning at 49.95 percent, or eighty-seven votes shy of a majority. Johnson and Eastland had polled enough of the white vote to keep Espy below 50 percent.[32]

That same morning, Betty Jo Hines, an official with the Washington County Democratic Executive Committee, called Johnnie Walls, the committee's chairman, and said, "Why don't we recount the boxes?" So the two of them spent the day painstakingly reviewing the returns from each precinct. Toward the end of the day, they realized one of the boxes that favored Espy had been incorrectly posted on the tabulation sheet, an error that gave Espy an additional 243 votes. Walls called Espy, and Hines called the state party.[33] Espy was the nominee.

Espy remembers the general election being a "love fest" within the Democratic Party. State officials campaigned on his behalf, and the national party provided money and other resources. Espy used his television commercials to talk about his family and his interest in agriculture—1985 and 1986 had been hard years for Delta farmers, and a summer drought in the middle of the election brought more misery. Franklin hurt himself when he said toward the end of the campaign, "We can't let the federal government support everybody who thinks he wants to be a farmer."[34] Espy countered by hosting a panel in Greenville featuring congressional agricultural leaders, Mississippi Agriculture Commissioner Jim Buck Ross, and Texas Agriculture Commission Jim Hightower.[35] The week before the election, Espy received a standing ovation from a mostly white Kiwanis Club luncheon in the Delta when he said, "I intend to be a Congressman for everybody."[36]

In the fifteen core Delta counties that formed the basis for both the 1982 district and the 1986 district, turnout was about the same, with Espy garnering about the same number of votes as Clark had previously. Both Clark and Espy squeaked by Franklin in these core counties. Espy defeated Franklin by 4,827 votes out of 141,411 cast. His efforts to reach out to white voters helped to increase his share of that vote by a modest amount, while his organizational campaign in the black communities across the district turned out more of his base vote than Franklin was able to accomplish in the white communities in this election, which had no presidential campaign to drive up voter turnout (the total number votes dropped from 182,520 in the 1984 presidential election year to 141,411 two years later). In the end, though, the changes made by the special three-judge panel federal court in 1983 provided the foundation for Espy's win. The court replaced the majority white counties of Choctaw,

Leake, Montgomery, and Webster from the 1982 district with the majority black counties of Claiborne and Jefferson along with a number of majority black precincts from Hinds County. In 1982, those four white counties had given Franklin a 4,500-vote margin. Four years later, Jefferson, Claiborne, and Hinds produced a 4,000-vote margin for Espy. Mississippi would be sending its first African American to Congress since John R. Lynch left office in March 1883.[37]

Only five Republican incumbents were defeated by Democrats that November across the country, and the overall number of incumbents defeated in the 1986 House elections was the lowest in postwar history.[38] Among those joining Espy as a newly elected member of Congress was John Lewis, a leader of the civil rights movement who had spent the better part of 1964 helping to organize Freedom Summer in Mississippi.[39] Still serving today, Lewis represents a district in Georgia.

A *Clarion-Ledger* editorial no doubt expressed the feelings of many right after the election: "The election of Mike Espy... represented the winds of change blowing over Mississippi."[40] The reality was a bit different: the state of Mississippi itself had fought the creation of the Delta district. And, on election day, racially polarized voting had characterized the outcome. But neither of those status quo indicators was as powerful as the substance and symbolism of Espy's election.

On the day in January 1987 when Espy took the oath of office, he hosted a reception in one of the committee rooms in the U.S. Capitol. Hundreds attended, including many of his county and precinct coordinators, who had rented a bus to join the occasion. Espy's former boss, Attorney General Ed Pittman, was there, along with his new colleagues, Congressman Wayne Dowdy and Senator Thad Cochran. Neither of Espy's parents was alive to witness the historic event, so in the ceremonial swearing in that highlighted the reception, his aunt and uncle stood in for his mother and father—Uncle Leon had journeyed from Chicago to seal the family bond all the way back to Cousin Tom.[41]

The 1986 election year was historic for another reason as well: Reuben Anderson became the first African American in the 169-year history of the state to be elected to a position on the Mississippi Supreme Court. Anderson was appointed to the post in 1985 by Governor Bill Allain and stood for election in 1986. He defeated a white challenger, who campaigned as a segregationist, by more than 37,000 votes, in a district without a majority black voting-age population. When Anderson retired from the court in 1991, Fred Banks, his friend since the fourth grade and former law partner, was appointed by Governor Mabus to fill the vacancy.[42]

FRANK PARKER AND HENRY KIRKSEY

The now legendary letter began: "This is the most audacious piece of presumptuousness that I have ever countenanced for a lawyer," and continued with, "Your request that anything be done with it will be thrown in the waste basket," and ended, "One has to possess a very warped mind to see anything derogatory, or insulting in the mural, and it will remain in this courtroom whether you like it or not." The February 18, 1971, letter was sent to Frank Parker from United States District Judge Harold Cox.

Parker moved to Mississippi in 1968 after graduating from Harvard Law School. For nearly fifteen years as an attorney with the Lawyers' Committee for Civil Rights Under Law, he litigated reapportionment, voting rights, job discrimination, and academic freedom cases.[43] It was Parker's complaint about a mural on Cox's courtroom wall that had provoked the judge. The mural had been painted on the wall behind the judge's bench in 1938 in connection with the construction of the courthouse. The mural purported to depict life in the state during this period: blacks were shown picking cotton and playing the banjo and were the only adults in the painting not wearing shoes. When Parker demanded that the mural be covered or removed because it "compromises the dignity of black litigants," Cox penned his letter. After Parker continued to raise objections, the mural was soon covered and remains covered to this day.[44]

For the last six years of the *Connor v. Johnson* reapportionment litigation, Parker headed the team of lawyers that brought that case to a resolution. For the three years that it took to create the majority black Delta congressional district, Parker would lead that legal team as well. But these were just two of the many civil rights cases that led his clients and co-workers to describe him as a "legal genius" who was "indispensable" to the success of the movement.[45] John Brittain was one of Parker's co-workers at the time and remembers this about Parker: "Frank's office was upstairs, a loft of sorts, and a half level from the ground floor. Frank would puff on fat stogie cigars that created a dense cloud of smoke and stunk up his office with the odor spreading downstairs all the while pecking on the old ribbon typewriter. But the greater the smoke, the more legal fire in his work against the state of Mississippi."[46] For Parker, politics was the vehicle blacks could use to control their own destiny.[47]

In his reapportionment cases, Parker handled the legal responsibilities, but he found he needed a partner to draw district lines. Early in Parker's tenure, Henry Kirksey started showing up at his office, at first just listening, but later offering suggestions. Kirksey had joined the army after Pearl Harbor, volunteering for the artillery. Having a knack for drawing things all his life, Kirksey discovered that artillery units needed soldiers who could draw maps to pinpoint the aim of their guns. The mapmaking skills he learned in the army would eventually help Parker win his reapportionment cases. For the remainder of Parker's time in Mississippi, he and Kirksey proved a formidable team as they went about redrawing state, county, and municipal district lines all across Mississippi. In 1979, Kirksey was elected to the state Senate with the campaign slogan: "He Made It Happen."[48]

It was several years after the resolution of the *Connor* case that then Attorney General Bill Allain filed his separation of powers lawsuit against the legislature. In the trial, Allain called both J. P. Coleman and Henry Kirksey as witnesses—Coleman as a former governor and Kirksey as an incumbent state senator, both of whom backed Allain's position. Kirksey once recalled that during Parker's reapportionment lawsuits, Coleman used to get "mad every time I showed up with my maps."[49] Looking to the back of the courtroom one day during the 1982 trial, Allain saw Coleman and Kirksey, sitting next to each other, "talking like old friends."[50]

POSTSCRIPT

Seen from the interstate highway that runs near downtown Jackson, the twenty-story Sillers State Office Building is the tallest building for miles around. For a number of years during the Christmas season, state officials would light the offices along the east wall of the building in such a way that a cross would be displayed up and down the side of the building. The Christmas cross of 1986 was to be the last. In response to an American Civil Liberties Union (ACLU) lawsuit, federal District Judge William Barbour ruled that the "purpose of the [state] in displaying the cross is to endorse the Christian religion," and thus held the practice unconstitutional.[51] The outcry was predictable. People marched on the offices of the ACLU, and one of the plaintiffs in the lawsuit was fired from his job.[52] In the end, the state declined to pursue an appeal, and a privately owned downtown skyscraper now lights a cross on the side of its building. Separation of church and state would reappear during the campaign of 2003, when Governor Ronnie Musgrove and Haley Barbour, his Republican challenger who was also Judge William Barbour's cousin, both vied for the honor of displaying the Ten Commandments in the state capitol.

CHAPTER 12

HIGHWAYS, BUDDIE NEWMAN, AND RAY MABUS

1987

It looks to me like the winds of change have turned into a tornado.
—SPEAKER BUDDIE NEWMAN[1]

I t happened gradually, though not inexorably. It took time, but also required a man who envisioned the possibilities. We may never know when Walter Sillers realized the position of Speaker of the House of Representatives could become the dominant political power in Mississippi. Before Sillers, other Speakers such as Thomas Bailey and Fielding Wright had used the position as a jumping off point for higher office. What Sillers surely grasped is that, in those days, the state constitution restricted the governor to one four-year term. No similar limit was imposed on the Speaker. Year after year, Sillers stayed put, shaping the position into the unquestioned reservoir of power in the state. Once elected in 1944, Sillers did not vacate the Speaker's office until the day he died in 1966. After Sillers's death, he was followed as Speaker by his protégé John Junkin, who served until 1976. Junkin was succeeded by yet another Sillers protégé, Buddie Newman. When the legislature convened on January 6, 1987, not only was Newman still the Speaker, but for the previous forty-three years, Sillers or one of his charges had wielded the power of the office. That era would come to an end during the course of the 1987 session.

Later in 1987, Ray Mabus would become the first Mississippi governor young enough to have missed participating in the civil rights movement. The year 1987 was historic for yet another milestone—the passage of a statewide four-lane highway program.

HIGHWAYS AND POLITICS

If you opened a Mississippi road map in 1987, your choice of four-lane highways was limited to the federal interstates, the section of Highway 49 from Yazoo City to Gulfport, and the section of Highway 82 from Greenville to Winona. Otherwise, you traveled two-lane roads. Not only were many of the two-lane roads extremely dangerous, but the lack of four-lane highways was blocking economic development throughout rural Mississippi.[2]

After removing legislators from executive branch agencies, Governor Allain turned his attention to the State Highway Department, which was governed by a three-member commission. Commissioners were elected from districts drawn east-west across the state, dividing the state into thirds. Allain sought to abolish the elected positions and vest management of the department in a director appointed by the governor. Allain's reform initiative reached a climax in the 1986 legislative session when he vetoed the Highway Department's funding bill.[3] After legislators failed to override his veto, they adjourned, leaving the department without legal authorization to spend money beyond July 1, the beginning of the state's fiscal year.[4] It was this unrelated crisis over the funding and management of the Highway Department that provided the impetus for the largest public works program in the state's history.

The Beginning

Two days after the 1986 legislature adjourned, Central District Highway Commissioner Sam Waggoner drove to Yazoo City for a dedication ceremony. Waggoner's concern that day was not the almost complete absence of four-lane highways, but the more immediate possibility that Allain would allow the Highway Department to shut down. At the dedication, Waggoner ran into Owen Cooper, a prominent Yazoo City businessman. After hearing Waggoner's concerns, Cooper asked a question that would prove crucial to the ultimate passage of the four-lane program: "What can I do to help?" Waggoner suggested a committee of Cooper's business and industry colleagues from around the state could convince Allain to convene a special session to authorize funding for the department. By the end of their conversation the following day, Cooper was fully behind the plan. They identified a group to invite to a May 7 meeting, all of whom readily agreed to attend. That meeting produced a public statement calling on Allain to provide funding. With the end of the state's fiscal year less than two months away, time was running out. Allain, on the other hand, saw a chance to force the legislature to act on his reorganization proposals.

About the same time, Waggoner paid a visit to Jackson contractor Tom Brown and asked him to finance a poll to gauge public opinion about appointed commissioners and the funding of highways. Brown agreed, and a week or so later the informal Cooper group released the results showing that 71 percent favored electing the commissioners. Allain called the special session for May 28, though he backed off asking lawmakers to consider his reorganization proposal when a series of meetings he had held around the state generated little enthusiasm for removing the elected commissioners.[5]

Toward the end of the special session—which approved the appropriation bill for the department—Senators Bob Montgomery, Eddie Briggs, Irb Benjamin, and Bill Canon engaged in the time-honored practice of converting a crisis into an opportunity. They asked Waggoner to develop a map showing the roads the department could afford to convert to four lanes with its existing legal authority to issue bonds to cover the costs. Waggoner came back with a map showing 300–400 miles could be constructed under those terms, with no new taxes. At Montgomery's urging, Waggoner set up a meeting with Cooper to review the map with him.[6] In Yazoo City, Waggoner rolled the map across Cooper's conference table. All the roads that would be four lanes were marked in red. Cooper "looked at the map for 20 minutes or more" and turned to Waggoner: "Sam, are you for this map?" After Waggoner assured him he was, Cooper observed, "Do you know that seventy percent of these roads are out of your district?" Gene Triggs, Cooper's right-hand man, was there and told Waggoner later, "If you had said you wanted your share of roads for your district, it would have been a dead program."[7]

But the program was alive. Cooper organized another meeting of business leaders from around the state for July 23 to consider Waggoner's proposals. The group had grown to about seventy-five, and the enthusiasm of the meeting convinced Cooper to request Waggoner to prepare a plan that would put every Mississippian within thirty to forty minutes of a four-lane highway. At this meeting, Meridian businessman Gil Carmichael proposed a nickel tax increase per gallon of motor fuel to fund the construction.[8] Cooper also concluded a permanent organization was needed. A steering committee was soon organized, but it needed a name. Waggoner turned to his friend and public relations consultant Harry Brown, whose recommendation was soon adopted: AHEAD (Advocating Highways for Economic Advancement and Development).[9] Within a few months, the organization had a name, a motto—"A Nickel Will Do It!"—and a consensus on the road program: construction of 907 miles to be four lanes at a cost of approximately $1.3 billion, financed by a five-cent motor-fuel tax.[10] When told that the legislature would never pass a tax increase, Cooper responded: "You are wrong. It's simply a matter of putting together a campaign to make them do it. We are on to something good and we are on to something big. You don't do things with little effort."[11]

Next stop for AHEAD was to recruit New Albany Representative John Pennebaker and Booneville Representative Billy McCoy—chairman and vice chairman, respectively, of the House Transportation Committee. After hearing the presentation, Pennebaker and McCoy embarked on a series of public hearings to consider various construction plans, to explore different funding approaches, and to meet with other legislators to convince them of the need for the program.[12] Along the way, they made two critical decisions. First, they recognized their underlying disagreement with the governor over the structure of the department would not be resolved. Allain wanted to change the system—by abolishing elected commissioners—before authorizing the expenditure of any new money. Pennebaker and McCoy realized that changing the system was impossible—legislators would never repeal an elected office. The alternative was to write into law exactly how any new money would be spent—remove discretion from the commissioners. That conclusion led them to the second critical decision: the determination that the specific roads to be built over the life of the program would be based on "nonpolitical" criteria such as traffic counts and safety considerations.[13] By the end of the year, Pennebaker and McCoy's hearings had attracted more than 1,200 people, helped to develop detailed proposals, and generated support for a comprehensive program. In the meantime, AHEAD had rented office space, employed full-time staff, built a mailing list, recruited endorsements from business and professional organizations, and made plans for a paid advertising campaign when the legislature convened in January.

On November 8, 1986, at the age of seventy-eight, Owen Cooper died of pancreatic cancer. Gene Triggs remembered Cooper calling him to his bedside just days before: "Gene, Mississippi needs this four-lane program. Please give it all you've got."[14] Indianola businessman Morris Lewis assumed the AHEAD chair and led the effort, along with Triggs and many others, to realize Cooper's initiative.

[189]

THE 1987 LEGISLATIVE SESSION

In the same way that William Winter had mobilized Mississippians five years earlier to support an education reform bill, AHEAD employed grassroots organizing, speeches, mailings, and advertising to sell a tax increase to fund the four-lane highway proposal. In 1987, the challenge would be even greater: legislators were being asked to oppose a governor and support a tax increase in the middle of an election year. The journey began on January 13 when Pennebaker's Transportation Committee approved the comprehensive bill and sent it to Representative Sonny Merideth's Ways and Means Committee, through which any tax increase must pass. The next day, Allain proposed his own four-lane highway program, funded without additional taxes, combined with a reorganized Highway Department. Allain challenged the legislature to let the voters decide in a statewide referendum if they wanted to pay additional taxes.[15] Even at this early stage in the legislative process, the reaction of key legislators indicated that momentum for a comprehensive highway program was in place. Lieutenant Governor Brad Dye remarked, "We have a democratic society and a representative form of government . . . having the people vote every time we have a tax decrease or tax increase would be shirking our responsibility," while Pennebaker complained that Allain's program "falls short of the state's transportation needs."[16] Rebutting Allain's call for appointed highway commissioners was left to Marshall County Senator Bill Minor: "If my people were smart enough to elect me, then they aren't too dumb to elect a highway commission."[17]

On January 27, the House Ways and Means Committee spent all day debating funding alternatives for the plan, with Merideth reminding House members, as he had with the 1982 education reform bill: "If you want to have a highway program you're going to have to put your money up." After the committee approved a series of increased taxes by a vote of 15–12, Merideth reported: "We finally got that baby delivered."[18] Two days later, the full House debated the bill, failing with sixty-four "yes" votes to fifty-three "no" votes—since the bill raised taxes, it needed a three-fifths margin to gain passage, or seventy-one votes. The challenge for supporters soon became apparent: of the thirty-one members from the Gulf Coast and Jackson metropolitan areas, only six supported the bill, both areas being largely left out of the new program because they were well served by the existing interstate system and Highway 49. But Merideth was undaunted: "I thought it would fail the first time." Merideth, Pennebaker,

McCoy, and others were engaged in a legislative tactic often used for controversial bills: bring a bill to the floor, get a recorded vote, and, if unsuccessful,
work overnight to convert targeted representatives who had voted "no."[19] That
night, legislative leaders lobbied their colleagues while AHEAD members contacted the targeted House members from their hometowns. By the next day,
they were ready for round two.[20]

When the red and green lights illuminate the voting boards at the front of the
House chamber, it is impossible for an onlooker to determine quickly whether
a three-fifths vote has been achieved. As the vote on round two was displayed
on the board, it appeared to have lost again, but Speaker Newman announced
the measure had been approved 69–45, exactly three-fifths. Several of those
who switched were lobbied by AHEAD members in their districts, while others changed out of deference to the Speaker and other legislators. How a small
group of businessmen and legislators were able to get this far was reflected in
an observation by Montgomery: "Look at where we were last spring. We were
fighting over the structure of the Highway Department. Now the question is
whether we do the most ambitious highway program in the history of the state
in 10 years or 13 years."[21]

The AHEAD public relations campaign reached a climax in late February
when it sponsored Highway Day in Jackson. More than 1,200 people from sixty-
two counties representing eighty-two organizations attended the pep rally.
Montgomery remarked, "Other than the [1985] teachers' marches, it was probably the largest citizens group, single issue meeting in the history of the state."
And the timing could not have been better. Within several hours, the highway
bill was approved by two Senate committees.[22] Two days later, the Senate, where
opposition to new taxes was less intense, approved the historic legislation 35–16,
with five votes to spare over the required three-fifths margin.[23]

The battle now returned to the House, but momentum was working in
favor of highways. On Wednesday, the House heard Pennebaker plead, "This is
the time. It may not come another time." The House, bolstered by the strong
Senate vote, concurred in the Senate version and sent it to the governor.[24] Five
days later, Allain vetoed the bill, declaring: "I am not willing to be a party to
any program which means an undue tax increase, coupled with a continuance
of present practices."[25] All eyes returned to the House floor when Pennebaker
brought the veto up for debate. The stakes were even higher. While a three-
fifths margin is required to pass a tax measure, a two-thirds vote is needed
to override a governor's veto. In the House, that could have meant finding as

many as eight votes more than had voted for the bill on original passage, if every member voted on the override effort.

In spite of all the lobbying by AHEAD and the legislative leadership, when Pennebaker walked on the floor, he didn't know if he had the votes to the override the governor's veto. Just as Pennebaker was preparing to open debate, Gulf Coast Representative Glenn Endris left his desk, approached Pennebaker, and asked about the vote count. Pennebaker confided that he just didn't know. Endris, who had earlier voted against the bill, told him: "This is not going to die on my vote." Endris walked back to his desk, where his seatmate, fellow Gulf Coast Representative Isiah Fredericks, was waiting for him. "What are you doing?" Fredericks asked. Endris said he was going to speak in favor of the override and vote to override. Whereupon, Fredericks says, "Well, I'm not gonna let you be by yourself."[26] The *Clarion-Ledger* reported the outcome on the front page the next morning: "Although proponents of the measure had preached the economic development virtues of new highways, several representatives held the House rapt by recounting personal and graphic experiences of deaths witnessed on perilous state roads. But the surprise of the afternoon was when Reps. Isiah Fredericks and Glenn Endris—both from Gulf Coast districts—took to the podium in support of the bill." For more than two hours, twenty-four representatives spoke for the measure, with only one voicing opposition. Before Pennebaker concluded the debate, Merideth walked over and whispered, "You're gonna win by one." The vote to override the veto was 79–38. Pennebaker and McCoy needed seventy-eight votes.[27]

Morris Lewis and Gene Triggs watched from the House gallery, and afterward Lewis leaned over to Triggs: "Gene, don't you know Owen Cooper is looking down at us now with a big smile on his face."[28] (On the west side of Highway 49 at the "Four Points" interchange at Yazoo City, there is a marker honoring the contribution of Owen Cooper.) Meantime, the Senate leaders— Dye, Montgomery, and Minor—knew they had the votes and, as if waiting for the baton to pass their way in a relay race, were standing by for the House to send them the veto. Pennebaker compared the Senate readiness to override the governor to "Babe Ruth pointing at the lights in center field." Montgomery was the only one who spoke on the floor: "Do not miss this point in the history. . . . When you look back at this time of service in the legislature, you will be able to say you . . . did the right thing at the right time." It took all of ten minutes for the Senate to override the veto 38– 11, five more votes than needed.

The highway bill was law. Over the next fourteen years, 1,077 miles of four-lane highways would be constructed at a cost of $1.6 billion, funded by an increase in the motor-fuels excise tax of 3.6 cents per gallon and a $5 increase in license tag fees.[29]

BUDDIE NEWMAN RETIRES

Buddie Newman took his first trip to the Mississippi House of Representatives in 1938 as a seventeen-year-old page. Walter Sillers had been there for twenty-two years and would stay another twenty-eight before he died in 1966. Newman returned as an Issaquena County representative in 1952.[30] When Speaker John Junkin took ill in late 1973, Newman and his lieutenants saw their chance to assume power. They circulated a petition in support of Newman's campaign to become Speaker Pro Tempore. When Robert Clark signed the petition, Newman had the majority he needed, and on January 17, 1974, Newman was elected to the number two leadership post.[31] When Junkin died in October 1975, it was a foregone conclusion Newman would be elected Speaker when the legislature convened in January 1976. Newman remained unchallenged until that fateful day in February 1982, when he walked off the dais ignoring the shouts of his colleagues for a roll call vote. Rather than oppose Newman directly, a small group of representatives began to work behind the scenes to amend the House procedural rules that vested the position of Speaker with almost absolute power. The goal was to disburse the power: allow the full House to elect the membership of some key committees; limit the number of terms a representative could serve as Speaker; require the Speaker, in appointing committees, to give preference to seniority; and vest in the position of Speaker Pro Tempore some of the powers that had been reserved exclusively to the Speaker.

Twelve members of the group held a press conference on December 13, 1983, to announce their proposed rule changes. When a newspaper reporter asked, "Well, I see only 12 of you here. What can you do with only 12 votes?" Tallahatchie County Representative Tommy Reynolds responded: "Well, Christ did pretty well with 12 spreading the word."[32] The first confrontation came at the beginning of the 1984 legislature, following the 1983 elections during which a number of candidates had won promising to challenge Newman. On January 3, when Representative Jim Simpson moved adoption of the House rules, Smith County Representative Eric Clark offered the alternative package of rules. Three hours of debate later, the vote recurred on Clark's proposal: twenty-five representatives joined Clark in this very public display of opposition to the Speaker, becoming known as the "Gang of 26."[33]

While the reformers failed on this vote, the issue refused to go away. Over the intervening three years, the tide turned when a number of Newman's young lieutenants abandoned him and joined with the Gang of 26. Why this switch happened remains a matter of debate to this day. Some claim the media continued to portray Newman as an impediment to progress and that supporting him became politically untenable. According to one former representative, Newman turned into a "lightning rod, a symbol of opposition to change. I could feel it back home. The tide of public opinion was turning against him." Another switched his vote when he realized he could no longer "defend Newman in [his] area of the state." Others concluded that Newman failed to learn any lessons from the uprising and refused to make any changes in the way he governed the House, or, as one former member observed, Newman was "bound in the history of Walter Sillers, and felt the need to continue his legacy." On the other hand, backers of Newman saw nothing but betrayal, arguing that the lieutenants who left Newman did so merely to arrogate power unto themselves, with some even positioning themselves to run for Speaker.[34] Newman's strongest supporter, Sonny Merideth, articulated this view: "Don't be fooled one minute that this is a distribution of power. This is a transfer of power."[35]

Newman compounded the problem by isolating the Gang of 26 and assigning them to meaningless committees.[36] Oktibbeha County Representative Cecil Simmons was one of the twenty-six, and found he had so much spare time that he enrolled at the Mississippi College Law School in Jackson. Living in the capital city with plenty of free time, Simmons soon found himself serving as the "negotiator" between the original twenty-six and small groups of other representatives who were becoming increasingly disenchanted with Newman.[37] When the legislature convened in January 1987, those negotiations upended the world of Mississippi politics. One reporter described what happened as "the legislative version of the Gunfight at the OK Corral." A package of rule changes negotiated by Simmons—all designed to reduce the power and influence of the Speaker—was adopted 75–45. It was this vote that led Newman to observe, "It looks to me like the winds of change have turned into a tornado."[38] Five days later, Simmons was elected Speaker Pro Tempore.[39] The Sillers legacy had ended.

Disillusioned with losing the rules fight and with the collective decision of some of his trusted lieutenants to abandon him, Newman soon announced his decision to retire at the end of the year. As he put it, "I just think it's best for Mississippi if I get out of the way."[40]

Newman apparently never understood what provoked the change, lamenting in an interview years later, "I wish that I knew the real reason for sure why some of them joined that movement. . . . I had put a lot of faith and a lot of trust in some young members of that legislature that I had a lot of respect for. I put them in key positions and gave them a chance to be in a leadership position."[41]

Toward the end of the 1987 session, the now larger group of "reformers" caucused and voted to support Lee County Representative Tim Ford for Speaker over his friend McComb Representative Tommy Walman. When asked years later why he won, Ford volunteered that he was the "least undesirable."[42] Oxford Representative Ed Perry assumed leadership of what was left of the Newman contingent, and over the summer and fall Ford and Perry waged their campaigns for Speaker. In the end, Ford's support among the group who had supported the rule changes was too strong, and Perry dropped out before the end of 1987. On January 5, 1988, Ford was elected Speaker by acclamation and became the first northeast Mississippi representative to hold that position since Sam Lumpkin, also from Lee County, was elected Speaker in 1940.[43]

An early supporter of Ed Perry's 1988 campaign for Speaker was DeSoto County Representative John Grisham. Suddenly out of favor with the new House leadership, Grisham found himself with little to do. He began writing a novel with the seemingly innocuous title of *The Firm*. Soon after he sent the final manuscript to his agent in late 1989, Grisham got a call on the first Sunday in 1990: Paramount Studios had purchased the movie rights to *The Firm* for $600,000. And the rest, as they say, is history. Grisham speculated in an interview years later that if Perry had won the Speaker's race in 1988, he would have been assigned to major committees and likely would have been too busy to write.[44]

THE 1987 CAMPAIGN FOR GOVERNOR

As the political players in Mississippi began to think about who would occupy the governor's mansion in 1988, one question loomed over all the prognostications. Would Bill Allain try to become the first Mississippi governor in modern history to succeed himself? The 1986 legislature had finally capitulated to years of editorials and lobbying by government reform groups and had sent to the voters a constitutional amendment allowing the governor to serve two consecutive terms. Later that year, the voters easily approved the amendment. Allain refused to tell anyone his plans, so the number of candidates who wanted the job of governor grew and grew during the months leading up to the June qualification deadline. Allain let the June 5 cutoff pass without making an announcement and without qualifying.[45]

The Democratic Primary

One candidate who had been planning and organizing for this campaign since 1985 was State Auditor Ray Mabus. A Harvard-educated lawyer from Choctaw County, Mabus had served as Governor William Winter's legal counsel and as a member of his "Boys of Spring" team that had helped pass the 1982 Education Reform Act. During early 1983, Winter had asked his legal counsel to check into allegations of fraud involving the Hinds County tax collector. In connection with his investigation, Mabus asked the state auditor's office for audits covering the last three years. He was sent reports for the years 1975, 1976, and 1977. Thinking there had been a mistake, he called the office but was informed those were indeed the three most current audits. "But that's five years ago," Mabus replied. "Yes, we're five years late," he was told. Mabus proceeded to read the laws governing the state auditor's office and realized it could be "the most powerful office in the state."[46] What Mabus discovered is that the office could audit or investigate virtually any local or state public agency. Later that year, at the age of thirty-four, he was elected state auditor, largely on the basis of promising to use the auditor's legal authority to police the spending practices of local governments. Taking on the "time-honored practice" that a little graft was part of the way county and municipal governments worked in Mississippi proved to be a compelling campaign theme.

Soon after his election, Mabus gave his first major speech to the annual meeting of county supervisors, a group of elected officials perceived as engaging in that "time-honored practice." Mabus knew he was in for a long four years after his exchange with Leflore County Supervisor Ray Tribble:

> Tribble: You're telling me I can't come to Jackson for a meeting and buy my wife a steak.
> Mabus: Sure, you can. You just can't use county money to pay for it.
> Tribble: What the hell you talking about?[47]

For the next four years, Mabus transformed the auditor's office, initiating high-profile investigations into the spending habits of public officials throughout the state. While some argued that county officials were critical to the success of a politician's career, Mabus banked on the equation that there are more people who pay taxes than those who spend taxes. He also identified the demographic shift that was taking place: while local officials like supervisors and sheriffs had their greatest influence in the state's rural areas, Mississippi was becoming more and more urban, yielding a politics less dependent on county officials. The crackdown on government corruption reached its peak in February 1987 when an FBI undercover investigation—known as "Operation Pretense"—went public with the first arrests and indictments of county supervisors. Eventually, fifty-seven officials would be charged statewide.[48] Mabus announced for governor four days after Operation Pretense was made public. Following Mabus's announcement, former Governor Bill Waller, unsuccessful 1978 U.S. Senate candidate Maurice Dantin, incumbent Attorney General Ed Pittman, perennial gubernatorial candidate John Arthur Eaves, and former 1983 gubernatorial candidate Mike Sturdivant all joined the field. Geography, once again, was the key. While the eleven counties of northeast Mississippi were home to only the fourth largest population among the state's distinct political regions, they had historically produced the highest number of votes of all regions on Democratic primary election days. Mabus was the only candidate in 1987 who called northeast Mississippi his home. Waller and Eaves lived in Jackson, Sturdivant was a Delta businessman and farmer, while Dantin and Pittman had their roots in south Mississippi.

Among the six candidates, Mabus had the fresh face and enjoyed the support of most editors and reporters for his record of attacking government corruption. Sturdivant, on the other hand, was willing to spend $1.3 million of his own money on the campaign. The first primary result, then, was almost preordained. Mabus took half the huge northeast Mississippi vote and added to it the large share he received in the state's urban centers that were supportive of his emphasis on government corruption. Sturdivant's financial advantage moved him above the others into the runoff. In the Democratic runoff, carrying the reformer's mantle and a fresh face into voters' living rooms each evening, Mabus won all but a handful of counties. He easily coasted to a 65 percent victory, the largest runoff win in the twentieth century.[49]

The General Election

The Republican nominee for governor was Jack Reed, a well-respected businessman with roots as deep as Mabus in northeast Mississippi. Reed had grown up and managed his family's retail and manufacturing businesses in and around Tupelo. And Reed's education credentials were as strong as Mabus's—Reed had chaired William Winter's education commission in 1980 and then served as one of the first members of the newly created State Board of Education. Believing that "education is to economic development what fertilizer is to the farmer," Reed had worked successfully to maintain local support for the public school system in Tupelo when the desegregation orders were issued in the late 1960s.[50] For many voters, the choice was between a younger and older version of the same candidate. Reed once admitted that he decided to run as a Republican because "it was the only chance I had to be elected," though as he later allowed, "In my heart I'm a Democrat and in my head I'm a Republican."[51]

The election outcome conformed to a rule once articulated by GOP activist Billy Mounger—the way to get Republicans excited about an election is to make the choice stark. The Democratic candidate has to be perceived as liberal while the Republican candidate has to be perceived as conservative. That choice was not available to the voters in 1987. Mabus's focus on education and government corruption appealed to many urban voters who tended to vote Republican in federal elections, while Reed took a moderate approach to his campaign that presented voters little philosophical contrast to Mabus. Mabus turned the Cliff Finch–Jimmy Carter formula on its head, marrying black voters with Republican-leaning urban voters while adding enough traditional Democratic rural voters from his home region to win with 53.4 percent of the vote.

POSTSCRIPT

In 1972, Jerry O'Keefe Jr. was serving as a state representative from Biloxi when the legislature considered a four-lane highway program. Funding the construction was the decisive issue. When an increase in the tax on liquor became an option, it dawned on legislators from the wet Gulf Coast counties that most of the roads would be built in the rural areas of the state, almost all dry at the time. Consequently, Gulf Coast Representative Jim Simpson, who chaired the critical subcommittee, agreed to release a liquor tax bill only after the House approved a bill to legalize liquor throughout the state. On March 16, the House debated legalization, defeating it 76–38, with Newton County Representative Raymond Comans leading the opposition and imploring his colleagues: "Don't shove that beer down our throats." After the vote, O'Keefe remembered Comans approaching Simpson and asking, "Jim, you don't think us killing that bill had any effect on whether or not you're going to pass that beer tax bill out of Ways and Means do you?" Jim says, "No, Raymond, I don't believe it has any more effect than the guillotine had on Marie Antoinette." And Raymond replied, "Who?"[52]

THE CAMPAIGN TO SUCCEED
JOHN STENNIS

1988

I took care of John Stennis's politics, and he took care of my conscience.
—JIM EASTLAND[1]

John Stennis came to the U.S. Senate in 1947, winning a special election following the death of the incumbent, Theodore Bilbo. He joined Jim Eastland, who had taken the oath of office nearly five years earlier. For the next thirty-one years, Mississippi voters would leave this team undisturbed.

When he announced his retirement in late 1987, Stennis was eighty-six and was widely, though not unanimously, recognized as the "conscience of the Senate," a man who had developed an unassailable reputation for protecting the honor of the Senate and for putting the interests of the country before the parochial interests of individual states.[2] Stennis made plain his style of governing as he closed his 1947 campaign speeches: "I want to go to Washington as a free and unfettered servant of the great body of people who carry the everyday burdens of life. I want to go there with express instructions from the people to pass on all matters fairly and impartially and with a view to the public good.... I want to plow a straight furrow right on down to the end of my row."[3]

The first test came early in his career. In the same way that it is practically impossible for a reader born after 1970 to comprehend adequately the reaction of white Southerners to the decision of *Brown v. Board of Education*, it is equally difficult to convey to later generations the country's obsession with Communism in the decades following World War II. The threat of Communist espionage in America became chillingly real in 1949 when Alger Hiss, a former State Department official, was convicted of spying for the Russians. Several months before the Korean War began in June 1950, a relatively unknown Republican senator from Wisconsin, Joseph McCarthy, delivered a speech claiming to know the names of spies in the State Department. For the next four years, the name McCarthy became synonymous with protecting America by rooting out Communist agents, actual or contrived. Reveling in the power and attention he obtained, McCarthy overreached in the spring and summer of 1954 by accusing innocent civilians and members of the armed forces of ties to the Communist Party. Consequently, a number of senators sought to publicly censure McCarthy for his tactics, a move that was postponed when the Senate agreed to a compromise: three Republicans and three Democrats would be chosen to conduct an investigation of McCarthy's conduct and determine if censure was warranted. Mississippi's John Stennis was one of the three Democrats chosen for this committee.

Concluding its work in September, the panel recommended censure. After McCarthy accused the members of being "unwitting handmaidens of the Community Party," Stennis rose on the floor of the Senate and delivered a speech that presaged his reputation. He called McCarthy's attack "a continuation of the slush and slime which have been poured on other committees ... another spot on the escutcheon of the Senate, another splash and splatter." If the Senate failed to censure McCarthy, Stennis argued, "then something big and fine will have gone from this chamber, and something wrong, something representing a wrong course, will have entered and gotten itself accepted as a proper standard of conduct." The impact of the speech was summed up by one witness: "If somebody had gotten up and said, 'I move to expel McCarthy,' the whole Senate would have stood up and expelled him."[4] The Senate later approved the censure motion 67-22. McCarthy never recovered from the defeat; he fell into obscurity and died in the spring of 1957.[5] The Republicans lost control of the Senate in the 1954 elections, partly because of McCarthy's antics. With the Democrats in control for the next twenty-six years, Jim Eastland would become Judiciary Committee chairman and Stennis would become Armed Services Committee chairman.

JOHN STENNIS AND RACE

The *Brown v. Board of Education* decision was also handed down in 1954, and it was Eastland who became associated with defiance in the strongest terms imaginable. Though Stennis was never the public agitator that Eastland became, their votes against civil rights legislation were identical. As someone once characterized the reputations of the two senators: "Blacks would always laugh and say, John Stennis or Jim Eastland. . . . You go knock on Jim Eastland's door to come in at home, and he'd shut the door in your face. He'd just say, 'You ain't coming in here.' You go to knock on John Stennis's door. He'd open the door, and he would bow and be nice to you but that's as far as you go."[6]

Stennis's approach to civil rights was more complicated than Eastland's. Largely avoiding the kind of public defiance Eastland favored, Stennis opted instead for the approach adopted by his close friend J. P. Coleman: work behind the scenes, counsel patience, support the right of the states to resolve the issue, postpone the inevitable for as long as possible.[7] The challenge facing Stennis's biographer will be peeling away the layers to expose Stennis's true motivations and whether his approach was more or less noble than Eastland's. According to one influential aide, Stennis believed that "blacks should have equal rights . . . equal protection of the courts . . . equal protection of the schools." At the same time, "He was more or less a strict constructionist of the Constitution and he believed that it was not proper for the federal government to usurp state's rights. And that did not mean that he didn't think that blacks should have an equal opportunity. He simply thought that it should be accomplished in a different fashion. . . . He did say, though . . . that states left to the problem could solve it. How long he thought it would take, I don't know."[8] Stennis himself, in a 1972 interview for the Lyndon Baines Johnson Presidential Library, disclosed his own feelings when he remarked about Johnson,

> But this so-called civil rights matter evolved slowly and got to where it was almost a religion, a zeal, and lost all portion of common sense, I thought. It was kind of a fever. . . . What I really blame [LBJ] for is after he became President, it seemed to me like he used the power of the office then to a very great extreme, to the detriment of other groups. There are groups beside minority groups, there are majority groups, and it's no sin to belong to the majority.[9]

Four years later, when Jimmy Carter came to Biloxi to campaign for president, he was joined by Eastland and Stennis. After endorsing Carter, Stennis told a reporter covering the event: "I never voted for a civil rights bill in my life. . . . Let me say just one thing about this integration. I'm against it, always have been and always will be, but it's a fact. I'm not a fool. It's a fact."[10] In 1982, when Haley Barbour opposed Stennis's reelection, Stennis voted to extend the Voting Rights Act, after first supporting amendments to weaken the act, all of which failed.[11] Later in the campaign, he endorsed Robert Clark's bid to become the state's first black congressman in the twentieth century.[12] Two years later, he refused to endorse Clark a second time.[13]

Another perspective was once offered by George Reedy, one of LBJ's press secretaries, who remembered a meeting with Stennis in New York City. When they broke for lunch, Reedy recalled: "You know what the lower East Side is like at lunchtime. The streets get jammed with people flowing in from all over the place. I don't think Stennis had ever seen that before. He kept looking, his eyes getting bigger, and bigger. He finally said, 'You know, George, if I lived in a place like this, I'd be for every bit of civil rights legislation there is. I can understand why they feel that way now.'"[14] Even though their approach to service in the Senate, their work on behalf of constituents, and their involvement in local politics was so dramatically different, everyone we interviewed for this book made clear that Eastland and Stennis were close friends and supported each other without hesitation.[15] Stennis articulated his position during a 1972 rally in Biloxi for Eastland: "You know, we've got a reputation up there. If you jump on me, you've got to whip Jim, and if you jump on Jim, you've got to whip me."[16] Unknown to history is the answer to a question that no one we interviewed was able to answer: following *Brown*, did Stennis ever counsel his colleague Jim Eastland to tone down his public remarks, to be less defiant, to take a different approach?

THE LATER STENNIS

Stennis played roles in two other critical issues of his time: Vietnam and Watergate. Stennis became chairman of the Senate Armed Services Committee in 1969, and while he harbored early concerns over committing ground forces in Vietnam, once that decision was made, he became a tireless backer of the war.[17] Vietnam represents another compelling challenge for the Stennis biographer: should he have been more critical of the war, based on the inside information he obtained as chairman of the Armed Services Committee?[18]

As the Watergate crisis was mounting in the fall of 1973, President Nixon attempted to exploit Stennis's reputation for honesty. After the existence of the tapes of White House conversations became public, Special Prosecutor

Archibald Cox demanded their release. Nixon maintained that the tapes were confidential and privileged. Cox would settle for nothing less than complete disclosure. The Nixon team proposed that Stennis would listen to the tapes, compare them with typed transcripts, and authenticate the accuracy of the transcripts. The Nixon administration would then make the transcripts available to Cox.[19] Cox balked, and the plan was dropped. The fight over release of the tapes ultimately led Nixon to order Attorney General Elliot Richardson, on Saturday, October 20, 1973, to fire Cox. Richardson resigned rather than carry out the order, as did his deputy, William Ruckelshaus. Robert Bork, next in line at the Justice Department, carried out the order that night, an infamous course of events now known as the "Saturday night massacre."[20]

Robert Bork resurfaced in 1987, when President Reagan nominated him to the Supreme Court. It became the most contentious and combative confirmation process in recent history. While initially disposed to support the president's nomination, Stennis soon asked his legislative aide, Fred Slabach, to "find out everything you can find about this fellow." The more Stennis learned about Bork, the more he believed Bork should not be seated on the Court, though he kept his opinion to himself because he "was worried about doing something that a lot of Mississippians would think was wrong." Stennis surprised almost everyone when he voted against Bork, arguing that "Judge Bork's nomination has been very divisive. I am confident that a nominee can be found who will be more acceptable." Stennis was the last of the hundred senators to reveal his decision in the matter, waiting until the day of the vote to disclose his opposition. Four days earlier, he had announced his decision not to seek reelection.[21] Stennis confided to Slabach that he was afraid Bork might convince the Court to overturn prior decisions, especially related to civil rights. Stennis remarked that Mississippi had already spent too much time and too many resources on those issues. "They're settled now," Stennis said. "It's time for us to get on about other business. We fought that battle before, and we lost."[22]

THE 1988 PRESIDENTIAL CAMPAIGN

In their wildest dreams, Republicans could not have imagined a political situation better suited to produce a Republican senator from Mississippi than what evolved during 1988. It had been twenty years since a presidential campaign was conducted without a sitting president running as one of the nominees.

Ronald Reagan was leaving office in 1988, and his vice president, George H. W. Bush, was vying to succeed him.

As for the Democrats, Massachusetts governor Michael Dukakis bested eight other candidates in the Democratic primaries, including Jesse Jackson and Tennessee Senator Al Gore. Over the course of Reagan's eight years as president and the nomination by the Democrats of Walter Mondale in 1984 and Dukakis in 1988, the image of the two national parties began to solidify in the minds of Mississippi voters—Republicans were conservative and Democrats were liberal. On all of the issues that define the political culture of Mississippi, Dukakis took what was characterized as the "liberal" position. In his acceptance speech at the Republican National Convention, Bush went through the list: Dukakis supported abortion and gun control, opposed the death penalty and school prayer, and had even vetoed a bill requiring teachers to lead their students in the Pledge of Allegiance. Bush then spoke directly to the issue of taxes with his infamous line: "Read my lips. No new taxes."[23] Throughout the campaign, Dukakis was attacked for being an "ultraliberal" who was "soft on crime."[24] When Neil Bush appeared at the Neshoba County Fair, he juxtaposed his father—who believed in "basic values, in family, in patriotism"—against the quintessential depiction of a liberal in Mississippi: Dukakis was "a card-carrying member of the American Civil Liberties Union."[25]

It was in the second nationally televised debate that Dukakis's campaign collapsed and the image of Democrats as soft on crime was hardened. The first question was posed to Dukakis by then CNN anchor Bernard Shaw: "Governor, if [your wife] Kitty Dukakis were raped and murdered, would you favor an irrevocable death penalty for the killer?" In their book on the 1988 campaign, Jack Germond and Jules Witcover described the reaction: "The question came matter-of-factly, almost conversationally, but it made a whole nation suck in its breath. A whole nation, that is, except for Michael Dukakis, who without indication or surprise or dismay proceeded to answer it calmly, concisely, unemotionally. . . . 'No, I don't Bernard. . . . And I think you know I've opposed the death penalty during all of my life.'"[26] Lanny Griffith served as Bush's southern campaign coordinator in 1988, and years later explained the influence of the Bush-Dukakis campaign for Mississippi: "I mean there were issues . . . but to me it's more than that, it's a cultural thing. Dukakis represented the ACLU, the liberals, sort of arrogant, we're smarter than you, look down on you, East Coast type thing, we scoff at your values." Bush's response was, "I respect your values, I believe in traditional values, I know how important things are like hunting, fishing, and your lifestyle." Griffith called it a "cultural divide." "For me," he remarked, "as a person in politics, '88 was, I knew instinctively what was happening [and] we exploited it . . . and we reaped huge benefits. I think it's the first time we ever fully realized how potent [the cultural issues] were."[27] Bush carried Mississippi with almost 60 percent of the vote, winning all but eighteen counties.

THE 1988 SENATE CAMPAIGN

In the campaign to replace John Stennis, Republican Congressman Trent Lott faced Democratic Congressman Wayne Dowdy. William Winter had the burden of running with Walter Mondale in 1984, and Wayne Dowdy had the burden of running with Michael Dukakis in 1988. Lott perfected what had become standard Republican campaign strategy in Mississippi, asking voters if they wanted, "a senator that is going to work with and vote with Thad Cochran, pulling like a team for Mississippi or do you want one that's going to vote with and work with Ted Kennedy in the U.S. Senate?"[28] As the campaign progressed, Lott continued with that theme: "It is a Dukakis-Dowdy ticket. I think you'll see he is much closer to the national Democratic leadership and the Dukakis campaign than he would lead you to believe."[29]

While political consultant Dick Morris would become nationally famous for his role in rehabilitating Bill Clinton's presidency after Republicans took control of the House in 1994, he was already well known in Mississippi. In the wake of helping to engineer Allain's 1983 victory, Morris suffered two losses in a row: with William Winter in 1984 and with Mike Sturdivant in 1987. But Morris emerged a winner in Lott's campaign for the Senate, developing what he called the "rock and snowball" strategy. Lott produced a television ad featuring a young, partially paralyzed woman who explained how Lott had helped her obtain a wheelchair. That was the "snowball." The "rock" came when the ad informed the voters that Dowdy had opposed the legislation making the wheelchair possible. As Lott's campaign manager once explained, "the soft puffy little snowball hits you and then the rock cuts your cheek."[30]

The only real spark in the campaign came when Dowdy discovered that Lott, then serving in a House leadership post, was assigned a $50,000-a-year driver by the Capitol Police. The driver's name was George Awkward, and Dowdy began telling voters that: "Let's don't cut the money for roads in

Mississippi. Let's tell the chauffeurs like George to hit the road."[31] When Morris urged the campaign to let Awkward respond to Dowdy on television, the staff sought the approval of Awkward's supervisor—the House sergeant at arms. The sergeant at arms just happened to be a Mississippian and a friend of Lott's. Next thing Dowdy knew, the issue was turned against him when Awkward appeared in a Lott television ad, wearing a large handgun, telling viewers that he had been a detective for twenty-seven years and that Dowdy's attack "offends every law enforcement officer who puts his life on the line every day." The spot ended with Awkward looking directly into the camera: "Mr. Dowdy. I'm nobody's chauffeur. Got it?"[32]

In the end, Lott garnered 54 percent of the vote. The margin of victory came from the home congressional districts of the two candidates: Lott received almost 80,000 more votes than Dowdy in his Fifth District, while Dowdy carried his Fourth District by only 3,200 votes.[33] The Lott-Dowdy race also offered evidence that a local issue still had the power to influence a campaign in Mississippi. Virtually all of the difference between Bush's 60 percent of the vote and Lott's 54 percent can be found in the eleven northeast Mississippi counties. Bush got 61 percent of that vote while Dowdy got 59 percent. Earlier in the year, the National Aeronautics and Space Administration (NASA) had announced plans for a new rocket manufacturing facility. Two sites prominently mentioned were the Stennis Space Center in Hancock County (in Lott's congressional district) and an abandoned Tennessee Valley Authority (TVA) nuclear power site in Tishomingo County, at the northeast corner of the state. Late in the campaign, local newspapers revealed that Lott had backed the Stennis site and had even made critical comments about Tishomingo County, speculating that northeast Mississippi could not attract the kinds of high-tech jobs necessary to staff the new facility.[34] Voters retaliated on election day.

THE 1988 CONGRESSIONAL CAMPAIGNS

In the campaign to replace Wayne Dowdy in Congress representing southwest Mississippi, nine candidates vied for the Democratic nomination and six for the GOP nomination. The primary winners were Mike Parker, a Brookhaven funeral home owner, for the Democrats, and Thomas Collins, a former Vietnam prisoner of war (POW) and businessman living in a small community on the outskirts of Jackson, for the Republicans. Parker won the Democrat primary chiefly because he was the only candidate who could spend a significant amount of his own money.[35] Collins rode his status as hometown war hero to victory in the GOP's six-man race.[36] In keeping with the geographical observations we made earlier about the difficulties faced by Jackson-area candidates, Parker won the general election, getting 55 percent of the vote and carrying all the counties in his southern part of the district.

In the campaign to replace Trent Lott in his coastal district, there were six candidates in the Democratic primary and five in the Republican primary. Larkin Smith emerged as the Republican nominee and Gene Taylor as the Democratic nominee. Smith was Harrison County sheriff at the time, while Taylor was a state senator. Taking advantage of the Bush and Lott coattails, and his own law enforcement record on the Coast, Smith won with 55 percent of the vote, carrying all but one county.

MISSISSIPPI'S CONSTITUTION

In the fifty years since Governor J. P. Coleman made passage of a new constitution his signature issue during a 1957 special legislative session, there has been only one other time when the legislature came close to giving the voters a chance to rewrite Mississippi's 1890 constitution. That was during the 1988 regular session. Constitutional reform was a signature issue for Governor Mabus, as it had been for Coleman. The House killed Coleman's initiative in 1957, and the House defeated Mabus's proposal in 1988.[37] Both initiatives failed for the same reason: entrenched groups believed a convention might dilute their power.

By 1988, federal courts had effectively removed from the 1890 state constitution all of the provisions for which it was originally enacted: voting restrictions barring African Americans from exercising the franchise, reapportionment provisions ensuring a rural-dominated white legislature, and sections requiring separate schools for white and "colored" children. By 1988, rewriting the state's constitution had become, in part, symbolic: Mabus argued in a speech to the legislature that rewriting the constitution "would show the rest of the country that Mississippi is willing to tackle the tough problems."[38] In 1957, however, the courts had not yet acted. The racial inequities of the nineteenth century document were still intact. And while Coleman likewise viewed the move as symbolic, he argued that the antibusiness provisions written into the 1890 charter by populist delegates were hindering economic development: "If we expect to get industry in Mississippi, we must take out everything in this present Constitution which applies to industry and proceed to write a new one based on the economic realities of 1957. . . . It will electrify the financial and industrial centers of the Nation when it is learned that what they supposed to be the most backward state in the country has proven itself [otherwise]."[39] Coleman made it plain that he sought to protect the segregated school system by removing constitutional provisions that federal courts could use to dismantle it.[40]

Walter Sillers, Speaker of the House, led the successful movement in the House to kill Coleman's proposal, arguing that any change Coleman wanted could be accomplished by amending specific sections. The special session came within two months of the Congress passing the 1957 Civil Rights Act, and Sillers was deeply worried what a convention might do to the provisions that denied blacks the right to participate in government, arguing that all of the state's energy and resources should be directed "at the attempts by the NAACP and the federal government to wrest from the white people of Mississippi the control of state and local government."[41] This was the same Walter Sillers who had driven to Ackerman in late 1955, offering to support Coleman's legislative program in exchange for Coleman's neutrality in the campaign for Speaker that William Winter was waging against Sillers. Less than eighteen months later, Sillers set the deal aside and led the opposition to the constitutional convention.

The fear of losing power is what drove the opposition to constitutional reform in 1957, and a similar fear fueled the opposition in 1988. But the way in which the stakes had shifted over the intervening thirty-one years represents the kind of irony that makes Mississippi politics so interesting and so frustrating. In 1988, black legislators killed the referendum. A document that had its historical roots in the disfranchisement of the black voter was protected by black House members out of a concern that a convention might backtrack on the victories blacks had achieved.[42] On May 4, 1988, the House crushed the call for a constitutional convention when seventy-four representatives voted against the proposal. Of those seventy-four members, fifteen were black. Without those fifteen votes, the move to defeat the convention proposal would have failed.[43]

POSTSCRIPT

A man and his wife from Mississippi were visiting Washington, D.C., and they went in to see Jim Eastland, who was sitting behind his desk, smoking a cigar, with his feet propped up on the desk. They came in and were introduced. He never got up, never said anything, talked to them a minute or two, grumped around. They then went down to John Stennis's office. He was there, all prim and proper as he always is, with his coat on. He got up and visited with them. He then took them to the elevator, rode down the elevator with them, and introduced them to the policeman at the door. The woman said to her husband, "Boy, isn't Senator Stennis nice?" And he replied, "Yeah, he is just a fine person and just a fine individual. But you know, ole Jim, he's our kind of people."[44]

CHAPTER 14

LIQUOR AND GAMBLING IN MISSISSIPPI

1989–1990

There is not one living person in the state or in the world that
ever dreamed what was going to happen. It's just a miracle.
—CHARLIE CAPPS, **Former State Representative**[1]

Few alive in November 1989 will ever forget the live televised pictures of thousands of people literally tearing down the wall dividing East Berlin from West Berlin. Three months later, the Soviet Union collapsed. That same month, Nelson Mandela was released from a South African prison. In the meantime, Tim Berners-Lee was cooking up his own little miracle, and on November 12, he published his World Wide Web proposal. The first known Web page was written the next day.

The years 1989 and 1990 also witnessed the creation of what some have described as the "Mississippi Miracle"—the legalization of casino gaming along the Gulf Coast and the Mississippi River. By 2005, the gaming industry had an annual payroll of $1 billion for its 40,000 employees, generated more than $320 million in state and local taxes each year, had invested more than $4.4 billion in capital construction, creating in excess of 15,000 new hotel rooms, along with golf courses and entertainment venues. Per capita income over this period grew by 79 percent in Harrison County, for example, and annual tourist visits to the Coast increased to 11.5 million, up from 1.5 million in 1992.[2]

By the summer of 2005, the casinos in Harrison and Hancock counties were generating $500,000 a day in tax revenues and employing more than 14,000 workers. On August 29, Hurricane Katrina devastated the entire Coast and its booming economy. The future prospects of the "Mississippi Miracle" on the

Coast would depend on the skills of a Republican governor and a Democratic state representative.

THE PRELUDE

Historically, the two cultural issues, apart from race, used by candidates in Mississippi to define each other were liquor and gambling. For generations, indulgence in these vices was allowed in certain parts of the state, so long as neither was legal. Prohibition was the first to fall. Mississippi joined the rest of the country in 1966 when the legislature authorized the sale and consumption of liquor.

A famous 1962 article in *Life* magazine called the nation's attention to Mississippi's "most peculiar situation. . . . The last dry state in the nation collected a tax on the illegal sale of liquor." Prohibition laws were generally enforced in the eastern side of the state, but in the Delta and along the Gulf Coast particularly, liquor was readily, though illegally, available. Where it was sold illegally, though foreign to the politics of today, the proceeds were taxed by the state. The attitude of local law enforcement officials in these counties was summed up by the Harrison County Sheriff quoted in *Life*: "If I tried to enforce the liquor laws, I'd bankrupt hundreds of businesses here. I'd cut the tourist trade by half . . . [then] the citizens would run me out of town."[3]

Two events coincided to motivate the legislature to repeal prohibition. On February 2, 1966, nearly two years after he had vetoed a local option bill, Governor Paul Johnson Jr. changed his mind and urged the legislature to "bring the matter to the voters," calling the "present situation of flaunting [sic] of dry laws shameful, disgraceful, indecent and scandalous."[4] Addressing the first regular session of the Mississippi legislature since passage of the 1965 Voting Rights Act, Johnson beseeched lawmakers, "Everyone is familiar with the changes that are taking place in the voting laws in this nation. I am confident that you will agree with me as to the urgency involved, for a number of reasons, including the wisdom of solving [the prohibition question] under existing voting conditions."[5]

Two days later, Johnson got an assist from the Hinds County Sheriff's office. The Jackson Country Club was playing host to a reception following the annual Carnival Ball that night. Around 7:00 P.M., sheriff's deputies raided the party. The *Clarion-Ledger* reported the next morning that "bottles by the hundreds, including champagne and the best of French wines were found. Deputies battered in the door while hundreds of men in evening dress and ladies wrapped in fur coats stood in a hallway nearby."[6] The "Country Club" trial took place in the middle of the 1966 session. Lawyers for the club subpoenaed local officials from around the state to testify about the sale of illegal liquor. The mayor of Indianola confirmed that liquor dealers in his hometown pled guilty every two weeks and paid nominal fines. When Leland's mayor was asked, "Do you make any attempt to control consumption in private homes?" he responded, "No sir, we don't. I'm afraid I'd get caught."[7] Four days of testimony offered conclusive proof that "legally dry Mississippi was wet in reality." Even then, the legislature might not have budged. Only after the judge threatened to order strict enforcement of the prohibition ban statewide was the legislature motivated to act—approving local option for each county and putting the state into the wholesale liquor business.[8]

State government maintained a similar posture toward illegal gambling, particularly along the Gulf Coast where "honky-tonks and supper clubs lined Harrison County's Gold Coast in the 1940s and 1950s like a string of neon pearls, beckoning tourists with gambling, liquor and women. . . . Gus Stevens Drive Inn, a swank supper club on Biloxi Beach was furnished with 13 slot machines, blackjack, and dice tables, two roulette wheels and a horserace wire. The Spot had 11 slot machines." Gulf Coast Senator Tommy Gollott remembers using his school lunch money to play the nickel slots in the corner grocery store on the way to school: "A lot of us didn't eat lunch in those days, and sometimes you would win fifty cents and man, you had plenty of money."[9]

Then, in the early 1950s, U.S. Senator Estes Kefauver and his Organized Crime Committee paid a visit to the Mississippi Gulf Coast. Testimony disclosed a "conspiracy by city and county officials to not only permit illegal gambling and alcohol to flourish on the Coast, but to use profits from the operations to load up government coffers." The committee publicized a 1951 survey that found that more than 320 bars, supper clubs, and other businesses in Harrison County were dealing in gambling and liquor in violation of state law. "Once Kefauver came," observed former District Attorney Boyce Holleman, "it was never the same."[10] Apparently, some "backroom casino and slot machines" could still be found into the early 1960s, but gambling was never to make a comeback until 1987. By that time, the Mississippi Gulf Coast was a shell of its former self. The crackdown on illegal gambling, the legalization of liquor, the destruction wrought by Hurricane Camille in 1969, and the opening of Interstate 10, allowing travelers to bypass Highway 90 along the beaches, had by the late 1980s nearly destroyed the region's tourism industry.

THE BUILDUP

The idea of a "cruise to nowhere" first showed up in an economic development planning document published by the city of Biloxi in 1985.[11] Gerald Blessey, who was mayor at the time, had organized a group of local businessmen and public officials to reenergize tourism along the Coast. The Biloxi Waterfront Master Plan was the product of their work.[12] The gambling cruise concept was simple: permit a ship to dock at a port, pick up passengers, and once in federal waters, allow gambling onboard the vessel. A few hours later, the ship would return. While it was illegal to gamble on Mississippi soil or in Mississippi waters, it was lawful in federal waters, generally recognized as three miles from the shoreline.

The Florida-based *Europa Star* was the first to try a "cruise to nowhere" from the newly renovated Biloxi port. In late 1987, as it was preparing to open for business, the *Star*'s lawyers belatedly discovered the barrier islands. Mississippi's barrier islands lie ten to twelve miles south of the Coast and more or less separate the shoreline from the Gulf of Mexico, thus forming the southern boundary of the Mississippi Sound. Sailing on water in the sound was no different than lying on the sandy beach in Biloxi. Gambling in the sound was just as illegal as if on land. Immediately, the economics of the gambling cruise no longer made sense. Making the trip to a destination three miles on the south side of the barrier islands—where gambling could legally begin—could easily take several hours. For a half-day cruise, those hours were critical if the boat was going to generate a profit. Ed Pittman was attorney general at the time, and he threatened legal action to enforce the gambling prohibition in the sound. Biloxi city officials and the *Star*'s owners needed time to get to the legislature to change the law. Harrison County Judge James Thomas gave it to them, offering the intriguing opinion that enforcement of Pittman's order would hurt the company and the community, while allowing the ship to operate within the sound would hurt no one.[13]

On the heels of that ruling, Gulf Coast Representative Glenn Endris enlisted a well-known capitol lobbyist, Buddy Medlin, to help the *Europa Star* obtain legislative approval to allow gambling in the sound. On January 22, 1988, Endris and nine other Gulf Coast representatives filed the legislation. Representative Sonny Merideth chaired the subcommittee that handled all gambling bills. Endris remembers Merideth approaching him, "Glenn, you got this gambling bill introduced over here. You want a dog and pony show or you want me to just go ahead and kill 'em?" After Endris assured Merideth he was serious about passing the bills, Merideth said, "Well, hell, let's go to work."

Merideth's committee held a hearing in early February, providing a platform for *Europa Star* owners and city officials to explain how the ship was living up to the vision of the Biloxi master plan: 6,900 passengers had boarded the ship in less than two months, easily surpassing projections; occupancy rates were higher at hotels and motels; and restaurants reported increased traffic. The Reverend Nathan Barber's arguments were typical of the opposition: legalized gambling would "unleash a predator." The committee opted for the economic potential and approved the bill, as did the full House a few days later. Endris told his colleagues, "This here is my baby. . . . I represent a city down there that is dying a death." Coahoma County Representative Delma Furniss objected: "Two thousand years ago a star in the East brought good news to the world. Now there's a star in the South to bring corruption to our state." Furniss's sermon triggered this rebuke from Forrest County Representative Bill Jones: "I am sick and tired of people telling my people they are going to hell because they gamble. The time has come to quit telling us we are not going to join Jesus because we go on the boat."[14]

By the end of February, the *Europa Star* was carrying near-capacity crowds, and its long-term prospects looked promising in light of the House action. But momentum ground to a halt when the Senate Finance Committee killed Endris's House bill. Senators remained unconvinced the economic opportunities outweighed the moral costs or the potential challenge from religious leaders to their reelection prospects.[15] Several months later, Judge Thomas was left with no choice but to conform to state supreme court decisions: he ruled the sound was in fact property of Mississippi and that gambling north of the barrier islands had to cease. The *Europa Star* departed soon thereafter.[16]

THE "MIRACLE"

Rick Carter was in the restaurant business with his partner, Terry Green, when they heard about the crowds the *Europa Star* was attracting.[17] Having grown weary of the food service business, they decided to explore operating their own "cruise to nowhere" at the Port of Gulfport. William "Si" Redd was also reading about the crowds, though from his office in Las Vegas. Redd had left his Neshoba County hometown years earlier and over time had become one of the most influential figures in the gambling industry. The company he founded developed and manufactured many of the slot machines used in the industry. Long interested in helping his home state, Redd saw a chance with the early success of the *Europa Star* on the Coast. After making contact with officials in Mississippi, he was told to call Carter.[18]

Carter would eventually describe Redd as the "Godfather of gaming in Mississippi," but when Si Redd called him in 1988, he was unaware of Redd's prestige in the gaming industry.[19] Their conversation went something like this:

> Carter: *Mr. Redd, a lot of people have called wanting to help us. I want to lay all our cards on the table. Do you have enough money to supply the resources we need to finance this cruise ship?*
> Redd: *Now, Rick, I like your style, cutting to the chase. Why don't you make a few calls and check me out.*
> Carter: *Okay, I'll be back in a few days.*

Carter called his partner, Terry Green, who quickly made a few inquiries in Las Vegas. Green hurriedly called Carter back: "Man. He's about the biggest fish you could have."

Within a few minutes, Carter had Redd back on the phone: "Mr. Redd, it didn't take me long to know when I got a big fish. We'll be at your office by noon tomorrow." Redd would eventually invest more than $20 million in the *Pride of Mississippi*.

The *Pride* made its first cruise from the port of Gulfport on February 19, 1989, though Carter and company realized almost immediately the venture would lose money unless gambling could begin soon after leaving the dock.[20] So, it was back to the legislature. Rick Carter called his friend Senator Tommy Gollott. Hugh Keating, Carter's lawyer, called his former law school classmate Scott Levanway, a lobbyist in Jackson. Buddy Medlin was recruited to join the team again. After being told by Endris that the House would wait for the Senate to send them a bill this time, the group got busy in the Senate. On March 20, 1989, Gulf Coast Senators Gollott, Claude Bilbo, and Gene Taylor introduced legislation to authorize gambling on cruise ships once they had traveled

1,500 feet from the shoreline. Over the intervening year, the economic prospects on the Coast had only worsened, especially with the withdrawal of the *Europa Star*, though the *Pride* could point to a continuing demand for business and a real impact on local businesses. It also helped that local Mississippians owned the *Pride* and had a well-respected partner—Si Redd—providing the financing. Bob Montgomery chaired the Senate Finance Committee and urged passage of the legislation. After the bills were approved by his committee on Wednesday afternoon, Montgomery was approached by Sonny Merideth with this advice: "If they wanted the bills passed, they had better get the bills to him before the weekend. . . . If the bills were still in the legislative process on Sunday, we would do nothing but lose ground. . . . They would be at every church, and every place would be covered up." [21]

Montgomery got the message, bringing the legislation up for a Senate floor vote the next morning. To gain passage, however, required the use of a tactic called "the walk." Since general bills are approved by a simple majority of those senators present and voting—as opposed to a majority of the total fifty-two senators—a senator trying to pass legislation can help his or her cause by asking a fellow senator, who might otherwise be opposed to the bill, to leave the chamber during the debate. An absent senator translates into one less "yes" vote proponents have to recruit. With Montgomery and Gollott lobbying their colleagues, the bill passed 23–17, with nine senators "absent" for the vote. [22] Montgomery once explained why senators were willing to absent themselves to help pass the bill: "They knew something had to be done on the Coast, or it was going to be lights out." It wasn't that they "were opposed to [gambling] in their gut . . . but they were viewing how this was going to play back home. . . . That's the reason we got so many for favoring the walk." The successful use of the tactic failed to impress Paul Jones, the spokesperson for the Mississippi Baptist Convention: "I really am disappointed that for something like this, almost a quarter of the Senate decided to take a walk. I really think the citizens of this state deserve better." [23]

Later that day, Merideth got the legislation from the Senate, and by Friday morning he had convened his committee, which approved the bills and sent them to the full House. On Friday morning, with the Gulf Coast delegation working the floor, the House approved the bills with eighteen absent House members. [24] Interviewed later by a reporter, Paul Jones expressed dismay that the House had voted so quickly, admitting to the reporter he had thought the House vote would come after the weekend. During the debate,

Representative Furniss reminded lawmakers the vote was occurring on Good Friday.[25]

As the year went by, the *Pride of Mississippi* was joined by two other cruise boats that began operations from Biloxi. More important, though, the Iowa legislature approved gambling aboard riverboats cruising the Mississippi River, leading Natchez Senator Bob Dearing, Gollott, and others to consider something similar for Mississippi.[26] At the beginning of the 1990 legislative session, Dearing and Gollott introduced a bill to allow gambling aboard riverboats traveling along the Mississippi River. Montgomery's Finance Committee approved the bill on a Friday late in January, and together they maneuvered the measure through the full Senate on the following Friday by the slim margin of 23–21, with several senators, again, agreeing to "take a walk."[27] The bill then moved to the House and to Merideth's domain.

Confronting Merideth was a bill that would authorize gambling on riverboats along the Mississippi River, once those ships were "underway making way"—the legal term to indicate a ship was no longer docked and was traveling. Representing the Delta community of Greenville, Sonny Merideth knew more about the Mississippi River than probably anyone else in the House. Greenville was the largest city on the river and home to the state's tugboat industry. Soon after the bill passed the Senate, Merideth asked Gollott to come over for a visit. Merideth told him, "We've got to take 'underway making way' out of the bill." Gollott protested, assuming that amendment would kill the bill; removing the restriction from the bill would allow gambling on ships docked to a pier, a change that no one had dared propose. While Gollott was not opposed to the practice, he couldn't believe the Senate would approve such a drastic departure from current law. Merideth persisted: "When you are moving down the Mississippi River and you turn around in the middle of the river, you will get into Arkansas [or Louisiana] waters. The authorities there can then confiscate that vessel and put all the people in jail." The other problem, as Merideth explained, was the treacherous nature of the river itself, particularly "where it intersects at Greenville. . . . So I thought it was best to come in and tie up and gamble." Gollott had no choice but to agree. Merideth's committee removed the three words—"underway making way"—from the bill. On March 7, Merideth steered the bill through the House, gaining approval on a vote of 66–52, but not before Lauderdale County Representative Roy Dabbs protested, "Next they'll want to run a canoe down the Chickasawhay River with a slot machine on it."[28]

In the Senate, Montgomery and Gollott were fearful their colleagues would reject Merideth's changes. Time and fatigue, however, were on their side. Before taking up the riverboat legislation, Montgomery asked the Senate to concur in some House amendments to a separate bill prescribing regulations for the cruise vessels on the Gulf Coast. It was toward the end of the day, the debate took several hours, and senators were getting tired and hungry. Right after the Senate finished work on the Gulf Coast bill, Montgomery called up the river-boat measure. Before he could explain the ramifications of Merideth's amend-ment, senators eager to adjourn started shouting, "Vote, Vote, Vote." Lieutenant Governor Brad Dye was presiding. He looked at Montgomery and Gollott, and they signaled him to call for a vote. Without discussion, the Senate approved the House amendments 22–20 and sent the bill to the governor; ten senators were "absent." [29] The Senate adjourned for supper, with all but just two or three senators unaware that they had enacted legal dockside gambling along the Mississippi River.

The Gulf Coast would get dockside gaming several months later when Gov-ernor Mabus called a special session for the legislature to consider his package of education reforms. Mabus included in the agenda for the special session a comprehensive bill to establish a Gaming Commission and regulations to gov-ern the state's newest industry. With dockside gambling the law for the Missis-sippi River, legislators agreed to give the Coast the same legal standing for its cruise vessels. Lieutenant Governor Dye helped the cause in the Senate when he appointed Greenville Senator Hainon Miller to chair a special committee to draft the Gaming Commission bill. While Miller had strongly opposed the gaming legislation, few senators were as well respected as Miller. Dye wanted an opponent of gaming to draft the legislation to regulate the industry. When asked years later why the legislation allowing dockside gambling on the Coast passed so easily during the special session, Gollott said simply, "because Hainon Miller was handling it."

Even after all of the emphasis from Harrison County to use gaming as an economic development incentive, the voters there turned it down in late 1990 in the first local referendum on the issue. During a second referendum some fourteen months later, though, the voters of Harrison County did approve it.[30] The *Isle of Capri* became the first dockside barge to open for business on August 1, 1992, in Biloxi, at virtually the same location at which the *Europa Star* had boarded passengers nearly four and a half years earlier.[31] Ironically, the *Isle of Capri* got its name from the Isle of Caprice, a barrier island twelve miles off the Gulf Coast that was a popular resort during the Roaring '20s, offering "swimming for families, dancing for lovers, and a casino for gamblers." The island is no longer there, with scientists believing that natural erosion made it sink beneath the water. One local legend, however, blames its disappearance on divine intervention.[32]

HURRICANE KATRINA

By 7:00 P.M. on Monday, August 29, 2005, the eye of Hurricane Katrina was thirty miles northwest of Meridian, and the hurricane was downgraded to a tropical storm.[33] The destruction that it left south of Interstate 20 in Mississippi was unprecedented in the history of the state—"miles upon miles of utter destruction [that] is unimaginable" was how Governor Haley Barbour described it. The thirteen casinos in Harrison and Hancock counties were no different than virtually every other structure along the Coast: if not completely destroyed, they had been rendered useless. The Copa Casino barge had been lifted by the storm surge and dropped 300 yards away in a parking lot. The 100,000-square-foot Grand Casino barge ended up on Highway 90.

A week after the hurricane, casino officers met and over a period of weeks determined that in order to begin rebuilding, they needed just one change to state law; they needed authorization to rebuild the casinos on land in order to secure them against future hurricanes. On September 27, 2005, Governor Barbour called the legislature into a special session to consider a number of initiatives related to reconstruction of the ravaged areas, including legislation sought by the casino owners. The Harrison County Board of Supervisors had recommended permitting land-based casinos within a 1,500-foot limit from the water, which is what Barbour recommended to the legislature. From that point on, the future of the bill rested with the chairman of the House Gaming Committee, Lincoln County Representative Bobby Moak, a Democrat, and Governor Barbour, a Republican. While Barbour and Moak had spent 2004 and 2005 on opposite sides of virtually every major public policy issue, they concluded that the move inland was necessary to protect the thousands of jobs generated annually by the Coast's $2 billion tourism industry. Partisan differences were set aside.

When the legislature convened in September 2005, many religious leaders were lying in wait, arguing: "This battle isn't about a little land and water. It is about our children's and our grandchildren's future. . . . Money has become more important than morals. . . . We must draw a line in the sand and say to the gamblers and those who support them: you can go no farther."[34] Barbour offered a practical response: "A few hundred feet on shore is not going to affect the moral fabric of Mississippi. . . . Now, all of these people who are outspoken against onshore, all voted for me. . . . But I have to do what's right, and I don't think it's a close call."[35]

After building a consensus for the move in the House, Moak introduced the bill allowing casinos to build inland 800 feet from the water and guided its passage though the House. A key factor in the bill's approval was Speaker of the House Billy McCoy, a twenty-five-year veteran from Prentiss County who had succeeded Tim Ford in 2004. Before voting against the legislation, McCoy told the House: "All of my official public life, and all of my adult life, I've opposed gaming. But I recognize the importance of this measure to our Gulf Coast." In not using the prestige of the Speaker's office to oppose the legislation, McCoy drew this praise from Barbour: "The speaker has shown true courage and leadership and statesmanship."[36] With Moak having delivered the bill through the House, Barbour turned to the Senate, where he persuaded a majority of the senators to approve the move inland.

At the time of the 1966 prohibition vote, the geographical regions of the state most likely to ignore the liquor ban were the Mississippi River counties and the Gulf Coast. Almost forty years later, little had changed. With but few exceptions, the legislators on the western side of the state and representing the Gulf Coast counties voted with Moak and Barbour, while the legislators representing the eastern side opposed the bill. The race or party affiliation of the legislator hardly mattered.

POSTSCRIPT

Harrison County Sheriff Larkin Smith had taken the oath of office as congressman from Mississippi's Fifth District in January 1989. Eight months later, he was killed when a small private plane in which he was flying crashed near Hattiesburg. A special election was called for October 3, 1989. The candidates were Tom Anderson, Trent Lott's top aide; Mike Moore, recently elected as the state's attorney general; and Gene Taylor, who had lost to Smith in the 1988 general election. Having served in the state Senate since 1984 and having waged a competitive campaign in 1988, Taylor was the odds-on favorite. Without a popular presidential candidate to motivate Republican voters, Gene Taylor took advantage of a low turnout in the same way Wayne Dowdy did in winning his 1981 special election and in the same way Mike Espy did in his 1986 off-year election. Taylor handily bested Moore in the "primary" and defeated Anderson by almost 40,000 votes in the runoff.

CHAPTER 15

REPUBLICANS GAIN THE GOVERNOR'S MANSION

1991

Mississippi will never be last again.
—RAY MABUS, 1987

That was the slogan Mabus, the candidate, used in his 1987 campaign for governor. The campaign of 1991 would be decided largely by voters making a relatively simple determination: had Mabus, the governor, fulfilled the expectations that slogan created?

THE 1991 CAMPAIGN FOR GOVERNOR

A campaign involving an incumbent is almost always a referendum on that incumbent.[1] For a challenger to unseat an incumbent, his or her campaign will generally be successful only if the voters share a predisposition that the incumbent does not deserve reelection. It is the challenger's job simply to run a mistake-free campaign and to reinforce preexisting attitudes. As the political year unfolded, Mississippi was experiencing the pain of the national economic recession that would cost George Bush his presidency in 1992. For Mississippi, the huge revenue gains from riverboat gaming were years away. In early 1991, Mabus had to impose drastic cuts in the budget to offset sagging revenues as required by state law.[2] For an administration associated firmly with change, it was an inauspicious beginning for a reelection campaign.

The first two years of the Mabus term represented a mixed record. On the plus side were a substantial pay raise for teachers; historic and substantive reform of county personnel, purchasing, and road-building operations; and funding for the repair and renovation of state agency, community college, and university facilities. On the negative side was the failure to adopt a call for a constitutional convention. And on the mixed ledger was a watered-down state government reorganization initiative that included the closure of the state's three charity hospitals. While the $7 million hospital appropriation was used to leverage an additional $21 million from the federal government for the Medicaid program, the closure was met with near unanimous and strident opposition in the three communities that were home to the hospitals—Laurel, Meridian, and Vicksburg. Along the way, Mabus appointed a well-known black civil rights lawyer to the state College Board, the first African Americans to the Public Service Commission and the State Tax Commission, and the first woman to head the State Department of Public Safety, home of the storied Mississippi Highway Patrol.

By 1990, Mabus had decided to make education the signature issue for the remainder of his term. Leading up to the 1990 session, Mabus and his staff employed many of the same basic organizing strategies that Winter and his staff, which had included Mabus, used in 1982 to pass the Education Reform Act. By the time the legislature convened in January 1990, the Mabus education program, known as BEST—Better Education for Success Tomorrow—had been publicized throughout the state and was clearly front and center at the state capitol. BEST would reward high-performing schools with cash grants and freedom from regulations, create comprehensive adult and family literacy programs, screen all three- and four-year-olds to ensure they were prepared for kindergarten, institute pilot programs in selected schools to eliminate grade levels K–3 and group students by ability, create accountability programs to help failing schools, establish health clinics in schools to combat teenage pregnancy, provide a school construction and repair fund, and develop a comprehensive program to reduce the dropout rate.

Unlike in 1982, when Winter and the legislature had disagreements about some of the reform programs, especially public kindergartens, the 1990 legislature ended up approving most of the content of Mabus's plan. Unlike in 1982, when Winter agreed at the beginning of the special session to support any revenue measure the legislature would pass to fund the program, Mabus refused to support an increase in the sales or income tax, arguing that "the working people of Mississippi pay enough taxes."[3]

To fund BEST, Mabus proposed a state lottery. There was, however, one small obstacle to overcome. In 1990, the state constitution specifically prohibited lotteries. For state government to operate a lottery, voters would have to amend the constitution, and for an amendment to be placed before the voters, Mabus would have to obtain the support of two-thirds of the Senate and the House. That requirement proved to be an insurmountable hurdle in the Senate. In the closing days of the 1990 regular session, the legislature agreed to approve BEST with one caveat—its education reforms would expire on June 30, 1990, unless sufficient funding was provided. Everyone knew that meant a special session, which Mabus called for June 18. Mabus gave the legislature a wide range of revenue options to consider—lottery, video poker, bingo taxes, and higher fees for government services—refusing again to allow consideration of an increase in sales and income taxes. The Senate once more rejected the lottery, and Mabus stood firm in his opposition to a tax increase, arguing that it was a common practice of the legislature to use a general tax hike to pay for other government programs in the name of education. He explained that the 1982 Education Reform Act had raised more than $1 billion in taxes during its six full years of operation, while the cost of the act was just $482 million.[4] Winter was willing to take that deal in 1982; Mabus was unwilling to do so in 1990. With Mabus maintaining his opposition to general tax increases, the legislature adjourned and left town. Mabus had worked for nearly a year promoting his education reform as the answer to "our children's dreams for a better and brighter Mississippi."[5] As the summer of 1990 began to heat up—and with an election year around the corner—the entire effort had led to nothing.

The Fallout

For those in the Mabus campaign listening to the opinions of average Mississippians participating in "focus groups" during the fall of 1990, the reaction to the special session was ominous. A "focus group" is a vastly downscaled poll. Instead of calling a random sample of 600 people around the state to gauge their attitudes and preferences, a focus group puts ten to twelve carefully screened voters around a table with a moderator for an hour and a half to discuss in detail the subject at hand—in this case, Mabus's performance in office. The people interested in what the voters say are either watching the discussion through one-way glass or in an adjoining room via closed-circuit television. The findings that night mirrored those identified by the Fordice campaign months later: in the wake of the loss of BEST, voters had forgotten all of Mabus's accomplishments that had preceded the special session. Rather than giving him credit for maintaining a principled stand against taxes, even if it meant losing BEST, voters morphed the legislative loss into the view that Mabus was unable to work with the legislature, and thus had not been successful. The Republican polling consultant was reading the same numbers in his own research: the voters wanted a change; they believed the state was moving in the wrong direction. In his own focus groups, the consultant identified the reason why voters believed Mabus was incapable of working with the legislature: he was "aloof" and did not identify with or care about the needs of "average" voters.

The Republicans

Many Republican leaders believed they had the perfect challenger. In early 1989, Pete Johnson, a lifelong Democrat who had succeeded Mabus as state auditor, switched parties and joined the GOP. Johnson continued to pursue government corruption as auditor while enjoying a name widely familiar to many older Mississippians—he was a grandson of former Governor Paul Johnson and a nephew of former Governor Paul Johnson Jr. One person who felt differently was Kirk Fordice. Unlike Johnson, Fordice had been a Republican long before it was popular. Fifty-six years old at the time, he had served in party positions for years, starting with the 1964 Goldwater campaign. Consequently, he knew longtime GOP activists all over the state. Fordice owned and operated a regional construction business based in Vicksburg and had served as national chairman of his company's trade group, the Associated General Contractors (AGC). When it was unpopular, for example, for national organizations to support Haley Barbour over John Stennis in 1982, Fordice made sure the AGC contributed to Barbour's campaign.[6] It was also this experience with AGC, which required him to work with Congress on issues important to the construction industry, that led him to conclude that more businessmen needed to serve in public office. Fordice's early polling results convinced him that many voters in Mississippi thought so, too.

Well into August, the *Clarion-Ledger* was reporting that "frontrunner Pete Johnson has dusted off the Rose Garden strategy of ignoring opponents and campaigning as if he's already won the GOP nomination."[7] What most people following the primary didn't know was that Fordice was recruiting committed activists—little known outside party circles—to his cause. One in particular was Billy Powell, who informally headed a group of budding Rankin County activists. A petroleum engineer by training, Powell had moved to Mississippi in 1969 to work in the energy department at Deposit Guaranty National Bank (now AmSouth). It was there he met Billy Mounger, who one day had this conversation with Powell:

Mounger: You're an engineer?
Powell: That's right.
Mounger: You must be conservative.
Powell: I am.
Mounger: Here's a form. Fill it out. You'll be giving $10 a month to the state
  Republican Party.[8]

Powell lived in historically conservative Rankin County, and over the years helped to build a group of neighbors and friends into the nucleus of an organized Republican Party in the county. Early in 1991, Powell got a call from a friend wanting him to visit with Fordice. After several meetings, Powell and his team signed on. They never heard from Pete Johnson. They got to work organizing the county for Fordice and decided to link Fordice's campaign with a young Republican candidate they were supporting for state representative—Phil Bryant. It was not long before the Fordice campaign asked Powell to take responsibility for Hinds and Madison counties—all of metro Jackson—as well. As Fordice would later remember it, "These guys had this entire countywide election command system built around Powell's kitchen table. And if you weren't in their plan, you weren't going to carry Rankin County."

After surprising most political observers by leading Johnson in a three-man primary election, Fordice won the Republican nomination, earning 31,753 votes to Johnson's 20,622 in an early October runoff. Fordice carried Rankin County with 68 percent of the vote and the Hinds/Rankin/Madison region with 64 percent. While he was skeptical of the party leaders who had recruited Johnson over a lifelong Republican, Fordice enjoyed their support in the general election, and the party united around a surprise candidate who looked able to deliver the Governor's Mansion for the first time in the century.

The Democrats

For Mabus, the Democratic primary was payback time from a variety of Democrats: county officials who had long resented Mabus's attacks, party officials who remained angry with Mabus for a failed 1988 attempt to unilaterally impose his own choice for party chair, and former Democratic officeholders who felt slighted by Mabus, most notably former Governor Bill Waller. As one reporter observed, "It dawned on state politicos that, just as important to Mabus as the actual taking on of 'deeply entrenched interests,' were statements that he was doing so. . . . In these dismissive phrases he was consigning his opponents to moral oblivion."⁹ Wayne Dowdy—former congressman from the southwest corner of the state and unsuccessful candidate against Trent Lott in 1988—became their candidate.

Dowdy announced in May 1991 with what would become common refrains: "Elected officials spend too much time attacking one another. I would be able to build a consensus with people in the Legislature. . . . We need to heal and bridge gaps in Mississippi, not pour salt on wounds. . . . Nothing has been accomplished to provide better schools. We want the voters of Mississippi to decide if they want four more years of feuding and fighting."¹⁰ In an artful turn of phrase, Dowdy converted Mabus's "never be last again" slogan into "Mississippi will never be lost again," exclaiming, "People get lost when they don't have strong leadership."¹¹

For the four months of the primary campaign, Mabus was forced to spend a significant amount of money, time, and energy to defend his record and his character, while undercutting Dowdy's appeal by criticizing his record in Congress. The attacks against Mabus left him a wounded candidate for the general election. The attacks Mabus made against Dowdy left many Democrats who had supported Dowdy unwilling to return to Mabus in the general election.

MABUS VERSUS FORDICE

The math confronting a Democrat running statewide in the early 1990s was this: on election day, assume 25 percent of the voters are African American and assume the Democrat gets 90 percent of that vote. A Democrat wins if he or she gets 38 percent of the white vote. The Mabus campaign knew it would split the urban/suburban white vote with Fordice: keeping voters along the Coast and in DeSoto County—where voters supported his reform agenda—but ceding those voters in areas that had become strongly Republican in recent years—suburban Rankin and Madison counties near the state capital, and the shifting populations around the medium-sized cities of Hattiesburg, Columbus, Meridian, and Laurel. That analysis left the rural white vote as the key demographic group that would determine the outcome of the election. The "bad news" for the Mabus campaign was that rural whites, especially in northeast Mississippi, but in other areas in southwest and east Mississippi as well, send their children to public schools, which in many cases served as anchors for their communities. It was in these areas where hopes had been high for BEST. At the same time, these voters are more culturally conservative, a trait Fordice would exploit in the campaign. The "good news" was that they had been more resistant to the overtures of the Republican Party than their urban/suburban counterparts.

By the time the general election kicked off, Fordice enjoyed the momentum that came with handily winning a primary campaign he was expected to lose, while Mabus was bloodied after an expensive and antagonistic primary he was not expected to have to run. The Mabus campaign concluded the only winning strategy was to make Fordice more unappealing than Mabus. On the other hand, the Fordice campaign had but one goal: keep the focus on Mabus and lend credence to the negative attitudes voters already embraced about the incumbent. The Mabus campaign went on the offensive, publicizing nearly every unfavorable piece of information about Fordice it could locate. In the meantime, the Fordice campaign was conducting its own polling and discovered the same general feeling expressed by the Mabus focus group participants—"he hasn't really accomplished all that much." That expression ultimately found its way into Fordice's most effective television commercial: a middle-age white man, dressed informally, in an outdoor setting, looking into the camera, talking about the campaign, ending with, "Well our Governor he's tried, but he's not accomplished much." It was a variant of the "rock and snowball" strategy Trent Lott had used in 1988. The "snowball" was the nice comment the man said about Mabus; the "rock" came with the ending—"the soft puffy little snowball hits you, and then the rock cuts your cheek."

Fordice reached out to the culturally conservative rural white vote in a number of ways. He claimed that "Ray Mabus [was] a devotee of Teddy Kennedy, the Kennedy dynasty, the Eastern liberal establishment. He was a strong supporter of fellow Harvard grad Michael Dukakis for president in 1988."[12] Fordice's campaign linked up with churches that had opposed the lottery and other gambling initiatives—Fordice liked to say that "hooking the education system to gambling is not a morally enhancing thing to do"[13]—and with right-to-life groups that had vowed to defeat Mabus after he had vetoed bills requiring the licensing of abortion clinics and a twenty-four-hour waiting period in advance of an abortion.[14] Toward the end of the campaign, Fordice aired a television commercial promoting "welfare reform" that contrasted white construction workers and a black mother and daughter shopping together with a young, forlorn-looking black woman holding her baby. The narrator ended with: "Welfare keeps people down. Workfare builds them up."[15]

By the last weekend, the polls being conducted by both the Mabus and Fordice campaigns showed the same trend: the race was getting tighter. For the campaign staffers who were privy to this information, one question worried—or thrilled—all of them over the weekend: was the trend unstoppable? There are certain bellwether precincts that can be used to predict a statewide election outcome. The Democrats use key precincts in the black community to determine if turnout is up to historical levels. The Republicans use key precincts in suburban white areas to do the same. Both campaigns identify boxes in rural white areas to determine who will win. We were getting those results called into our respective campaign offices on election night. It wasn't until we began writing this book that we learned each of us was engaged in the same precinct targeting process on election night. As we received the results from the key precincts in rural Mississippi, we both realized early in the evening that Fordice had won the race.

Fordice ended up with 50.8 percent of the vote. A shift in 11,521 votes to Mabus—or less than 2 percent of the 711,212 votes cast—would have given the election to Mabus. There's a rule of thumb employed in political analysis: the closer an election, the more difficult and contentious the analysis. When a candidate loses by a small percentage, as did Mabus, pundits are prone to say, "Well, if he had just done 'x', then he would have won." On the other hand, a defeat by a large margin usually results in something like, "Well, the voters were just ready for a change." In light of the narrow margin of the Mabus/Fordice election, analysts have been filing in the blank "x" with a variety of reasons ever since.

We examined the geographical/political regions of the state that Mabus won in 1987 but lost in 1991. Of the ten commonly recognized regions, only two changed sides in the 1991 election: the eleven counties that define northeast Mississippi and the fourteen counties that define southwest Mississippi. In both elections, Mabus carried northwest Mississippi, central Mississippi, the Delta, Hinds County, and the Gulf Coast; in both elections, he lost east Mississippi, southeast Mississippi, and the six large suburban counties.

Northeast Mississippi has the highest concentration of rural whites and is arguably the region where public schools have long enjoyed their strongest overall support. Mabus carried it by 1,991 votes in 1987, despite having a GOP challenger from the same region. Mabus lost it in 1991 by 4,176 votes. Southwest Mississippi is home to the congressional district that Wayne Dowdy represented for seven years. In 1987, Mabus carried it by 12,916 votes. Four years later, he lost it by 3,562 votes, a shift of almost 16,500 votes. The most revealing statistic about the rural white vote was not available until a year later, when the legislature finally sent the voters a constitutional amendment to remove the prohibition on lotteries. While the initiative passed with 53 percent, the bulk of that vote came from the river and Coast counties. The strongest opposition came from northeast Mississippi, where more than 60 percent voted against the amendment. In the thirty-five counties that opposed the lottery, Mabus lost their vote in 1987 by a combined 2,785. In 1991, his margin of loss was 44,591.

Over the years, another reason has been given for Mabus's defeat: the failure of black voters to aid the Democratic incumbent with the enthusiasm they showed in 1987. Twelve counties in Mississippi are home to a black voting-age population greater than 60 percent. Mabus won those counties in 1987 by a margin of 15,534. Four years later, his margin of victory was 16,238.[16] In the presidential campaign a year later, with its much higher turnout, Bill Clinton was able to generate a margin of only 18,286 votes in these counties. In the 1995 gubernatorial election, in which the Democratic nominee Dick Molpus spent more than $500,000 specifically devoted to increasing black voter turnout, his winning margin in these twelve counties was 16,351. While Ray Mabus had political problems in 1991, his problems were not with black voters.

In the end, the 1991 campaign was not a referendum on the ideology of the Republican Party; it was a referendum on Ray Mabus. Fordice's polling consultant said as much after the election: "Kirk Fordice had won because he was not Ray Mabus."[17] The challenge for Fordice was to take the opportunity and convert it into permanent GOP gains.

THE AFTERMATH

Reapportionment—the decennial legislative nightmare—revisited Mississippi in 1991. Unable to realign their district lines in a timely manner, legislators were forced to stand for election in back-to-back campaigns—during the regularly scheduled elections in 1991 and then in special elections in 1992.

During the 1992 session—sandwiched between these two elections—the issue of funding education returned, provoking Governor Fordice's first clash with the legislature. As the session progressed, it became clear that the national recession was continuing to take its toll on the state treasury, eating dramatically into funds available for all functions of state government, including education. Toward the end of the session, the legislature responded by enacting a one-cent increase in the state's sales tax—from 6 percent to today's rate of 7 percent. Fordice vetoed the measure, explaining that "Mississippians don't want more state money pumped into public schools because they're displeased with the product being turned out."[18]

With just a few months before the special legislative election, the House overrode the veto 82–37. The margin in the Senate was even more lopsided: 40–8.[19] Republicans in both houses supported the move to raise taxes. Lee County GOP Senator Roger Wicker spoke for many when he explained: "I intend to support the governor when I can. But each of us answers to the local districts we represent. My sense was that there was such widespread support for education back home that a vote to override was called for." BEST was never mentioned in the debate.

SONNY MERIDETH

A House colleague approached Sonny Merideth one day: "Sonny, I heard you told Homer Smith that I was a son of a bitch." Sonny looked at him and said, "I don't know where you got that information. That is not the truth. I don't know how he found it out."[20]

After thirty-one years in the legislature, Sonny Merideth retired at the end of 1991. In the legislative battles profiled in this book, Merideth was in the middle of all of them—funding the 1982 Education Reform Act and the 1987 Highway Bill, drafting the 1984 reorganization legislation in response to Bill Allain's lawsuit, and helping to maneuver to passage the bill that established dockside gaming. One of his colleagues once said of Merideth, "His mind was about three weeks ahead of everybody else."[21]

When the largest public employee strike in the state's history took place during the 1985 legislative session, Merideth once again played a pivotal role. The issue was teacher pay. On January 18, 1985, more than 10,000 teachers marched on the state capitol. A month later, the Mississippi Association of Educators voted to authorize strikes. By the middle of March, the strike had reached fifty-seven school districts: 9,260 teachers had walked off the job, affecting more than 170,000 students. Soon thereafter, the legislature approved a three-year $4,400 raise for teachers, but not without a measure of retribution drafted by Merideth. The pay bill included a provision that outlawed any strike or work stoppage by any public employee, with harsh criminal sanctions for anyone violating the law.[22]

Merideth was one of those few legislators with whom one might regularly disagree, but could never afford to ignore. His recipe for legislative success is rarely used these days:

If you've got your facts and that led you to a conclusion, then you factor in the political process.... You don't factor in political factors until you've reached a decision on facts. Put on blinders, go out there and get a decision, here's what the facts show. Then you start to factor in the political considerations ... It was unusual for a constituent to write or call. I had people say, "I'm sorry you voted for that bill or I was against that bill." ... They pretty well knew if it was a serious matter I'd thought it out and made a decision I thought best. I've had people tell me, "I disagreed with what you did but I think you felt like you were doing it for the right reasons." ... I guess I was there long enough till they felt there's no point in talking to the crazy bastard, you can't change his mind."[23]

POSTSCRIPT

In 1993, with Fordice's blessing, Billy Powell was elected chairman of the Republican Party in Mississippi. In 1996, when then Democratic State Auditor Steve Patterson resigned, Governor Fordice had an opportunity to appoint a successor for the remaining term of this statewide position. He looked no further than Rankin County and a young state representative named Phil Bryant.

In July 2004, Wayne Dowdy was elected chair of the state Democratic Party. In an interview a year later with the *Clarion-Ledger*, Dowdy admitted, "I do regret running for governor in 1991. Ray Mabus had some good achievements as governor, and frankly, I think that our spirited primary contributed to his loss for re-election. I do regret that."[24]

CHAPTER 16

THE POLITICS OF REAPPORTIONMENT

1992–1993

There are occasions when loyalty, integrity and friendship go by the boards.
One of those occasions is legislative redistricting.
—THOMAS B. EDSALL, **Washington Post**[1]

The 1990s represented another decade, another census, and another reapportionment in Mississippi. This latest round of district boundary realignment would prove to be the most contentious since Judge W. T. Horton's 1962 order. Compounding the ever-present desire for self-preservation among incumbents was aggravation caused by two unrelated imperatives.

First, black leaders decided to push for dramatic increases in their numbers in the legislature. At the conclusion of the 1991 session, the 122-member House had twenty African Americans while the fifty-two-member Senate had only two, constituting 13 percent of the legislature in a state where 36 percent of its constituents were black. Those numbers were unacceptable to the black leadership.

Second, the struggle to redraw district lines became intertwined with a simmering leadership conflict in the House. Those supporting Speaker Tim Ford and those wanting his removal adopted rival reapportionment plans, both designed to emasculate the districts of their political opponents. By 1991, many of the reformers who had supported Ford in 1987 and 1988 had switched sides to oppose him. In this chapter, we examine why that happened and how it affected reapportionment. It is a reminder that the quest for power oftentimes trumps ideology, friendship, and political constituencies.

HOUSE LEADERSHIP

Almost as soon as Tim Ford became Speaker in January 1988, he came to the stark realization that his coalition was composed of competing factions with different approaches to the conduct of business in the House.[2] The Gang of 26 and their followers believed strongly that Ford should disperse the power and involve more members in the management of the House. Many of the late-comers to the coalition, having been appointed by Ford to chair key commit-tees, saw the need to consolidate power to facilitate the passage of legislation. Almost all of the representatives who had supported Ed Perry's abortive cam-paign for Speaker against Ford were out of power, and many of them decided to test the mettle of these newly elected "reform" leaders by generally creat-ing havoc. One representative summed up the challenge facing Ford when he referred to Ford's coalition as "revolutionaries without governing skills."

The result was a relentless contest for control of the House. For two years, the power struggles dominated much of the House business until a group who had supported Buddie Newman in 1987, led by Representatives John Pennebaker and Billy McCoy, approached Ford and offered to work with him to build a governing coalition. The new alliance went public on January 5, 1990. In a move to restore some of the power stripped from the Speaker in 1987, Ford and his new supporters sought to amend the rules. The vote was 71–49 in their favor, but they needed seventy-two to win.[3] Of the twenty-three members of the Gang of 26 still in the House, only two switched sides to vote with Ford. On the other hand, of the twenty-seven representatives who opposed the 1987 changes and who were still in the House, twenty-five voted with Ford. While Representatives Eric Clark, Cecil Simmons, and others hailed the vote to retain the rules as a "victory for democracy," they also recognized that Ford had assembled a strong governing majority. He was now in control.[4] Simmons and others concluded that retaliation was in order for Ford's betrayal on the rules. They would search for a new Speaker. Their candidate of choice: Ed Perry.

Ford and his new coalition saw reapportionment as the means to consoli-date their power by protecting the districts of their supporters and rearrang-ing lines so as to make it tougher for their opponents to win reelection. In one of Ford's plans, for example, Natchez Representative Barney Schoby, an African American who opposed Ford, discovered that changes to his district would "give [him] the largest white vote in the county," diluting the district's 63 percent voting-age black population to 43 percent.[5] Into this internecine power struggle came the Legislative Black Caucus and its desire to expand dramatically the number of districts from which black representatives could get elected.

LEGISLATIVE BLACK REPRESENTATION

By 1992, the use of "impact districts" to maintain Democratic control—as advanced by former Representative Tommy Campbell and others during the early 1980s—had lost all traction among black leaders. Undermining the strategy of "impact districts" were white Democrats themselves, specifically those who represented districts with substantial black populations, but many of whom had spent the previous ten years voting against legislation beneficial to their black constituents. African American leaders concluded that a black Democrat was more reliable on votes of importance to their constituents than a white Democrat, even if creating a larger share of majority black districts would also yield a larger number of districts with fewer black voters.[6]

During the early stages of reapportionment, Canton Representative Ed Blackmon emerged as the spokesperson for the Legislative Black Caucus. He was once asked if creating majority black and majority white districts would not lead to "racially polarized voting," whereas "a truly integrated society [would] have blacks being elected by whites and whites being elected by blacks." His answer is filled with frustration:

> That's political utopia, but it doesn't exist. What is the alternative? Do we wait for the good will of white citizens and politicians to come around, or do we try to maximize our influence and see how that works? I think the latter is something we need to do since we (blacks) have waited 400 years for the other system to come around and work. I don't see waiting another 100 years to see if . . . men and women of goodwill will come forward and see things not in terms of color but in terms of merit.[7]

The die was cast. Legislators would be forced to confront three major issues at once: first, applying the one-person, one-vote reapportionment rule in counties such as DeSoto, Rankin, and Madison and along the Gulf Coast, where growth had left legislative districts severely overpopulated in terms of the one-person, one-vote principle; second, responding to the demands to create additional majority black districts; and, third, resolving the contest between competing leadership factions in the House.

The Tim Ford faction drafted its version of the reapportionment plan for the House while his opponents, led by Representative Cecil Simmons, Adams County Representative Ayres Haxton, Lincoln County Representative Bobby Moak, Tallahatchie County Representative Tommy Reynolds, and Blackmon, drafted their own, which became known as the "alternative" plan. The showdown—"pure, unadulterated, hardball politics"—occurred on April 27, 1991, when both plans were debated in the House.[8] While each faction's proposal sought to undermine the ability of its opponents to get reelected, the "alternative" plan dramatically increased the number of districts from which blacks would have a greater chance of getting elected. On the eve of the vote, both sides were predicting the outcome to be close. The Ford team prevailed 64–58, holding together its governing coalition forged from the 1990 rules challenge. All twenty black representatives voted against the Ford plan.[9] Of the twenty-two members of the Gang of 26 still in the House, twenty-one voted against the Ford plan.

In the end, political realities had made it impossible for the white incumbents allied with Ford and the white incumbents in control of the Senate—where only two blacks were members—to threaten the reelection prospects of their colleagues by maximizing the number of majority black districts. Both the House plan and the Senate plan, which was adopted on the same day, failed to meet the demands of black leaders.

While Haxton and Blackmon went to Washington to brief Justice Department officials on the "alternative" plan, civil rights activists began an all too familiar journey to federal court, asking a three-judge panel to overturn the legislature's reapportionment blueprint on the grounds that it diluted black voting strength. "It's the politics of race," lamented Carroll Rhodes, the Copiah County lawyer who filed the suit.[10] Acting pursuant to the preclearance provisions of the Voting Rights Act, the Justice Department refused to approve the reapportionment plans, making a determination that it "would appear that the legislature avoided the creation of a significant number of compact districts in which black citizens could elect candidates of their choice."[11] One other reason was given for the denial. The Justice Department staff learned that during the debate on the House floor, the "alternative" plan was repeatedly referred to as the "Black Caucus Plan"; in private, some legislators had lobbied against it by labeling it as "the nigger plan"; and a representative had commented in one meeting that if the "alternative" plan "gets passed, we're either going to have to move to Arizona or learn to eat watermelon."[12]

Once the Justice Department refused to preclear the legislature's plan, everyone realized that more black districts were about to be a political reality in Mississippi. There was still, however, one unresolved issue: who would wield power in the House? As one reporter observed: "Opponents of Speaker Tim Ford now have a chance to protect districts of white members who voted against the speaker in House factional fighting. In effect, it transfers a power struggle in the legislature into the court and is crucial if Ford and his conservative backers are to have a chance at holding a majority in the House. Much of the fight now is over strengthening or weakening whites involved in a power struggle over the rule of Ford."[13] Or as Tishomingo County Representative Bill Wheeler, a supporter of the "alternative" plan, declared: "It's a question of who gets sacrificed."[14]

By the time the federal judges had scheduled a hearing on Monday, July 29, more than eleven different plans for redistricting the Senate and the House had been submitted. The legislature had deteriorated into a number of different factions, and the court heard from them all.[15] Over the weekend before the hearing, though, there was a major new development. Haxton remembers that on Sunday night, Blackmon came into the room where the Ford opponents met to develop their strategies and announced, "I've got to tell you guys something. I've made a deal with Tim [Ford]." In the twin hopes of gaining Justice Department approval and maintaining its power, the Ford group had joined forces with Blackmon. In return for increasing the number of majority black districts, Blackmon would support Ford in his bid for reelection as Speaker.

Blackmon was unrepentant: "You've got to decide which set of good ol' boys you're going to line up behind."[16] Or as he told another reporter: "I have to be focused. I can't be emotional about this." The Speaker's fight, he said, was the whites' affair. His business was to maximize black representation.[17] Wheeler, however, described the impact of Ford's plan on the white districts of his group: "It looked like we would be destroyed. [The Ford plan] would have eliminated 15 of the 38 progressive whites." Blackmon's move also split the Black Caucus, with Natchez representative Barney Schoby bitterly complaining that Blackmon had abandoned an alliance with progressive whites to join with "the speaker's forces, who had formerly called our plan the 'nigger plan.'" Blackmon readily agreed that "they [in the conservative faction] are [racist], there is no question about it," but, he argued, the decision was made on a gamble that it would best serve the interests of blacks in Mississippi.[18]

Black and white legislators, in the House and the Senate, were stunned. But even the striking of the new deal did not resolve the issue. A substantial number of black representatives refused to join Blackmon, and a substantial number of white senators refused to approve a compromise plan increasing the number of majority black districts in the Senate.[19] The timing presented one additional problem: 1991 was an election year, and with the date for the elections getting closer and closer, and with no prospect in sight for any compromise within the legislature, the federal court punted: "[With] the troubling political winds that have unfailingly roared through the courtroom at every turn of this litigation . . . it became apparent at the hearings that [the failure to settle the dispute] was, among other things, part of the ongoing contest for Speaker of the House—a pure political controversy, that can be given no consideration by this court." The judges ordered legislative elections to be held in the old districts.[20]

For the remainder of 1991, the campaign for Speaker would consume the House. Four years after Cecil Simmons and other members of the Gang of 26 had helped to engineer Ford's election as Speaker over Ed Perry, Simmons and his followers found themselves campaigning on behalf of Perry against Ford. With Blackmon's defection, however, the race was all but over. And if black representatives recruited by Blackmon needed another reason to join Ford's team, Ford gave it to them when he chose Holmes County Representative Robert Clark to stand with him as Speaker Pro Tempore.

Toward the end of December, Perry got within two to five votes of winning, depending on who was counting. But everyone agreed he lacked a majority. Several of his supporters wanted a recorded vote. For his part, Perry released those who had committed to him so they would not have to take a public stand against an incumbent Speaker. When the legislature convened on January 7, 1992 the first order of business was election of Speaker. Not since Walter Sillers defeated William Winter in 1956 had House members publicly recorded their choice for Speaker. The vote was eighty-five for Ford and thirty-five for Perry. By this time, the Gang of 26 was divided. Of the nineteen members still in the House, nine voted with Ford and ten stayed with Perry. The black members in the House also split, nine voting for Ford and eleven with Perry. The Republicans likewise divided their vote—eighteen went with Ford while five voted for Perry.[21]

Unlike the reaction of Buddie Newman in 1984, when his opponents were relegated to insignificant House roles, Ford gave key committee assignments to some of Perry's supporters and recruited others to help him draw new district lines. Within five weeks, the House leadership had a plan acceptable to most members that dramatically increased the number of majority black districts. The full House approved the plan 102–16.[22] The Senate likewise adopted new districts that met the demands of the civil rights lawyers. After the Justice Department precleared the new districts, the only business left for the federal judges was to order special elections to be held in the new districts to coincide with the 1992 federal elections.[23] After election day in 1992, the number of black legislators increased from twenty-two to forty, while the number of Republicans grew from twenty-six to thirty-five.

Finally, after four years, Ford was in firm control of the House, enjoying support from almost all its members. As Ford was consolidating his power in the House, newly elected Lieutenant Governor Eddie Briggs was working in the Senate on an issue that would further, if unintentionally, strengthen the power of the House Speaker. Briggs had defeated three-term incumbent Brad Dye in the 1991 elections, making many of the same charges about the unilateral power exercised by the lieutenant governor in presiding over the state Senate that the Gang of 26 had made against Buddie Newman. Briggs's proposed solution, and a primary campaign plank during his 1991 run against Dye, was similar to that of the House reformers—limit the lieutenant governor to two terms. Briggs persuaded the legislature to send the voters a constitutional amendment to do just that, and during the November 1992 elections, the voters overwhelmingly approved the change.

Less than two months later, on January 28, 1993, supporters of Tim Ford led the House to a 76–43 vote to remove the two-term limit imposed on the Speaker by the 1987 rule reforms.[24] The constitution now restricted the governor and the lieutenant governor to two four-year terms. The Speaker could now serve indefinitely. Walter Sillers would be proud.

Toward the end of the 1999 legislative session, after thirty-two years of service in the House, Ed Perry announced his retirement. As he was packing up his belongings, Ford came by and asked, "What you gonna do when you get home? How would you like to be Clerk?"—as in Clerk of the House, the senior House staff person. Even though the full House elects the Clerk, it is a ratification of the Speaker's recommendation. On January 4, 2000, Perry was nominated and elected to the post by acclamation.[25]

THE 1992 CAMPAIGN

A governor from Mississippi's neighboring state was elected president in 1992, defeating the incumbent George H. W. Bush. Yet Mississippi gave Bush his best vote of the campaign, while Bill Clinton collected fewer votes across the state than Jimmy Carter received twelve years earlier. For federal elections, at least, the shift in rural white voters had matured; even a southern governor could not overcome the ideological positions of his national party. Northeast Mississippi gave Bush 50 percent to Clinton's 40 percent, while the eastern part of the state gave Bush 58 percent to 35 percent for Clinton. The cultural issues dividing Democrats from Republicans were given a boost in favor of the GOP when the legislature placed on the November ballot a constitutional amendment to authorize a state lottery, prompting a campaign against it by organized religious groups.[26]

Lanny Griffith worked at the Bush White House and once offered this explanation for what happened in 1992:

> I worked with [Bill Clinton] a lot when he was governor. I went to the White House to get away from politics. I wanted something different. My instructions were to work with all the governors, Republicans and Democrat. . . . I ended up working with a bunch of Democrats and among those was Bill Clinton. . . . Just in terms of raw political ability, he's the best of a generation and we'll never see any better, he's the best I'll ever encounter in my lifetime. . . . When he ran, a lot of people were saying a womanizing, dope smoking draft dodger is not going to be hard to beat. I said "Oh no, you're wrong. You've got your hands full." And part of it was . . . that he was a really gifted politician, second is he was from Arkansas, not from Massachusetts, and third is he did understand the issues, he understood what was going on, he understood what we were doing to win and he was going to change that.[27]

CONGRESSIONAL REAPPORTIONMENT

Population shifts from 1980 to 1990 also forced the legislature to realign the state's congressional district boundaries. The Second District, commonly referred to as the "Delta district," had lost more than 40,000 people over the decade. The issue confronting legislators was: should more black voters be added to the Delta district to ensure the election prospects of a black candidate, or should the adjoining congressional districts, especially the Fourth, then occupied by Democrat Mike Parker, and the Third, then occupied by Democrat Sonny Montgomery, retain those black voters and their influence that would otherwise be transferred into the Second District? The incumbent Delta congressman, Mike Espy, supported the impact theory and argued for retaining black voters in the other districts, since he could maintain his reelection with a district that had a black population of 58 percent.[28] While they agreed that Espy could most likely win reelection, other black leaders were worried about the day when Espy would not be a candidate. Consequently, they advocated adding black voters to the district to increase the black population to 65–67 percent.[29] In the end, the legislature compromised, drawing the district lines so that the black population for the Delta district was 63 percent.[30]

Mike Espy went on to win his 1992 reelection campaign handily that November. Then, on Christmas Eve, newly elected president Bill Clinton nominated Espy as the first African American secretary of agriculture in the nation's history. At once, the concerns of the black leadership about congressional politics after Mike Espy were made real.

THE 1993 CONGRESSIONAL CAMPAIGN

After the adoption of the new Delta district, most political activists in Mississippi thought only in terms of the overall black population, which had increased from 58 percent to 63 percent. Most failed to notice—or care— where black voters actually lived within the district. When a special election was called for 1993 to replace Espy, one who knew and understood was Hinds County Supervisor Bennie Thompson.

After living through the civil rights movement and graduating from Tougaloo College in 1968, Thompson immersed himself in the day-to-day task of registering voters in his hometown of Bolton. During the municipal elections of 1969, he campaigned successfully for a position on the Bolton Board of Alderman. When the white mayor refused to certify the results, Thompson asked Frank Parker for help. One lawsuit and a few weeks later, a federal judge upheld Thompson's election. Later, the local all-white draft board notified Thompson he was going to Vietnam. Frank Parker was called again. Finally, the Madison County School District where Thompson was a teacher notified him that his contract would not be renewed. Frank Parker was called for the third time.

For four years, the white mayor of Bolton opposed every Thompson initiative, so in 1973, Thompson ran for mayor and won. Six years later, he was elected to the Hinds County Board of Supervisors. Along the way, he helped to form the Association of Black Mayors, the Association of Black Supervisors, and the Mississippi Institute for Small Towns. From time to time, Thompson showed up as a plaintiff in civil rights cases. Aaron Henry, the longtime head of the state NAACP, once said of Thompson, "It's like good cop, bad cop. Bennie's the bad cop. He's rough and tumble and brusque." [31]

Thompson knew that counties in the southern part of the district where he lived and worked—the counties not normally considered "Delta" counties— were rich in votes. There are no party primaries in special elections in Mississippi. All candidates run in an initial election, and unless a candidate wins a majority, there is a runoff between the top two vote-getters. By the March 30 "primary," the Republicans had coalesced behind Yazoo City native and Fordice aide Hayes Dent. [32] The Democrats failed to achieve that kind of party unity—seven Democrats joined Dent in the special election, including Thompson and Mike Espy's brother, Clarksdale Mayor Henry Espy.

Those who had not looked at the demographics of the district believed it was a foregone conclusion that Henry Espy was the heir apparent. Taking advantage of his brother's new national notoriety, Henry Espy liked to point out that the Agriculture Department controlled many of the programs important to the Delta: "Access is a tool. Let him who has the tools use them." [33] Thompson took a different approach, telling voters that he would represent "those who do not have a traditional voice. . . . I'm an activist. I want to make things happen. You must get people to start talking and you don't do that by holding your peace. I don't believe in the status quo." [34] As the election drew near, Henry Espy made a mistake that cost him. At a candidate's forum in Greenwood, Espy said he would consider repealing key provisions of the 1965 Voting Rights Act, apparently trying to broaden his appeal to white voters. [35] For the remainder of the election, however, those comments found their way into radio commercials and printed handouts, courtesy of the Thompson campaign.

On election day, party and geography determined the outcome. Dent was the only Republican in the field of eight, and Thompson was the only candidate from the southern part of the district. Dent led the field with 34 percent of the vote; Thompson came in second with 28 percent; Espy trailed with 20 percent. Thompson got 14,715 votes from the five counties in the southern part of the district—Hinds, Jefferson, Claiborne, Warren, and Madison—compared to 4,608 for Espy. In the nineteen counties in the northern part of the district, in what is commonly thought of as the Delta, Thompson managed to stay close, getting 14,326 votes to 16,192 for Espy. The runoff between Dent and Thompson was over before it began. Thompson won with 55 percent, focusing almost exclusively on maximizing the black voter turnout. In Hinds County alone, Thompson got 12,817 votes to 1,735 for Dent.

POSTSCRIPT

Shortly after winning reelection in 1992, Mike Espy, knowing he was rotating off the House Budget Committee, decided to try for a seat on the House Appropriations Committee then chaired by Mississippi's own Jamie Whitten. Congressmen wanting to serve on the Appropriations Committee have to campaign among their fellow Democrats for election to the committee, though having the support of the chairman would be invaluable. So Espy paid a visit to Whitten: "I told him I had checked and there was nobody else from my region who was in line to be on the committee, and I was coming into my fourth term, and I was pretty senior by then, and I asked Jamie for a commitment that I would be a member of the appropriations committee . . . and he told me to send him a résumé. I was shocked. . . . He said I would have to get voted on like everybody else." Espy campaigned for the position regardless, and lost on the sixth ballot. The same evening that Espy was told he was out of the running, he was scheduled to be a speaker at a formal dinner honoring President-elect Clinton in Washington, D.C. Espy remembers what happened next: "That night was a celebratory event for Bill Clinton, and I knew I would be at the head table. So between 5 o'clock and 7:30 I decided to run for the position of Secretary of Agriculture. . . . I had the invitation in my hand, and I turned it over and wrote 10 reasons why I should be considered for secretary of agriculture." On entering the reception, Espy found Warren Christopher, the chairman of Clinton's transition team, and gave him the note. When Clinton entered the room "he started shaking hands around the table. When he got to me, I said, 'Mr. President-elect, I've given a note to Warren Christopher for you.' I figured next week they'd get to it. And he said to Christopher, where's

Mike's note? Christopher gave it to him and [Clinton] put it in his breast pocket." Later that evening, when Espy rose to make his appointed speech, "as I was about to begin my speech, [I saw Clinton] reading my note, and when he finished, he looked up and gave me thumbs up. . . . I wanted to stay in Congress. I didn't want to leave. If Whitten had said 'yes,' I would have been there a lot longer."[36] In early 1993, Mike Espy took the oath of office as secretary of agriculture.

CHAPTER 17

THE GOP CONSOLIDATES POWER

1994–1996

It's pork barrel when it's in somebody else's district. When it's in yours,
it's good government.
—JAMIE WHITTEN, on federal spending[1]

As 1994 began, Mississippi's two U.S. senators were Republican, and all five congressmen were Democrats. The governor was Republican, though the overwhelming majority of legislators were Democrats. Three years later, Republicans held three of the five congressional posts and had made modest progress in picking up seats in the state legislature. Like virtually all Republican gains in the state, thanks to the power vested with incumbents, these advances were made by winning open-seat elections or convincing incumbent officeholders to switch parties. The first of these open contests occurred in northeast Mississippi, home to the First Congressional District.

JAMIE WHITTEN

When Jamie Whitten announced his retirement from Congress on April 5, 1994, he had served longer than anyone else in the history of the U.S. House of Representatives.[2] Having won a special election in 1941, Whitten took the oath of office less than three weeks before Pearl Harbor. While he led the House Appropriations Committee from 1979 to 1992, it was the forty-one years he served as chair of the Appropriations Subcommittee on Agriculture that earned him the title of "Permanent Secretary of Agriculture" and his reputation as "one of the nation's most influential figures on agricultural policy." For Mississippi, with an economy dependent on agriculture, Whitten's seniority was critical.

Like every other white politician in Mississippi whose career spanned the 1960s, Whitten was forced to come to terms with black voters. After spending the first forty years of his tenure opposing civil rights, he succumbed to the reality of Mississippi's demographics by hiring black staff members and supporting the renewal of the Voting Rights Act in 1982. One group Whitten rarely befriended, however, was environmentalists. He confronted them often, for his subcommittee had jurisdiction over a broad range of consumer and environmental issues. The most famous conflict occurred after the 1962 publication by Rachel Carson of her influential book *Silent Spring*, which decried the pervasive use of pesticides and provoked the ban on DDT. Several years later, Whitten published his own book—*That We May Live*—to rebut and undermine Carson's theme. Unfortunately for Whitten, the media discovered that his book had been "conceived by and subsidized by pesticide industry executives." Whitten also fought the environmental community relentlessly over the construction of the $500 million Tennessee-Tombigbee Waterway, an expenditure of federal dollars that is widely cited as one of history's most notorious examples of the federal pork barrel, and even its longtime supporters will often admit that the economic development opportunities for which it was originally proposed have only recently been realized.

The end of Whitten's career, however, was anticlimactic. Having suffered a mild stroke early in 1992, Whitten was unable to manage the work of his committee, though he refused to retire or yield his chairmanship. Following the 1992 elections, Whitten was removed as chairman of both the Appropriations Committee and the Agriculture Subcommittee.[3] In spite of this extraordinary action taken against him, Whitten refused to say if or when he would be retiring, preventing local Democrats from organizing effective campaigns to succeed him. Three days before the deadline to qualify for the 1994 election, Whitten announced his retirement.

THE 1994 CONGRESSIONAL CAMPAIGN

The First Congressional District emerged largely intact from reapportionment. Historically defined by the counties of northeast Mississippi, the political character of the district was rapidly changing due to the influence of the fastest-growing county in the state—DeSoto—and its thousands of conservative, white voters who were leaving Memphis to find a new home. Not only was the recent electoral performance working against the Democrats—George H. W. Bush easily carried this district in 1988 and in 1992—but the national Republican Party, under the leadership of chairman Haley Barbour, embarked on a comprehensive initiative to win control of Congress in 1994, with the most widely publicized component being the "Contract with America." Six weeks before the election, more than 350 Republican House incumbents and challengers held a signing ceremony on the steps of the U.S. Capitol for the ten-point Contract with America, which focused on law enforcement, welfare reform, balancing the budget, tax cuts, term limits, and excessive government regulations. The move paid off: for the first time in forty years, the GOP gained control of the House, electing seventy-three new Republicans. As *Congressional Quarterly* observed, "the Democratic debacle was truly national in scope. For unrelieved misery for Democrats, though, no region could touch the South."[4]

One of the Republicans in Washington to sign the contract that day was Roger Wicker, a Republican state senator from Tupelo.[5] Wicker had defeated five other Republicans in the June primary, prompting Haley Barbour to proclaim that winning Whitten's seat "will be a precursor of Republican gains in the South."[6] Wicker's opponent was Bill Wheeler, a state representative from Tishomingo County who had defeated two other Democrats in the primary, including the sitting Speaker of the House, Tim Ford. Wicker never deviated from a Republican strategy that was proving to be a winner in Mississippi elections: he complained Wheeler was "selling out" to labor unions,[7] and that "the people of this district are ready to elect someone who is going to go to Washington and oppose the Clinton agenda. . . . They have seen what the liberal, labor dominated agenda has brought to the federal government."[8] Wicker would declare, "I can't imagine any congressional candidate in the nation more closely tied to Bill Clinton than Billy Wheeler," and Wheeler would respond defensively with, "I am not running to represent the president. I disagree with him on a lot of issues."[9] In one television ad, Wicker went for the jugular by reminding voters that Wheeler had campaigned for Dukakis in 1988, ending the ad with: "Any questions?"[10] The voters had none: Wicker carried the district with 63 percent.

KIRK FORDICE AND THE 1995 CAMPAIGN

From time to time, Kirk Fordice would "ask God to prevent him from being transformed into a politician."[11] If you believe a "politician" is someone who measures his or her choice of words very carefully and who may not actually believe everything that comes out of his or her mouth, then Fordice's prayers were answered. There was nothing pretentious about Fordice; unvarnished candor was his defining characteristic. A voter may not always agree with him, but knowing where he stood involved no guesswork. Just three days after he was sworn into office, Fordice was asked what he would do if a federal judge ordered the state to raise taxes in order to upgrade the three historically black universities. The governor's reaction presaged more to come: "We may have to call out the National Guard, because I'm just not going to do it." While he later apologized for invoking the standard refrain of Mississippi politicians during the 1960s, he ended with: "I'm sorry I ever said that, but, come on people, if you can't use a metaphor."[12]

Later that year, at a conference in Washington, D.C., Fordice was asked if he favored relaxing the party's opposition to abortion. He remarked that such questions imply "there is a demise of Christianity in American. I totally reject that. The United States of America is a Christian nation. The less we emphasize the Christian religion the further we fall into the abyss of poor character and chaos." South Carolina's Governor Carroll Campbell hurried to the microphone to add, "The value base of this country comes from the Judeo-Christian heritage." According to a newspaper reporter, Campbell told Fordice, "I just wanted to add the 'Judeo' part," which prompted Fordice to respond, "If I wanted to do that, I would have done that."[13]

Fordice's penchant for candor got personal in the spring of 1993. The governor was finishing up what was supposed to have been a routine interview with Sid Salter, a political columnist for the *Jackson Clarion-Ledger*. Salter said something that led Fordice to believe that Salter knew he and his wife, Pat, were having difficulties. As one friend remembered Fordice saying afterward, "He asked me a question. I thought he knew the answer. I felt I needed to be honest with him." The next morning, on the top of the front page, was Fordice's admission: "I regret to announce that Mrs. Fordice and I are enduring irreconcilable marital differences. I pledge to the people of Mississippi that my personal difficulties will not diminish my commitment to serve as ably and honorably as I know how."[14] The next day, Pat Fordice, who was unaware of her husband's conversation with Salter, had her own statement for the press: "Governor's Wife Says No Divorce."[15] Several days later, reporters were notified by the governor that "Mrs. Fordice and I are working very hard to strengthen our marriage. We want to thank all of the people of Mississippi for their concerns and prayers."[16]

Pat Fordice stayed in the Governor's Mansion, and the issue largely dropped off the public radar screen until Dick Molpus, the Democratic nominee for governor, told a Gulf Coast crowd: "The current governor and I, if we were married, would have what would be considered irreconcilable differences about the future of the state." For Molpus, it was a way of using a commonly understood metaphor to describe the public policy gulf separating him from the incumbent governor. For Fordice, it was personal. A month or so later, more than 400 people came to Mississippi College in Clinton for a debate between Fordice and Molpus. After introducing his wife, Sally, Molpus proceeded to talk about jobs, education, and the state's economy. A reporter described what happened next: "A hush fell over the crowd when Kirk and Pat Fordice walked onstage together, holding hands. Pat Fordice stood quietly—lips pursed, eyes staring over the heads of the audience—as her husband talked about their nearly 40-year marriage." After he finished, Fordice looked at his challenger: "Mr. Molpus, when you started your public campaign . . . with a thinly veiled cheap shot at that 40-year marriage . . . we decided that what we would do is make a direct statement to you about our marriage and about the fact that we just don't believe it is any of your business." Then he did something not even his campaign manager anticipated: he leaned over and kissed his wife before she left the stage. The photo of the kiss ran in the next day's *Clarion-Ledger* with the caption: "Smacks of politics."[17]

THE 1995 GENERAL ELECTION

Dick Molpus, native of Neshoba County, member of Governor William Winter's staff, and one of the 1982 "Boys of Spring," was elected secretary of state in 1983. Education was Molpus's passion, and he had made a name for himself by overhauling and enforcing sixteenth-section land leases throughout the state, generating millions of dollars for local school districts that had been leasing those lands to private landowners for pennies on the dollar. He had also helped found Parents for Public Schools.

Knowing that Molpus would stress education, the Fordice campaign decided to take the offensive and propose their own education reform based on the state's recently revived initiative law: they called their effort PRIME, or People's Right to Initiate Model Education. Fordice and his staff wanted to articulate a conservative set of principles for public education—"something other than being for less money for education." PRIME offered a way for parents to determine educational policy "instead of the bureaucrats," reflecting Fordice's view of conservativism. Molpus argued that "Gov. Fordice [was trying] to sell PRIME under the persuasive words of local control, when what it really meant was allowing districts to abandon standards and allow private groups access to public school dollars." But Molpus found himself in the untenable position of debating Fordice's education platform rather than his own. [18]

The 1995 campaign turned out to be the last time voters have been offered a substantive debate about tax policy in Mississippi. Unless handled very carefully, Democrats almost always lose a public contest if the topic is tax policy. Fordice initiated the debate when he called on the legislature to reduce the state's income tax by $78 million over three years: "Please don't listen to any of this liberal talk about, 'We have these needs.' We have all been horn swaggled to a degree at one time or another in this state out of a lot of tax money by saying 'the little children' and 'education.'"[19] There was nothing subtle about Fordice. Molpus and Democratic legislators took the bait and offered an alternative: reducing the sales tax on food. As one legislator argued: "If we want real tax reduction . . . if we want to affect 100 percent of the people, let's cut the sales tax."[20] Molpus himself explained that reducing the sales tax on groceries would help all Mississippians, including retirees and people who earned too little to pay income taxes. The problem for Molpus was his support for a 1992 sales tax increase for education that had been approved over Fordice's veto.

The lines were drawn. Even though the sales tax on food affects every Mississippian, it falls more heavily on the low-income population, which is how the Democrats characterized their position. Fordice, as usual, was unembarrassed about the reason he advocated an income tax cut: an income tax cut would help those who pay the most for government programs.[21] In the end, the 1995 Senate passed Fordice's income tax reductions, while a divided House killed the Fordice plan and the Democrats' proposal. The legislature left the public policy issue unsettled, though the voting public knew precisely where the candidates stood.

Then came the "Great Debate." The annual Neshoba County Fair was in early August, a perfect setting, the Fordice campaign decided, for a debate. As one Fordice campaign worker remarked, "It was just vintage Fordice. How could you not turn the guy loose doing what he was the very best at? Especially since Neshoba County is Molpus's home!" For years, the fair had sponsored speeches by political figures, but never in its 106-year history had the fair been host to a head-to-head debate. More than 3,000 people showed up to listen. One reporter described the scene: "I don't remember from a lifetime of listening to stump speeches ... [anything] that even approached the in-your-face tenor of the exchanges between ... Fordice and ... Molpus. ... They don't like each other. They don't agree with each other politically. And when both view the other, they see the antithesis of everything they believe in from the standpoint of public policy and the practice of governing." Another reporter wrote: "Never in 47 years of going to the Neshoba County Fair have I seen such a show as the Great Debate."[22] The crowd was packed with supporters from both campaigns. When Fordice accused Molpus of changing his position on the sales tax—"You've flip-flopped since 1992"—the Fordice partisans in the audience waved hundreds of pairs of flip-flops that had been distributed prior to the event.

The heat and the dust and the surging, pushing, and shoving crowd added to the tension when Sid Salter, the moderator, asked Fordice how he could reconcile talking about family values while trying to leave his wife:

> *Fordice: Sid, this goes for you, Molpus, any of the rest of you. In about a week, the first lady and I will have been married 40 years. We have ... eight grandchildren. When any of y'all get in that shape and get them all educated and have gone through all the things we've done and ... instilled in them their moral values and all that, you come and we'll have that argument then, either one of you.*
>
> *Molpus: Mr. Fordice, you're pointing your finger at me? ... I didn't invite that. I don't owe anyone an apology in this state. It's you that owes the apology.*
>
> *Fordice: Sid, let's get out of there.*
>
> *Molpus: Let me tell you something very clearly. Your private life doesn't interest me.*
>
> *Fordice: Good. Good.*
>
> *Molpus: Your public life is what appalls me.*
>
> *[By this time the crowd was getting out of hand, and the candidates' voices had become roars.]*
>
> *Fordice: You're losing it Sid.*
>
> *Salter: No sir. I've got control of it just fine. If you want to debate me, you can come up on the porch tonight and we'll do it.*

Fordice won the award for the best comeback when Salter asked him to defend the $145,000 in contributions he had received from gaming executives while, as governor, he had the duty to appoint the board members who regulated the industry.

Salter: Mississippi has sent highway commissioners to prison for accepting donations from road builders. What's the difference?
Fordice: I'm not in prison is one difference.[23]

The antagonism continued later in the campaign when Molpus produced a television commercial featuring his wife criticizing Fordice's education plan, an attack that provoked Fordice to mimic her tone of voice in a conversation with reporters. Rising to his wife's defense, Molpus declared he was going to take Fordice "to the woodshed." At their next encounter—a televised debate late in the campaign—Fordice pulled Molpus aside: "You said last Friday that you wanted to take me to the woodshed. You tell any more lies about me, and this 61 year old man will take you to the woodshed and I'll whip your ass."[24]

For all the political theater that voters enjoyed free of charge, the Molpus campaign knew early on that the campaign was uphill, though a campaign Molpus felt was necessary. In March, a Molpus poll had Fordice ahead 59-32. When white voters were asked in the poll to choose between a "moderate Democrat" and a "conservative Republican" for governor, they favored a "conservative Republican" candidate by a margin of 68-18. Molpus's consultant offered this advice: "It is obvious from these results that the Molpus campaign simply cannot allow the gubernatorial election to be defined as Democrat versus Republican. We need to make this race into a contest between two individuals (preferably two conservative candidates), and the campaign's top priority over the next few months should be to provide voters with an image of Dick Molpus that goes beyond his party label." It is advice that rings true even today.

Fordice won his election convincingly, getting 55.4 percent of the vote. Many Democrats claimed his campaign was nothing but code words and strategies to draw a black-white distinction—for example, Fordice vetoed a bill containing minority set-asides, arguing, "I believe it is wrong for a building program to become a social program."[25] Fordice's supporters, on the other hand, claimed it was his stewardship of the economy and his forthrightness and basic conservative principles that earned the victory.[26] While Molpus received 25,000 more votes than Mabus had received in 1991, Fordice increased his vote total over 1991 by almost 95,000. Fordice carried northeast Mississippi with 56.7 percent, the suburban counties with 68.1 percent, and the Gulf Coast with 58 percent.

The enormous turnout surprised everyone. In 1991, 711,212 people voted; in 1995, the turnout surged to 819,471; four years later, it dropped to 763,937. How can that phenomenon be explained? We identified two reasons. One, both Molpus and Fordice were well funded; both believed passionately in their positions; and because those positions were about as far apart ideologically as any campaign in recent memory, the voters were presented with clear choices and motivated to vote for fear "the other guy" might get elected. Two, toward the end of the campaign, Molpus broadcast an advertisement exclusively on radio stations with a predominantly African American audience. The ad included a dialogue in which a rider was instructed to "Go to the back of the bus," followed by the narration: "Fordice wants to send us all to the back of the bus." Taking advantage of the gift, Fordice's campaign recorded the Molpus ad and added to it this introduction: "This is Governor Kirk Fordice. I want to play you an ad run by my opponent that should be offensive to all Mississippians, black and white." The Fordice campaign then purchased as much broadcast time as it could locate on every gospel and country radio station in the state. The hundreds of times the ad played until election day no doubt had the desired impact of generating turnout.

The extent of the GOP win, however, stopped with Fordice. Incumbent Republican Lieutenant Governor Eddie Briggs lost his reelection bid to Ronnie Musgrove, a Democratic state senator. The Democratic incumbents in the other statewide offices all won by convincing margins, even though the Republicans offered serious challenges to most of them. While the Republicans increased their number in the legislature from thirty-five to fifty, these gains came from incumbents switching parties or Republican candidates winning open-seat elections. Republican legislative challengers defeated four Democratic incumbents, while Democratic challengers defeated five GOP incumbents. Another way to look at the election of 1995 is this: Fordice was able to give voice to very popular conservative positions—vetoing the sales tax increase, urging a cut in income taxes—while the voters were never allowed to feel the impact of those policies because the Democratic-controlled legislature overrode the vetoes and opposed any tax cuts, and thus any reduction in state spending.

A few days after Fordice's win, the Republicans picked up their second congressional seat in as many years when the incumbent Democrat for the Fourth District, Mike Parker, switched parties, saying: "The (Democratic) Party became increasingly more liberal."[27] Two down, one to go.

AARON HENRY

Knowing "when to fold your cards" remains a challenge for almost all politicians. The allure of the office is often too tempting to abandon, as Aaron Henry discovered the hard way in 1995. Few men or women, black or white, were as central to the success of the civil rights movement in Mississippi as Aaron Henry, who led the state NAACP for over thirty-three years. After serving with the army during World War II, Henry used his GI benefits to earn a pharmacy degree and returned home to Clarksdale, where his Fourth Street drugstore became a focal point for the civil rights struggle and the movement to unify the state Democratic parties. When the Mississippi Freedom Democratic Party fielded candidates for the 1963 Freedom Vote, Henry was the candidate for governor. As one scholar of the civil rights period wrote: "Aaron Henry's position in the Mississippi movement was both unique and essential.... More than any other Mississippi leader, the Clarksdale pharmacist united blacks across lines of age, ideology, and social class to present a consolidated front against the forces of white supremacy."[28] Of the seventeen African Americans who were elected to the legislature in 1979, one of the most rewarding victories went to Henry in the House. Voters reelected him in 1983, 1987, and 1991, but on August 8, 1995, they chose a new face: Leonard Henderson defeated Henry by sixty-five votes.

By 1995, nearly thirty years had passed since Henry's heyday as a civil rights leader. The younger voters had no memory of that time. One day in the middle of June 1975, a *New York Times* reporter came to a similar conclusion as he was writing an article about the city of Jackson opening nine new public swimming pools, "a dozen years after it drained its old pools and let trees spring up through their cracked bottoms rather than desegregate them." The reporter asked an eleven-year-old black swimmer if he knew anything about the trouble that had forced the closure of the pools. "I don't know what sort of trouble you're talking about," the boy answered. The reporter thought: "The name Medgar W. Evers meant nothing to [these kids]."[29]

SONNY MONTGOMERY

It was the day after the June 1966 primary election, and Sonny Montgomery desperately wanted to avoid a runoff. A state senator for ten years, Montgomery had joined three other candidates in the Democratic primary for the congressional seat being vacated by the Republican incumbent Prentiss Walker. Montgomery avoided a runoff by 112 votes, and in an interview years later, he explained how: "There were about five boxes in Winston County, and I carried them pretty good, like two to one. Then one box, I lost it. That didn't quite make sense, so we had the circuit clerk go back in and look at it. . . . He didn't want to. . . . However, he went back and looked and the figures had just been reversed [on the tabulation sheet] . . . so that put me over the top."[30] Thirty years later, Sonny Montgomery retired from his congressional seat. Montgomery chaired the Veterans Affairs Committee from 1981 until the Republicans assumed power in 1995, and he was described by one reporter as "the nation's armed services . . . greatest friend in Congress."[31] Montgomery once said his most notable accomplishment was the enactment of the "Montgomery G.I. Bill," legislation that requires the federal government to match funds military personnel put aside for education. At one count, more than two million participants were enrolled in the program.[32]

When Sonny Montgomery retired, he was the last of the Democrats who had formed the core of the Mississippi congressional delegation since the 1940s—a group who had transformed relatively easy reelection campaigns into 200 years of seniority and critical leadership positions—Jim Eastland and John Stennis in the Senate and William Colmer, Jamie Whitten, and Sonny Montgomery in the House. They were all replaced by Republicans.

THE 1996 CONGRESSIONAL CAMPAIGN

Like the First District to the north, the Third Congressional District was changed little by the authors of the reapportionment legislation. Anchored by Columbus and Starkville in the north, Meridian to the south, and Rankin County in the west, this area of east Mississippi contains the most politically conservative white voters in the state. For both the 1992 and 1996 presidential elections, the district gave the GOP presidential candidate his best vote in Mississippi.

Three candidates vied for the Democratic nomination, while nine Republicans filed for the chance to succeed Montgomery. The eventual nominees were Democrat John Arthur Eaves Jr., son of a well-known Jackson trial lawyer who had made three gubernatorial campaigns, and Trent Lott aide Chip Pickering, son of a Mississippi federal judge and former state party chairman. By the time the polls opened on election day 1996, Republicans had controlled the House for two years, leaving voters with a simple calculation: did they want to send a representative to join the House majority party or the minority party? In one debate, Eaves made that point, arguing that the voters could do better than sending "[GOP Leader] Newt Gingrich another player." Pickering's response: "I guess the choice is sending Bill and Hillary [Clinton] another player."[33] For the voters, the choice was easy. Pickering carried the district with 61 percent.

POSTSCRIPT

The most powerful position in the U.S. Senate is majority leader. The party in control of the Senate elects one senator to be its leader, who in turn, for all practical purposes, controls the flow of legislation and thus the public policies considered by the full Senate. When Kansas Republican Senator Bob Dole— the Senate majority leader—resigned in 1996 to campaign for president, the nation's capital witnessed something truly out of the ordinary. Trent Lott, who held the second most powerful position in the Senate—majority whip—and Thad Cochran, who held the number three position—Republican Conference chairman—ran against each other for majority leader. In a secret vote among the fifty-two Senate Republicans, Lott was elected. For the first time in history, a single state's two senators vied for the post, and for the first time, a Mississippian was elected to the post.

CHAPTER 18

TOBACCO

1997–1998

*The U.S. tobacco industry is facing a string of history-making trials this
year in what is emerging as the biggest and costliest showdown in the
annals of American civil litigation. . . . More than 500 law firms and thousands of individual attorneys have already been mobilized for the escalating
fight. . . . So far, 23 states have sued the [tobacco] industry to recover tax
funds they allege were spent treating indigent victims of smoking-related
illnesses . . . key showdowns: Mississippi's Medicaid case.*
—*LOS ANGELES TIMES*, March 17, 1997

One billion dollars. That's the total of Mississippi's budget deficit
during the five years between 2000 and 2005. To make up the difference, the legislature tapped something called the "Health Care
Trust Fund." The Health Care Trust Fund exists to receive the proceeds of a
$3.4 billion settlement the state reached with the tobacco industry on July 3,
1997.[1] The settlement came about because a group of attorneys general from
around the country—headed by Mississippi's Mike Moore—and a group of
private lawyers—headed by Mississippi's Richard Scruggs—decided to wage
war against the firms that manufacture tobacco products. They were successful
in large part because the two most significant whistleblowers in the history of
the tobacco industry—Jeffrey Wigand and Merrell Williams—embarked on
journeys that led them to Mississippi.

THE PLAYERS

By the time our story begins in 1993 with Mike Lewis sitting down for breakfast
with Richard Scruggs and Don Barrett, all the players are in place.[2]

• Mike Moore was in his second term as attorney general when he set in motion Mississippi's five-year odyssey with the tobacco industry. He was serving as Jackson County district attorney when Ray Mabus was elected state auditor in 1983 and had just completed a successful and widely publicized prosecution of local county supervisors. The two became allies, and when Mabus was elected governor in 1987, the voters chose Moore as his attorney general, the first statewide official from the Gulf Coast in more than a century. Moore grew up in the same Pascagoula neighborhood with Scruggs and was a law school classmate at the University of Mississippi with Scruggs and Mike Lewis. As he was once aptly described: "While [Moore] got along with a lot of people, he wasn't afraid to not get along."[3]

• Richard Scruggs had just turned forty-seven years old when Mike Moore asked him to meet with Mike Lewis. Scruggs had been practicing law in Pascagoula since 1980, and by 1993 had made a small fortune representing thousands of workers who had been exposed to asbestos, many of them former and current workers at the Ingalls Shipyards in Jackson County. Attracted to their crusading styles, Scruggs supported Mabus and Moore in 1987 and became fast friends with both. A year later, he switched sides and campaigned for Trent Lott against Democrat Wayne Dowdy—no doubt owing to his 1971 marriage to Diane Thompson, whose older sister, Tricia, was married to Lott. Before entering law school, Scruggs served as a navy pilot, flying A-6 fighter-bombers from aircraft carriers in the Mediterranean Sea. A writer once observed: "The character traits required of naval aviators are a propensity for risk, steely nerves, and a capacity for instantaneous decision-making. In Scruggs's case, he has brought them to the practice of law."[4] The breakfast meeting with Lewis took place in Greenville, where Scruggs was litigating a case with his friend Don Barrett.

• Don Barrett, a Holmes County lawyer whose family planted its roots there in the 1890s, was the first Mississippi lawyer to sue a cigarette company on behalf of someone with smoking-related illnesses and one of the first lawyers in the country to bring a lawsuit to trial. From January 1988 through September 1990, Barrett represented Nathan Horton against American Tobacco Company. Barrett's first trial ended in a hung jury, his second in a mistrial, and his third with what the jury thought was a compromise verdict: they sided with Horton but awarded him zero damages. Barrett came to believe that "cigarette companies were too strong to be taken on one case at a time." Though they had known each other briefly while undergraduates at the University of Mississippi, Scruggs and Barrett had nurtured their friendship during a series of legal collaborations. In the summer of 1993, Scruggs was in Greenville helping Barrett with yet another trial against American Tobacco when they had breakfast with Lewis. A year later, Barrett was the first lawyer in Mississippi to hear from Merrell Williams.

• Merrell Williams was in Louisville, Kentucky, in early 1988 when he accepted a job with a local law firm reviewing and classifying documents for one of the firm's major clients: Brown and Williamson Tobacco Corporation. That fall, he began secretly removing documents from the office, copying and returning them—a smuggling operation that lasted until Williams's last day of work in early 1992. The significance of the Williams documents was once summarized by a reporter:

> *Internal documents from a major tobacco company show that executives struggled with whether to disclose to the Surgeon General what they knew in 1963 about the hazards of cigarettes.... The executives of the company, Brown and Williamson, chose to remain silent, to keep their research results secret, to stop work on a safer cigarette and to pursue a legal and public relations strategy of admitting nothing. In more than 100 documents ... the officials spoke of the hazards of cigarettes and state plainly to one another that nicotine is addictive.*[5]

Williams had family on the Mississippi Gulf Coast, had met his first wife while attending the University of Mississippi, and had followed Barrett's lawsuit on behalf of Nathan Horton.

• Jeffrey Wigand had a Ph.D. in biochemistry when he joined Brown and Williamson in 1989 as the company's director of research and development. By early 1993, company executives had concluded that Wigand was not a team player, so he was fired and forced to sign a confidentiality agreement. Wigand ended up doing some freelance consulting with *60 Minutes* producer Lowell Bergman and over time began to reveal what he had learned while at Brown and Williamson, information that corroborated the explosive disclosures in the Merrell Williams documents. It was when CBS wanted to televise an interview with Wigand, over the frenzied objections of Brown and Williamson, that Scruggs came to represent Wigand.

THE BEGINNING

Mike Lewis had lived in the Mississippi Delta most of his life, interrupted with service in the air force, and by the summer of 1993 he had established a successful law practice with his wife, Pauline, in Clarksdale. It was then that he approached Mike Moore with an idea. While returning from a visit with his secretary's mother, who was dying of smoking-related illnesses, a thought occurred to him: why shouldn't cigarette manufacturers owe money to the government since government health care programs were paying for much of her treatment? In other words, why should the taxpayers cover the cost? Moore was intrigued and encouraged Lewis to follow up with Scruggs, someone both of them knew had the financial resources and experience to pursue it. Breakfast was arranged in Greenville, and by the time Lewis had finished his explanation, Scruggs and Barrett were excited about the possibilities.

Scruggs returned to the Coast and a trial he was sharing with Ron Motley, a South Carolina lawyer who would become a leading collaborator in the epic legal struggle. Scruggs shared Lewis's idea and remembered that "Motley immediately caught on to it, and I almost had to strap him to his chair, he was ready to get up and file that afternoon." Over the next several months, the idea was researched, and a team of lawyers was assembled under the aegis of the attorney general's office. They all met in New Orleans around Thanksgiving to develop strategy and hear from Dick Morris, Trent Lott's 1988 campaign consultant whom Scruggs had retained to poll prospective jurors. The results were not promising—more people were opposed to the idea than supported it—thus resolving one piece of the strategy: the lawsuit would be filed in chancery court instead of circuit court. Circuit court cases are tried in front of a jury; chancery court cases are tried before a single judge.

Early in 1994, as Moore and his team continued with lawsuit preparations, three unrelated events took place that, on their own, would not have proven deadly to tobacco interests. Occurring almost simultaneously, they turbocharged the Mississippi initiative.

• The Food and Drug Administration (FDA) announced an investigation into allegations that tobacco companies had manipulated nicotine levels to keep smokers addicted. The publicity surrounding that announcement led to a congressional hearing on April 14, 1994, in which seven tobacco executives stood before the committee and testified under oath they did not believe nicotine was addictive.

• Between the FDA announcement and the congressional hearing, Merrell Williams had his first meeting with Barrett, who had invited Scruggs to join them. Several weeks earlier, Williams had faxed a note to Barrett: "One of these days I may call you. We ought to talk."[6] Barrett followed up and arranged the meeting.

• During this same period, Jeffrey Wigand began consulting with CBS *60 Minutes* producer Lowell Bergman. The more time Bergman spent with Wigand, the more Bergman learned about the role of nicotine in the manufacture of cigarettes and that the congressional testimonies may not have been truthful.

A few weeks later, Scruggs met with Williams again, who this time handed over the documents he had copied, including a 1963 memo from the company's legal counsel: "We are . . . in the business of selling nicotine, an addictive drug." Scruggs could hardly believe his good fortune: "it was a verifier of everything we thought was true, we could see it in black and white." The material was so compelling that Scruggs and Moore delivered a set to the congressman who had convened the hearings. When asked why he was unmoved by the argument that he was peddling "stolen" documents, Moore explained: "Look, I am the Chief Law Enforcement Officer of this state and these documents [were] evidence of a crime and so therefore nobody has the legal right to own them or keep them out of the public domain."[7]

On May 23, 1994, the state of Mississippi sued thirteen cigarette manufacturers seeking the recovery of money the state had spent providing medical care to residents with smoking-related illnesses. The lawsuit was filed with Jackson County Chancery Court Judge William Myers. Moore explained to the press: "This is a taxpayers' lawsuit. The bottom line is the [taxpayers] are paying hundreds of millions of dollars a year to treat people who have tobacco related disease. This is not a smoker's case. We're not suing to get money back for poor smokers. We're suing to get money back for all the taxpayers of Mississippi."[8] That evening, Governor Fordice signaled the onset of what remains the longest, most vitriolic duel between the state's top executive officer and its top legal officer: "I just want to throw up."[9]

THE LITIGATION

Over the course of the summer and fall, lawyers argued over whether the lawsuit would remain in chancery court or be transferred to circuit court, as advocated by the tobacco companies. As Scruggs once remarked: "If we were going to lose, we wanted to lose early and cheap." On February 21, 1995, Judge Myers, appointed to the bench by Governor Fordice a few years earlier, sided with the Mississippi team, allowing the litigation to proceed. There was no turning back.

A year and a half after securing the help of Merrell Williams, Scruggs—who by now was generating headlines across the country—got a call from a San Francisco attorney hired by CBS to represent Wigand. Would Scruggs be interested in assisting his client? The answer was easy, and over the course of the next few months, Scruggs earned Wigand's confidence, became his attorney, and secured his participation in the Mississippi lawsuit. Wigand's assistance came in the form of a deposition on November 29, 1995, in Pascagoula. In a civil suit, witnesses may be interrogated under oath, or "deposed," in advance of the trial. In this case, the Mississippi lawyers would ask the questions, in the presence of attorneys representing the tobacco defendants. In requesting Wigand to submit to a deposition, Scruggs hedged nothing: "Your testimony . . . is a mortal threat not only to Brown and Williamson but also to the entire tobacco industry. Obviously they will resort to all means . . . to discredit and intimidate you." [10] In spite of possible sanctions for violating the confidentiality agreement he had earlier signed, Wigand agreed to help.

The tension of the day is captured in the movie *The Insider*—while tobacco lawyers jam the room where the deposition will be held and hundreds of reporters "were wondering if this guy was going to testify," Wigand was back at Scruggs's house, experiencing a last-minute case of "should I really go through with this?" A state judge in Wigand's hometown in Kentucky had issued a gag order seeking to prevent Wigand's testimony, though Judge Myers had ruled that Kentucky law did not apply in Mississippi—"no Kentucky judge is going to tell me who can testify and who can't." Regardless, local authorities were threatening to jail him when he returned home. Scruggs remembered what happened:

> Wigand was nervous that if he goes back to Kentucky they would lock him up immediately and we couldn't tell him that wouldn't happen. All we could tell him was that we will do everything we can. . . . Lowell Bergman was there, and he and Bergman were close. . . . And Wigand was pacing around in my front yard and I said, "Look Jeff, if you are not comfortable with this, don't do it, nobody is going to think any less of you. . . . I feel like I have pushed you way too far to do this."

A few minutes later Wigand looked at Scruggs and said, "Let's go." [11]

The testimony Wigand gave in that deposition corroborated and expanded on the information provided in the Williams documents, and it formed the basis for his famous February 4, 1996, interview on *60 Minutes*, which included this exchange:

Mike Wallace: And that's what cigarettes are for?
Jeffrey Wigand: Most certainly. It's a delivery device for nicotine.

The verbal warfare between Fordice and Moore erupted again several weeks later when Fordice launched his own legal action, this one against the attorney general, seeking an order from the state supreme court to halt the lawsuit. Fordice's reasoning was twofold: "I oppose the lawsuit not only because it is improper … but also because I firmly believe that this irresponsible action has the potential to seriously damage our efforts to attract jobs to our state," and "When Mike Moore is in *Time Magazine*, nothing else matters. We're off on another publicity binge.… That's what it's about. It's people in *Time Magazine* and certain plaintiff's lawyers making a whole lot of money." Moore's oft-quoted response: "The tobacco companies have been looking for a new Marlboro Man and they have found him. He already had his hat. He already had his boots. And his name is Governor Daniel Kirkwood Fordice."[12]

On March 13, 1996, the Mississippi team recorded its first win, though it had virtually nothing to do with the merits of the litigation. As it happened, Bennett S. LeBow had financial control over the Liggett Group, the smallest of the five major cigarette manufacturers. LeBow was waging a fight to gain control of RJR Nabisco, parent company of R. J. Reynolds Tobacco. By negotiating an end to the Mississippi lawsuit and arranging for those terms to apply to any other tobacco company, the settlement would aid his takeover attempt. As Scruggs described it: "He would be able to sell the shareholders of RJR Nabisco a 'Get-Out-of-Jail-Free' card." Regardless of the motivations, the Mississippi team earned a substantive legal victory and consequently reaped a public relations bonanza when LeBow agreed to settle the claims against Liggett. For Scruggs, the Liggett settlement "was huge, huge, huge … a validator for the other state Attorneys General." Only four other states joined Mississippi in the Liggett settlement: Florida, Louisiana, West Virginia, and Massachusetts. But the phones in Mississippi started ringing once the settlement was final.

For the next twelve months, the Mississippi team moved on three fronts: preparing for a July 1997 trial; recruiting other states to join the litigation to increase public pressure; and entering into secret negotiations with representatives of the tobacco companies with the possibility of achieving a settlement. By the end of 1996, nineteen states had joined the lawsuit.

The team earned another win on March 13, 1997, when the supreme court ruled against Fordice: "This court finds that it is without jurisdiction to act as a trial court in this matter, and dismisses the Governor's petition."[13] The ruling that the trial could proceed resulted in a sell off of tobacco stocks.[14] While unintended by Fordice, this legal victory gave the Mississippi team valuable momentum. Moore observed, "We're feeling pretty strong now and the rest of the attorneys general have been calling me. The green light is on."[15]

By this time, the tobacco companies had made a calculation that winning the July trial in Mississippi was not a sure thing and that even if they won in Mississippi, other state trials were on its heels; stockholders were jittery; the media had, by and large, turned against them; and there was no end in sight for the litigation costs. They sent an emissary to Moore: could anything be worked out? Moore's reply: "Okay, I will meet with you, but I will only meet with CEOs of the companies, I don't want to meet with a bunch of lawyers. . . . I want to see the CEOs across the table from me and I want to look into their eyes and see that they are serious." A few days later, the chief executive officers sat down at a conference table in a suburban Washington, D.C., hotel to strike a deal with Mike Moore and his team of other attorneys general and lawyers.

When the *Wall Street Journal* broke the story about the settlement talks two weeks later, forty states had signed up. The negotiations were all-consuming, contentious, and emotional, and broke down several times. Two items not negotiable were legal claims made against Merrell Williams and Jeffrey Wigand; getting Brown and Williamson to back off of those claims was the last hurdle to completing the negotiations. On June 20, 1997, the agreement was announced by Moore to a jammed press conference in Washington, D.C. The reporters for the *Los Angeles Times* described the event:

In a landmark settlement that is easily the largest in the history of litigation, lawyers representing 40 states announced that cigarette makers had agreed to pay $368.5 billion over 25 years and submit to unprecedented new rules that aim to dramatically scale back tobacco's hold over people's lives. The remarkable settlement, which must be approved by Congress and the White House,

would acknowledge the government's authority to regulate nicotine, repay bil-
lions of dollars to the states for smoking-related health care costs, and fund free
stop-smoking programs for whoever wants them. It would also shrink tobacco's
profile across the nation, sharply restricting the advertising of cigarettes while
funding a massive anti-smoking campaign and ordering up bigger and blunter
notices on cigarette packs.[16]

Among its many provisions, the settlement contained limits on lawsuits against tobacco companies and new FDA regulatory authority over tobacco products, all of which proposed to amend federal law. Later that day, Moore told the negotiators, "Next week, let's sit down and talk about what we are going to do about my trial date." Since the national settlement would only take effect if passed by Congress and approved by the president, the cigarette industry still faced a showdown in Judge Myers's court over the specific Mississippi case. The tobacco companies offered Moore $50 million to move the date until after Congress had time to consider the deal. "I knew I would never ever have as much leverage to get a settlement as I had right [then]," remembered Moore, "So I said no, I'm not moving the trial date. . . . Y'all will just have to pay [Mississippi]."

Several weeks later, on July 3, in the rotunda of the state capitol, Mike Moore came home to announce the Mississippi agreement: $3.4 billion, to be paid no matter what Congress did with the proposed national settlement. As other states followed suit and settled with the tobacco companies, a special section in the Mississippi accord took effect. Called a "most favored nation" provision, it stipulated that if other states negotiated more favorable terms with the tobacco industry, those terms would likewise apply to Mississippi. For example, when Florida settled a month later, the companies agreed to remove their billboards and their ads in stadiums. Consequently, similar advertising ended in Mississippi.

THE AFTERMATH

For an entire year, Moore, Scruggs, and their allies lobbied Congress, albeit unsuccessfully, to enact the settlement. They blame the failure on public health activists who refused to compromise on any point with the tobacco industry, whose only strategy was zealotry. Michael Pertschuk, a former chairman of the Federal Trade Commission with a long history in the field of public health advocacy agreed: "the collective leadership of the tobacco control movement . . . blew the opportunity of a lifetime."[17] The two people singled out by Scruggs and Moore as the prime architects of the congressional defeat of the settlement were C. Everett Koop, former surgeon general, and David Kessler, FDA commissioner for much of this period.

On September 8, 2004, Peter Jennings narrated an ABC News special about the failed tobacco deal. Jennings interviewed, among others, Arizona senator John McCain, who handled the settlement legislation in Congress, and Koop and Kessler, whom McCain characterized as "two of the most respected men in America on this issue."

> *Jennings: Senator McCain said that you gave him assurance that you would support the bill with liability protection in it. But you changed your mind and he doesn't know why.*
>
> *Kessler: It really was the, you know, the ultimate bargain put in front of you. Everything you ever worked for, everything you ever wanted, you could have. But there's only one catch. Why do you have to tie those public health measures to legal liability protection for the industry?*
>
> *Jennings: Perhaps it's the only way to get a deal.*
>
> *Kessler: Why? Because you have to pay off the industry?*
>
> *Jennings: And you were prepared to ignore all the public health components based on the $6.5 billion liability protection on an annual basis?*
>
> *Kessler: It's not about the dollars. It's about assuring the industry its future. . . .*
>
> *Jennings: The legislation died in the full Senate. Senator McCain is convinced to this day that landmark legislation was defeated by the two great pillars of the public health community, Kessler and Koop.*
>
> *McCain: I think history will show that they squandered a historic opportunity. And now, we have a situation where none of their goals are being met. . . .*
>
> *Jennings: It was the most comprehensive anti-tobacco bill ever.*
>
> *Kessler: And we will get there, Peter.*
>
> *Jennings: But have you ever thought that you might have to wait a very long time in order to get the public health components that would satisfy you? And that it would take so long that many people might needlessly die?*
>
> *Kessler: I understand that there are down sides, to waiting. The—regrettably, people continue to die. But we need to get this right. And we need to get this right for the duration.*

Jennings: In the six years since the McCain bill failed, the Congress has not passed a single piece of tobacco control legislation, and two and a half million more Americans have died from smoking.[18]

POSTSCRIPT

Three years after switching parties, Fourth District congressman Mike Parker chose not to seek reelection in 1998. The general election for Parker's seat featured Democrat Ronnie Shows against Republican Delbert Hosemann. During the 1992 reapportionment fight, when black voters were reallocated from the Fourth District to the Delta congressional district, white Democrats feared a Republican would later have an improved chance of winning the Fourth District seat. The GOP, however, made the mistake of nominating a Jackson lawyer—Hosemann—to oppose Shows, an elected transportation commissioner whose hometown of Bassfield was deep in the southern part of the district. Geography always trumped party in this district on election day: Shows won with 53.4 percent of the vote.

CHAPTER 19

THE LEGACY OF KIRK FORDICE

1999

*Four years from now, Lord willing, on January 11, 2000, we will meet here
one last time. On that day I will be sitting in one of the chairs right behind
me now as a spectator just like you. I hope for many things on that day, but,
most of all, I hope and pray that as I look into that crowd I will be able to
tell by the smiles on your faces that we were successful in our mission.*
—GOVERNOR KIRK FORDICE[1]

K irk Fordice expressed that longing as he spoke to the crowd gathered in early January 1996 for his second inaugural, the first time in
the 179-year history of Mississippi that a popularly elected governor had succeeded himself in office. When he was called upon to perform the
role of spectator four years later, it was a Democrat who addressed the crowd
as the state's newest governor. If Fordice's mission had been to recast the politics of the state, to lead a Republican takeover fueled by a conservative ideology, his mission met with little short-term success. Fordice's legacy suggests
that irony may sometimes be the most satisfying way to appreciate Mississippi
politics.

THE LEGACY OF KIRK FORDICE

Within weeks of assuming office in 1992, Kirk Fordice responded to a query
about gambling: "None of this gambling adds value to anything. It just causes
people to throw their money away and I don't see how that can enhance
Mississippi's moral values."[2] Nonetheless, Fordice had inherited legalized
casino gaming along the Gulf Coast and the Mississippi River and was charged

with making the first appointments to the newly created Mississippi Gaming Commission, the state agency vested with regulating the nascent industry.

In one of the most successful decisions of his eight-year tenure, Fordice adopted an "absolute litmus test" for the commission posts—"if you wanted the job, you were disqualified." As a result, all three of Fordice's appointments— Stuart C. Irby Jr., sixty-nine, of Jackson; Robert C. Engram, seventy-two, of Gulfport; and Bill Gresham Jr., sixty-seven, of Indianola—had to be convinced to take the job. Irby, a conservative Republican, a successful businessman, and a prominent philanthropist, turned Fordice down twice before he finally said "yes," and then only after Fordice appealed to his sense of patriotic duty: "Stuart, I don't like this. I would have vetoed it, if I'd had a chance, but I didn't and it's the law, and I need you to do this." Robert Engram, a retired navy captain and manager of a cargo handling company, told a reporter he had "not spent one dime in" any of the Coast casinos.[3] Clarke Reed, who helped Fordice identify and recruit possible appointees, remembers flying around the state for several months with his friend and fellow Delta businessman Bill Gresham interviewing possible appointees, and getting turned down one after the other. Late one night, after their latest recruit had refused their entreaty, he called Gresham:

Reed: Bill . . .
Gresham: I told my wife last night you were gonna call me.
Reed: Well, you're right. You've got to do it.

Fordice appointed three white, very conservative, financially independent men to a post none of them wanted. All three had managed thriving businesses, enjoyed successful careers, and weren't looking for another entry on their résumés. In turn, they ensured that the regulation and growth of the gaming industry would be accomplished without a hint of corruption or favoritism. Once chosen, Fordice left them alone. Engram later remarked that Fordice "never once interfered with any of the decisions the gaming commission made. For a politician, that's saying a helluva lot."[4] Engram was also the author of the most far-sighted decision the commission made: requiring casinos to build hotels, restaurants, golf courses, and other land-based developments as a condition for receiving their licenses. As Engram said: "The future of Mississippi gaming and long-term prospects are going to be based on tourism development."[5] The first casino in Mississippi opened its doors eight months after Fordice took the oath of office; by the time he was a "spectator" eight years later, twenty-eight casinos had generated over $3.3 billion in state and local taxes, were employing more than 40,000 people, and had financed a multibillion dollar building boom. In Tunica County alone, the number of hotel rooms had grown from 20 to more than 6,000.[6]

Legislators, on the other hand, were not a group Fordice could "leave alone." At one point he became so frustrated with their refusal to pass one of his proposals that he accused several legislators of winning their campaigns "because of voter fraud."[7] He once told the assembled representatives and senators: "Even though I have been a participant in the legislative process for almost eight years now, I sometimes have trouble comprehending the method to the madness."[8] No doubt Fordice was aggravated by the willingness of many Republican legislators—who, by the time he left office, constituted nearly a third of the membership—to put local political considerations or public policy positions in front of unilaterally siding with a Republican governor.

Despite Fordice's oftentimes stormy relationship with the legislature, he left the state in sound financial shape, successfully urging the legislature to create a "rainy day" fund for future fiscal emergencies and to adopt a policy of spending only 98 percent of expected revenues in any given budget year. At the end of his eight-year tenure, the "rainy day" fund was flush with some quarter of a billion dollars. Ironically, the legislature was sometimes the source of this political charity. The growth of the state treasury during Fordice's eight-year tenure—from $4.8 billion to $10 billion—and the ensuing budget surpluses were partly a result of initiatives Fordice opposed: the one-cent sales tax the legislature enacted over his veto in 1992 and the revenue produced by the surging casino industry, legislation he would have vetoed had he been governor in 1989 and 1990 when it passed.

Back on the home front, Fordice was less successful. On election day, 1996, Fordice was driving back to Jackson when he lost control of his Jeep Grand Cherokee and ended up off the road in a crash that nearly killed him.[9] Though no one knew it at the time, Fordice had been in Memphis having lunch with his childhood sweetheart, Ann Creson. The story died until the evening of June 8, 1999, when the Jackson NBC affiliate, WLBT-TV, reported that Fordice had vacationed in France the week before with Creson. Fordice's exchange in the front yard of his privately owned Madison County home with Bert Case, a longtime WLBT reporter, made headlines around the state and nation. "Let me tell you something, you invade my privacy this way, six months from now,

I'll whip your ass. You have no damn business playing these games."[10] This time the story wouldn't go away. Two days later, Fordice announced his intention to divorce his wife of forty-four years and marry Creson.[11] As in 1993, Pat Fordice refused to commit to a divorce. At one point, she apologized to "all of the people of this state for having to endure the embarrassment and possible humiliation associated with the failure of her marriage."[12] Fordice's divorce was finalized in 2000, and he subsequently married Creson. They, too, were later divorced.

Despite the notoriety of Fordice's personal difficulties, Pat Fordice conducted herself and managed her family's activities with a dignity that endeared her to Mississippians. Although the Fordices were not married at the time of his illness and death in 2004, Pat Fordice provided care for her former husband in the final months of his life. She filled the role of matriarch of her entire family and former First Lady during the highly public funeral and memorial services that attended the death of her former husband.

THE ELECTION OF 1999

In the latter part of the twentieth century, the Republican Party began an inexorable march to political power in Mississippi by taking advantage of the process by which the Republican Party became known as conservative and the Democratic Party became known as liberal.[13] In 1999, though, the Republicans hit a bump in the road: the Democrat who succeeded Fordice owed his rise in some ways to the very man he was succeeding. The campaign that year for the opportunity to live in the Governor's Mansion—featuring Democrat Ronnie Musgrove and Republican Mike Parker—actually began four years earlier. On November 7, 1995, Musgrove, a two-term state senator from Panola County and whose support for public education mirrored that of William Winter, Ray Mabus, and Dick Molpus, defeated the Republican incumbent lieutenant governor, Eddie Briggs. The victory left Musgrove with a platform from which to launch a gubernatorial campaign. Three days later Fourth District Congressman Mike Parker switched to the Republican Party.

While Fordice's 1995 campaign was generating the largest turnout Mississippi had ever produced for a state election, and Fordice's campaign team was using that turnout to defeat Dick Molpus by some 90,000 votes, fellow Republican Briggs failed to benefit from that voter largesse. The reason: Fordice offered no help to Briggs, and Briggs had made no effort to join his campaign to Fordice's, in fact purposely distancing himself from Fordice. Fordice was the only businessman elected governor in Mississippi in the twentieth century with no prior government experience. He brought to the job a "top-down" CEO approach—he ran the ship of state, and everyone else was expected to fall in line and perform their jobs. Fordice assumed Briggs, as the second-highest state Republican officeholder, would faithfully follow his lead. But before Briggs switched parties in 1991 to oppose Democratic incumbent Lieutenant Governor Brad Dye, he had served as a Democratic state senator from Lauderdale County for eight years. Briggs believed Fordice should listen to those who had public sector experience and work as a team. Their contrasting viewpoints were never reconciled.

The disagreement reached a peak in 1994. By this time, Briggs had been openly critical of Fordice in public speeches and smaller meetings—comments that party activists made sure Fordice heard about. At one point, Briggs hinted broadly that he might oppose Fordice's reelection. While Fordice was vacationing that summer, Briggs, acting as governor in Fordice's absence, amended a proclamation for a special legislative session that Fordice had issued before leaving town. Fordice was unforgiving for this breach of protocol: "When the cat is away the mice will play. We'll set the agenda. That's what the Governor does."[14] Relations became so tense that state GOP chairman Billy Powell orchestrated a reconciliation meeting between the two. While the meeting resulted in Fordice and Briggs swearing public allegiance to the GOP, the actual reconciliation never materialized.[15]

Consequently, the two men ran separate campaigns in 1995. In the meantime, Musgrove executed a well-financed and aggressive campaign and exploited this breach at the top of the ticket. On election night 1995, Republican Governor Kirk Fordice won his reelection in a landslide, while the Republican Lieutenant Governor Eddie Briggs lost his reelection bid to a Democrat, Ronnie Musgrove. It was no secret that Fordice and Briggs disliked each other and that Briggs had distanced his campaign from Fordice. Andy Taggart managed Fordice's campaign and was with him and a few others that night awaiting returns. One campaign staffer said he had heard that a number of strong Fordice Republicans were actually crossing over to vote for Musgrove against Briggs. Taggart responded that he couldn't believe that was happening. Just then, he looked over at Fordice, who sheepishly raised one finger. With an embarrassed smile, Taggart's wife then raised her hand.

Musgrove upset Briggs's attempt at reelection, and began a four-year drive for governor. At practically the same time, Mike Parker, at the urging of Billy Powell, Billy Mounger, and Trent Lott, switched parties, giving the usual explanation—"I want you to understand I am not simply leaving the Democratic Party. The Democratic Party left me a long time ago."[16] This change of party label coincided with the Republicans gaining the majority in the U.S. House of Representatives. Parker was reelected in 1996 and then announced his retirement in 1997. While most pundits assumed he left Congress to prepare a campaign for governor in 1999, Parker had grown tired of the constant travel between Mississippi and Washington, D.C., and of the prospect of a competitive election every two years. As one of his former staffers described him, "he was a man without a country."[17] Only later did he agree to run for governor, when he was heavily recruited by GOP leaders.

In contrast to the 1995 election between Fordice and Molpus—in which the candidates articulated clear ideological positions and argued them forcefully and passionately—the 1999 campaign represented the reverse. Musgrove matched the Republican position on the big-ticket social issues—he became a leading opponent of abortion and the first Democrat to advertise extensively on Christian radio stations—and turned the election into a referendum on education and Parker's ten-year voting record in Congress. Parker, on the other hand, opted to make the election a referendum about nothing other than his personal appeal. The campaign was noteworthy for the absence of hard-hitting dueling television ads that presented voters with contrasting ideological positions. The Parker ads focused on his hometown, his family, and his career. While Musgrove complained about Parker's "issueless" campaigning, Parker ignored him, declaring that voters were "tired of the past and negative campaigning," and that he was not "going to play this 'gotcha politics.'"[18]

The 1999 campaign was also noteworthy for Parker's decision to devote virtually all of his money and resources to radio and television advertising, spending little time traveling around the state, meeting with groups of voters, and organizing supporters to get their friends and neighbors out to vote on election day. The campaign was aptly captured on the front page of the *Jackson Clarion-Ledger* only days before the election, where side-by-side articles featured the two candidates.

The Musgrove piece began: "By the time he arrived at the Mississippi School for Math and Science at 3:25 Wednesday afternoon, Ronnie Musgrove had been on the campaign trail for 8½ hours straight. And he would continue making appearances for almost another 8½ hours, mingling at a Methodist dinner, worshipping at a Baptist service and schmoozing at a private reception in Meridian."

The Parker piece began with: "Mike Parker was faced with a dilemma Wednesday. His ball was in the middle of the fairway, but he was facing a difficult, over the water shot on the eighteenth hole at Annandale Golf Club in Madison, where he was participating in a charity pro-am tournament." [19]

Without a clear ideological difference between the two candidates to motivate the voters, the turnout conformed to the Billy Mounger "rule of thumb" described earlier—the way to get Republicans excited about an election is to make the choice between the candidates clear, almost stark. Turnout dropped by 60,000 votes from 1995, and Musgrove won with 379,033 votes to Parker's 370,691.

Some political observers gave Musgrove credit for the win: "[Musgrove] was a non-Mabus and a non-Molpus. He had an appeal to blue-collar whites that (Mabus and Molpus) didn't." [20] While Musgrove had indeed received more than 12,000 votes than Molpus did in 1995, he received fewer votes than Mabus's 1987 win. On the other hand, Fordice netted 455,261 votes in 1995, while Parker could only garner 370,691 four years later. Even in Parker's Fourth Congressional District, Parker got fewer votes than Fordice. The Democrats didn't win the election of 1999; the Republicans lost it. Years later, Billy Mounger, Parker's finance chairman, observed that Parker "did as little or nothing as you can do and run for office." [21]

Two decisions made in 2002—one by Governor Musgrove and one by Haley Barbour—would put the Republicans back on track. Musgrove would call a special legislative session to enact tort reform, and Barbour would decide to leave Washington, D.C., and return home to consider a campaign for governor. But first, Mississippi returned to the past.

THE ELECTORAL COLLEGE

The first legislative session of the twenty-first century was Mississippi's first legislative session in any century to fully test Mississippi's Electoral College. Section 141 of the Mississippi Constitution provides that for a person to be elected governor, he or she must obtain a majority of the popular vote and a majority of the vote in each of the state House districts. If a candidate fails to satisfy both of those criteria, then the election outcome is determined by the House of Representatives. This is Mississippi's version of the Electoral College.

In 2000, the Electoral College was the last remnant of the sophisticated scheme embedded in the 1890 constitution to guarantee white supremacy. In the unlikely event that the federal government overturned the franchise restrictions imposed on Mississippi's black residents, the framers conceived the Electoral College as the safety net. They fashioned the 1890 House district boundaries in such a way as to ensure that the majority of representatives would come from counties with a majority white population, thus erecting "an impregnable barrier to any possible organization of the Negro majority." [22]

When the final results of the 1999 gubernatorial election were tabulated, Musgrove led by 8,344 votes, but fell short of an absolute majority because of the presence in the race of two independent candidates. While everyone in the state waited for the secretary of state to receive the certified returns from each county and then allocate those votes into each of the House districts, Parker refused to concede. At one point, Fordice urged him to give it up, admitting that "there's just a huge amount of work that needs to be done for the new governor." [23]

Once the secretary of state calculated the results for each of the 122 House districts, the two men were tied, with each winning 61 districts. [24] The net result: although Musgrove was the clear leader in the popular vote, he had failed to satisfy either of the two criteria required by the constitution of 1890. When Mississippians looked to Parker for an indication of his intentions, Parker opted to let the House decide the election: "We are not challenging or contesting the popular vote. We are simply allowing the constitution to work."

On the afternoon of January 4, 2000, as the name of each member of the House was called alphabetically, he or she stood and announced a vote for Musgrove or a vote for Parker. The historic procedure—broadcast live—put Ronnie Musgrove in the Governor's Mansion, by a margin of 86-36. Of the 86 Democrats in the House, 84 voted for Musgrove; of the 33 Republicans, 31 voted for Parker; all three independents voted for Parker. [25] Of those House members who cast their electoral votes for a candidate other than the one who carried the majority of the votes in their districts, none was defeated in his or her 2003 reelection campaigns on account of that vote.

POSTSCRIPT

From the winter day in 1982 when Buddie Newman walked off the dais, no institution of government has been subjected to more ridicule than the Mississippi legislature. During his eight years as Governor, Kirk Fordice was the unofficial cheerleader of the anti-legislature movement. On two different occasions during Fordice's tenure, citizens' groups attempted to harness that criticism into an effort to impose term limits on elected officials. The first initiative appeared on the statewide ballot in 1995 and would have subjected almost all of Mississippi's public officials, including legislators, to an eight-year limit on their terms in office. It lost by more than 61,000 votes. Operating under the belief that the first measure was too broad, affecting local as well as state politicians, the group came back in 1999 and tried again, this time limiting the proposed constitutional amendment to legislators, seeking to restrict their terms to eight years. It still lost, this time by more than 65,000 votes. Voters may decry the institution, but they prefer the rewards that come with a local legislator who has seniority.

CHAPTER 20

THE STATE FLAG AND CONGRESSIONAL REAPPORTIONMENT

2000–2001

*A new banner is intrusted today, as a battle-flag, to the safe keeping of the
Army of the Potomac. Soldiers: Your mothers, your wives, and your sisters
have made it. Consecrated by their hands, it must lead you to substantial
victory, and the complete triumph of our cause.
It can never be surrendered.*

—CONFEDERATE ADJUTANT GENERAL THOMAS JORDAN,
November 1861[1]

T he world of presidential politics was roiled in 2000 when the U.S. Supreme Court ruled that George W. Bush had won Florida's electoral votes and would become the nation's forty-third president, in spite of getting fewer popular votes than Al Gore. The world of international politics and domestic security changed forever on September 11, 2001. The world of business and commerce was transformed on December 2, 2001, when Enron filed for bankruptcy, followed eight months later by WorldCom. In Mississippi during these years, the political world was visited by ghosts of the past.

THE MISSISSIPPI STATE FLAG

For nearly 107 years, Mississippi had flown a state flag distinguished by the presence in the upper left corner of the Confederate battle flag—developed at the insistence of General P.G.T. Beauregard so as to identify the Confederate troops from the Union troops and presented to the army at a Centerville, Virginia, camp by General Thomas Jordan.[2]

As the 2000 regular session of the legislature was winding down, the state supreme court surprised virtually everyone when it issued a ruling in a seven-year-old case: Mississippi's state flag was not a legally adopted state flag. The legal journey began on April 19, 1993, when the state NAACP brought suit against Mississippi, asking the court, for a variety of reasons, to prohibit display of the flag.[3] The Mississippi Division of the United Sons of Confederate Veterans joined the litigation in support of the flag. By 1999, the case had worked its way to the state supreme court. While the court dismissed the arguments advanced by the NAACP, purely on its own initiative it presented a summary of the flag's history. The court revealed this fact: in 1906, when the laws of the state were first assembled into a uniform code, the 1894 act of the legislature creating the flag was not included. "Consequently," the court declared, "the state of Mississippi has no existing law establishing or promulgating a flag for the state."[4]

The dilemma facing Governor Musgrove and the legislature was as politically dangerous as a public policy issue could get in Mississippi: keep the flag as is or use the opportunity created by the court to design a new flag without the Confederate symbol. Musgrove punted: he appointed a commission to study the issue, hear from citizens, and make a recommendation. What the commissioners heard could be summed up this way: critics of the 1894 flag maintained it represented a defense of slavery; supporters argued it represented southern heritage. Through public hearings, letters to editors across the state, and in countless conversations and arguments in homes, restaurants, clubs, and churches, there was no reconciling the two viewpoints.

• At a hearing in Meridian, opponents of the 1894 flag were referred to as "these scalawags [who] want to spit on the graves of my ancestors."[5]

• In the Delta, feelings were rawer. While David Jordan, a black state senator from Greenwood, was arguing for a change—"I'm for redesigning it because it's the right thing to do"—someone in the audience yelled "watermelon." A leader of the movement to retain the 1894 flag pointed at William Winter, the commission head, and yelled: "You have been nothing but a parasite your entire career. You are a sorry lawyer. You're gutless. You are worthy of being tarred and feathered."[6]

• At one meeting an African American testified, "Some traditions are made to be kept. Some need to be thrown away," while a white spokesperson rebutted with: "I don't see how the blacks can say this has anything to do with slavery. That's ignorance. Once this is over and done with, what's next?"[7]

• More than 800 people showed up at the last hearing in Jackson to hear a white opponent of the 1894 flag testify: "Christian love would dictate that almost half the population of our state not be offended by what the majority clings to." A white man clearly had had enough and rose to declare, "The last 40 years, we have had this junk jammed down our throat, day in and day out." A black man then spoke of his great-great-grandfather who was a slave: "It is my heritage to resist it with every fiber of my being." At this point, a white supporter of the 1894 flag raised the "slippery slope" argument: "What's truly divisive is this escalating . . . assault on Confederate heritage. When does it stop?"[8]

• Responding to a poll about voter attitudes, one respondent said: "I don't think we should change something we hold sacred to make a point to (Northerners). I don't believe in turning to what the colored people want. We've got our rights too."[9]

• The Mississippi Religious Leadership Conference's endorsement of the new flag provoked this letter to the editor: "If these ministers want to strike a blow in the name of human rights, they should blow their holier-than-thou hot air in a direction where it might do some good for the entire human race. Their desire to see the flag changed will only satisfy a bunch of spoiled brats."[10]

While the commission adopted a new design for the state flag—which removed the Confederate battle flag—it also recognized that public opinion would not be abated; voters should have the final say. They recommended that the legislature authorize a statewide referendum: let the voters choose the 1894 flag or the new flag design. The 2001 legislature quickly sided with the commission and ordered the referendum for April 17.[11]

Polling conducted on behalf of a group supporting the new flag showed their cause to be a loser by a long shot: whites would turn out in record numbers and vote overwhelmingly for the 1894 flag, while many black voters, especially younger black voters, failed to see the relevance of the dispute. As a result, the group decided to focus its resources on identifying its supporters and encouraging them to vote; it opted not to wage a high-profile media campaign for fear that it would generate an even higher turnout among the proponents of the 1894 flag.

In the closing days of the campaign, the *Jackson Clarion-Ledger* ran profiles of two middle-age white voters whose relatives had fought in the Civil War.

At age 7, Tommy Walker and his grandfather crept across the hallowed ground of the Battle of Shiloh where the old man once fought. His 90 year old grandfather leaned against his gold headed walking stick and pointed at trees and memories he could never forget. "He knew everything that happened there," recalled Walker, 72 of Meridian. . . . "What I cannot understand is that people do not comprehend the people who support the 1894 flag. We are not segregationists. We are not separatists. We are not the KKK. We're just people who feel it's a part of us."

Emotions swell inside Eunice Milton Benton, the great-great-granddaughter of a Southern secessionist governor, when she sees a Confederate battle flag: "As a child I saw it sentimentally and thought it was glorious and wonderful. Now, I see it with eyes that have lived for 57 years and I do not want a flag that is offensive to people I love."[12]

THE VOTE

On April 17, 2001, more Mississippians went to the polls than voted in the 1999 governor's election. The 1894 flag prevailed over the alternative 494,323 votes to 273,359. Those totals only obscure a more dramatic reality.

• Of Mississippi's eighty-two counties, sixty-two have a majority white voting-age population; only two of those counties—Madison and Oktibbeha—voted for the new flag.

• Of the 1,311 majority white precincts in the state, 43 supported the new flag. Of those 43, 18 were in the Jackson metro area, and 12 were in university towns.

• Mississippi has 43 precincts with no African American residents. The margin in favor of the 1894 flag in those precincts was 5,887 to 221, or 96.4 percent voting in favor. In the 408 precincts that have fifty or fewer African Americans, the margin in favor of the 1894 flag was 89,112 to 8,014, or 91.8 percent supporting the 1894 flag.

• According to the 2000 federal census, only two precincts have no white residents. The margin in favor of the new flag in those two precincts was 421 to 5, or 98.8 percent voting for the new flag. In the 94 precincts with fifty or fewer white residents, the margin in favor of the new flag was 23,098 to 1,115, or 95.4 percent voting for the new flag.[13]

Ninety percent of white voters supported the 1894 flag, and 95 percent of black voters supported the new flag design. Although there were a number of different reasons why white voters backed the 1894 flag, the vote was nothing less than a referendum on the civil rights movement. Voters did not necessarily oppose the political and legal rights that had been restored to black Mississippians, but the vote did offer them a chance to voice their opposition to the way it was done—through the "movement"—and the humiliation and ridicule the state suffered as a result. For nearly forty years, the civil rights movement and the federal government had pushed the collective back of the white voter up against the wall, and on April 17, 2001, came the response. It was surely part resentment, but it was also a message: forty years of affirmative action, quotas, busing, and boycotts were enough.

The vote was also something else: in more recent military conflicts, such as Vietnam and Iraq, opponents of those causes have sought to pay tribute to the courage of the individual soldier while criticizing the wars in which they fought. For supporters of the 1894 flag, the passage of 136 years had obliterated that distinction: the courage and honor of the soldiers had become the sole cause for which Confederate soldiers had fought. Loss had been transformed into honor, and honor had coalesced into heritage. "The heritage of Mississippi is tied up with that flag," is how one supporter of the 1894 flag put it, "I'm offended they want to tear it down."[14]

In the end, the ambivalence expressed by one voter—"she wanted a new flag, but she doesn't want the current flag's role in history to be forgotten"— captured what may be the essential purpose of a flag: a somber reminder of the past.[15] In Mississippi, it's a different past, worthy or unworthy depending on your race.

Nonetheless, one should not read more into the flag vote than what it actually represents. Consider the case of Senate District 4, which occupies the far northeastern corner of the state and includes all of Alcorn County and parts of Tippah and Tishomingo counties. Less than 10 percent of its voters are African American, and since 1992, Travis Little has served as its senator. If there is a family that is synonymous with the local politics of a county, it is the Little family in Alcorn County. In 2003, Little switched parties and ran for reelection as a Republican. His lone Democratic opponent was Eric Powell, a native of Alcorn County and a former coach and teacher in the public schools who worked at the local paper mill in Tishomingo County. What makes this story noteworthy is that Powell is black. The new flag received 2,161 votes in this district compared to 12,865 for the 1894 flag. Only in one other senate district did the 1894 flag prevail by a greater margin. In the 2003 general election, however, Powell came close to winning, receiving 7,819 votes to Little's 8,449 votes. The contrast was even more telling in Powell's home county of Tishomingo, where the 1894 flag won 2,262 to 163 in those precincts allocated to his senate district. Powell defeated Little in those same precincts 1,664 to 1,271. The flag vote was about principle. The vote for state senator was about personal relationships and partisan politics.

CONGRESSIONAL REAPPORTIONMENT

Four decades and four censuses had come and gone in Mississippi since the U.S. Supreme Court upended the balance of political power with its 1962 *Baker v. Carr* reapportionment decision.[16] In the intervening years, legislators had raised taxes and resisted attempts to cut taxes, repealed prohibition, enacted casino gambling, revoked Sunday blue laws, authorized women to serve on juries, and confronted all other manner of controversial legislation. Reapportionment, on the other hand, was something they could not do. Federal courts imposed legislative districts following the 1960, 1970, and 1990 censuses and congressional districts following the 1980 census. They would do so again in 2001. But as the legislature convened that year, there was a new twist.

Following the census of 1900, Mississippi was allocated eight representatives in the U.S. Congress. That number was reduced to seven in 1930, to six in 1950, and to five in 1960. With Mississippi's population growing more slowly than other states', the census of 2000 would reduce the allocation by one more. It had been forty years since the state had too many incumbent congressmen and too few districts. When legislators gathered in the winter of 1962, the civil rights movement was in full swing, James Meredith was making application to the University of Mississippi, and Speaker of the House Walter Sillers, Lieutenant Governor Paul Johnson Jr., and Governor Ross Barnett were in charge. Of the six incumbent congressmen, only one failed the racial litmus test— Frank Smith. His district was combined with Jamie Whitten's district and was configured in such a way to give the electoral advantage to Whitten.[17]

Legislators faced the same disappearing district challenge in 2001—the only way geographically to squeeze five congressmen into four districts would be to force a conservative Republican congressman—Chip Pickering in the Third District—to run against a less conservative Democratic congressman— Ronnie Shows in the Fourth District. The legislature faced the question: Would the boundaries of the combined district be drawn in such a way to favor

Pickering or Shows? In other words, would the district include more traditional Republican voters or more traditional Democratic voters? In the Mississippi of 2001, that meant the equation was reduced to one variable: the number of black voters to be allocated to this newly combined district.

In 2001, Tim Ford was beginning his fourteenth year as Speaker of the House. The Senate, however, was under new leadership. Amy Tuck, a Democrat and a former state senator from Webster County, had won the 1999 campaign for lieutenant governor when Ronnie Musgrove vacated the post to campaign for governor. Most national political observers assumed the Mississippi legislature, dominated by Democratic members and led by a Democratic lieutenant governor and a Democratic Speaker, would craft a district that would favor Shows. It was a perfectly normal assumption, but was dead wrong.

Ford, his reapportionment leader Representative Tommy Reynolds, and the House supported a plan that would favor the Democrat. It became known as the "tornado plan" because a "funnel" left Congressman Roger Wicker's existing district in the north and headed due south to take in Rankin County, a bastion of white Republican voters in suburban Jackson. With Rankin County safely in Wicker's district, Democrats reasoned, the black voting-age population of the newly combined district would be 38 percent, enough to make it a competitive race for Shows against Pickering. Tuck, on the other hand, took a different approach, explaining: "We need to be sure we do what's fair and what's in the best interest of this whole state. And to do that, we have to be very objective when we draw those lines." She led the Democrats in the Senate to support the "block plan," which kept the northern district compact and inserted Rankin County in the new district, also more compact, yielding a black voting-age population of 34 percent.[18]

These two conflicting views were well established by early August, and the terms of the debate never changed. The House position was summed up by a representative: "I just believe that we ought to adhere to the political realities of the makeup of our state and do what's in the best interests of the majority party in state government."[19] Linking Rankin County to northeast Mississippi—to which it bore no resemblance or cultural similarity—was untenable for Tuck. Her Elections Committee chairman explained the Senate's position: "I don't know of any ditch in which the Senate is prepared to die more so than that particular ditch."[20] The legislature convened on November 1 in a special session to enact a plan. Seven days later, neither the House nor the Senate would change its basic position. Legislators left the state capitol empty-handed.

By this time, a group of Democrats had filed a lawsuit in Hinds County Chancery Court asking a state judge to draw the district lines. Republicans countered with their own lawsuit in federal court, asking a three-judge panel to configure the districts. The state judge assigned to the case was Patricia Wise. The three federal judges assigned to the case were Grady Jolly, David Bramlette, and Henry Wingate. Wise is black. Jolly and Bramlette are white; Wingate is black. Wise was elected in 1989; all three federal judges were appointed by Republican presidents.

Staring everyone in the face was a March 1, 2002, deadline for candidates to qualify for the congressional elections. A plan adopted by a state court would require approval by the Justice Department under the Voting Rights Act. No such requirement was needed for a plan prescribed by a federal court. To approve a reapportionment plan, the Justice Department imposed a sixty-day review period. The Democrats were under the gun: the state judge had to adopt her plan before the end of December. Judge Wise began her trial on December 14, and by this time, the Democrats had appropriated the language of Tuck's argument, maintaining that it was only "fair" to give both incumbents an equal opportunity at reelection: a lower number of black voters put Shows at a disadvantage. On December 21, Wise sided with the Democrats, holding: "Ultimately the key issue is equity. The problem was caused by the loss of a seat. The resolution must be one that is fair." The Republicans, meanwhile, complained bitterly that "the citizens of Mississippi will be outraged to know one judge sitting in Hinds County has drawn the congressional districts for the entire state."[21]

The sixty-day clock started ticking. On January 16, 2002, the federal judges refused to extend the qualifying deadline and announced they would develop their own plan if the Justice Department failed to act by the end of February. Three weeks later, the federal court promulgated the specific plan it would adopt in the event the state court plan was rejected.[22] To the dismay of Democrats, the federal court created a variant of Tuck's "block plan," but lowered the black voting-age population in the newly combined district to 30.4 percent. The court utilized a number of what it called "neutral" criteria to draw its districts, none of which included the need for a "fair" district.[23]

About this time, the Mississippi Republican lawyers paid a visit to the Department of Justice in Washington, D.C., taking the opportunity to explain to the officials the problems with a single state judge drawing congressional districts. The *Clarion-Ledger* disclosed the meeting on February 9, provoking

Rob McDuff, the lawyer for the Democrats: "What bothers me is the apparent political manipulation of the Voting Rights Act by top-level Republican officials in the Justice Department who seem to be delaying a decision on preclearance so that the federal court can substitute its plan for the state court plan."[24] The GOP lawyers echoed concerns raised earlier by the federal court: "The wide-ranging implications of . . . giving a single chancery judge the power to reapportion the entire state's congressional districts . . . raises uncertainties whether the [procedure] will be precleared. . . . At the very least [the Department of Justice] . . . might perhaps request more information."[25] On February 14, the Department of Justice did just that, asking the state to more fully explain "the legal basis for the Mississippi Supreme Court decision to vest a chancery court with jurisdiction to create and implement a statewide redistricting plan."[26] In requesting additional documentation from the state, however, the sixty-day clock was restarted, which moved the Justice Department's deadline past March 1. The game was up. Two weeks later, the federal court imposed its plan, a decision later upheld by the U.S. Supreme Court.[27]

The key was the March 1 qualifying deadline. With a federal court unwilling to push back that date, the fate of the Democrats was in the hands of the Bush administration's Justice Department. All the officials in Washington had to do was request additional information, which they did near the end of the initial sixty-day review period. In an interview months later, McDuff claimed that he had never "seen the Department manipulate the Voting Rights Act for political purposes in the way it did here. . . . It is just one of the most blatantly improper things I have seen come out of the Civil Rights Division in a long time."[28] The lead lawyer for the GOP, Michael Wallace, defended the decision in a separate interview: "I think it's simply enough to say that in 37 years of experience under the Voting Rights Act, the Justice Department had never been presented with a question of whether a judicial redistricting plan was something that the Court's assumption of jurisdiction has to be pre-cleared under Section 5. . . . It's certainly not arbitrary and capricious to ask a few questions about it before making a decision."[29]

In the wake of *Baker v. Carr*, conservatives in Mississippi—then Democrats—complained about the role of the federal courts in drawing legislative and congressional districts. It was a matter reserved for the states, they argued. Ironically, forty years later, conservatives in Mississippi—now Republicans—turned to the federal courts to halt the actions of a state judge.

For all the criticism that was visited upon Amy Tuck for her role in opposing the move by the Democratic Party to help Ronnie Shows, she adopted the same "we need to be sure we do what's fair and what's in the best interest of this whole state" approach the next year in drawing the district lines for the state senators. To the consternation of many Republicans, she allowed Monroe County Senator Hob Bryan, her reapportionment committee chairman, to fashion a plan for all fifty-two districts that, on balance, provided more opportunities for Democrats to win in the future than Republicans.

POSTSCRIPT

For all the uproar and energy and resources that were devoted to crafting the district, the actual contest between Pickering and Shows was anticlimactic. Pickering prevailed by more than 63,000 votes, receiving nearly 64 percent of the total vote. Even removing heavily Republican Rankin County from the district would not have changed the outcome. Two years earlier, George W. Bush had defeated Al Gore in the district by 64 to 36 percent.

CHAPTER 21

THE CONSEQUENCES OF TORT REFORM

2002

In the thirty years I was in the Legislature, [tort reform] was the most contentious, the most divisive piece of legislation since I was there. It made reapportionment pale.
— ED PERRY, Former State Representative[1]

Early on the morning of August 23, 2002, Governor Ronnie Musgrove hosted a breakfast meeting of close friends and key financial contributors from his earlier campaigns. They were all trial lawyers, and Musgrove proceeded to notify them he would be convening a special session of the legislature to consider tort reform. The rumors about a possible special session had been around for months; now they were confirmed. When the lawyers in attendance objected, Musgrove claimed the political pressure had become too intense. Twenty years had passed since William Winter perfected the use of a special session to focus the public's attention on a single issue. Now a Democratic governor would begin the process by which the single largest source of funding for Democratic candidates would be permanently undermined.

The special session called by Musgrove lasted eighty-three days, the longest in the history of the state. When it ended on November 26, the legislature had indeed enacted sweeping tort reform for doctors, nursing homes, hospitals, and businesses. In the election year that followed, the Democrats would lose more campaigns to Republicans in Mississippi than in any year since Reconstruction.[2]

THE ISSUE

"Tort reform" is a term widely popularized by the media to describe changes to laws that govern the use of courts by persons who claim to have suffered injury while using a defective product or because of someone's negligence (the collapse of a poorly designed building or a car wreck, for example) or who claim to have been victims of medical malpractice.[3] Persons seeking compensation in lawsuits against defendants—including physicians, manufacturers, nursing homes, and insurance companies—are represented by plaintiffs' lawyers, or "trial lawyers," as they are more commonly called.

The saga of tort reform is included in this book because of its immense political implications, particularly in Mississippi. Modern political campaigns are heavily dependent on money, primarily for advertising. In Mississippi, there have been four sources of funding for Democratic and Republican politicians: labor unions, teacher organizations, trial lawyers, and businesses. The first three typically supported Democrats, while the business community traditionally made contributions to candidates of both parties. By the time of Musgrove's breakfast, Democrats could count on little money from labor or teachers—both organizations had failed, for a variety of reasons, to stay financially healthy through the 1990s. Trial lawyers, on the other hand, began in the early 1980s to use the courts and the law in innovative ways to successfully recover large sums of money on behalf of their clients. Along the way, a sizable number of lawyers earned millions of dollars of fees and gave generously to political candidates, almost all Democrats.

The pursuit of tort reform became the most emotional and influential wedge issue Mississippi politics had spawned in thirty years, and it aided Republicans by separating business campaign contributions from Democrats and by drying up trial lawyer campaign contributions to Democrats. In a way that had not been accomplished since the civil rights movement, the tort reform initiative drew a line in the proverbial sand of Mississippi politics. Trial lawyers were on one side opposing tort reform, and businesses, joined by health care professionals, were on the other side advocating reform. A public official was forced to choose sides. There was no middle ground, no compromise. In 1987 or 1995, for example, a Ray Mabus or a Dick Molpus could knit together a coalition of trial lawyers and teachers and businesses to adequately fund a campaign because tort reform was not on the menu of public policy issues facing the state. In post–tort reform Mississippi, the political dynamic has forever changed. For businesses and their political allies, a candidate who accepts contributions from trial lawyers becomes radioactive.

While your authors agree on the political ramifications of tort reform, we disagree on the merits of the issue. Taggart argues that the civil justice system was in dire need of changes, was being abused regularly by trial lawyers, was hurting economic development efforts in the state, and was contributing to the inability of health care professionals to obtain reasonable malpractice insurance. Nash, on the other hand, believes the "crisis" that came to exist in 2001 and 2002 had little to do with tort laws and the court system and more to do with insurance companies failing to manage their finances and medical professions failing to police themselves and revoke the licenses of unqualified practitioners, and with businesses creating a phantom crisis for political purposes. Taggart believes that tort reform was successful because the facts carried the day. Nash is convinced that tort reform was successful because the supporters were able to change the focus of the debate from the victims who were injured or killed to the lawyers who represented them. Finally, Taggart concludes that tort reform corrected the opportunities for abuse of the judicial system but maintained protections for actual victims. Nash believes the tort reform measures adopted by the legislature and the Supreme Court since 2002 will ultimately prevent many victims from obtaining fair compensation and will effectively remove the deterrent that trial lawyers posed for businesses that manufactured defective products. The divide that separates the two authors is repeated across the entire state's political landscape.

THE BEGINNING

The incubator of tort reform in Mississippi can be found in the coastal hamlet of Pascagoula. It was there in 1938 that Alabama businessman Robert Ingalls located his shipbuilding business. The United States' entry into World War II a few years later proved that timing is just as important for business as it is for politics. Ingalls Shipyard became a prime contractor for the American armed forces, building hundreds of ships and vessels. Ingalls, later to become a part of the Northrop Grumman Corporation, emerged as Mississippi's largest employer, reaching a peak of 25,000 workers in 1977.[4] Ingalls was also home to thousands of workers who had been exposed to asbestos, a substance the manufacturers of which had known for many years could cause cancer and other life-threatening diseases to those who worked directly with it.[5]

While 1964 is the year remembered for the famous surgeon general's report on the hazards of cigarette smoking, it was also the year that major research studies received wide public attention emphasizing the dangers of asbestos.[6] The first asbestos lawsuit was filed in 1966 in Texas, and two years later a jury awarded the plaintiff $79,000.[7] The first Mississippi asbestos cases were filed in the late 1970s, and the first asbestos plaintiff to take his case to trial, an Ingalls Shipyard worker named James Jackson, was represented by Jackson attorney Danny Cupit. In June 1982, a federal jury in Biloxi awarded Jackson more than $1 million from two manufacturers of asbestos products.[8] By this time, a small group of Mississippi lawyers were specializing in asbestos litigation and had filed almost 1,000 lawsuits in federal court, mostly on behalf of Ingalls Shipyard employees. Then Pascagoula attorney Richard Scruggs changed the playing field.

It was in early 1984, and Scruggs had lost an unrelated trial in federal court. He explains what happened next:

> *I was on about my second or third Gin and Tonic, licking my wounds that night at home, and the telephone rang: "Mr. Scruggs, this is Lonnie Parden. . . . I wonder if you handle any of these asbestosis cases?" He was a welder at the ship yard and I guess about a minute or so into the conversation, he realized that I wasn't quite sure who he was. . . . And he said, "I was on your jury over in Federal Court." And then I immediately knew who he was, and I said, "Well, maybe you called the wrong lawyer, I lost the case." He was very complimentary of me, he said, "No, I thought you did a great job . . . you just had a lousy client." He came to see me a couple days later and I got him tested.*

Scruggs had called a friend, secured the name of a doctor, and sent Parden to get diagnosed. Scruggs continues:

> *[Parden] had been a welder for 20 some odd years and he had asbestosis. . . . And then the next thing I know, Parden sends me some of his buddies. . . . I was paying [for the test] myself, I thought everybody was, I didn't know any better, and I didn't realize that all those [other lawyers] were charging the patient for cost of the physical, and that kept the number down because the several hundred dollars was more than most of these guys had just to go get tested.*

Before he knew it, Scruggs was benefiting from word of mouth and free testing, and his asbestos practice mushroomed.[9]

For Scruggs, his cases had come late and were therefore at the end of a long line waiting for a hearing in federal court. Rather than file hundreds of individual cases in federal court, and pay a separate filing fee for each case, Scruggs decided to lump all of his cases together in one lawsuit and pay one filing fee, and, more important, do it in state court, where he could get a quicker resolution. Knowing the danger inherent in this approach, the asbestos companies immediately convinced the federal judge to transfer Scruggs's lawsuits back to federal court.

About the same time, the Mississippi Supreme Court issued a ruling on an unrelated matter that would ultimately provide a way for Scruggs to reassign, or "remand," his cases back to state court and try them as one. The problem was that Scruggs knew nothing about it. But his friend Don Barrett did. Barrett had used this ruling to keep his lawsuits against the American Tobacco Company in a Holmes County state court. Scruggs remembers talking with Barrett one day:

> at some point during our conversations, I asked him, "How did you keep the cases in state court?" And he said, "Well they did remove me [to federal court]." And I said, "Well, how did you get it remanded?" He said, "Well, on the Vicksburg Coca Cola Bottling case," and I said, "Damn, what case is that?" He got me the case . . . and my eyes popped out, I said "WOW!, this is the leverage we need to get it back in state court," and sure enough that's what happened.[10]

In due time, Scruggs and his colleagues prevailed in several major trials, winning hundreds of millions of dollars for their clients and earning millions of dollars in fees in subsequent cases.[11] The asbestos industry soon began to settle with lawyers throughout Mississippi—representing in excess of 6,000 asbestos clients according to one count—and by the early 1990s a good number of Mississippi trial lawyers were netting huge sums of money. Many of these same attorneys used earnings from their asbestos litigation to pay the $10–$15 million in expenses associated with the tobacco litigation.

Ironically, though, it was not the asbestos litigation that led to the first sustained initiative by business to enact tort reform at the state legislature: it was Don Barrett's lawsuits against the American Tobacco Company.

TORT REFORM: ACT I

The laws governing the way in which a tobacco lawsuit would be handled by a judge and ultimately decided by a jury are collectively known as product liability laws. Key issues include whether the product (cigarette) was defective, whether the company knew it, what responsibility did the user of the product have, and the like. In Mississippi, product liability law had been developed over the course of years through decisions in a number of state supreme court decisions, though these rulings had never been codified by the legislature as a comprehensive set of statutes. Consequently, each was subject to change by the supreme court, on a case-by-case basis. Faced with the Barrett litigation, concerned that the court could alter product liability rules at any time, and wanting to make the law as favorable as possible, the tobacco industry plunged into legislative politics.

At that time, a Mississippian, Gene Ainsworth, was in charge of governmental relations with the R. J. Reynolds Tobacco Company. As it happens, Ainsworth had worked served years earlier on Congressman Sonny Montgomery's staff with another Mississippian, Bob Montgomery. As Barrett's lawsuit was preparing for trial, Ainsworth contacted Montgomery, who by this time was a prominent lawyer in Canton and a state senator. He asked Montgomery to recommend a lobbyist the industry could retain to represent it at the legislature. Montgomery suggested Steve Dickson, also from Canton, who was working for the Mississippi Manufacturers Association (MMA), which for several years had been promoting tort reform, albeit unsuccessfully.

In January 1988, when Don Barrett was making his opening arguments to a Holmes County jury, lawyers from the Washington, D.C., firm of Covington and Burling, legal counsel for R. J. Reynolds, paid a visit to Jackson and met with Dickson and other MMA officials and offered to help with their tort reform program in the 1988 legislative session. Three months later, the effort had met with little success because Tim Ford, having just been elected Speaker with the help of African American representatives, had appointed Percy Watson, an African American lawyer from Hattiesburg who was sympathetic to trial lawyers and their clients, to chair the House committee to which all tort reform legislation was referred. In the other chamber, Lieutenant Governor Brad Dye had appointed another sympathetic Hattiesburg lawyer, Senator Rick Lambert, to chair the corresponding committee in the Senate.

At the end of the session, Dickson met with the Covington and Burling team to assess the outcome of the session. At one point, they asked the question: "What would it take to get the package passed?" Knowing that changes would have to occur in the membership of the legislature before it would ever seriously consider any tort reform, Dickson proposed a candidate recruitment, training, and fund-raising plan, focused on the 1991 elections. Covington and Burling agreed that tobacco companies would primarily fund the plan and expanded the group to include other law firms and other business interests. Over the intervening months, Mississippians for a Fair Legal System (M-FAIR) was created to raise and spend the money, businesses and other proponents of tort reform were recruited to join, and the initiative began.

As discussed earlier, reapportionment litigation resulted in the 1991 legislative elections being held in the districts that had existed for the previous ten years, and political allegiances had shifted in the House, resulting in another campaign for Speaker, with Ed Perry opposing Tim Ford. M-FAIR took advantage of both opportunities. The coalition helped to elect a number of new representatives and senators, enough, in fact, to present a formidable obstacle to Ford's reelection. The price for the group's support of Ford: a new committee chairman. On January 7, 1992, Tim Ford was reelected Speaker of the House. Six days later, Monroe County Representative Mike Mills became the new committee chairman, replacing Percy Watson, the only returning chairman of a major committee to lose his chairmanship. Mills had been one of the original Gang of 26 in 1984 and had supported his friend Ed Perry in 1988. Mills once explained why he changed his vote in favor of Ford in 1992: "I had spent eight years on the back row. . . . If you can't be in a position to influence after a couple of terms, then you need to go home and let someone else serve. That's the way I looked at it. It's a hard, cold reality. I knew Tim was going to win." Mills was also recommended to Ford by M-FAIR.

M-FAIR also started 1992 with two advantages it had not anticipated: the election of Kirk Fordice as governor and Eddie Briggs as lieutenant governor. When Briggs replaced Rick Lambert with Greenville senator Hainon Miller, tort reform looked like a sure winner. Mills's committee reported out a bill that was soon passed by the full House.[12] A few days later, Briggs referred it to Miller's Senate Judiciary Committee; but it died there, unexpectedly: Miller surprised almost everyone by concluding tort reform was unnecessary. The fight would have to wait another year. Trial lawyers and M-FAIR spent the intervening nine months preparing for the 1993 legislative session. In the weeks leading up to the January session, M-FAIR raised a substantial amount of money and used it to embark on an unprecedented advertising campaign that depicted trial lawyers as "greedy" and uninterested in their clients. One famous billboard they used said simply: "Fairness, Yes. Greed, No."[13] As the session was set to open, the *Jackson Clarion-Ledger* described the scene: "It's a modern-day Mississippi version of the Hatfields and McCoys. It's a big-bucks dispute between two of the most powerful groups in Mississippi politics. In one corner are Mississippi's trial lawyers. . . . Opposite are Mississippi's business leaders."[14]

The products liability legislation was introduced on January 18 by Gulf Coast Representative Mark Garriga. Ford referred it to Mills's committee, who explained what happened next:

Senators were coming to me saying can you please send us something again. We need to vote on something. And members of the House were saying we want to vote on something . . . so I felt like the best thing to do was for people who had an interest to work it out, if possible. And what I did was told the leaders of both sides, I said it publicly in the committee, that this bill has been introduced. There's something in here for everybody and there's something in here that none of you can stand. And we're going to pass something that I assure you will upset everyone unless the two of you, the two large groups, work it out.[15]

For the next three weeks, the Mississippi Trial Lawyer Association, represented by Jackson attorneys Danny Cupit, Crymes Pittman, Bill Liston, and Jim Brantley, negotiated the provisions of the bill with Steve Dickson, Bob Montgomery, and others on behalf of M-FAIR.[16] The compromise was approved by Mills's committee, and when he brought the bill up on the House floor for a final vote, he made sure Cupit and Dickson were sitting next to each other in the House gallery. As Mills was explaining the provisions of the compromise, he signaled to both of them to stand and indicate that the bill was indeed acceptable. The bill passed the House 97–25.[17] In order to prevent Senator Miller from using his committee as a graveyard, Briggs referred the bill to the friendlier Insurance Committee, which promptly approved it. The full Senate soon passed the legislation 43–6 and sent it to Governor Fordice, who hailed it as a major reform on behalf of business for Mississippi.[18]

For Mills, tort reform was done for the rest of the term: "[it] enabled us to put that issue behind us so we could deal with other issues." The tobacco companies got the law they wanted, and they moved on to other states. Mississippi businesses, happy with the outcome, turned their attention to other issues.

Mississippi's trial lawyers, however, rebounded. During the remainder of 1993, the asbestos lawyers would win a major trial in Pascagoula, and Don Barrett would host the meeting in Greenville between Richard Scruggs and Michael Lewis that would eventually lead to Mike Moore's lawsuit against the tobacco industry. In the meantime, Cupit, Brantley, Pittman, Scruggs, Liston, and others would form a new political committee to raise money and campaign on behalf of specific legislative candidates. For the 1995 and 1999 statewide and legislative elections, and the 1996 and 1998 judicial elections, lawyers associated with this new organization (known as ICE PAC) would spend well over $1 million helping to elect candidates opposed to more tort reform. Not until 2000 would the business community return to the fight in any organized way.

TORT REFORM: ACT II

While the product liability legislation had indeed imposed changes to tort laws, it had done nothing to disturb the basic framework trial lawyers had subsequently perfected to litigate their cases: join clients with similar complaints together and bring one comprehensive lawsuit, almost always against a national company, in a state court before a local jury. The 1993 bill had also failed to restrict the amount of money a jury could award to a plaintiff. Legislators at the time were reluctant to tie the hands of jurors by establishing a uniform limit applicable to all cases.

The tide began to change in 1998 when a Holmes County jury issued a $145 million verdict against Ford Motor Company.[19] And when a Jefferson County jury awarded five people who had taken the diet drug fen-phen a total of $150 million in a December 1999 trial, business groups were motivated to revisit tort reform in Mississippi.[20] Their first opportunity came with the 2000 Mississippi Supreme Court elections. The supreme court not only has the authority to review and overturn any jury award of a lower court, but it promulgates the procedures that govern how lawsuits are handled. Four of the nine incumbent judges were up for reelection that year, and the trial lawyer and tort reform organizations were each supporting opposing candidates in each of the four races.

Three weeks before the election, candidates backed by the trial lawyers had raised and spent more money than their opponents and were in command of the campaign. Then, the U.S. Chamber of Commerce showed up, and by the time the election was over, it had financed $1 million in commercials on behalf of the four business-backed candidates. While some Mississippi reporters and editors decried the Chamber's initiative, and while the secretary of state and the attorney general tried in vain to force the Chamber to disclose which companies were paying for the advertising, the unprecedented move was successful. Instead of losing all four races, the business coalition was able to elect two of their candidates.[21] The Chamber explained its motivation this way: "Business is now stepping up to the plate to respond to the new political influence of the trial lawyers in the wake of the tobacco settlement."[22] While the 2000 election changed the way in which judicial campaigns were financed and managed in Mississippi, momentum to enact additional tort reform laws failed to gain a foothold, either with the general public or in the legislature. By the end of 2001, however, tort reform proponents would have all the momentum they needed.

First, the state and national press turned against trial lawyers. It started on June 17, 2001, when Mississippians woke up to a front-page *Jackson Clarion-Ledger* headline: "Hitting the Jackpot in Mississippi Courtrooms." The newspaper explained to its readers that a series of articles would examine

> *how multimillion-dollar verdicts and settlements have created a war inside and outside Mississippi courtrooms, spurring debate over whether reform of civil laws is needed. . . . Until 1995, lawyers say there was no verdict, including punitive damages, that surpassed $9 million here. Since then, there have been at least 19—together totaling more than $2 billion. . . . These Lotto-like verdicts, many of which are handed down in poor and rural counties, are enticing out-of-state lawyers and clients to sue here.*[23]

The term "jackpot justice" soon became synonymous with the campaign to enact tort reform, and it became irresistible to the media. Headlines across the country picked up the theme: "Mississippi Town Becomes Lawsuit Central" and "Jackpot Justice Is a Black Eye for State" and "Mississippi Gaining a Lawsuit Mecca" and "Poor Southern County That's Big on Lawsuits."[24]

Second, the business lobby secured the services of new allies in the fight for tort reform: doctors, hospitals, and nursing homes. In the summer and fall of 2001, insurance companies providing medical malpractice coverage began to raise their rates dramatically or stopped writing the policies all together. "Jackpot justice" soon encompassed Mississippi's malpractice insurance crisis. A typical article appeared in the *Mississippi Business Journal*: "Medical liability insurance premiums are skyrocketing in Mississippi, squeezing health care costs and creating unfavorable situations for doctors that practice in rural areas."[25] In December, the St. Paul Insurance Company announced it was quitting the malpractice insurance business, leaving more than 400 physicians without coverage.[26] Pamphlets and posters urging an end to "lawsuit abuse in Mississippi's courts" started showing up in the waiting rooms of doctors and hospitals throughout the state.

By the time the legislature convened for its 2002 regular session in January, business leaders, health care workers, physicians, nursing home owners, reporters, and editors had one group in their sights: trial lawyers. A reporter for the *Memphis Commercial Appeal* captured the emotions at the state capitol:

> *Business owners, doctors, nursing home operators and others here are launching the most aggressive push in years for legislation to protect themselves from what they perceive as a growing threat of lawsuits and financially devastating jury awards. Hiring a platoon of lobbyists and public relations specialists, they are taking their concerns to state lawmakers as well as trying to explain to the public that they feel overwhelmed by a legal climate run amok.*[27]

Trial lawyers argued that the insurance companies had manufactured the crisis and that making changes to the laws governing malpractice lawsuits would do nothing to lure companies like St. Paul back into the state. Legislators sympathetic to the trial lawyers' point of view were in control of the key House and Senate committees, and after holding hearings on the many tort reform bills that had been introduced, they decided against adopting any of them.

MUSGROVE'S SPECIAL SESSION

For the proponents of tort reform, the good fortune of timing came to their rescue in the summer and fall: 2002 was an election year. In addition to the bitter congressional contest between Republican Chip Pickering and Democrat Ronnie Shows—Pickering had supported tort reform in Congress while Shows had opposed it—incumbent Judge Chuck McRae was on the November ballot for reelection to the state supreme court. McRae was a trial lawyer before his election to the court in 1990 and in the intervening twelve years had become one of the state's most vocal and flamboyant opponents of tort reform. While he was famous for his Harley Davidson motorcycle journeys, he was also infamous for two DUI arrests and for a *Reader's Digest* article that named him one of America's worst judges.[28] By the time an opinion poll was conducted in McRae's district in advance of his campaign, only 14 percent of the respondents said they would vote to reelect him. Verne Kennedy was overseeing polls for tort reform proponents that year and expressed astonishment in an interview for this book that the trial lawyers had not convinced McRae to retire from the court and avoid a reelection campaign. For Kennedy's clients, McRae was a lightning rod for their cause. As one confidential memorandum to doctors around the state put it: "*Chuck 'Motorcycle' McRae is in line to be the next Chief Justice of the Supreme Court.* WE SIMPLY CANNOT LET THIS HAPPEN. . . . Let the war begin!"[29]

The U.S. Chamber of Commerce returned to Mississippi after the session, buying full-page ads in newspapers exclaiming that "its members and other businesses are at significant risk from a flawed legal system when doing business in the state of Mississippi." President Bush visited the state late in the summer, making tort reform one of his principal themes. At the annual meeting of the Mississippi Economic Council, delegates were told that "doctors are drowning in lawsuits and leaving the state because of it."[30] By the end of the summer, the issue had become so emotional that some doctors were refusing to examine or treat trial lawyers and members of their families. Trial lawyers responded with their own media campaign, focusing on victims who had been injured because of negligent physicians or businesses.

Into this cauldron of raw emotion, intense media scrutiny, and election dynamics, Governor Musgrove called legislators into a special session. The timing could not have been more advantageous for those advocating tort reform: Ronnie Shows, Chuck McRae, and trial lawyers versus local doctors, pharmacists, and small businesses. Public relations consultants yearn for those rare situations where one event feeds off of another—they call it synergy. Every time Pickering complained about Shows's votes against tort reform in Congress or every time McRae's opponent—Gulf Coast lawyer Jess Dickinson— complained about McRae's record of opposing tort reform on the supreme court, it bolstered the lobbying efforts of their allies at the state capitol.

With Mike Mills having since been named to the federal bench, Representative Percy Watson was back as chairman of the House committee that considered tort reform measures. He and other opponents held out for as long as they could. They lasted thirty days before finally agreeing to a comprehensive tort reform bill for doctors and others in the health care industry. They lasted another two months before Tim Ford forced Watson to agree to a tort reform bill for other businesses, fearing that the stalemate "was damaging the House." In the meantime, Pickering defeated Shows, and Dickinson defeated McRae.

THE AFTERMATH

The Christmas season was a time of rejoicing for all the individuals and interest groups who had supported tort reform. It was especially rewarding for Republicans. They had succeeded beyond their highest hopes. Laws were enacted to restrict the ability of trial lawyers to continue collecting multimillion dollar verdicts for their clients. And in the eyes of the public, the Democratic Party was married to trial lawyers, ensuring the end of business support for Democratic candidates. The Republicans could give thanks for a Democratic governor who called a special session.

In the election year that followed, Ronnie Musgrove's opponent—Republican Haley Barbour—would make tort reform a central part of his campaign message. He campaigned as if the 2002 special session had never happened, complaining that Mississippi still needed tort reform. Musgrove failed to collect any political benefits from presiding over the enactment of tort reform. Governor Barbour made good on his campaign commitment when he called a special session of the legislature in the spring of 2004 and was successful in lobbying legislators to pass yet additional tort reform proposals.

POSTSCRIPT

The one Mississippi Republican politician who experienced anything but a joyous holiday season that year was Trent Lott. Strom Thurmond, South Carolina senator and former presidential candidate for the 1948 Dixiecrat Party, turned 100 years old during the first week of December. Serving as Senate majority leader, Lott was one of the guests chosen to speak at a birthday party for Thurmond. He closed his remarks with an "off the cuff" comment: "I want to say this about my state. When Strom Thurmond ran for president, Mississippians voted for him. And if the rest of the country had followed our lead, we wouldn't have had all these problems over the years either." There was little to no reaction to Lott's comments at the party, which were not even covered by newspapers the next day. But the comment was making the rounds of Internet sites, and within a couple of days, Lott found himself engulfed in a controversy that two weeks later cost him his Senate leadership position.[31]

CHAPTER 22

THE HALEY BARBOUR YEARS

2003–2006

*It's the morning after the election and Haley Barbour is asleep in his hotel
room when the phone rings. His wife, Marsha, answers the phone: "Haley,
Arnie is on the phone." Trying to wake up, rubbing sleep out of his eyes, he's
wondering, "Why is Arnie calling me so early?" Arnie Hederman, that is,
computer whiz kid of the campaign, their numbers specialist. Then it hits
him: "Oh damn, something happened with the vote tabulations over night,
we didn't win after all! Arnie wouldn't dare call this early unless something's wrong." Barbour picks up the phone, still waking up, he can hardly
understand what the person on the other end of the phone is saying. About
thirty seconds into the conversation he realizes, it's not Arnie Hederman, it's
Arnold Schwarzenegger, offering congratulations.*

—HENRY BARBOUR[1]

E stimates of the crowd ranged from 25,000 to 75,000. They gathered at
Biloxi's Keesler Air Force Base on the evening of September 8, 1969,
to greet President Richard Nixon. Three weeks earlier, Hurricane
Camille had nearly obliterated much of the Mississippi Gulf Coast, and
Nixon had come to view the damage himself and offer assurances of federal
assistance.[2]

Helping with the arrangements for Nixon's visit was Haley Barbour, then
a twenty-one-year-old sometime student at the University of Mississippi and
a budding Republican operative. By the time Barbour welcomed President
George W. Bush to the Gulf Coast thirty-six years later to witness the destruction of Hurricane Katrina, he was not only governor of Mississippi, but his
career had mirrored the rise of the Republican Party in the state he was now
serving as its chief executive officer.[3]

Barbour's first campaign came in the spring of 1968 when he helped his older brother become Yazoo City's first Republican mayor. A few months later, Barbour left the University of Mississippi to join Nixon's presidential campaign, raising money in the state. Impressed by Barbour's organizational skills, Republican Party leaders recommended him for the job of coordinating the 1970 census operation in Mississippi—one of the few state-level patronage jobs still available to political parties. As Barbour would remember several years later, "The Census is pretty good organizational training for an organizational politician."[4] Barbour soon became executive director of the state Republican Party, worked in campaigns through the 1970s, and then became a candidate himself, opposing Senator John Stennis in 1982. He returned to Yazoo City to practice law until President Ronald Reagan asked him in 1985 to join the White House staff as political director. In 1993, Barbour was elected chairman of the national Republican Party and was a leader of the team that engineered the GOP takeover of Congress in 1994. After creating one of the most successful lobbying businesses in Washington, he left it in 2003 to wage a campaign for governor.

THE 2003 CAMPAIGN

By the time Barbour announced for governor, the friends, clients, and allies he had made over the course of a career would serve him well.[5] The value of his long history in party affairs was once articulated by Ed Gillespie, the national Republican Party chairman. After proclaiming that the national party would "do everything that we're legally allowed to do" on behalf of Barbour, a reporter asked Gillespie about other Republican races in 2003, Gillespie explained: "They're all important to us, but Haley Barbour and I go way back."[6] With years of campaign experience, Barbour was "somebody who understood money, who understood grassroots, who understood message, fundraising, mail, everything. And he'd seen it. He knew it. He understood it."[7]

Those connections and that experience would translate into a campaign that raised and spent $13.5 million, more than three times what any candidate had ever spent in a statewide campaign in Mississippi.[8] That money would translate into nine million pieces of direct mail, hundreds of thousands of phone calls to voters, a paid staff of more than sixty people, eight months of continuous television advertising, 40,000 volunteers, and three presidential visits. In some ways it was a campaign unlike any before it in Mississippi. In one very significant way, though, it was reminiscent of most campaigns that had preceded it in the state—cultural issues trumped economic issues.

In the middle of the 2003 election season, the role of religion in politics dominated the news for several weeks when a federal judge, over the protests of Alabama Supreme Court Chief Justice Roy Moore, ordered the removal of a two-and-a-half-ton granite monument of the Ten Commandments from the rotunda of the Alabama Supreme Court building. For weeks, supporters of Moore had maintained vigils outside the court building, urging officials to retain the monument in the building, and generating nationwide headlines. On the day in August when the monument was removed, Haley Barbour's campaign manager and nephew, Henry Barbour, heard the news and thought, "Oh my, what an opportunity," and immediately drafted a press release declaring: "Tell Judge Moore, who is a hero to so many of us, that if they don't want the monument in Alabama, we want it in Mississippi." Almost simultaneously, and not wanting to cede one inch of conservative political ground to the Republicans, Governor Ronnie Musgrove released his own letter to Moore, this one on official stationery: "For too long our courts and politicians have interpreted every American freedom of religion as freedom from religion. It would be my honor to host this monument as a symbol of every Mississippian's dedication to the fundamental principles of the Ten Commandments."[9] Judge Moore eventually decided to keep the monument in Alabama, but the Mississippi candidates had scored points back home.

Abortion then took center stage when the National Right to Life political action committee (PAC) endorsed Barbour for governor and Amy Tuck for lieutenant governor. A few days later, Barbara Blackmon, a member of the state Senate and the Democratic nominee for lieutenant governor, held an extraordinary news conference in which she challenged Tuck to sign an affidavit "attesting to the fact" that Tuck had never had an abortion. Editorial writers around the state joined Tuck in calling it "one of the sleaziest political attacks in Mississippi history." The tactic backfired when Tuck signed the affidavit in late October. Blackmon made the mistake of raising an issue that helps only Republicans, and then, for all intents and purposes, she made an egregious personal accusation without any evidence. Henry Barbour was polling for his candidate throughout the fall and found that "one of the biggest moves that we saw on our tracking [polling] was when Barbara Blackmon went crazy on this abortion accusation about Amy Tuck. She looked like a crazed woman. . . . It made a bigger move than when the President came in September. . . . I mean, it just ended that race." When asked if it hurt Musgrove, Barbour said, "No question."[10]

The statistic confronting the Musgrove and Barbour campaigns in the fall of 2003 was this: the average vote in Mississippi for Democratic gubernatorial candidates over the previous four elections was 368,000, while the average vote for Democratic presidential candidates over the same period was 392,000. The average vote for Republican gubernatorial candidates over the previous four elections was 382,000, while the average vote for Republican presidential candidates was 515,000. Over the course of the last thirty years, Mississippi has grown more Republican voters than Democratic voters. The challenge for the Barbour campaign was to turn them out.

The challenge for the Musgrove campaign was identical to that faced by Ray Mabus in the 1991 general election against Kirk Fordice. After four years of constant fighting with the legislature, after a very public divorce from his wife of twenty-four years, after becoming identified with the losing side of the 1894 flag election, and after presiding over the deterioration of state finances as a result of a national recession, there was little that Musgrove could say about himself that would move voters his way. His only hope was to prevent voters from supporting Barbour, and that meant an unrelenting attack on his opponent. To finance that assault, Musgrove raised and spent $7.7 million, twice what any Democratic candidate had ever spent in any general election. But in 2003, Musgrove faced a candidate who believed that election day turnout could make or break an election and who would leave nothing to chance. As former Kansas senator Bob Dole once described Barbour: "He's this. He's that. He's everywhere. He's like fog. Get up in the morning, there's Haley, a cloud hanging over somewhere."[11]

No other county symbolized the battleground more than DeSoto County. Forty years ago, when Republicans began their rise in Mississippi, DeSoto County had a population of 9,248 whites and 14,643 blacks. Soon after busing was ordered for Memphis schools in the late 1960s, the demographics in DeSoto County began to change. With Memphis crime soaring in the 1970s and 1980s, white families there moved south in even greater numbers. By election day 2003, the influx of whites from Memphis had transformed the county into the classic suburb that has long formed the base of the Republican Party. The 2000 census found 91,950 whites and 12,216 blacks in the county. The Parker campaign essentially ignored DeSoto County in the 1999 election, allowing Musgrove to come within a few hundred votes of carrying the county: Parker received 9,300 votes to Musgrove's 9,144. The Barbour campaign vowed to double the DeSoto County vote.

Targeting urban and suburban counties all over the state, but especially in DeSoto County, the Barbour campaign implemented what Republicans have come to call the "Seventy-Two-Hour Program"—an intensive effort over the last seventy-two hours of the campaign designed to do nothing but identify Republican voters and motivate them to go vote. The Barbour campaign recruited several thousand workers, most of them "sixteen- to twenty-two-year-olds who have got a lot of energy," many from Mississippi but a significant share who came from out of state, to canvass neighborhoods and knock on doors, make phone calls, put up signs, distribute literature, and work at the polls on election day.

In DeSoto County, the program started on the Saturday morning before the Tuesday election when President Bush became the first U.S. president to ever visit the county. Merle Flowers, the Barbour county chairman, "knew they had won the election" when he arrived at the civic center at 6:00 that morning, four hours before the scheduled start of the event, to find 3,000 people already in line. More than 10,000 packed the center to cheer Bush, and as the crowd was leaving, the Barbour campaign had buses, vans, and cars waiting for volunteers to donate their afternoon distributing literature throughout the county. By election day, a Barbour volunteer had knocked on "nearly every door in the county." When the polls closed, Barbour's vote tally in the county came to 18,869 compared to Musgrove's 8,876. Overall, the five major suburban counties in Mississippi increased their turnout over 1999 by 28.3 percent, the highest of any of the state's ten geographic regions.

The "Seventy-Two-Hour Program" works well for urban and suburban areas where people live in well-populated neighborhoods that allow for intensive door-to-door canvassing. In rural areas, that kind of program is more difficult to implement. In order to motivate voters in the rural areas, the Barbour campaign made good use of the Blackmon/Tuck abortion controversy by linking Musgrove to Blackmon, and they made good use of Musgrove's support for a new state flag. The region of the state with the highest concentration of rural white voters, northeast Mississippi, produced the highest vote for the 1894 flag, nearly 78 percent. Henry Barbour characterized the campaign perspective: "We stood with our flag . . . whereas Governor Musgrove turned his back on our flag. . . . We are proud of it and don't think we should be embarrassed to be proud of our state flag. . . . There was clearly an opportunity coming down the home stretch to use that to help turn out the vote. It was a way to kind of turbo power your turnout, there are a lot of folks that, who are not as likely to vote and you have to give them something to go vote for." The northeast region increased its turnout over 1999 by 27.3 percent, the second highest performance after the suburbs, and gave Barbour a 10,000-vote margin.

With both candidates spending record amounts of money and generating intense interest in the campaign, turnout statewide increased over 1999 by 17 percent to a record 894,487 votes. Musgrove increased his share of the vote from 1999 by 30,000 votes, but Barbour increased his share from Parker's 1999 dismal showing by 100,000, leaving him the winner with 53 percent of the total vote.

THE AFTERMATH

Amy Tuck won her race with 61 percent of the vote. A Republican was elected state treasurer for the first time in Mississippi's history, and a Republican was reelected state auditor. Not since Reconstruction had more Republicans been elected to the state legislature. In fact, it had been more than 170 years since a Republican governor had been elected with a "veto proof" legislature. In Mississippi, a governor's veto can be overridden by a two-third's vote of both houses of the legislature. Or, to look at the equation another way, a governor needs only one-third of the members to sustain a veto. After the 2003 elections, Barbour and his party had well over a third of the members in the House and almost half the members in the Senate.[12]

Not since William Winter had Mississippians elected a governor who had as deep a history in the affairs of his political party as Haley Barbour. At the same time, Mississippians had never elected a governor as skilled and experienced in partisan conflict as Barbour. With Barbour in the Governor's Mansion and with seventy-one Republicans in the legislature, a political dynamic emerged at the capitol that was unique in the state's history—issues were debated from a Democratic perspective and a Republican perspective. Prior to the convening of the 2004 session, geography, race, and economic status influenced the votes legislators cast on public policy issues. The rules changed when Barbour took the oath of office. Political party began to matter.

The first two years of Barbour's administration were consumed with arguments about the appropriate level of funding for education, the number of Mississippians who should be covered by Medicaid, the level at which cigarettes should be taxed, and balancing the state's budget. With a Republican lieutenant governor in charge of a Senate where almost half of its members were Republicans, it soon became apparent to anyone at the capitol that the governor and the Senate were acting as a team. The House, with a greater margin of Democrats than the Senate, and headed by a lifelong Democrat from northeast Mississippi—Speaker Billy McCoy—became the repository of the Democratic opposition. How a legislator voted on education, health care, and taxes and spending was determined in large part by the party label appended to his or her name. This movement toward a distinctly partisan legislature was put on "pause" on August 29, 2005.

THE HURRICANE

In addressing the special session of the Legislature he called soon after Katrina had affected the life of nearly every Mississippian, Haley Barbour ended his speech by reaching back into Mississippi's history:

I am a seventh generation Mississippian. My family has seen us survive disasters before. The worst disaster, man made not natural, was the Civil War. . . . After the great flood of 1927, the federal government tried to help us. The Hoover Commission's work got lost in the Depression, and we stayed on the bottom. After Camille in 1969, another opportunity was lost. Nothing changed. After two months they were building service stations on the beach. I'm determined we will not miss this fourth chance. We must not fail our citizens.[13]

Barbour named a commission of community and business leaders, headed by former Netscape CEO Jim Barksdale, to develop aggressive rebuilding plans for south Mississippi, he led the effort to allow land-based casino development, and he joined with Mississippi's Congressional delegation to secure a multi-billion dollar package of tax credits and federal grants from Congress to assist with the recovery.

Consequently, Barbour has escaped the harsh criticism leveled at Louisiana officials and FEMA managers. As we go to press, nearly a year after Katrina, many areas of the three Gulf Coast counties look the same as they did a few weeks after the hurricane hit landfall—driving along Highway 90 still is not for the faint of heart. But Katrina is different from Camille in two important ways: the amount of federal aid that is now forthcoming and the presence of the casino and condominium businesses that were not there in 1969 to serve as economic engines for recovery. What seems clear is that the rebuilding of Mississippi's Gulf Coast will take place quicker and with more development than what occurred after Camille. While the verdict on the public policy challenge posed by Barbour will not be known for years, the political verdict will be returned in the 2007 election for governor. A politician rarely gets an opportunity to single handedly determine the success or failure of his or her career. The response of the Barbour administration to the hurricane's devastation represents that opportunity.

CONCLUSION

*We haven't had a partisan revolution in Mississippi. We've had an evolu-
tion. In retrospect, it seems like a natural progression, though it didn't feel
like it along the way.*
—HALEY BARBOUR[1]

Commenting in early 2006 on the evolution of partisanship in Mississippi,
Haley Barbour was referring to the rise of the Republican Party in Mississippi,
though the same observation could be made about almost all of the movements we have chronicled—reapportionment, legislative power struggles,
education funding, and tort reform. While each of them took years to accomplish and was made possible by underlying changes in the political fabric of
the state—often spurred by national trends—the actual movement in Mississippi occurred because men and women decided to challenge the status quo.
And, no doubt, the men and women who forged these cataclysmic changes
often wondered along the way if they would ever be successful.

That fomenting substantive political change is not for the faint of heart
is demonstrated by two anniversaries that occurred as we were finishing this
manuscript in the early spring of 2006—a date memorializing the creation of
the both the modern Republican and Democratic parties in Mississippi. Fifty
years ago, Wirt Yerger Jr. and his Young Republicans joined forces with E. O.
Spencer and his Citizens for Eisenhower to wrest control of the state Republican Party from the Lily-White and the Black and Tan factions and began their
journey. That odyssey ran from Little Rock to Rubel Phillips to Barry Goldwater to the southern strategy to Richard Nixon to Watergate to Gil Carmichael

to Ronald Reagan to the Christian Coalition to Kirk Fordice—all the way to George W. Bush and the party of Thad Cochran, Trent Lott, Roger Wicker, Chip Pickering, and Haley Barbour. And thirty years ago, the Regular Democrats set aside their segregationist past and merged with the Loyalist Democrats in an effort to preserve the political power the party had exercised since the adoption of the 1890 constitution. First confronted in 1964 by the Mississippi Freedom Democratic Party (MFDP) and later by the Loyalists, the Regulars resisted overtures to integrate party ranks for twelve years, until its all-white membership became untenable in a state that over the previous decade had witnessed the transformation of its black residents into black voters.

That transformation was forced on Mississippi by the Voting Rights Act of 1965. In addition to repealing literacy tests and residency requirements, the act required public officials in Mississippi to obtain approval of the Justice Department before enacting any voting laws or changing any election districts. Those preclearance provisions were renewed in 1970, 1975, and 1982, the most recent extension for twenty-five years. They were set to expire in 2007, though as this book was going to press in July 2006, the Congress reauthorized them for another twenty-five years. Coincidentally, 2007 is also the fortieth anniversary of the election of Robert Clark—the first African American elected to the state legislature since the 1890s. Clark secured his seat because the Voting Rights Act enfranchised black Mississippians and because a lawsuit filed by the MFDP forced a federal court to reapportion state legislative district boundaries to give meaning to the votes African Americans cast. Over the next forty years, the Voting Rights Act would intersect with the one-person, one-vote decisions of the U.S. Supreme Court to spawn countless reapportionment lawsuits and end a state legislature that had been dominated by rural white Democrats. The one-person, one-vote decisions of the U.S. Supreme Court in the early 1960s required the legislature to reconfigure its district boundaries to account for the growing urban and suburban areas. The Voting Rights Act forced the legislature to draw district lines to give African Americans a fair chance to elect one of their own to the state House and Senate.

For the seventy years following the adoption of the 1890 constitution, the legislative district boundaries never changed. By the time the U.S. Supreme Court imposed reapportionment on Mississippi, the state had 920,000 black citizens—more than 42 percent of the total population—and a 174-member state legislature with no black representatives or senators. Mississippi was also a state where the 16,826 residents of Noxubee County sent three representatives to the state House and the 119,489 residents of Harrison County sent just one representative to the state House. Today, the vote of a person living in a DeSoto County or Lamar County suburb has the same weight as the vote of a person living in rural Prentiss or Covington County. Today, one of Mississippi's four congressmen is an African American, and the state legislature now has forty-seven African Americans among its number. The public policy consequences wrought by reapportionment have been enormous. As the legislature's membership became more urban, suburban, Republican, and African American, the legislature began to address issues that rural white legislators had ignored for decades.

The 2010 federal census will require legislators once again to confront reapportionment. While the prizes owned by the majority party in the legislature are many, the big one is reapportionment. The party that controls the legislature controls how those district lines will be redrawn and which party the boundaries will favor. Republicans know this from experience. After the 2000 census forced the relocation of four House districts and one Senate district from areas of the state that had lost population to those areas that had experienced rapid growth, all five incumbents who saw their districts disappear in those areas that had lost population were Republicans.

When the legislature convened early in 2006, the state House had seventy-five Democrats and forty-seven Republicans. The margin was even smaller in the state Senate, where there were twenty-eight Democrats and twenty-four Republicans. A swing of fifteen House seats and three Senate seats in the 2007 elections will yield control of the legislature to the Republican Party for the first time since 1875. For the Democrats to retain their majority, the challenge is this: Barbour carried twenty-six of the seventy-five House districts represented by Democrats in 2003; of the twenty-eight Senate districts represented by Democrats, Barbour carried eleven. In that 2003 election, incumbent Democratic governor Ronnie Musgrove prevailed in only one Senate district and only one House district represented by a Republican.[2]

The Democratic Party not only must overcome this numerical disadvantage and the campaign fund-raising handicaps brought on by the passage of tort reform, it must confront the motivations of the typical white voter in Mississippi. Ever since Ronald Reagan used Supreme Court decisions on issues like school prayer, busing, abortion, and affirmative action and organizations like the Moral Majority and Christian Coalition to knit together a Republican Party that voters would come to view as conservative on a wide range of cultural issues, Mississippi Democrats have been in a quandary: how to reconcile their national party's "liberal" platform with a majority of Mississippi voters who are not only culturally conservative, but whose votes are motivated more by their cultural perspective than their economic status. Reagan's campaigns were a culmination of years of work by party activists and presaged the "culture wars" that now pervade national politics. The response of Mississippi Democrats has been to fashion a state party they could claim was separate and apart from the national party. In the 1960s, when the national party asserted leadership on civil rights, state Democratic leaders campaigned feverishly to assure voters that a Mississippi Democrat was different. An early Republican activist remembers how it went: "When I would hear somebody say 'I'm a Mississippi Democrat,' I would say, 'You're not. You're a Democrat.' They would take exception to that and say, 'No, I don't believe in what the national party does, but we have our own party down here.' This facade went on for many years, and they got away with it."[3]

In more recent times, with a larger palette of cultural issues defining the difference between the two parties, history is repeating itself. In May 2004, the state Democratic Party adopted a platform that mirrored the positions of the Republican Party on abortion and gay marriage.[4] One could almost hear the insistent voices of Ross Barnett, Paul Johnson, and John Bell Williams— "Mississippi Democrats are one of a kind!"—as their successors sought to distance the state party from the national party. Ever since Harry Truman persuaded the national Democratic Party to adopt his civil rights proposals in 1948, the Mississippi Democratic Party has sought to orient itself to positions shared by a majority of Mississippians, all the while hoping voters wouldn't hold the platform of the national party against its Democratic candidates. Their dilemma was once summed up by Trent Lott: "If they subscribe to the national Democratic Party's principles, they are clearly going to alienate the overwhelming majority of the white people in Mississippi.... So, if they go with the typical national Democrat base, they wind up with blacks and labor and your more liberal, social-oriented Democrats, white people. Put those groups together and they are a minority in Mississippi."[5] Ronnie Musgrove recognized the wisdom of this analysis, which is why he courted prolife activists in his gubernatorial campaigns, advertised on Christian radio stations, and tried to place a monument of the Ten Commandments in the state capitol during his 2003 reelection campaign.

The ability of the state Democratic Party to overcome this dilemma in the years ahead is complicated by a phenomenon long known to political consultants: the majority of black Mississippians tend to be conservative on many of these same cultural issues. Since obtaining the right to vote, African Americans have supported the party they perceived would protect their vote and would offer them economic opportunities. These public policy issues were more important than abortion, gay marriage, and school prayer. Nevertheless, as the passing years undermine the memory of the civil rights era, as the economy continues to grow the black middle class, and as nondenominational churches become more prominent in the black community, the danger for the Mississippi Democratic Party is that more and more African Americans may over time prefer to base their votes on their faith rather than their pocketbook. There's already evidence of this phenomenon. When the state House approved legislation in early 2006 to prohibit virtually all abortions in Mississippi, nine African American representatives rebuffed their national party's platform and supported the move, joining all of the body's Republicans. Similarly, when the 2004 legislature approved a constitutional amendment banning gay marriage in Mississippi, twenty-three black representatives and senators voted for the ban.[6] Should these cultural forces continue to gain strength, as we believe they will, Republicans will have an opportunity to broaden their base considerably.

The political implications of substantial numbers of African Americans moving to the Republican Party are, of course, enormous. In the same way that it took decades for whites to leave the Democratic Party, any movement of black voters to the Republican Party will certainly be gradual and will take time, if, indeed it happens. If, however, Republicans seize the opportunity and if African Americans respond, then the issue of race would at last begin to lose its potency in the contest for political power in Mississippi. The extent to which that happens in the coming generations is a subject for a book of Mississippi political history someone else will write later this century.

SOURCES AND NOTES

GENERAL

A book about Mississippi political history necessarily encompasses two academic disciplines—southern political science and southern history—that have produced a wealth of original research, analysis, and writing. The problem for the average reader is that most of it is not readily accessible, mainly because it is in the form of oral histories, graduate student papers, scholarly journal articles, or books no longer in print. One aim of this book was to mine that wealth of material, looking for information we could combine with our own interviews and personal experiences and turn into what we hope is a coherent and engaging history of the state's contemporary politics. In the end, we could have written a book three times as long and still not had room for all the poignant stories, humorous anecdotes, and insightful analysis.

We risk being second-guessed with our next observation, but if the reader is looking for recommendations of books that provide details of the political history of Mississippi from Reconstruction to the 1976 campaign, there are three that cover a period more or less where one leaves off and the other begins: Albert D. Kirwan, *Revolt of the Rednecks: Mississippi Politics, 1876–1925* (New York: Harper and Row, 1951); Neil R. McMillen, *Dark Journey: Black Mississippians in the Age of Jim Crow* (Chicago: University of Illinois Press, 1989)—from the early 1900s to the advent of World War II—and John Dittmer, *Local People: The Struggle for Civil Rights in Mississippi* (Chicago: University of Illinois Press, 1994)—from the end of World War II to the mid-1960s. All three are extremely well written and are packed with anecdotes as well as analysis. The last two each won the Bancroft Price, the equivalent of the Pulitzer Prize for a work of history.

Three dissertations we used extensively in our research deserve to be converted into books: William Charles Sallis, "The Color Line in Mississippi Politics, 1865–1915" (Ph.D. diss., University of Kentucky, 1967); Jesse L. White Jr., "Mississippi Electoral Politics, 1903–1976: The Emerging Modernization Consensus" (Ph.D. diss., Massachusetts Institute of Technology, 1979); and Leslie B. McLemore, "The Mississippi Freedom Democratic Party: A Case Study of Grass-Roots Politics" (Ph.D. diss., University of Massachusetts, 1971). The Sallis dissertation provides a huge amount of detail for the period beginning with the close of the Civil War and ending with the rise of the Vardaman era. White's 623-page dissertation has to be the definitive accounting of political campaigns in Mississippi for the first seventy-five years of the twentieth century. And McLemore, who participated in the civil rights move-ment about which he writes, combines a first-hand account with scholarly analysis to give his reader a thorough understanding of the beginnings of the modern Democratic Party.

Almost any book on southern politics pays homage to the classic work by V. O. Key Jr., *Southern Politics in State and Nation* (New York: Alfred A. Knopf, 1949). His analysis of Mississippi politics is now dated, but it contains much of the early history and remains to this day fun to read just because it is so well written. Books that have taken Key's approach, profiling each of the southern states and providing some overall interpretations, include William C. Havard, ed., *The Changing Politics of the South* (Baton Rouge: Louisiana State University Press, 1972); Neal R. Peirce, *The Deep South States of America* (New York: W. W. Norton, 1974); Jack Bass and Walter DeVries, *The Transformation of Southern Politics* (New York: Basic Books, 1976), Neal R. Peirce and Jerry Hagstrom, *The Book of America: Inside the 50 States Today* (New York: W. W. Norton, 1983), Robert H. Swansbrough and David M. Brodsky, eds., *The South's New Politics* (Columbia: University of South Carolina Press, 1988); Alexander P. Lamis, *The Two Party South*, 2nd ed. (New York: Oxford University Press, 1990); Alexander P. Lamis, ed., *Southern Politics in the 1990s* (Baton Rouge: Louisiana State University Press, 1999); and Charles S. Bullock III and Mark J. Rozell, eds., *The New Politics of the Old South*, 2nd ed. (New York: Rowman and Littlefield, 2003).

Books that analyze the politics of the South as a whole and that we found useful include three by the team of brothers Earl Black and Merle Black, *Politics and Society in the South* (Cambridge, Mass.: Harvard University Press, 1987), *The Vital South: How Presidents Are Elected* (Cambridge, Mass.: Harvard University Press, 1992), and *The Rise of Southern Republicans* (Cambridge, Mass.: Belknap Press of Harvard University Press, 2002). Others include Alexander Heard, *A Two-Party South?* (Chapel Hill: University of North Carolina Press, 1952); Monroe Lee Billington, *The Political South in the Twentieth Century* (New York: Charles Scribner's Sons, 1975); James F. Lea, ed., *Contemporary Southern Politics* (Baton Rouge: Louisiana State University Press, 1988); David Lublin, *The Republican South: Democratization and Partisan Change* (Princeton, N.J.: Princeton University Press, 2004); James M. Glaser, *Race, Campaign Politics, and the Realignment in the South* (New Haven, Conn.: Yale University Press, 1996); Charles L. Eagles, ed., *Is There a Southern Political Tradition?* (Jackson, University Press of Mississippi, 1996); and Richard K. Scher, *Politics in the New South*, 2nd ed. (New York: M. E. Sharpe, 1997).

While the following books examined political trends from a national perspective, we found them especially helpful in our study: Wayne Greenhaw, *Elephants in the Cottonfields* (New York: MacMillan, 1982); James L. Sundquist, *Dynamics of the Party System*, rev. ed. (Washington, D.C.: Brookings Institution, 1983); Thomas B. Edsall and Mary D. Edsall, *Chain Reaction* (New York: W. W. Norton, 1991); Dan T. Carter, *The Politics of Rage* (New York: Simon and Schuster, 1995); and Dan T. Carter, *From George Wallace to Newt Gingrich* (Baton Rouge: Louisiana State University Press, 1996). For information on political parties and their candidates through the years, one should start with the multivolume set *History of U.S. Political Parties*, Arthur M. Schlesinger Jr., gen. ed. (Philadelphia: Chelsea House).

Every two years the Department of Political Science and Criminal Justice at The Citadel hosts the Biennial Citadel Symposium on Southern Politics. It has been doing this since 1978 and has published numerous books based on the papers that were presented at the conferences. Three that we found helpful were Robert P. Steed, Laurence W. Moreland, and Tod A. Baker, eds., *Party Politics in the South* (New York: Praeger Publishers, 1980); Robert P. Steed, Laurence W. Moreland, and Tod A. Baker, eds., *The Disappearing South?* (Tuscaloosa: University of Alabama Press, 1990); and Robert P. Steed, Laurence W. Moreland, and Tod A. Baker, eds., *Southern Parties and Elections* (Tuscaloosa: University of Alabama Press, 1997).

For a book that has less political science analysis and more history of the politics of the region, and the politicians, it would be hard to beat Dewey W. Grantham, *The Life and Death of the Solid South: A Political History* (Lexington: University of Kentucky Press, 1988). If you only have time to read one book on the history of southern politics, this is the one to get.

For books that chart the overall history of the South, including politics, culture, business, labor relations, and religion, our standard reference was the History of the South series. We relied on the last three volumes: C. Vann Woodward, *Origins of the New South, 1877–1913* (Baton Rouge: Louisiana State University Press, 1951); George B. Tindall, *The Emergence of the New South, 1913–1945* (Baton Rouge: Louisiana State University Press, 1967); and Numan V. Bartley, *The New South, 1945–1980* (Baton Rouge: Louisiana State University Press, 1995). A very readable book that packs the essentials of that same historical period into one volume is Dewey W. Grantham, *The South in Modern America: A Region at Odds* (New York: HarperCollins, 1994).

Personal memoirs and observations of time spent in the South and essays about the South abound. Those that we read that contained specific information about Mississippi include Harry S. Ashmore, *An Epitaph for Dixie* (New York: W. W. Norton, 1957); Robert Coles, *Farewell to the South* (Boston: Little, Brown, 1963); John Egerton, *The Americanization of Dixie: The Southernization of America* (New York: Harper and Row, 1974); John Egerton, *Shades of Gray: Dispatches from the Modern South* (Baton Rouge: Louisiana State University Press, 1991); and Peter Applebome, *Dixie Rising: How the South Is Shaping American Values, Politics and Culture* (New York: Random House, 1996).

For works that focus on Mississippi history, the most comprehensive is the two-volume set by Richard A. McLemore, ed., *A History of Mississippi* (Hattiesburg: University and College Press of Mississippi, 1973), a project that was funded by the state in connection with the celebration of the American Revolution Bicentennial. A much shorter one-volume history of the state was written as part of the States and the Nation Series: John Ray Skates, *Mississippi: A Bicentennial History* (New York: W. W. Norton, 1979). A more recent one-volume history of the state is Wesley F. Busbee Jr., *Mississippi: A History* (Wheeling, Ill.: Harlan Davidson, 2005). In 1987, the Mississippi Historical Society sponsored Edward N. Akin, *Mississippi: An Illustrated History* (Northridge, Calif.: Windsor, 1987). That book was updated by Charles C. Bolton and re-released in 2002: Edward N. Akin and Charles C. Bolton, *Mississippi: An Illustrated History* (Sun Valley, Calif.: American Historical Press, 2002). A book that tells the history of Mississippi by highlighting key documents is Bradley G. Bond, *Mississippi: A Documentary History* (Jackson: University Press of Mississippi, 2003). Of all the textbooks on Mississippi history, the most famous is James W. Loewen and Charles Sallis, *Mississippi: Conflict and Change* (New York: Pantheon Books, 1974), which the state textbook procurement board tried to prevent schools from purchasing because Loewen and Sallis included information about segregation and the rise of the civil rights movement. Two books that contain biographies of Mississippi political figures are Cecil L. Sumners, *The Governors of Mississippi* (Gretna, La.: Pelican, 1980), and George A. Sewell and Margaret L. Dwight, *Mississippi Black History Makers*, rev. ed. (Jackson: University Press of Mississippi, 1984). A compilation of noteworthy writings by Mississippi authors and by other authors about Mississippi is Marion Barnwell, ed., *A Place Called Mississippi: Collected Narratives* (Jackson: University Press of Mississippi, 1997).

For the early political history of Mississippi, we relied on Eric Foner, *A Short History of Reconstruction: 1863–1877* (New York: Harper and Row, 1990); Otto H. Olsen, ed., *Reconstruction and Redemption in the South* (Baton Rouge: Louisiana State University Press, 1980); Vernon Lane Wharton, *The Negro in Mississippi, 1865–1890* (New York: Harper Torchbooks, 1947); Stephen Cresswell, *Multiparty Politics in Mississippi, 1877–1902* (Jackson: University Press of Mississippi, 1995); and Bradley G. Bond, *Political Culture in the Nineteenth Century South: Mississippi, 1830–1900* (Baton Rouge: Louisiana State University Press, 1995).

For personal accounts of Mississippi history, we used Trent Lott, *Herding Cats: A Life in Politics* (New York: ReganBooks, 2005); Erle Johnston, *Mississippi's Defiant Years, 1953–1973* (Forest, Miss.: Lake Harbor, 1990); Erle Johnston, *Politics: Mississippi Style* (Forest, Miss.: Lake Harbor, 1993); Bill Minor, *Eyes on Mississippi* (Jackson, Miss.: J. Prichard Morris Books, 2001); Curtis Wilkie, *Dixie: A Personal Odyssey through Events That Shaped the Modern South* (New York: Scribner, 2001); and Adam Nossiter, *Of Long Memory: Mississippi and the Murder of Medgar Evers* (New York: Addison-Wesley, 1994).

Books that focus specifically on Mississippi politics and government include Robert B. Highsaw and Charles N. Fortenberry, *The Government and Administration of Mississippi* (New York: Thomas Y. Crowell, 1954); David B. Ogle, *Strengthening the Mississippi Legislature* (New Brunswick, N.J.: Rutgers University Press, 1971); David M. Landry and Joseph B. Parker, eds., *Mississippi Government and Politics in Transition* (Dubuque, Iowa: Kendall/Hunt, 1976); Thomas E. Kynerd, *Administrative Reorganization of Mississippi Government: A Study in Politics* (Jackson: University Press of Mississippi, 1978); Dale Krane and Stephen D. Shaffer, *Mississippi Government and Politics: Modernizers versus Traditionalists* (Lincoln: University of Nebraska Press, 1992); and Joseph B. Parker, *Politics in Mississippi*, 2nd ed. (Salem, Wis.: Sheffield, 2001). Shaffer is a professor of political science at Mississippi State University who has posted on his Web site at the university virtually all of the scholarly papers he has published over the years. We read them all and used many as references.

Election data were obtained from three basic sources. For state returns, we relied on the figures published every four years in the *Official and Statistical Register* as well as F. Glenn Abney, *Mississippi Election Statistics, 1900–1967* (Oxford, Miss.: Bureau of Governmental Research, University of Mississippi, 1968). For national returns, we used the *Guide to U.S. Elections*, 3rd ed., published by Congressional Quarterly in 1994, and subsequent updates issued by Congressional Quarterly. For specific information on actions in the state legislature, we referred to the House and Senate Journals. Court cases we used are fully cited in the text or notes. Articles we used from state newspapers came from the files of the Mississippi Department of Archives and History. Articles from other newspapers were obtained from the relevant archives. The oral histories we used are listed below, as are the interviews personally conducted by the authors.

ORAL HISTORIES CONDUCTED BY THE AUTHORS

Ainsworth, John Ed, Jackson, Mississippi; recording, February 7, 2005

Allain, William A., Jackson, Mississippi; recording, December 17, 2004

Anderson, Reuben V., Jackson, Mississippi; recording, June 17, 2004

Banks, Fred L., Jr., Jackson, Mississippi; interview, February 17, 2004

Barbour, Haley, Jackson, Mississippi; recording, February 15, 2006

Barbour, Henry L., Jackson, Mississippi; recording, March 24 and May 12, 2005

Barefield, Stone, Hattiesburg, Mississippi; interview, March 30, 2004

Barksdale, Claiborne, Oxford, Mississippi, interview, May 11, 2005

Benton, Paul, Gulfport, Mississippi; interview, August 25, 2004

Blass, Joel, Gulfport, Mississippi; interview, July 30, 2004

Blessey, Gerald, Biloxi, Mississippi; recording, May 5, 2005

Bowie, Harry, McComb, Mississippi; recording, November 4, 2004

Bronstein, Alvin, Washington, D.C.; recording, July 15, 2004

Brown, Walter, Natchez, Mississippi; recording, March 31, 2004

Bryan, Hob, Amory, Mississippi; interview, October 12, 2004

Carmichael, Gil, Meridian, Mississippi; recording, March 9, 2004

Carnathan, Gary, Tupelo, Mississippi; recording, October 13, 2004

Carpenter, Tim, New Orleans, Louisiana; recording, November 22, 2004

Carter, Hodding, III, Miami, Florida; recording, July 7, 2004

Carter, Rick, Gulfport, Mississippi; recording, July 27, 2004

Clark, Charles, Jackson, Mississippi; recording, January 24, 2005

Cochran, Thad, Washington, D.C.; recording, September 26, 2005

Cole, Ed, Jackson, Mississippi; recordings, November 9 and December 8, 2004

Confidential interviews, Jackson, Mississippi, February 9 and August 9, 2004

Confidential interview, Jackson, Mississippi, September 14, 2005

Confidential recording, Jackson, Mississippi, September 21, 2004

Connor, Peggy, Hattiesburg, Mississippi; recording, February 3, 2005

Cooper, Danny, Jackson, Mississippi; interview, March 12, 2004

Crews, David, Oxford, Mississippi; recording, September 12, 2004

Cupit, Danny E., Jackson, Mississippi; recordings, August 19 and September 30, 2004, and interviews, March 29, 2004, and September 28, 2005

Dantin, Maurice, Columbia, Mississippi; recording, November 4, 2004

Derian, Patt, Miami, Florida; recording, November 19, 2004

Dickson, Steve, Jackson, Mississippi; interviews, June 29 and August 31, 2004

Dye, Brad, Jackson, Mississippi; recording, December 21, 2004, and interview, February 16, 2004

Edwards, Wayne, Nashville, Tennessee; recording, June 23, 2004

Ellington, Ed, Jackson, Mississippi; interview, October 5, 2004

Endris, Glenn, Biloxi, Mississippi; recording, December 20, 2004

Espy, Mike, Jackson, Mississippi; recording, July 2, 2004

Evers, Charles, Jackson, Mississippi; interview, February 16, 2004, and recording, July 19, 2004

Flowers, Merle, Southaven, Mississippi; recording, November 18, 2004

Ford, Tim, Jackson, Mississippi; recordings, April 21 and May 18, 2005

Fox, Grant, Tupelo, Mississippi; interview, September 13, 2004

Garrett, Tone, Jackson, Mississippi; interview, August 11, 2004

Golden, Wilson, Washington, D.C.; interview, February 15, 2004

Gollott, Tommy, Biloxi, Mississippi; recording, July 28, 2004

Gordon, Jack, Okolona, Mississippi; recording, October 29, 2004

Griffith, Lanny, Washington, D.C.; recordings, July 13 and 14, 2004

Grisham, John, North Garden, Virginia; interviews, October 5 and 6, 2004

Guyot, Lawrence, Washington, D.C.; recording, July 14, 2004

Guyton, Steve, Jackson, Mississippi; recording, September 7, 2004

Haxton, Ayres, Natchez, Mississippi; interviews, March 31 and November 4, 2004

Hazard, Mark, West Point, Mississippi; recording, October 12, 2004

Henegan, John, Jackson, Mississippi; interview, March 11, 2004

Holloman, John, Jackson, Mississippi; recording, April 7, 2005

Jones, Bill, Montgomery, Alabama; interview, April 11, 2005

Kennedy, Verne, Pensacola, Florida; recording, January 4, 2005

Kirchmayr, Steve, Jackson, Mississippi; recording, August 16, 2004

Kirksey, Henry, Jackson, Mississippi; recording, June 22, 2004

Klumb, Charles, Fairhope, Alabama; recording, January 4, 2005

Langston, Joey, Booneville, Mississippi; recording, September 13, 2004

Leonard, Jerris, Washington, D.C.; recording, July 14, 2004

Levanway, Scott, Biloxi, Mississippi; recordings, October 6 and December 20, 2004

Lipman, David, Miami, Florida; interview, April 27, 2004

Liston, Bill, Winona, Mississippi; interview, October 12, 2004

Lott, Trent, Washington, D.C.; interview, October 24, 2005

Mabus, Ray, Jackson, Mississippi; recordings, June 8, 2004, and May 3, 2005

Mavar, Victor, Biloxi, Mississippi; recording, July 28, 2004

Maxey, John, Jackson, Mississippi; recording, June 24, 2004, and interview, October 7, 2005

McBride, Eddie, Jackson, Mississippi; interview, February 17, 2006

McClendon, B. B., Jackson, Mississippi; interview, March 25, 2004

McDuff, Rob, Jackson, Mississippi; interview, February 13, 2004

McKellar, Charles, Holly Springs, Mississippi; recording, September 14, 2004

McLemore, Les, Jackson, Mississippi; recording, March 10, 2004

McMillen, Neil, Hattiesburg, Mississippi; recording, February 3, 2005

McTeer, Victor, Greenville, Mississippi; interview, June 21, 2005

Medlin, Buddy, Jackson, Mississippi; recording, July 21, 2004

Merideth, H. L., Jr., Jackson, Mississippi; recordings, June 29 and July 23, 2004

Mills, Mike, Oxford, Mississippi; recording, October 19, 2004

Moak, Bobby, Bogue Chitto, Mississippi; interviews, November 4, 2004, and October 13, 2005

Molpus, Dick, Jackson, Mississippi; recording, July 20, 2004

Montgomery, Bob, Canton, Mississippi; recording, October 26, 2004

Moore, Mike, Jackson, Mississippi; recording, September 9, 2004

Mounger, William D., Jackson, Mississippi; interviews, February 24 and March 19, 2004, and recordings, May 13 and August 19, 2004, and April 22, 2005

Patterson, Steve, New Albany, Mississippi; recordings, May 11 and September 13, 2004

Peden, James A. Jr., Jackson, Mississippi; interview, October 22, 2004

Pennebaker, John, New Albany, Mississippi; recording, September 14, 2004

Percy, LeRoy, Greenville, Mississippi; interview, February 17, 2004

Perry, Ed, Oxford, Mississippi; recording, September 14, 2004

Phillips, Rubel, Jackson, Mississippi; interview, March 4, 2004

Pickering, Charles, Hattiesburg, Mississippi; interview, March 30, 2004

Pittman, Crymes G., Jackson, Mississippi; recording, April 2, 2004

Powell, Billy, Jackson, Mississippi; recording, November 10, 2004

Reed, Clarke, Greenville, Mississippi; recordings, June 25 and November 5, 2004, and May 20, 2005, and interview February 17, 2004

Reed, Jack, Tupelo, Mississippi; recording, October 13, 2004

Reynolds, Tommy, Charleston, Mississippi; recording, September 20, 2004

Russell, Dan M., Jr., Gulfport, Mississippi; interview, May 5, 2005

Scruggs, Richard, Oxford, Mississippi; recordings, October 19 and November 1, 2004

Simmons, Cecil, Maben, Mississippi; recording, October 12, 2004

Spell, William E., Clinton, Mississippi; recording, September 6, 2004

Stennis, John Hampton, Jackson, Mississippi; interviews, February 16 and March 12, 2004, and recording, April 12, 2004

Stevens, Stuart, Washington, D.C.; interview, March 10, 2004

Stubbs, Terrell, Mendenhall, Mississippi; recording, May 6, 2005

Taylor, George P., Birmingham, Alabama; interview, June 8, 2004

Thompson, Bennie G., Bolton, Mississippi; interview, July 13, 2004, and October 9, 2005

Triggs, Gene, Clinton, Mississippi; recording, August 18, 2004

Waggoner, Sam, Jackson, Mississippi; recording, September 21, 2004

Walls, Johnnie, Greenville, Mississippi; recording, November 5, 2004

Walman, Tommy, McComb, Mississippi; recording, May 18, 2005

Watkins, David, Jackson, Mississippi; recording, September 24, 2004

White, Jesse L., Jr., Durham, North Carolina; interview, March 8, 2004

Williams, T. Clovis, Jackson, Mississippi; interview, March 24, 2004

Winter, William F., Jackson, Mississippi; recordings, April 14 and December 29, 2004, and interview on February 20, 2004

Wroten, Joseph E., Aberdeen, Mississippi; recording, October 14, 2004

Yerger, Wirt A., Jr., Jackson, Mississippi; recordings, June 24, July 22, and September 8, 2004

Zucarro, Joe, Natchez, Mississippi; recording, March 24, 2004

ORAL HISTORIES OBTAINED FROM OTHER SOURCES

Department of Archives and History,
State of Mississippi Oral History Program, Jackson

Barnett, Ross R., 1981
Blessey, Gerald H., 1975
Campbell, Hayden, 1976
Cossar, George Payne, 1973
Deaton, Charles M., 1975
Evers, Charles, 1981
Henry, Aaron, 1981
Junkin, John R., 1975
Percy, LeRoy, 1979
Thompson, Bennie G., 1977
White, Jesse L., Jr., 1973
Wiesenburg, Karl, 1976

Lyndon B. Johnson Library, Austin, Texas

Eastland, James O., 1971
Evers, Charles, 1974
Henry, Aaron, 1970

Mississippi State University Libraries,
John C. Stennis Oral History Project,
Congressional and Political Research Center, Starkville

Barbour, Haley, 1991
Blount, Joe, 1991
Brunini, Edmund L., Sr., 1991
Carmichael, Gil, 1991
Clark, Robert G., 1991
Cochran, Thad, 1991
Cole, Ed, 1991
Dean, Kenneth, 1992
Derian, Patt, 1991
Hailman, John R., 1990
Montgomery, G. V., 1991
Overby, Charles, 1991
Ready, George, 1992
Seal, Leo, Jr., 1991
Slabach, Fred, 1991

Speakes, Larry, 1991
Spell, William E., 1990
Stennis, John, 1972
Stennis, John, and J. P. Coleman, 1977
Stennis, John Hampton, 1975
Winter, William F., 1991 and 1992
Wroten, Joseph E., 1992

University of North Carolina at Chapel Hill, Southern Oral History Program Collection (4007), Southern Historical Collection, Wilson Library

Carmichael, Gil, A-99, 1974
Carter, Hodding, III, A-100, 1974
Clark, Robert G., A-101, 1974
Cochran, Thad, A-103, 1974
Coleman, J. P., A-102, 1974, and A-338, 1990
Derian, Patt, A-105, 1974
Henry, Aaron, A-107, 1974
O'Keefe, Jerry, Jr., A-111, 1974
Reed, Clarke, A-113, 1974
Williams, John Bell, A-117, March 29, 1974

University of Southern Mississippi, Center for Oral History and Cultural Heritage, Hattiesburg

Abernethy, Thomas G., vol. 23, 1973
Adam, Bidwell, vol. 34, 1976
Alexander, W. B., vol. 346, 1974
Alford, Sam, vol. 177, 1981
Anderson, Reuben V., vol. 320, 1986, and vol. 320, pt. II, 1997
Armstrong, Louis, vol. 295-2, 1979
Banks, Fred L., Jr., vol. 706, 1998
Barber, Frank, vol. 667, 1990 and 1993
Barber, Rims, vol. 626, 1995, and vol. 690, 1997
Barbour, Haley, vol. 301, 1978
Barnett, Ross R., vol. 26, 1971
Blass, Joel, vol. 639, 1977
Blessey, Gerald, vol. 747, 2001
Brady, Thomas P., vol. 2, 1972
Bramlett, Leon, vol. 205, 1980
Carmichael, Gil, vol. 176, 1981

Capps, Charles W., Jr., vol. 748, 1999
Chain, Bobby, vol. 51, 1977
Coleman, J. P., vol. 203, 1982
Colmer, William M., vol. 43, 1974
Cooper, Owen, vol. 57, 1972
Corlew, John G., vol. 221, 1983
Crews, David, vol. 737, 1991
Davis, Russell C., vol. 55, 1974
Deaton, Charles M., vol. 737, 1991
DeCell, Herman B., vol. 207, 1977
Dye, Brad, vol. 737, 1991, and vol. 467, 1993
Edwards, Wayne, vol. 91, 1976
Evers, Charles, vol. 7, 1971
Giordano, Thomas S., vol. 129, 1980
Glazier, Herman, vol. 485, 1993, and vol. 485, pt. II, 1991
Godwin, George, Jr., vol. 463, 1993, and vol. 695, 1997
Griffin, Charles H., vol. 191, 1981
Guyot, Lawrence, vol. 673, 1996
Henegan, John, vol. 737, 1991
Henry, Aaron, vol. 33, 1972
Holleman, Boyce, vol. 484, 1976
Johnson, Pete, vol. 441, 1993
Knight, Thomas, Sr., vol. 410, 1992
Ladner, Heber, vol. 30, 1977, and vol. 30, pt. II, 1983
Lane, Dewey, vol. 338, 1979
Mavar, Victor, vol. 350, 1979
McKellar, Charles, vol. 93, 1977
Merideth, H. L., Jr., vol. 737, 1991
Minor, Bill, vol. 737, 1991
Mounger, W. D., vol. 311, pts. I and II, 1977
Moye, James, vol. 216, 1981
Newman, C. B., vol. 447, 1992, and vol. 737, 1991
Overby, Charles L., vol. 737, 1991
Pierce, Clarence A., vol. 336, 1979
Ramsay, Claude, vol. 215, 1981
Retzer, Mike, vol. 209, 1980
Robertson, James L., vol. 325, 1986
Rogers, George W., vol. 652, 1977
Shanks, Doug, vol. 291, 1980
Simmons, William J., vol. 372, 1979
Simpson, James C., vol. 497, 1992
Slaughter-Harvey, Constance, vol. 695, 1997
Smith, Theodore, vol. 218, 1984

Sturdivant, Mike P., vol. 109, 1979
Thompson, Bennie G., vol. 339, 1974
Triggs, Gene, vol. 385, 1975
Walker, Prentiss, vol. 208, 1976
Walker, Robert, vol. 695, 1997
Walman, Thomas H., vol. 737, 1991
West, Phillip, vol. 629, 1980
White, Jesse L., Jr., vol. 65, 1976
Williams, John Bell, vol. 106, 1978
Williams, Kenneth O., vol. 470, 1993
Winter, William F., vol. 417, 1978, and vol. 737, 1989, 1990 and 1991
Wroten, Joseph E., vol. 476, 1993
Yerger, Swan, vol. 265, 1978
Yerger, Wirt A., Jr., vol. 204, 1978
Young, Stanford, vol. 396, 1991

Tougaloo College, Civil Rights Documentation Project, Jackson, Mississippi

Allen, Willie T., 2000
Clark, Robert G., 2000
Young, Charles L., Sr., 1998

The remainder of our reference materials are itemized according to the specific chapter, listed below.

INTRODUCTION

1. Gil Carmichael, MSU Oral History, 10.
2. Robert Highsaw and Charles N. Fortenberry, *The Government and Administration of Mississippi* (New York: Thomas Y. Crowell, 1954), 11.
3. Frank R. Parker, *Black Votes Count: Political Empowerment in Mississippi after 1965* (Chapel Hill: University of North Carolina Press, 1990), 6.
4. James C. Simpson, USM Oral History, 16.
5. Thomas S. Giordano, USM Oral History, 9–11.
6. Nick Kotz, *Judgment Days: Lyndon Baines Johnson, Martin Luther King, Jr., and the Laws That Changed America* (New York: Houghton Mifflin, 2005), 154.
7. Gil Carmichael, UNC Oral History, 8; Gil Carmichael, USM Oral History, 28.
8. Julie Goodman, "Growing Partisanship Leaves Budget, Ed Funding in Limbo," *Jackson Clarion-Ledger*, April 5, 2004.
9. Neil McMillen, interview with the authors.

CHAPTER 1. HISTORY OF MISSISSIPPI DEMOCRATS, 1948–1975

The scope of material published on the civil rights period in this country is enormous. Just shy of enormous is the number of works published on the civil rights movement in Mississippi; the sheer volume is nearly overwhelming. Even for the small piece of the movement on which we focus—the creation of the modern Democratic Party—there is a wealth of primary and secondary sources.

For coverage of the civil rights movement generally, we relied on Taylor Branch, *Parting the Waters: America in the King Years, 1954–1963* (New York: Simon and Schuster, 1988), and Taylor Branch, *Pillar of Fire: America in the King Years,* 1963–1965(New York, Simon and Schuster, 1998). The third volume of Branch's collection was released as this book was going to press. For the full impact of this period, there is no substitute for the *Eyes on the Prize* television series produced for PBS in the late 1980s. The companion volume to the series does a superb job of covering the highlights of the movement in 300 pages: Juan Williams, *Eyes on the Prize: America's Civil Rights Years, 1954–1965* (New York: Viking, 1987). We also found the following books useful: David J. Garrow, *Bearing the Cross: Martin Luther King, Jr. and the Southern Christian Leadership Conference* (New York: William Morrow, 1986); Anthony Lewis and the *New York Times, Portrait of a Decade: The Second American Revolution* (New York: Random House, 1964); Robert Mann, *The Walls of Jericho: Lyndon Johnson, Hubert Humphrey, Richard Russell, and the Struggle for Civil Rights* (New York: Harcourt, Brace, 1996); Pat Watters and Reese Cleghorn, *Climbing Jacob's Ladder: The Arrival of Negroes in Southern Politics* (New York: Harcourt, Brace and World, 1967); Manning Marable, *Race, Reform, and Rebellion: The Second Reconstruction in Black America, 1945–1990* (Jackson: University Press of Mississippi, 1991); and Nick Kotz, *Judgment Days: Lyndon Baines Johnson, Martin Luther King, Jr., and the Laws That Changed America* (Boston: Houghton Mifflin, 2005).

For coverage of campaign politics related to the periods of massive resistance and the civil rights movement, we used Earl Black, *Southern Governors and Civil Rights: Racial Segregation as a Campaign Issue in the Second Reconstruction* (Cambridge, Mass.: Harvard University Press, 1976), and Numan V. Bartley and Hugh D. Graham, *Southern Politics and the Second Reconstruction* (Baltimore: Johns Hopkins University Press, 1975).

For coverage of the years immediately preceding and following the *Brown* decision, we used Kari Frederickson, *The Dixiecrat Revolt and the End of the Solid South, 1932–1968* (Chapel Hill: University of North Carolina Press, 2001); Richard Kluger, *Simple Justice: The History of* Brown v. Board of Education *and Black America's Struggle for Equality* (New York: Alfred A. Knopf, 1975); Stephen J. Whitfield, *A Death in the Delta: The Story of Emmett Till* (New York: Free Press, 1988); Michael R. Belknap, *Federal Law and Southern Order* (Athens: University of Georgia Press, 1987); Neil R. McMillen, *The Citizens' Council: Organized Resistance to the Second Reconstruction, 1954–1964* (Chicago: University of Illinois Press, 1971); Hodding Carter III, *The South Strikes Back* (New York: Doubleday, 1959); Numan V. Bartley, *The Rise of Massive Resistance: Race and Politics in the South during the 1950's* (Baton Rouge: Louisiana State University Press, 1969); Richard D. Chesteen, "Mississippi Is Gone Home: A Study of the 1948 Mississippi States' Rights Bolt," *Journal of Mississippi History* 32

(February 1970); Susan Weill, "The Dixiecrats and the Mississippi Daily Press," *Journal of Mississippi History* 64 (Winter 2002); and Richard C. Ethridge, "Mississippi's Role in the Dixiecrat Movement" (Ph.D. diss., Mississippi State University, 1971).

For coverage of the movement in Mississippi, in addition to Dittmer's *Local People*, we relied on Charles M. Payne, *I've Got the Light of Freedom: The Organizing Tradition and the Mississippi Freedom Struggle* (Berkeley: University of California Press, 1995); J. Todd Moye, *Let the People Decide: Black Freedom and White Resistance Movements in Sunflower County, Mississippi, 1945–1986* (Chapel Hill: University of North Carolina Press, 2004); John R. Salter Jr., *Jackson, Mississippi: An American Chronicle of Struggle and Schism* (Hicksville, N.Y.: Exposition Press, 1979); Frederick M. Wirt, *"We Ain't What We Was": Civil Rights in the New South* (Durham, N.C.: Duke University Press, 1997); Yasuhiro Katagiri, *The Mississippi Sate Sovereignty Commission: Civil Rights and States' Rights* (Jackson: University Press of Mississippi, 2001); Howell Raines, *My Soul Is Rested* (New York: G. P. Putnam's Sons, 1977); Howard Zinn, *SNCC: The New Abolitionists* (Boston: Beacon Press, 1964); Kenneth T. Andrews, *Freedom Is a Constant Struggle: The Mississippi Civil Rights Movement and Its Legacy* (Chicago: University of Chicago Press, 2004); William McCord, *Mississippi: The Long, Hot Summer* (New York: W. W. Norton, 1965); David R. Davies, ed., *The Press and Race: Mississippi Journalists Confront the Movement* (Jackson: University Press of Mississippi, 2001); Douglas O. Linder, "Bending Toward Justice: John Doar and the Mississippi Burning Trial," *Mississippi Law Journal* 72 (Winter 2002); William F. Winter, "Development of Educational Policy in Mississippi," *Mississippi Law Journal* 58 (Fall 1988); Charles C. Bolton, "The Last Stand of Massive Resistance: Mississippi Public School Integration, 1970," *Journal of Mississippi History* 61 (Winter 1999); Sarah Rowe-Sims, "The Mississippi State Sovereignty Commission: An Agency History," *Journal of Mississippi History* 61 (Spring 1999); J. Michael Butler, "The Mississippi State Sovereignty Commission and Beach Integration, 1959–1963: A Cotton-Patch Gestapo?" *Journal of Southern History* 68 (February 2002); and Judge Billy G. Bridges and Wendy E. Walker, "The Forty Year Fight to Desegregate Public Education in the Fifth Circuit and in Particular, Mississippi," *Mississippi College Law Journal* 16 (Spring 1996). As we were going to press, a superb book detailing the history of public education in our state was published: Charles C. Bolton, *The Hardest Deal of All: The Battle Over School Integration in Mississippi, 1870–1980* (Jackson: University Press of Mississippi, 2005).

For the role of the Mississippi Freedom Democratic Party and the creation of the Loyalist Democratic Party and the subsequent merger with the Regular Democratic Party in Mississippi, we relied on a number of graduate research papers, in addition to the McLemore dissertation: Anne Cooke Romaine, "The Mississippi Freedom Democratic Party Through August 1964" (Master's thesis, University of Virginia, 1970); Kenneth T. Andrews, "Freedom Is a Constant Struggle: The Dynamics and Consequences of the Mississippi Civil Rights Movement, 1960–1984" (Ph.D. diss., State University of New York, 1997); Jan H. Lewis, "Mississippi's Experiments in Biracial Politics, 1960–1973: A Challenge to White Supremacy" (Master's thesis, Mississippi State University, 1974); Charles H. Baer, "The New Black Politics in Mississippi: A Quantitative Analysis" (Ph.D. diss., Northwestern University, 1970); Vanessa Lynn Davis, "Sisters and Brothers All: The Mississippi Freedom Democratic Party and the Struggle for Political Equality" (Ph.D. diss., Vanderbilt University, 1996); Paul

J. Stekler, "Black Politics in the New South: An Investigation of Change at Various Levels" (Ph.D. diss., Harvard University, 1982); Robert Sabin Montjoy, "The Negro and Mississippi Politics: The 1967 Democratic Primaries" (Master's thesis, University of Alabama, 1973); and Gary H. Brooks, "Inter- and Intragroup Conflict in Black Politics: A Case Study of the Mississippi Freedom Democratic Party" (Master's thesis, Tulane University, 1970). Journal articles we found helpful include William Simpson, "The Birth of the Mississippi Loyalist Democrats (1965–1968), *Journal of Mississippi History* 45 (February 1982); Lawrence Guyot and Mike Thelwell, "The Politics of Necessity and Survival in Mississippi," *Freedomways* (Spring 1966); and Peter H. Wood, "I Did the Best I Could for My Day: The Study of Early Black History during the Second Reconstruction, 1960–1976," *William and Mary Quarterly* 35 (April 1978).

In addition to Dittmer's *Local People*, books that had relevant information on the Mississippi Freedom Democratic Party and the other events of 1964 include Len Holt, *The Summer That Didn't End* (London: Heinemann, 1966); Nicolaus Mills, *Like a Holy Crusade* (Chicago: Ivan R. Dee, 1992); John Dittmer, "The Transformation of the Mississippi Movement, 1964–1968: The Rise and Fall of the Freedom Democratic Party," in *Essays on the American Civil Rights Movement* (College Station, Tex.: Texas A&M Press, 1993); John Dittmer, "The Politics of the Mississippi Movement, 1954–1964," in Charles W. Eagles, ed., *The Civil Rights Movement in America* (Jackson: University Press of Mississippi, 1986); and Hanes Walton Jr., *Black Political Parties* (New York: Free Press, 1972).

For coverage of the James Meredith debacle at Ole Miss, we used William Doyle, *An American Insurrection: The Battle of Oxford, Mississippi, 1962* (New York: Doubleday, 2001); Walter Lord, *The Past That Would Not Die* (New York: Harper and Row, 1965); Nadine Cohodas, *The Band Played Dixie: Race and the Liberal Conscience at Ole Miss* (New York: Free Press, 1997); Victor S. Navasky, *Kennedy Justice* (New York: Atheneum, 1971); and Ellen Douglas, *A Long Night* (Jackson, Miss.: Nouveau Press, 1986).

In trying to understand the mindset of white Mississippians during the civil rights era, it is still hard to beat James W. Silver, *Mississippi: The Closed Society* (New York: Harcourt, Brace and World, 1964), and Anne Moody, *Coming of Age in Mississippi: An Autobiography* (New York: Dial Press, 1968).

Autobiographical and biographical works that we found useful include Mrs. Medgar Evers with William Peters, *For Us, the Living* (Garden City, N.Y.: Doubleday, 1967); Erle Johnston, *I Rolled with Ross: A Political Portrait* (Jackson, Miss.: Moran, 1980); Eric Burner, *And Gently He Shall Lead Them: Robert Parris Moses and Civil Rights in Mississippi* (New York: New York University Press, 1994); Aaron Henry with Constance Curry, *Aaron Henry: The Fire Ever Burning* (Jackson: University Press of Mississippi, 2000); Chana Kai Lee, *For Freedom's Sake: The Life of Fannie Lou Hamer* (Chicago: University of Illinois Press, 1999); Dennis J. Mitchell, *Mississippi Liberal: A Biography of Frank E. Smith* (Jackson: University Press of Mississippi, 2001); Charles Marsh, *God's Long Summer: Stories of Faith and Civil Rights* (Princeton, N.J.: Princeton University Press, 1997); Reed S. Derr, "The Triumph of Progressivism: Governor Paul B. Johnson, Jr. and Mississippi in the 1960s" (Ph.D. diss., University of Southern Mississippi, 1994); John Ray Skates Jr., "A Southern Editor Views the National Scene: Frederick Sullens and the Jackson, Mississippi, *Daily News*" (Ph.D.

diss., Mississippi State University, 1965); Michael H. Hoffheimer, "L.Q.C. Lamar:1825–1892," *Mississippi Law Journal* 63 (Fall 1993); and Sandra Stringer Vance, "The Congressional Career of John Bell Williams:1947–1967" (Ph.D. diss., Mississippi State University, 1976).

For background on the presidential campaigns of this period, we used Theodore H. White, *The Making of the President 1960* (New York: Atheneum, 1961), Theodore H. White, *The Making of the President 1964* (New York: Atheneum, 1965); Theodore H. White, *The Making of the President 1968* (New York: Atheneum, 1969), Theodore H. White, *The Making of the President 1972* (New York: Atheneum, 1973); Lewis Chester, Godfrey Hodgson, and Bruce Page, *An American Melodrama: The Presidential Campaign of 1968* (New York: Viking Press, 1969); and Lewis L. Gould, 1968: *The Election That Changed America* (Chicago: Ivan R. Dee, 1993).

Finally, for anyone who wants to examine the darkest side of recent Mississippi history, one has only to read the two books that provided the intellectual justification for segregation and white supremacy: Theodore G. Bilbo, *Take Your Choice: Separation or Mongrelization* (Poplarville, Miss.: Dream House, 1947), and Tom P. Brady, *Black Monday: Segregation or Amalgamation . . . America Has Its Choice* (Winona, Miss.: Association of White Citizens' Councils, 1954).

1. Cited in Leslie Burl McLemore, "The Mississippi Freedom Democratic Party: A Case Study of Grass-Roots Politics" (Ph.D. diss., University of Massachusetts, 1971), 254.

2. Gary H. Brooks, "Inter- and Intragroup Conflict in Black Politics: A Case Study of the Mississippi Freedom Democratic Party" (Master's thesis, Tulane University, 1970), 37; Charles M. Hills, "State Democrats Delay Decision on Candidate," *Jackson Clarion-Ledger*, July 29, 1964; Jan H. Lewis, "Mississippi's Experiments in Biracial Politics, 1960–1973: A Challenge to White Supremacy" (Master's thesis, Mississippi State University, 1974), 25.

3. Glover Moore, "Separation from the Union, 1854–1861," in *A History of Mississippi*, ed. Richard A. McLemore, vol. 1 (Hattiesburg: University and College Press of Mississippi, 1973), 441.

4. William Charles Sallis, "The Color Line in Mississippi Politics, 1865–1915" (Ph.D. diss., University of Kentucky, 1967), 74–87.

5. James W. Loewen and Charles Sallis, eds., *Mississippi: Conflict and Change* (New York: Pantheon Books, 1974), 159–163; Sallis, "Color Line in Mississippi Politics," 212–217; see also Vernon Lane Wharton, *The Negro in Mississippi, 1865–1890* (New York: Harper and Row, 1965), 195–197; and William C. Harris, "Mississippi: Republican Factionalism and Mismanagement," in *Reconstruction and Redemption in the South*, ed. Otto H. Olsen (Baton Rouge: Louisiana State University Press, 1980), 105.

6. Bradley G. Bond, *Political Culture in the Nineteenth-Century South: Mississippi, 1830–1900* (Baton Rouge: Louisiana State University Press, 1995), 180; see also Albert D. Kirwan, *Revolt of the Rednecks: Mississippi Politics, 1876–1925* (New York: Harper and Row, 1951), 3–4; "Voting in Mississippi," Report of the United States Commission on Civil Rights (Washington, D.C.: Government Printing Office, 1965), 2; Warren

A. Ellem, "The Overthrow of Reconstruction in Mississippi," *Journal of Mississippi History* 54 (May 1992): 175–201; and William L. Coker, "The United States Senate Investigation in the Mississippi Election of 1875," *Journal of Mississippi History* 37 (February–November 1975): 143–163.

7. Loewen and Sallis, *Mississippi*, 163.

8. Kari Frederickson, *The Dixiecrat Revolt and the End of the Solid South, 1932–1968* (Chapel Hill: University of North Carolina Press, 2001), 76–80; Numan V. Bartley, *The New South: 1945–1980* (Baton Rouge: Louisiana State University Press, 1995), 74–76; Dewey W. Grantham, *The Life and Death of the Solid South* (Lexington: University Press of Kentucky, 1988), 121–123; Richard D. Chesteen, "Mississippi Is Gone Home: A Study of the 1948 Mississippi States Rights Bolt," *Journal of Mississippi History* 33 (February 1970): 43–59.

9. Frederickson, *Dixiecrat Revolt*, 130–131, 139; see also Governor Fielding Wright's "Statement of Democratic Party Leaders" in January 1948, reprinted in Arthur M. Schlesinger, Jr., gen. ed., *History of U.S. Political Parties*, vol. 4 (Philadelphia: Chelsea House, 2002), 3399–3401.

10. Sources for these paragraphs include Neil R. McMillen, *Dark Journey: Black Mississippians in the Age of Jim Crow* (Chicago: University of Illinois Press, 1989); C. Vann Woodward, *The Strange Career of Jim Crow*, new and rev. ed. (New York: Oxford University Press, 1957); and Reuben Anderson, interview.

11. Sallis, "Color Line in Mississippi Politics," 345.

12. Bartley, *New South*, 84–85; C. Vann Woodward, "From the First Reconstruction to the Second," *Harper's*, April 1965, 129–130.

13. Monroe Lee Billington, *The Political South in the Twentieth Century* (New York: Charles Scribner's Sons, 1975), 88–90.

14. William F. Winter, "New Directions in Politics, 1948–1956," in McLemore, *History of Mississippi*, vol. 2, 144.

15. Bartley, *New South*, 78.

16. Jesse L. White Jr., "Mississippi's Electoral Politics, 1903–1976: The Emerging Modernization Consensus" (Ph.D. diss., Massachusetts Institute of Technology, 1979), 340–403; Neil McMillen, "Development of Civil Rights, 1956–1970," in McLemore, *History of Mississippi*, vol. 2, 157–159.

17. Bartley, *New South*, 99–103; White, "Mississippi's Electoral Politics," 375–378; Davis R. B. Ross, "The Democratic Party:1945–1960," in Schlesinger, *History of U.S. Political Parties*, 2691–2695.

18. Sandra Stringer Vance, "The Congressional Career of John Bell Williams:1947–1967" (Ph.D. diss., Mississippi State University, 1976), 141.

19. Bartley, *New South*, 160.

20. McMillen, interview.

21. "Go Slow Attitude Urged by Governor in Court Decision," *Jackson Clarion-Ledger*, May 18, 1954.

22. "Bloodstains on White Marble Steps," *Jackson Daily News*, May 18, 1954.

23. Winter, "New Directions," 151–152.

24. Anthony Lewis and the *New York Times*, *Portrait of a Decade: The Second American Revolution* (New York: Random House, 1964), 204.

25. Tom P. Brady, *Black Monday: Segregation or Amalgamation . . . America Has Its Choice* (Winona, Miss.: Association of White Citizens' Councils, 1954, 1955).

26. Claude Sitton, "Inquiry into the Mississippi Mind," *New York Times Magazine*, April 28, 1963, as quoted in Lewis, *Portrait of a Decade*, 208.

27. Neil R. McMillen, *The Citizens' Council: Organized Resistance of the Second Reconstruction, 1954–1964* (Chicago: University of Illinois Press, 1971), 25–28, 235.

28. Douglas Starr, "Legislature OKs School Abolition," *Jackson Clarion-Ledger*, September 17, 1954; House Journal, 1954 Extraordinary Session, 40.

29. Joel Blass, USM Oral History, 40–41.

30. Robert A. Caro, *Master of the Senate: The Years of Lyndon Johnson* (New York: Alfred A. Knopf, 2002), 706–707, 769; see also Stephen J. Whitfield, *A Death in the Delta: The Story of Emmett Till* (New York: Free Press, 1988); Clenora Hudson-Weems, "Resurrecting Emmett Till," *Journal of Black Studies* 29 (November 1998): 179–188. Notably, at this writing, fifty-one years after the murder of Emmett Till, the FBI and supporting agencies have exhumed the body of Till with a view to pursuing charges against living participants in the crime.

31. Bartley, *New South*, 178–184.

32. Sarah Rowe-Sims, "The Mississippi State Sovereignty Commission: An Agency History," *Journal of Mississippi History* 61 (Spring 1999): 29–36; see also Yasuhiro Katagiri, *The Mississippi State Sovereignty Commission: Civil Rights and States' Rights* (Jackson: University Press of Mississippi, 2001).

33. Bartley, *New South*, 198–199; "Manifesto Branding Segregation Ruling as Abusive Is Filed," *Jackson Clarion-Ledger*, March 12, 1956.

34. In the third volume of his biography of Lyndon Johnson, *Master of the Senate*, Robert Caro uses more than 220 pages to describe how the 1957 legislation was passed.

35. Brad Dye, interview with the authors; Bill Spell, interview with the authors; Larry Speakes, MSU Oral History, 29.

36. Hank Klibanoff, "Winds of Time Moving Some, but Not All, Segregationists," *Jackson Clarion-Ledger*, June 19, 1983.

37. Vance, "John Bell Williams," 218–219; Bill Minor, *Eyes on Mississippi: A Fifty-Year Chronicle of Change* (Jackson, Miss.: J. Prichard Morris Books, 2001), 11; Joe Wroten, interview with the authors; Charles Clark, interview with the authors.

38. Bartley, *New South*, 298–303.

39. "Racial Violence Erupts at Biloxi," *Biloxi Daily Herald*, April 25, 1960; J. Michael Butler, "The Mississippi State Sovereignty Commission and Beach Integration, 1959–1963: A Cotton-Patch Gestapo?" *Journal of Southern History* 68 (February 2002): 107–148.

40. McMillen, "Development of Civil Rights," 159; see also Hodding Carter III, "Citadel of the Citizens Council," *New York Times Magazine*, November 12, 1961; Patt Derian, MSU Oral History, 4–6; and Patt Derian, interview with the authors.

41. McMillen, "Development of Civil Rights," 160.

42. Charles M. Hills, "Barnett's Colonels Hear Elector Plan," *Jackson Clarion-Ledger*, October 11, 1960; Minor, *Eyes on Mississippi*, 74–78.

43. "State Has Own Debate," *Jackson Clarion-Ledger*, October 31, 1960; Edmund Noel, "Sen. Russell Long in Demo Pep Rally," *Jackson Clarion-Ledger*, November 4, 1960.

44. Bartley, *New South*, 306–312.

45. Les McLemore, interview with the authors.

46. Nadine Cohodas, *The Band Played Dixie: Race and Liberal Conscience at Ole Miss* (New York: Free Press, 1997), 62; Douglas Starr, "In Custody of Patrol, King Says He's Through," *Jackson Clarion-Ledger*, June 6, 1958.

47. McMillen, "Development of Civil Rights," 161.

48. James W. Silver, *Mississippi: The Closed Society* (New York: Harcourt, Brace and World, 1963), 114; Jack Bass, *Unlikely Heroes* (New York: Simon and Schuster, 1981), 172.

49. William L. Peart, "Barnett Receives All-Out Support," *Jackson Clarion-Ledger*, September 14, 1962; Joe Wroten, USM Oral History, 27–28; House Journal, 1962 First Extraordinary Session, 52.

50. Charles M. Hills, "Ross Halts Negro for Second Time," *Jackson Clarion-Ledger*, September 25, 1962.

51. Taylor Branch, *Parting the Waters: America in the King Years, 1954–1963* (New York: Simon and Schuster, 1988), 659. Video of the speech by Barnett at the football game was used in the PBS *Eyes on the Prize* series, program no. 102, entitled "Fighting Back: 1957–1962."

52. Curtis Wilkie, *Dixie: A Personal Odyssey through Events That Shaped the Modern South* (New York: Scribner, 2001), 105; see also Gerald Blessey, USM Oral History; William Winter, interview with the authors; Gary Carnathan, interview with the authors; Buddy Klumb, interview with the authors.

53. Branch, *Parting the Waters*, 647–672; Walter Lord, *The Past That Would Not Die* (New York: Harper and Row, 1965), 98–112, 139–235; Silver, *Mississippi*, 107–133; John Dittmer, *Local People: The Struggle for Civil Rights in Mississippi* (Chicago: University of Illinois Press, 1994), 138–142; McMillen, "Development of Civil Rights," 161–163.

54. Erle Johnston, *Politics: Mississippi Style* (Forest, Miss.: Lake Harbor, 1993), 161; William Doyle, *An American Insurrection: The Battle of Oxford, Mississippi, 1962* (New York: Doubleday, 2001), 83–85, 120–124.

55. Johnston, *Politics*, 161; Minor, *Eyes on Mississippi*, 211–216; Joel Blass, USM Oral History, vol. 639, 1977, 54–55.

56. Brooks, "Intragroup Conflict," 30–34; Anne Cook Romaine, "The Mississippi Freedom Democratic Party through August, 1964" (Master's thesis, University of Virginia, 1970), 22.

57. Spell, interview.

58. White, "Mississippi's Electoral Politics," 418–429.

59. Mary Ann Pardue, "Miss. Delegation Raps CR Stand," *Jackson Clarion-Ledger*, November 28, 1963.

60. John Hebers, "Beckwith Placed at Evers Meeting," *New York Times*, January 30, 1964.

61. Richard C. Ethridge, "Mississippi's Role in the Dixiecrat Movement" (Ph.D. diss., Mississippi State University, 1971), 143–146; Purser Hewitt, "Mississippi Delegate Fight

in Convention Limelight," *Jackson Clarion-Ledger*, July 18, 1952; Frederick Sullens, "State Democrats May Face a Bitter Fight at Chicago," *Jackson Clarion-Ledger*, July 8, 1956; Spell, interview; Winter, interview.

62. McLemore, "Mississippi Freedom Democratic Party," 106–108; Brooks, "Intragroup Conflict," 36–38.

63. Jimmie Gates, "Volunteers Brought Vision to Mississippi," *Jackson Clarion-Ledger*, July 1, 1984; Brooks, "Intragroup Conflict," 34–36; Lawrence Guyot, interview with the authors.

64. McLemore, "Mississippi Freedom Democratic Party," 119.

65. Charles M. Hills, "Governor Urges Unity of State Conservatives," *Jackson Clarion-Ledger*, July 29, 1964.

66. "Brief Submitted by the Mississippi Freedom Democratic Party," prepared by Joseph L. Rauh Jr. (1964), copy in authors' possession.

67. Kotz, *Judgment Days*, 194–196.

68. Vanessa Lynn Davis, "Sisters and Brothers All: The Mississippi Freedom Democratic Party and the Struggle for Political Equality" (Ph.D. diss., Vanderbilt University, 1996), 95.

69. Kotz, *Judgment Days*, 205–206; Dittmer, *Local People*, 287–288.

70. McLemore, "Mississippi Freedom Democratic Party," 142.

71. Theodore H. White, *The Making of the President 1964* (New York: Atheneum, 1965), 291–292.

72. Charles Marsh, *God's Long Summer: Stories of Faith and Civil Rights* (Princeton, N.J.: Princeton University Press, 1997), 10–20; Len Holt, *The Summer That Didn't End* (New York: William Morrow, 1965), 168–170; McLemore, "Mississippi Freedom Democratic Party," 141–144.

73. Davis, "Sisters and Brothers," 95.

74. Kotz, *Judgment Days*, 205; Taylor Branch, *Pillar of Fire* (New York: Simon and Schuster, 1998), 458–460.

75. Davis, "Sisters and Brothers," 72–118; Kotz, *Judgment Days*, 200–202.

76. William Simpson, "The Birth of the Mississippi Loyalist Democrats," *Journal of Mississippi History* 45 (February 1982): 27; Brooks, "Intragroup Conflict," 53–54.

77. Kotz, *Judgment Days*, 199–212; Dittmer, *Local People*, 291–298.

78. Davis, "Sisters and Brothers," 103–106; Dittmer, *Local People*, 297–299; Harry Bowie, interview with the authors; McLemore, interview; Guyot, interview; McLemore, "Mississippi Freedom Democratic Party," 149; Brooks, "Intragroup Conflict," 54–56; Davis, "Sisters and Brothers," 102–104, 113–116; Romaine, "Mississippi Freedom Democratic Party," 39–40.

79. McLemore, "Mississippi Freedom Democratic Party," 151; Purser Hewitt, "State Group Votes 53-3 for Boycott," *Jackson Clarion-Ledger*, August 26, 1964.

80. Jack Bass and Walter DeVries, *The Transformation of Southern Politics* (New York: Basic Books, 1976), 204; Hodding Carter III, interview with the authors.

81. White, "Mississippi's Electoral Politics," 437; "Separate but United Goldwater Vote Urged," *Jackson Clarion-Ledger*, August 30, 1964.

82. Dan Russell, interview with the authors. We doubted the veracity of Russell's tale until we entered the 1964 election results into our computer and programmed it to calculate the county percentages for LBJ and rank them in descending order.

83. Guyot, interview; Carter, interview; Bowie, interview.

84. Davis, "Sisters and Brothers," 100–103; see, for example, Hodding Carter III, UNC Oral History, A-100, April 1, 1974, 15–16.

85. Carter, interview.

86. McLemore, "Mississippi Freedom Democratic Party," 413–416; Simpson, "Mississippi Loyalist Democrats," 30–31; Lewis, *Portrait of a Decade*, 43–44; Carter, interview.

87. White, "Mississippi's Electoral Politics," 465.

88. Vance, "John Bell Williams," 232–246; White, "Mississippi's Electoral Politics," 469.

89. White, "Mississippi's Electoral Politics," 464–489; Johnston, *Politics*, 191–195.

90. Lewis Chester, Godfrey Hodgson, and Bruce Page, *An American Melodrama: The Presidential Campaign of 1968* (New York: Viking Press, 1969), 4–20; Richard C. Wade, "The Democratic Party:1960–1972," in Schlesinger, *History of U.S. Political Parties*, 2838–2840.

91. McLemore, "Mississippi Freedom Democratic Party," 409–411; Carter, interview.

92. McLemore, "Mississippi Freedom Democratic Party," 424–425.

93. Simpson, "Mississippi Loyalist Democrats," 37.

94. McLemore, "Mississippi Freedom Democratic Party," 421; Dittmer, *Local People*, 420–422; Guyot, interview.

95. McLemore, "Mississippi Freedom Democratic Party," 437–455; Lincoln Warren, "Loyalist Democrats Select Delegate Slate," *Jackson Clarion-Ledger*, August 12, 1968.

96. Simpson, "Mississippi Loyalist Democrats," 44; Tom Ethridge, "Mississippi Notebook," *Jackson Clarion-Ledger*, August 29, 1968.

97. "Committee Delays Miss. Demo Ruling," *Jackson Clarion-Ledger*, August 20, 1968.

98. Brooks, "Intragroup Conflict," 99; McLemore, "Mississippi Freedom Democratic Party," 475; Carter, interview; Derian, interview.

99. "Conservative Unity Urged by Bramlett," *Jackson Clarion-Ledger*, August 25, 1968.

100. Derian, interview.

101. White, "Mississippi's Electoral Politics," 493–494.

102. William F. Winter, "Development of Educational Policy in Mississippi," *Mississippi Law Journal* 58 (Fall 1988): 230–232; Charles C. Bolton, "The Last Stand of Massive Resistance: Mississippi Public School Integration, 1970," *Journal of Mississippi History* 61 (Winter 1991): 329–342.

103. Loewen and Sallis, *Mississippi*, 319–320; Minor, *Eyes on Mississippi*, 251–253; see also Timothy Spofford, "Lynch Street: The Story of Mississippi's Kent State—The May 1970 Slayings at Jackson State College" (Ph.D. diss., State University of New York, 1984). At the time of the shootings, Jackson State University was known as Jackson State College.

104. Johnston, *Politics*, 218; see also Tom Normand, "Campaign Pays Visit to Neshoba Fair," *Jackson Daily News*, August 3, 1967.

105. White, "Mississippi's Electoral Politics," 501–522; Johnston, *Politics*, 215–225; Spell, interview; Charles McKellar, interview with the authors. Ironically, some years later Waller would locate his active law practice at a prominent Capitol Street address in downtown Jackson.

106. Lewis, *Portrait of a Decade*, 62–75; Paul Jeffrey Steckler, "Black Politics in the New South: An Investigation of Change at Various Levels" (Ph.D. diss., Harvard University, 1982), 174–179; Carter, interview; Ed Cole, interview with the authors; Wayne Edwards, interview with the authors; Charles McKellar, USM Oral History, 40–41.

107. White, "Mississippi's Electoral Politics," 536–558; Johnston, *Politics*, 253–267; Minor, *Eyes on Mississippi*, 15–17; Bill Jones, interview with the authors.

108. See, for example, the analysis of this race by Tip H. Allen Jr. and Dale A. Krane, "Class Replaces Race: the Reemergence of Neopopulism in Mississippi Gubernatorial Politics," *Southern Studies* 19 (Summer 1980): 182–192.

109. Steve Patterson, interview with the authors; Joey Langston, interview with the authors.

CHAPTER 2. HISTORY OF MISSISSIPPI REPUBLICANS, 1955–1975

For the history of the Republican Party in Mississippi, we relied on Martha H. Wilkins, "The Development of the Mississippi Republican Party" (Master's thesis, Mississippi College, 1965); Alexander J. Simpson Jr., "George L. Sheldon and the Beginnings of the Lily White Movement in Mississippi, 1909–1932" (Master's thesis, Mississippi State University, 1962); Neil R. McMillen, "Perry W. Howard, Boss of Black-and-Tan Republicanism in Mississippi, 1942–1960," *Journal of Southern History* 47 (May 1982); James Edward Cliatt III, "The Mississippi Republican Party:1952–1960" (Master's thesis, Mississippi State University, 1964); David J. Ginzl, "Lily-Whites versus Black-and-Tans: Mississippi Republicans during the Hoover Administration," *Journal of Mississippi History* 42 (1980); Guy Paul Land, "Mississippi Republicanism and the 1960 Presidential Election," *Journal of Mississippi History* 40 (February 1978); and Hanes Walton Jr., *Black Republicans: The Politics of the Black and Tans* (Metuchen, N.J.: Scarecrow Press, 1975). Before he died, Erle Johnston began a book of Republican history called "The Thunder of Elephants in Mississippi: From Bayonets to Ballots." Bubby Johnston, Erle Johnston's son, provided us with a copy of the first half of the book, covering the period up to 1955, as well as drafts of unfinished subsequent chapters. A comprehensive account of the two campaigns of Rubel Phillips can be found in Billy B. Hathorn, "Challenging the Status Quo: Rubel Lex Phillips and the Mississippi Republican Party, 1963–1967," *Journal of Mississippi History*, 47 (1985). For the years leading up to 1976, we relied on Frederick G. Slabach, "The Mississippi Republican Party Critical Election Years:1967–1978" (Honors paper, Mississippi College, 1979).

Books dealing with the "southern strategy" as adopted and implemented by the Republican Party over the last four decades, as well as the general rise of the Republican Party, include Kevin P. Phillips, *The Emerging Republican Majority* (New Rochelle, N.Y.: Arlington House, 1969); Reg Murphy and Hal Gulliver, *The Southern Strategy* (New York, Charles Scribner's Sons, 1971); Harry S. Dent, *The Prodigal South Returns to Power* (New York: John

Wiley and Sons, 1978); Louis M. Seagull, *Southern Republicanism* (New York: John Wiley and Sons, 1975); Joseph A. Aistrup, *The Southern Strategy Revisited* (Lexington: University of Kentucky Press, 1996); and David Lublin, *The Republican South: Democratization and Partisan Change* (Princeton, N.J.: Princeton University Press, 2004). The number of articles found in scholarly journals on the topic of race and the Republicans is truly astounding. One we found especially useful was John C. Kuzenski and Michael K. Corbello, "Racial and Economic Explanations for Republican Growth in the South: A Case Study of Attitudinal Voting in Louisiana," *American Review of Politics* 17 (Summer 1996).

For background on the presidential campaigns of this period, we used Theodore H. White, *The Making of the President 1960* (New York: Atheneum, 1961), and Theodore H. White, *The Making of the President 1964* (New York: Atheneum, 1965). For background on Barry Goldwater and the early conservative movement, we used Rick Perlstein, *Before the Storm: Barry Goldwater and the Unmaking of the American Consensus* (New York: Hill and Wang, 2001).

1. These first two paragraphs are based on the narrative history of early Mississippi found in Dunbar Rowland, ed., *The Official and Statistical Register, State of Mississippi* (Nashville, Tenn.: Press of the Brandon Printing Company, 1908), 153–154, 195; see also Sallis, "Color Line in Mississippi Politics," 16–17; Yerger, interview.

2. George A. Sewell and Margaret L. Dwight, *Mississippi Black History Makers* (Jackson: University Press of Mississippi, 1984), 9–10.

3. Sallis, "Color Line in Mississippi Politics," 144–160; Rowland, *Official and Statistical Register*, 155.

4. Rowland, *Official and Statistical Register*, 195.

5. Rowland, *Official and Statistical Register*, 203.

6. Martha H. Wilkins, "The Development of the Mississippi Republican Party" (Master's thesis, Mississippi College, 1965); Alexander J. Simpson Jr., "George L. Sheldon and the Beginnings of the Lily White Movement in Mississippi, 1909–1932" (Master's thesis, Mississippi State University, 1962). The information about Sheldon in the legislature is from Erle Johnston's unpublished book, "The Thunder of Elephants in Mississippi: From Bayonets to Ballots," in the chapter on 1963.

7. Alexander Heard, *The Two Party South?* (Chapel Hill: University of North Carolina Press, 1952), 23, 33, 98.

8. Earl Black and Merle Black, *The Vital South* (Cambridge, Mass.: Harvard University Press, 1992), 184.

9. Wilkins, "Mississippi Republican Party," 14–26.

10. White, "Mississippi Electoral Politics," 377–379.

11. Wilkins, "Mississippi Republican Party," 27–32; Wirt Yerger Jr., interview with the authors.

12. The information about Yerger is from Wirt Yerger Jr., USM Oral History, vol. 204, 1978, and from interviews with the authors.

13. Wilkins, "Mississippi Republican Party," 33–42; Yerger, USM Oral History; Yerger, interview.

14. Wilkins, "Mississippi Republican Party," 33–42; Yerger, USM Oral History; Yerger, interview; Harold Foreman, "Ex-Democrats Take Over Top Post in State GOP; Spencer Gets No. 1 Spot," *Jackson Clarion-Ledger*, March 23, 1956; B. B. McClendon, interview with the authors.

15. Wilkins, "Mississippi Republican Party," 36–42; Yerger, USM Oral History; Yerger, interview; "Mississippi's Split GOP Delegation Seated Together," *Jackson Clarion-Ledger*, August 21, 1960; Jack K. Russell, "Howard Says Race Platform Is Acceptable," *Jackson Clarion-Ledger*, August 22, 1956.

16. Robert E. Clark, "Ike Declares Action," *Jackson Clarion Ledger*, September 25, 1957.

17. Sources for these two paragraphs include articles in the *Jackson Clarion-Ledger*, *Meridian Star*, and *Laurel Leader-Call*, September 12–30, 1957; and Bartley, *New South*, 227–230.

18. McClendon, interview.

19. Wilkins, "Mississippi Republican Party," 44.

20. Sources for these two paragraphs include Wilkins, "Mississippi Republican Party," 43–47; and "E. O. Spencer Quits GOP Patronage Post Over Use of Troops," and "Yerger Says He'll Stay within GOP Framework," *Jackson Clarion-Ledger*, October 2, 1957.

21. Clarke Reed, Wirt Yerger Jr., B. B. McClendon, Victor Mavar, Billy Mounger, and Buddy Klumb, interviews with the authors.

22. Earl Black and Merle Black, *The Rise of Southern Republicans* (Cambridge, Mass.: Belknap Press for Harvard University Press, 2002), 24. In the political science literature covering this time period, there is a debate as to whether in organizing the party, the Republicans should have started at the presidential and statewide levels and worked their way down to the municipal and county levels in electing officials (the so-called top-down approach) or started at the lowest levels and worked their way up (that is, focus on the grassroots and city aldermen and county supervisor positions). While we have no room in this book to participate in that debate, we think the Republicans in Mississippi did it the only way they could.

23. Theodore H. White, *The Making of the President 1960* (New York: Antheneum, 1961), 222.

24. Purser Hewitt, "GOP May Draft CR Plank Mississippi Can Live With," *Jackson Clarion-Ledger*, July 23, 1960; Yerger, interview.

25. Norman Walker, "Nixon Takes Command of Fight for Tough CR," *Jackson Clarion-Ledger*, July 26, 1960.

26. Purser Hewitt, "State Group Joins Show for Goldwater," *Jackson Clarion-Ledger*, July 28, 1960.

27. Bob Pittman, "Nixon Knew Right Topics," *Jackson Clarion-Ledger*, September 25, 1980; Wilkins, "Mississippi Republican Party," 53; Minor, *Eyes on Mississippi*, 78–79.

28. Jerry DeLaughter, "Nixon Makes Bid Here for State's Eight Votes," *Jackson Clarion-Ledger*, September 25, 1960; Klumb, interview.

29. Bass and DeVries, *Transformation of Southern Politics*, 27. Background information on "Operation Dixie"—Goldwater's attempt to focus the organizing energies of the

Republican Party in the South—can be found in Joseph A. Aistrup, *The Southern Strategy Revisited* (Lexington: University Press of Kentucky, 1996), 5–11.

30. Reg Murphy and Hal Gulliver, *The Southern Strategy* (New York: Charles Scriber's Sons, 1971), 2–3.

31. Harry S. Dent, *The Prodigal South Returns to Power* (New York: John Wiley and Sons, 1978), 75; see also Dewey W. Grantham, *The South in Modern America: A Region at Odds* (New York: Harper Collins, 1994), 282–283.

32. Murphy and Gulliver, *Southern Strategy*, 3.

33. Jerry DeLaughter, "Sen. Goldwater Invites State into Republican Party's Fold," *Jackson Clarion-Ledger*, November 30, 1962; Yerger, interview; Klumb, interview; Rick Perlstein, *Before the Storm: Barry Goldwater and the Unmaking of the American Consensus* (New York: Hill and Wang, 2001), 168, 181, 186.

34. Klumb, interview.

35. Sources for these paragraphs on the Phillips campaign include Billy Burton Hathorn, "Challenging the Status Quo: Rubel Lex Phillips and the Mississippi Republican Party, 1963–1967," *Journal of Mississippi History* 47 (November 1985): 240–264; "Democrats Stand Up For Johnson," *Jackson Clarion-Ledger*, October 9, 1963; "Let's Don't Play with Fire," *Jackson Clarion-Ledger*, November 4, 1963; and Rubel Phillips, interview with the authors.

36. Yerger, USM Oral History, 44; Yerger, interview.

37. "Senate Unit for Change in Elections," *Jackson Clarion-Ledger*, March 18, 1964.

38. Yerger, USM Oral History, 45; Yerger, interview.

39. Charles M. Hills, "House Rejects Action on Election Changes," *Jackson Clarion-Ledger*, April 30, 1964.

40. White, *Making of the President 1964*, 228.

41. Yerger, USM Oral History, 67; Yerger, interview; Klumb, interview.

42. Charles M. Hills, "Appeasement Hit by Sen. Thurmond," *Jackson Clarion-Ledger*, October 21, 1964.

43. William D. Mounger, USM Oral History, vol. 311, 1977, 41.

44. Charles and Barbara Whalen, *The Longest Debate* (Cabin John, Md.: Seven Locks Press, 1985), 212.

45. James Saggus, "State Goes for Barry; Rep. Winstead Beaten," *Jackson Clarion-Ledger*, November 4, 1964.

46. Minor, *Eyes on Mississippi*, 89–90; Yerger, interview.

47. Mounger, USM Oral History, 40.

48. Thomas B. Edsall and Mary D. Edsall, *Chain Reaction: The Impact of Race, Rights and Taxes on American Politics* (New York: W. W. Norton, 1991), 40.

49. Charles M. Hills, "Legislature Approves Private School Tuition," *Jackson Clarion-Ledger*, July 16, 1964; Yerger, interview; Billy Mounger, interview with the authors.

50. Clarke Reed, interview with the authors; Klumb, interview; Yerger, interview.

51. Bass and Devries, *Transformation of Southern Politics*, 214.

52. Mounger, USM Oral History, 42–44; Mounger, interview.

53. Yerger, interview; Mounger, USM Oral History, 45b; Charles Smith, "Yerger Resigning as GOP Chairman," *Jackson Clarion-Ledger*, February 8, 1966; "Rep. Walker Announces for Senate," *Jackson Clarion-Ledger*, February 8, 1966.

54. Yerger, USM Oral History, 43; Yerger, interview.

55. Mounger, interview; Phillips, interview.

56. Frederick Gilbert Slabach, "The Mississippi Republican Party, Critical Election Years: 1967–1978" (Honors paper, Mississippi College, 1979), 12; White, "Mississippi's Electoral Politics," 483–484.

57. White, "Mississippi's Electoral Politics," 485–487; John Pearce, "GOP Hopeful Challenges Whites to Aid Negroes," *Laurel Leader-Call*, October 4, 1967.

58. White, "Mississippi's Electoral Politics," 488.

59. Clarke Reed, interview.

60. Mounger, USM Oral History, 73–83; Carmichael, UNC Oral History, 11; Clarke Reed, interview; Dent, *Prodigal South*, 95–101; Chester, Hodgson, and Page, *American Melodrama*, 438–450.

61. Tom Cook, "Air Force One Due at 7 P.M.," *Biloxi Daily Herald*, September 8, 1969; Tom Cook, "Mississippians Standing Tall," *Biloxi Daily Herald*, September 9, 1969.

62. Edsall and Edsall, *Chain Reaction*, 88–89.

63. Mounger, USM Oral History, 139; Mounger, interview; Thad Cochran, interview with the authors; Charles Evers, interview with the authors; Cochran, UNC Oral History, A-103, 14; Eddie McBride, interview with the authors.

64. Dewey Lane, USM Oral History, vol. 338, 12; Victor Mavar, interview with the authors; Trent Lott, *Herding Cats: A Life in Politics* (New York: Regan Books, 2005), 52–55; Trent Lott, interview with the authors.

65. Carmichael, UNC Oral History, 17; see also Clarke Reed, UNC Oral History, 27; Gil Carmichael, interview with the authors; Clarke Reed, interview.

66. Thomas Giordano, USM Oral History, vol. 129, 12; Carmichael, MSU Oral History, 16; Carmichael, UNC Oral History, 27; Mounger, interview; Carmichael, interview.

67. Mounger, USM Oral History, 170–174; White, "Mississippi's Electoral Politics," 532–535; Carmichael, interview. Among the other high ironies represented by Kleindienst's announcement is the fact that it violated a generations-long rule of presidential cabinet politics. Historically, the lower-ranking members of a president's cabinet have actively campaigned in pursuit of the president's political aims, but the higher-ranking, supposedly nonpolitical cabinet secretaries, including the attorney general and the secretary of state, have refused to engage in partisan campaign efforts or appearances.

68. Mounger, USM Oral History, Part II, 29.

69. Carmichael, UNC Oral History, 21.

70. Nancy Stevens, "Rain-Soaked Crowd Attends Agnew Rally," *Jackson Clarion-Ledger*, October 30, 1972; "Carmichael Brands Eastland 'Bogus Republican,'" *Biloxi Daily Herald*, October 30, 1972.

71. Carmichael, UNC Oral History, 20; Carmichael, MSU Oral History, 29; Carmichael, interview.

72. Carmichael, MSU Oral History, 17; Carmichael, interview.

73. Clarke Reed, UNC Oral History, 27.
74. Mounger, USM Oral History, 175.
75. Carmichael, USM Oral History, 89; Carmichael, interview.
76. Mounger, USM Oral History, Part II, 21; see also Steve Guyton, interview with the authors; Lanny Griffith, interview with the authors; Bass and DeVries, *Transformation of Southern Politics*, 215–216.
77. Mounger, USM Oral History, Part II, 30–34; Mounger, interview.
78. Bass and DeVries, *Transformation of Southern Politics*, 215–216.
79. Tim Carpenter, interview with the authors.
80. Carmichael, USM Oral History, 102; Carmichael, interview.
81. Mounger, interview.

CHAPTER 3. THE BEGINNING OF THE END, 1976

In covering the presidential election of 1976, the starting point for anyone must be Jules Witcover's 683-page *Marathon: The Pursuit of the Presidency, 1972–1976* (New York: Viking Press, 1977), which has two chapters devoted exclusively to the role of the Mississippi GOP delegation in choosing the Republican nominee. Also published that year was Elizabeth Drew, *American Journal: The Events of 1976* (New York: Random House, 1977); Martin Schram, *Running for President 1976* (New York: Stein and Day, 1977); and Kandy Stroud, *How Jimmy Won: The Victory Campaign from Plains to the White House* (New York: William Morrow, 1977). Harry Dent's, *The Prodigal South Returns to Power*, mentioned earlier, has one chapter on Mississippi in 1976. Published some twenty-eight years later, Craig Shirley, *Reagan's Revolution: The Untold Story of the Campaign That Started It All* (Nashville, Tenn.: Nelson Current, 2005), focuses on the influence of Reagan's campaign on the politics within the Republican Party that followed the pivotal year of 1976. Additional information came from David Keene, "Why Reagan Chose Schweiker: An Insider's Account," *The Alternative: An American Spectator* (November 1976).

1. Quoted by John Hampton Stennis, interview with the authors.
2. Danny Cupit, interview with the authors.
3. Cupit, interview.
4. Mark Hazard, interview with the authors.
5. Jules Witcover, *Marathon: The Pursuit of the Presidency, 1972–1976* (New York: Viking Press, 1977), 10–12; Elizabeth Drew, *American Journal: The Events of 1976* (New York: Random House, 1977), 532; *Jackson Clarion-Ledger*, November 4, 1976.
6. Witcover, *Marathon*, 210–214.
7. Witcover, *Marathon*, 215–216.
8. Fredric N. Tulsky and Bob Zeller, "Joint Caucuses to Test Unity of State Party," *Jackson Clarion-Ledger*, January 24, 1976; see also Paul Jeffrey Stekler, "Black Politics in the New South: An Investigation of Change at Various Levels" (Ph.D. diss., Harvard University, 1982), 179–186.

9. Fredric N. Tulsky, "Party Seems to Survive New Demo Caucus System," *Jackson Clarion-Ledger*, January 25, 1976; Bob Zeller, "Wallace Leads Caucus Voting," *Jackson Clarion-Ledger*, January 25, 1976.

10. Bob Zeller, "Almost 30% Pledged," *Jackson Clarion-Ledger*, February 15, 1976.

11. Cupit, interview.

12. Bob Zeller, "Unity Move Prevails at Democratic Meet," *Jackson Clarion-Ledger*, March 1, 1976.

13. Cupit, interview; Guyton, interview; Carter, interview; Hazard, interview; Fred Banks, interview with the authors; McKellar, interview.

14. Jack Elliott, "Delegates Urged Not to Switch," *Jackson Clarion-Ledger*, May 27, 1976; Fredric M. Tulsky, "Wallace Move May Cement Party Unity," *Jackson Clarion-Ledger*, June 10, 1976; Cupit, interview.

15. Fredric N. Tulsky, "State Democrats—No Feuds Is Good News," *Jackson Clarion-Ledger*, July 12, 1976; Fredric N. Tulsky, "State Democrats' Harmony in N.Y. Wins Nations Eye," *Jackson Clarion-Ledger*, July 13, 1976.

16. Mounger, USM Oral history, vol. 311, Part II, 267; Mounger, interview.

17. Otis L. Sanford, "State GOP Chief to Resign after Convention," *Jackson Clarion-Ledger*, January 23, 1976; Clarke Reed, interview.

18. Mounger, USM Oral History, vol. 311, Part II, 54–56; Clarke Reed, interview.

19. Stephanie Saul, "State GOP Bloc Vote Decision May Give Delegates to Reagan," *Jackson Clarion-Ledger*, April 11, 1976; Mounger, USM Oral History, 119.

20. Dent, *Prodigal South*, 31.

21. Stephanie Saul, "Reagan: 27 State Votes Expected," *Jackson Clarion-Ledger*, June 25, 1976.

22. Doug Shanks, USM Oral History, 38–40.

23. "State GOP Leaders: Key Held by Truly Undecided," *Jackson Clarion-Ledger*, July 8, 1976.

24. "172 Uncommitted GOP Votes Remain," *Jackson Clarion-Ledger*, July 19, 1976.

25. Stephanie Saul, "GOP Delegation May Reveal Choice Early," *Jackson Clarion-Ledger*, July 20, 1976.

26. Stephanie Saul, "Big Names Seek State GOP Votes," *Jackson Clarion-Ledger*, July 23, 1976.

27. Haley Barbour, USM Oral History, 55.

28. Carmichael, USM Oral History, 120–122.

29. Sam Alford, USM Oral History, vol. 177, 1981, 49–52; Mounger, interview.

30. "Focus on State GOP Bloc," *Jackson Clarion-Ledger*, July 25, 1976; Mounger, USM Oral History, 104–105.

31. David Keene, "Why Reagan Chose Schweiker: An Insider's Account," *The Alternative: An American Spectator*, November 1976, 13; Mounger, USM Oral History, 117.

32. Barbour, USM Oral History, 45.

33. Keene, "Why Reagan Chose Schweiker," 14.

34. Stephanie Saul, "State GOP Bloc Silent on Choice," *Jackson Clarion-Ledger*, July 26, 1976; Dent, *Prodigal South*, 41–42; James M. Naughton, "Mississippi Slate Delays Endorsing until GOP Meets," *New York Times*, July 26, 1976.

35. Mounger, USM Oral History, 108–109; Clarke Reed, interview; Keene, "Why Reagan Chose Schweiker," 15–16.
36. Barbour, USM Oral History, 56; Dent, *Prodigal South*, 42–43; Clarke Reed, interview.
37. Mounger, USM Oral History, 127–135; Mounger, interview.
38. Craig Shirley, *Reagan's Revolution: The Untold Story of the Campaign That Started It All* (Nashville, Tenn.: Nelson Current, 2005), 293.
39. Mounger, USM Oral History, 141.
40. Keene, "Why Reagan Chose Schweiker," 15; Dent, *Prodigal South*, 42–44; see also Sanford J. Ungar, "Campaigning I: Clarke Reed of Mississippi," *Atlantic Monthly*, November 1976, 9–24.
41. Fredric N. Tulsky and Stephanie Saul, "Schweiker Damaging Reagan Bid," *Jackson Clarion-Ledger*, July 28, 1976.
42. Shirley, *Reagan's Revolution*, 293.
43. Yerger, USM Oral History, 60.
44. Shirley, *Reagan's Revolution*, 294; Witcover, *Marathon*, 468.
45. Dent, *Prodigal South*, 44.
46. Mike Retzer, USM Oral History, vol. 209, 1980, 24; Mounger, interview; Clarke Reed, interview.
47. Keene, "Why Reagan Chose Schweiker," 15.
48. Fredric N. Tulsky and Stephanie Saul, "Reed Move to Ford May Injure Reagan," *Jackson Clarion-Ledger*, July 29, 1976.
49. Giordano, USM Oral History, 19. In an interview for this book, Mounger maintained that Giordano had moved to Ford weeks earlier.
50. Fredric N. Tulsky, "Reed—Eyes of the Nation upon Him," *Jackson Clarion-Ledger*, July 30, 1976; Stephanie Saul and Fredric N. Tulsky, "Ford Seeks Votes Today in Mississippi," *Jackson Clarion-Ledger*, July 30, 1976.
51. Stephanie Saul, "Delegates Unswayed by Visit," *Jackson Clarion-Ledger*, July 31, 1976; Robert Paynter and Otis L. Sanford, "1,200 Well-Wishers Strain Necks—Few Get View of Ford," *Jackson Clarion-Ledger*, July 31, 1976.
52. Stephanie Saul, "GOP Bloc Talks Today to Reagan, Schweiker," *Jackson Clarion-Ledger*, August 4, 1976; Dent, *Prodigal South*, 45.
53. Shanks, USM Oral History, 38–55; Stephanie Saul, "Schweiker Strives to Shed Image," *Jackson Clarion-Ledger*, August 5, 1976; Fredric N. Tulsky, "Reagan Visit to State No Bloc-Buster," *Jackson Clarion-Ledger*, August 5, 1976; Mounger, interview.
54. Barbour, USM Oral History, 60; see also "Coaxing and Coddling a Delegation," *Time*, August 16, 1976, 10.
55. Fredric N. Tulsky and Stephanie Saul, "Nomination: A Heavy Burden to Carry," *Jackson Clarion-Ledger*, August 10, 1976.
56. Lane, USM Oral History, 52.
57. Mounger, USM Oral History, 206.
58. Retzer, USM Oral History, 25.
59. Shanks, USM Oral History, 38–40.
60. Mounger, USM Oral History, 215.

61. Barbour, USM Oral History, 66.

62. Witcover, *Marathon*, 497; Mounger, interview.

63. Barbour, USM Oral History; Charles Pickering, interview with the authors; Mounger, interview.

64. Ungar, "Campaigning," 23.

65. Drew, *American Journal*, 387.

66. Mounger, USM Oral History, 255–257; Mounger, interview.

67. Stephanie Saul and Fredric N. Tulsky, "Can Leaders Salve GOP Wounds," *Jackson Clarion-Ledger*, August 20, 1976.

68. Shanks, USM Oral History, 45; Giordano, USM Oral History, 31–33.

69. Barbour, USM Oral History, 73.

70. Drew, *American Journal*, 390.

71. Lane, USM Oral History, 44.

72. Barbour, USM Oral History, 43.

73. "Reed Voted to National GOP Post," *Jackson Clarion-Ledger*, August 24, 1976.

74. Bob Zeller, "Carter Hits Ford Tactic, Visits Coast," *Jackson Clarion-Ledger*, September 18, 1976.

75. Bob Zeller, "He Will Win Deep South, Ford Claims," *Jackson Clarion-Ledger*, September 26, 1976.

76. "Ford Swing to Include Gulf Coast," *Jackson Clarion-Ledger*, September 17, 1976.

77. Bob Zeller, "Ford Promotes Defense on Coast," *Jackson Clarion-Ledger*, September 27, 1976; Stephanie Saul, "This Is Writing Off the South?" *Jackson Clarion-Ledger*, September 27, 1976.

78. Witcover, *Marathon*, 561–567.

79. "Ex-Baptist President Backs Carter," *Jackson Clarion-Ledger*, October 22, 1976; Cupit, interview.

80. Carter, interview.

81. Sharon Peters, "Finch Predicts Ford Loss Over Tenn-Tom," *Jackson Clarion-Ledger*, September 28, 1976.

82. Witcover, *Marathon*, 597–598.

83. Witcover, *Marathon* 7, 621–622.

84. "Reed Gives Tight State Race to Ford," *Jackson Clarion-Ledger*, October 19, 1976; "Both Campaigns Say State Polls Show Their Man Ahead," *Jackson Clarion-Ledger*, October 19, 1976.

85. Cupit, interview; see also Hazard, interview.

86. Stephanie Saul, "Wallace Defends Carter Support," *Jackson Clarion-Ledger*, October 23, 1976; Edwards, interview; Guyton, interview; Cupit, interview.

87. As quoted in Dent, *Prodigal South*, 16–18.

88. Stephanie Saul, "Carter Has Firm Lead in State," *Jackson Clarion-Ledger*, November 3, 1976.

89. Carter, interview.

90. W. D. Mounger letter to Dr. Charles Pruitt Jr., December 1, 1976, copy obtained from Mounger's Oral History file at USM.

91. "Waller May Run for U.S. Senate," *Jackson Clarion-Ledger*, November 30, 1976.

92. Carter, interview.

93. Danny Cupit and Mark Hazard, interviews with the authors.

CHAPTER 4. THE CAMPAIGN TO SUCCEED
JIM EASTLAND, 1977–1978

There is no biography of the most colorful and powerful politician Mississippi has produced in contemporary times—Jim Eastland. Tragically, there has been no attempt by any person or institution to systematically record oral histories of people who were close to Eastland. In the early 1990s, Mississippi State University recorded oral histories with a number of people who were part of the life and career of John Stennis; so far as we can tell, nothing similar has been done for Eastland.

We found two journal articles on specific aspects of Eastland's early career: Wolfgang Schlauch, "Representative William Colmer and Senator James O. Eastland and the Reconstruction of Germany, 1945," *Journal of Mississippi History* 34 (August 1972); and Dorothy M. Zellner, "Red Roadshow: Eastland in New Orleans, 1954," *Louisiana History* 33 (Winter 1992).

In addition to citations of Eastland in the various books we have cited thus far (and there are many), we found information about him in Robert Sherrill, *Gothic Politics in the Deep South: Stars of the New Confederacy* (New York: Grossman, 1968); Virginia Foster Durr, *Outside the Magic Circle* (University: University of Alabama Press, 1985); Harry McPherson, *A Political Education* (Boston: Little Brown, 1972); and Larry Speakes, *Speaking Out: Inside the Reagan White House* (New York: Charles Scribner's Sons, 1988).

Three books have been published that cover the early career of Charles Evers: Jason Berry, *Amazing Grace: With Charles Evers in Mississippi* (New York; Saturday Review Press, 1973); Charles Evers and Grace Halsell, *Evers* (New York: World, 1970); and Charles Evers and Andrew Szanton, *Have No Fear: The Charles Evers Story* (New York: John Wiley, 1997).

1. In addition to the specific sources hereinafter cited, this portrait was developed through interviews the authors had with Steve Patterson, John Hollomon, Danny Cupit, Brad Dye, Mark Hazard, and Ed Cole.

2. Virginia Foster Durr, *Outside the Magic Circle* (University: University of Alabama Press, 1985), 171–172; Tom Eppes, "Powerful Peers Pay Homage to Eastland," *Jackson Daily News*, March 9, 1975.

3. Frank Barber, USM Oral History, 26; Hazard, interview; Cole, interview; Patterson, interview.

4. Minor, *Eyes on Mississippi*, 14.

5. "Mississippi's Jim Eastland," *Time*, March 26, 1956.

6. Bartley, *New South*, 117–118.

7. Bass, *Unlikely Heroes*, 17; see also McMillen, *Citizens' Council*, 9; and Johnston, *Politics*, 112–113.

8. Caro, *Master of the Senate*, 767; McMillen, *Citizens' Council*, 117; Numan V. Bartley, *The Rise of Massive Resistance: Race and Politics in the South during the* 1950's (Baton Rouge: Louisiana State University Press, 1969), 106; Stephen B. Oates, *Let the Trumpet Sound: The Life of Martin Luther King, Jr.* (New York: Harper and Row, 1982), 91–92.

9. Kotz, *Judgment Days*, 163–164.

10. Eppes, "Powerful Peers."

11. "Kennedy Urges Bravery for Justice," *Jackson Daily News*, May 15, 1978.

12. Arthur M. Schlesinger Jr., *Robert Kennedy and His Times* (Boston: Houghton Mifflin, 1978), 289.

13. Bass, *Unlikely Heroes*, 312; Clark, interview.

14. Bass, *Unlikely Heroes*, 146–147.

15. Ed Cole, MSU Oral History, January 7, 1981, 27–29; Cole, interview; see also Bob Gabriel, "Eastland, Farmer to Heartbeat from President," *Jackson Clarion-Ledger*, March 22, 1978; confidential interview with the authors.

16. Wilkie, *Dixie*, 252–253.

17. David Bates, "Waller to Run for Senate," *Jackson Clarion-Ledger*, March 10, 1978.

18. David Bates, "Waller to Run Against 'Tradition,'" *Jackson Clarion-Ledger*, March 21, 1978; McKellar, interview.

19. David Bates, "Eastland Rules Out Re-Election," *Jackson Clarion-Ledger*, March 22, 1978.

20. Stephanie Saul, "Eastland's Stepping Down Shakes Up Political Scene," *Jackson Clarion-Ledger*, March 22, 1978.

21. Maurice Dantin, interview with the authors; Patterson, interview; Cupit, interview; Carnathan, interview; McKellar, interview.

22. Johanna Neuman, "Pressured for Finch Contributions, Bankers Say," *Jackson Clarion-Ledger*, May 17, 1978.

23. Johanna Neuman, "Finch's TV Ads Liven Up Campaign," *Jackson Clarion-Ledger*, June 22, 1978.

24. Cochran, interview.

25. Pickering, interview; Cochran, interview; Lott, interview; Claiborne Barksdale, interview with the authors; Mounger, USM Oral History, 286; Barbour, USM Oral History, 84–85.

26. Barbour, USM Oral History, 86.

27. Jason Berry, *Amazing Grace: With Charles Evers in Mississippi* (New York: Saturday Review Press, 1973), 17–19; Charles Evers, USM Oral History, 6–7; Evers, interview; Charles Evers, MDAH Oral History, 3, 23–24, 43.

28. Bowie, interview.

29. Johanna Neuman, "Evers: Blacks Should Vote for Independents," *Jackson Clarion-Ledger*, May 29, 1978.

30. Edwards, interview; Evers, interview; McKellar, interview; see also Joe Sterling, "The 'Greatest' Stalks the Campaign Trail," *Jackson Clarion-Ledger*, October 23, 1978; Johanna Neuman, "Evers' Star-Studded Delta Drive," *Jackson Clarion-Ledger*, November 6, 1978.

31. Recollection of one of the authors.

32. Evers, interview; see also Charles Evers and Andrew Szanton, *Have No Fear: The Charles Evers Story* (New York: John Wiley and Sons, 1997), 286.

33. Carmichael, USM Oral History, 44; Carmichael, UNC Oral History, 24.

34. Dave Kubissa, "Hinson Scores Stunning Win," *Jackson Clarion-Ledger*, November 8, 1978.

35. As quoted in "Fannie Lou Hamer," editorial in *Greenville Delta Democrat-Times*, March 17, 1977; Romaine, "Mississippi Freedom Democratic Party," 216–217.

36. Craig Roberton, "Mrs. Hamer: Loving and Stalwart," *Greenville Delta Democrat-Times,* March 21, 1977.

37. Andrew Young, *An Easy Burden: The Civil Rights Movement and the Transformation of America* (New York: HarperCollins, 1996), 141–150, 302–309.

CHAPTER 5. DEMOCRATS WIN ONE AND REPUBLICANS LOSE ONE, 1979

Sources on William Winter include his oral histories and our interviews with him, along with Bethany Lamar Baskin, "The Rise of William Forrest Winter" (Master's thesis, Mississippi State University, 1992), and Erskine Alvis, "Winter's Young Men: The Boys of Spring in Recent Mississippi Politics" (History Honors paper, Centre College, 1984).

1. Bethany Lamar Baskin, "The Rise of William Forrest Winter" (Master's thesis, Mississippi State University, 1992), 72.

2. Frederickson, *Dixiecrat Revolt*, 11.

3. James P. Coleman, USM Oral History, 188; James P. Coleman, UNC Oral History, A-102, 1974, 34.

4. William Winter, USM Oral History, 30; Baskin, "William Forrest Winter," 11; William Winter, MSU Oral History, 1992, 7–9.

5. Charles M. Hills, "Speaker Given Wide Margin," *Jackson Clarion-Ledger*, January 4, 1956.

6. "Mrs. Bailey Dies Saturday in Meridian," *Jackson Clarion-Ledger*, April 1, 1956.

7. Winter, MSU Oral History, 1991, 16–17; Winter, MSU Oral History, 1992, 8–9; Winter, interview.

8. Coleman, USM Oral History, 188.

9. "Winter Sworn In as Tax Collector," *Jackson Clarion-Ledger*, April 4, 1956.

10. Winter, USM Oral History, 44–45; Winter, interview.

11. "Campaign Headquarters Head for the Big Silence," *Jackson Clarion-Ledger*, August 4, 1979; Jones, interview; David Crews, interview with the authors.

12. Mounger, interview.

13. Mounger, interview.

14. Jo Ann Klein, "GOP Falls Short of '79 Goal," *Jackson Clarion-Ledger*, June 8, 1979.

15. Jo Ann Klein, "Clarksdale Businessman, Farmer Begins Gubernatorial Campaign," *Jackson Clarion-Ledger*, June 16, 1979; Leon Bramlett, USM Oral History, vol. 205, 1980, 24; Yerger, interview.

16. Carmichael, USM Oral History, 104–107.

17. David Bates, "Candidates Promise Corruption Crackdown," *Jackson Clarion-Ledger*, April 3, 1979.

18. Winter, MSU Oral History, 1992, 18–19; Winter, interview.

19. David W. Kubissa, "Winter Enters Race with Swipe at Gandy," *Jackson Clarion-Ledger*, June 7, 1979; Winter, MSU Oral History, 1992, 20.

20. Winter, interview.

21. Joseph B. Parker, "New-Style Campaign Politics: Madison Avenue Comes to Dixie," in James F. Lea, ed., *Contemporary Southern Politics* (Baton Rouge: Louisiana State University Press, 1988), 161–164; "Robert Squier's Media Miracles in Dixie: An Exclusive C&E Interview," *Campaigns and Elections*, (Summer 1980): 29–41; Lois Romano, "Pollsters: The Figures Candidates Count On," *Washington Post*, January 15, 1984; Bill Peterson, "The Kingmaker of the 30-Second Spot: Robert Squier," *Washington Post*, November 27, 1979; David Bates, "From Soap Box to Idiot Box," *Jackson Clarion-Ledger*, August 2, 1979; Jo Ann Klein, "Gandy Back at No. 2 Spot, Silent about Future Plans," *Jackson Clarion-Ledger*, August 30, 1979; Winter, interview; confidential interview.

22. David W. Kubissa, "Winter Celebrates End of Long Quest," *Jackson Clarion-Ledger*, August 29, 1979; Crews, interview.

23. Carmichael, interview.

24. Carmichael, USM Oral History, 109.

25. Mounger, interview.

26. Winter, MSU Oral History, 1992, 21.

27. Winter, USM Oral History, 1978, 30.

28. David Bates, "Pickering Ads Claim Allain against Blacks," *Jackson Clarion-Ledger*, November 5, 1979.

29. Edwards, interview.

30. David Bates, "Pickering Says Ads Didn't Have His OK," *Jackson Clarion-Ledger*, November 6, 1979; Norma Fields, "Allain Calls Pickering Ads a Lie," *Northeast Mississippi Daily Journal*, November 6, 1979.

31. Edwards, interview.

32. Pickering, interview.

33. Bates, "Pickering Says Ads Didn't Have His OK."

34. Fields, "Allain Calls Pickering Ads a Lie."

35. David Bates, "Allain Clings to 2 Percent Lead in Attorney General Election," *Jackson Clarion-Ledger*, November 7, 1979.

36. "Pickering Blames Loss on Radio Advertisements," *Meridian Star*, November 8, 1979.

37. David Bates, "Pickering Aide Admits Ads Shouldn't Have Run," *Jackson Clarion-Ledger*, November 9, 1979.

38. Pickering, interview; Stuart Stevens, interview with the authors.

CHAPTER 6. THE ORIGINS OF REAPPORTIONMENT, 1890–1979

While there have been slightly fewer books written about reapportionment than the civil rights era, the difference has more than been made up by the overwhelming number of law review articles and scholarly journal articles on the impact of the Voting Rights Act of 1965 and the influence of the U.S. Supreme Court decisions on reapportionment, not to mention the hundreds of state and federal court decisions that the voting rights litigation inspired.

Several indispensable references guided our writing of this chapter: Frank R. Parker, *Black Votes Count: Political Empowerment in Mississippi after 1965* (Chapel Hill: University of North Carolina Press, 1990); "Voting in Mississippi," Report of the United States Commission on Civil Rights (Washington, D.C.: U.S. Government Printing Office, 1965); "The Voting Rights Act: Ten Years After," Report of the United States Commission on Civil Rights (Washington, D.C., January 1975); Morton Stavis, "A Century of Struggle for Black Enfranchisement in Mississippi: From the Civil War to the Congressional Challenge of 1965—And Beyond," *Mississippi Law Journal* 57 (December 1987); Neil R. McMillen, "Black Enfranchisement in Mississippi: Federal Enforcement and Black Protest in the 1960s," *Journal of Southern History* 43 (August 1977); and Armand Derfner, "Racial Discrimination and the Right to Vote," *Vanderbilt Law Review* 26 (April 1973).

Graduate research papers we relied on included Steven Andrew Light, "There's More Than Meets the Eye: Southern Cities and Minority Political Empowerment Following the 1965 Voting Rights Act" (Ph.D. diss., Northwestern University, 1999); William A. Butts, "The Relationship of Economic and Social Variables to Population Change and Negro Voter Registration in Mississippi, 1950–1966" (Ph.D. diss., Southern Illinois University, 1968); and Hugh Stephen Whitaker, "A New Day: The Effects of Negro Enfranchisement in Selected Mississippi Counties" (Ph.D. diss., Florida State University, 1965).

For information on Mississippi's 1890 constitution, we used Eric C. Clark, "The Mississippi Constitutional Convention of 1890: A Political Analysis" (Master's thesis, University of Mississippi, 1975); David G. Sansing, "Mississippi's Four Constitutions," *Mississippi Law Journal* 56 (April 1986); Albert D. Kirwan, "Apportionment in the Mississippi Constitution of 1890, *Journal of Southern History* 14 (May 1948); and Eric C. Clark, "Legislative Apportionment in the 1890 Constitutional Convention," *Journal of Mississippi History* 42 (November 1980).

Other books we used included Steven F. Lawson, *Black Ballots: Voting Rights in the South, 1944–1969* (New York: Columbia University Press, 1976); Steven F. Lawson, *In Pursuit of Power: Southern Blacks and Electoral Politics, 1965–1982* (New York: Columbia University Press, 1985); J. Morgan Kousser, *The Shaping of Southern Politics: Suffrage Restrictions and the Establishment of the One-Party South, 1880–1910* (New Haven, Conn.: Yale University Press, 1974); Howard Ball, Dale Krane, and Thomas P. Lauth, *Compromised Compliance: Implementation of the 1965 Voting Rights Act* (Westport, Conn.: Greenwood Press, 1982); David Lublin, *The Paradox of Representation* (Princeton, N.J.: Princeton University Press, 1997); Mary DeLorse Coleman, *Legislators, Law and Public Policy* (Westport, Conn. Greenwood Press, 1993); Richard K. Scher, Jon L. Mills, and John J. Hotaling, *Voting Rights and Democracy: The Law and Politics of Redistricting* (Chicago: Nelson-Hall, 1997);

Hanes Walton Jr. and Robert C. Smith, *American Politics and the African American Quest for University Freedom* (New York: Longman, 2000); Chandler Davidson and Bernard Grofman, eds., *Quiet Revolution in the South: The Impact of the Voting Rights Act, 1965–1990* (Princeton, N.J.: Princeton University Press, 1994); Charles E. Fager, *Selma, 1965: The March That Changed the South*, 2nd ed. (Boston: Beacon Press, 1985); and Thomas I. Emerson, David Haber, and Norman Dorsen, *Political and Civil Rights in the United States*, 3rd ed. (Boston: Little, Brown, 1967).

We found law journals across the country filled with articles about the enactment of the Voting Rights Act, its implementation, the three times it has been extended by Congress, and its impact on reapportionment. Among those articles we found useful include Laughlin McDonald, "The 1982 Extension of Section 5 of the Voting Rights Act of 1965: The Continued Need for Preclearance," *Tennessee Law Review* 51 (Fall 1983); Laughlin McDonald, "The Quiet Revolution in Minority Voting Rights," *Vanderbilt Law Review* 42 (1989); Frank R. Parker, "County Redistricting in Mississippi: Case Studies in Racial Gerrymandering," *Mississippi Law Journal* 44 (June 1973); Francis B. Stevens and John L. Maxey II, "Representing the Unrepresented: A Decennial Report on Public Interest Litigation in Mississippi," *Mississippi Law Journal* 44 (June 1973); Thomas Vocino, John H. Morris, and D. Steve Gill, "The Population Apportionment Principle: Its Development and Application to Mississippi's State and Local Legislative Bodies," *Mississippi Law Journal* 47 (November 1976); Frank R. Parker, "Protest, Politics, and Litigation: Political and Social Change in Mississippi, 1965 to Present," *Mississippi Law Journal* 57 (December 1987); Kathryn Healy Hester, "Mississippi and the Voting Rights Act:1965–1982," *Mississippi Law Journal* 52 (December 1982); Carroll Rhodes, "Enforcing the Voting Rights Act in Mississippi through Litigation," *Mississippi Law Journal* 57 (December 1987); and "Judicial Performance in the Fifth Circuit," *Yale Law Journal* 73 (1963).

Sources for the courts and lawyers we used include Leon Friedman, ed., *Southern Justice* (New York: Pantheon Books, 1965); Charles V. Hamilton, *The Bench and the Ballot: Southern Federal Judges and the Black Vote* (New York: Oxford University Press, 1973); Jack Bass, *Unlikely Heroes* (New York: Simon and Schuster, 1981); Charles V. Hamilton, "Southern Judges and Negro Voting Rights: The Judicial Approach to the Solution of Controversial Social Problems," *Wisconsin Law Review* 65 (Winter 1965); Alexander M. Bickel, "Impeach Judge Cox," *New Republic*, September 4, 1965; Mary Hannah Curzan, "A Case Study in the Selection of Federal Judges: The Fifth Circuit, 1953–1963" (Ph.D. diss., Yale University, 1968); Fred L. Banks Jr., "The United States Court of Appeals for the Fifth Circuit: A Personal Perspective," *Mississippi College Law Journal* 16 (Spring 1996); and Carol Caldwell, "Harold Cox: Still Racist After All These Years," *American Lawyer* 1 (July 1979).

Court Cases

Sproule v. Fredericks, 69 Miss. 898 (1892)
Williams v. Mississippi, 170 U.S. 213 (1898)
Smith v. Allwright, 321 U.S. 634 (1944)
Colegrove v. Green, 328 U.S. 549 (1946)

Baker v. Carr, 369 U.S. 186 (1962)

Gray v. Sanders, 372 U.S. 368 (1963)

Wesberry v. Sanders, 376 U.S. 1 (1964)

Reynolds v. Sims, 377 U.S. 533 (1964)

United States v. Mississippi, 229 F.Supp. 925 (1964)

United States v. Mississippi, 380 U.S. 128 (1965)

South Carolina v. Katzenbach, 383 U.S. 301 (1966)

United States v. Mississippi, 256 F.Supp. 344 (1966)

Connor v. Johnson, 256 F.Supp. 962 (1966)

Connor v. Johnson, 265 F.Supp. 492 (1967)

Allen v. State Board of Elections, 393 U.S. 544 (1969)

Connor v. Johnson, 330 F.Supp. 506 (1971)

Connor v. Johnson, 402 U.S. 690 (1971)

Connor v. Johnson, 330 F.Supp. 521 (1971)

Evers v. State Board of Election Commissioners, 327 F.Supp. 640 (1971)

Connor v. Williams, 404 U.S. 549 (1972)

Connor v. Waller, 396 F.Supp.1308 (1975)

Connor v. Waller, 421 U.S. 656 (1975)

Connor v. Waller, No.3830(A), So. Dist. Miss., unreported case dated July 11, 1975

Connor v. Waller, 396 F.Supp.1308 (1975)

Connor v. Waller, 421 U.S. 656 (1975)

Connor v. Coleman, 425 U.S. 675 (1976)

Connor v. Finch, 419 F.Supp.1072 (1976)

Connor v. Finch, 419 F.Supp.1089 (1976)

Connor v. Finch, 422 F.Supp.1014 (1976)

Connor v. Finch, 431 U.S. 407 (1977)

Connor v. Finch, 440 U.S. 612 (1979)

State of Mississippi v. United States, 490 F.Supp. 569 (1979)

State of Mississippi v. United States, 444 U.S.1050 (1980)

1. Davis, "Sisters and Brothers," 70. The civil rights worker was Ivanhoe Donaldson, and the Jackson police officer had a gun to his face while yelling at him in the back of a police car.
2. Sallis, "Color Line in Mississippi Politics," 294.
3. Kirwan, *Revolt of the Rednecks*, 6–13, 58–61; C. Vann Woodward, *Origins of the New South:1877–1913* (Baton Rouge: Louisiana State University Press, 1951), 326–328.
4. Sallis, "Color Line in Mississippi Politics," 286; Kirwan, *Revolt of the Rednecks*, 58; James P. Coleman, "The Mississippi Constitution of 1890 and the Final Decade of the Nineteenth Century," in McLemore, *History of Mississippi*, vol. 2, 8–12; Woodward, *Origins*, 327.
5. Sallis, "Color Line in Mississippi Politics," 292–293; see also J. Morgan Kousser, *The Shaping of Southern Politics: Suffrage Restrictions and the Establishment of the One-Party South*, 1880–1910 (New Haven, Conn.: Yale University Press, 1974), 30–33, 139–141; Kirwan, *Revolt of the Rednecks*, 59–60; Vernon Lane Wharton, *The Negro in Mississippi: 1865–1890*

(New York: Harper Torchbooks, 1947), 206–210; "Voting in Mississippi," 3; Mayre Dabney, "Keynote Address at the Reunion of the Survivors of the Constitutional Convention of 1890, November 1, 1910," in *Pamphlets of Great Historical Value to Mississippi*, 12, Mississippi Department of Archives and History; Charles N. Fortenberry and F. Glenn Abney, "Mississippi: Unreconstructed and Unredeemed," in William C. Havard, ed., *The Changing Politics of the South* (Baton Rouge: Louisiana State University Press, 1972), 476; Sallis, "Color Line in Mississippi Politics," 296.

6. Woodward, *Origins*, 321–322; Kirwan, *Revolt of the Rednecks*, 77–78.

7. *United States v. Mississippi*, 229 F.Supp. 987 (1964); Judge R. H. Thompson, "An Address Delivered Before the Mississippi State Bar Association, May 2 and 3, 1923," in *Pamphlets of Great Historical Value to Mississippi*, 16–17, Mississippi Department of Archives and History.

8. Eric C. Clark, "The Mississippi Constitutional Convention of 1890: A Political Analysis" (Master's thesis University of Mississippi, 1975), 113–114; Sallis, "Color Line in Mississippi Politics," 310–311.

9. Clark, "Mississippi Constitutional Convention," 154–157; see also Wharton, *Negro in Mississippi* (1947), 214.

10. Sallis, "Color Line in Mississippi Politics," 320.

11. "Voting in Mississippi," 5. The presidential turnout figures come from *Guide to U.S. Elections*, published by Congressional Quarterly; what makes this figure all the more remarkable is that women earned the right to vote in 1920. The eligible white electorate was doubled when women achieved the right to vote through the ratification of the Nineteenth Amendment.

12. *Sproule v. Fredericks*, 69 Miss. 898 (1892).

13. *Williams v. Mississippi*, 170 U.S. 213 (1898). Notably, the makeup of the 1898 Court was, but for the replacement of one retiring justice, the same as the Court that handed down one of the nation's most infamous judicial edicts. Just two years previously, almost the same Supreme Court had ruled that "separate but equal" public accommodations were sufficient to satisfy constitutional requirements of equal treatment among the races in *Plessy v. Ferguson*, 163 U.S. 537 (1896).

14. "Voting in Mississippi," 7–8; see also Kousser, *Shaping of Southern Politics*, 75–77.

15. *Smith v. Allwright*, 321 U.S. 649 (1944).

16. William A. Butts, "The Relationship of Economic and Social Variables to Population Change and Negro Voter Registration in Mississippi" (Ph.D. diss., Southern Illinois University, 1968), 157.

17. Neil R. McMillen, "Black Enfranchisement in Mississippi: Federal Enforcement and Black Protest in the 1960s," *Journal of Southern History* 43 (August 1977): 351–352.

18. "Voting in Mississippi," 9–10; see also Hugh Stephen Whitaker, "A New Day: The Effects of Negro Enfranchisement in Selected Mississippi Counties" (Ph.D. diss., Florida State University, 1965), 28–33.

19. Gerald M. Stern, "Judge William Harold Cox and the Right to Vote in Clarke County, Mississippi," in Leon Friedman, ed., *Southern Justice* (New York: Pantheon Books, 1965), 172–174.

20. Romaine, "Mississippi Freedom Democratic Party," 12–13; Dittmer, *Local People*, 109–110.
21. "Voting in Mississippi," 13–15.
22. David J. Garrow, *Bearing the Cross: Martin Luther King, Jr. and the Southern Christian Leadership Conference* (New York: William Morrow, 1986), 397–408; Charles E. Fager, *Selma, 1965: The March That Changed the South*, 2nd ed. (Boston: Beacon Press, 1985), 133–136; Kotz, *Judgment Days*, 283–285, 308–310.
23. Morton Stavis, "A Century of Struggle for Black Enfranchisement in Mississippi: From the Civil War to the Congressional Challenge of 1965—And Beyond," *Mississippi Law Journal* 57 (December 1987): 640–665; McLemore, "Mississippi Freedom Democratic Party," 229–249; Dittmer, *Local People*, 352; McMillen, "Black Enfranchisement," 368–369; Lawrence Guyot, USM Oral History, vol. 673, 19; Guyot, interview.
24. Frank R. Parker, "Protest, Politics, and Litigation: Political and Social Change in Mississippi, 1965 to Present," *Mississippi Law Journal* 57 (December 1987): 680.
25. Kathryn Healy Hester, "Mississippi and the Voting Rights Act: 1965–1982," *Mississippi Law Journal* 52 (December 1982): 805. Laughlin McDonald, "The 1982 Extension of Section 5 of the Voting Rights Act of 1965: The Continued Need for Preclearance," *Tennessee Law Review* 51 (Fall 1983): 27–29, points out that Congress first banned literacy and other tests in 1965 only in the jurisdictions covered by Section 5. In the 1970 amendments, Congress extended the ban for five years and at the same time made it nationwide. Then in 1975 Congress made the ban permanent.
26. Hester, "Mississippi and the Voting Rights Act," 805; McDonald, "Voting Rights Act of 1965," 29.
27. "Four More Counties Get U.S. Registrars," *Jackson Clarion-Ledger*, December 21, 1965.
28. Hester, "Mississippi and the Voting Rights Act," 809–811; McDonald, "Voting Rights Act of 1965," 30–33. McDonald points out that by the time the 1975 amendments to the act were implemented, the preclearance provisions covered twenty-two states or parts of states.
29. "Another Stab at South," *Jackson Daily News*, August 7, 1965.
30. *South Carolina v. Katzenbach*, 383 U.S. 301 (1966); McDonald, "Voting Rights Act of 1965," 26.
31. James Saggus, "State Files Action against Registrars," *Jackson Clarion-Ledger*, September 8, 1965.
32. Parker, *Black Votes Count*, 37–41.
33. *Allen v. State Board of Elections*, 393 U.S. 544 (1969); *Whitley v. Johnson*, filed by the Lawyers Constitutional Defense Committee (LCDC), concerned the onerous new qualifying requirements for independent candidates. *Fairley v. Patterson*, filed by the Lawyers Committee for Civil Rights Under Law, concerned the counties that had switched to countywide elections for supervisors. *Bunton v. Patterson*, filed by the Lawyer's Committee, concerned the law that changed elected school superintendents to appointive in eleven counties.
34. Parker, *Black Votes Count*, 98–99; see also Armand Derfner, "Racial Discrimination and the Right to Vote," *Vanderbilt Law Review* 26 (April 1973): 577.

35. Parker, "Protest, Politics, and Litigation," 680; Hester, "Mississippi and the Voting Rights Act," 803. The constitutional amendment applied to federal elections; litigation filed by the federal government ultimately abolished poll taxes for state elections. See *Harper v. Virginia State Board of Elections*, 383 U.S. 663 (1966).

36. In strictly legal terms, "redistricting" is the term used to describe the process by which political district lines are drawn. "Reapportionment" is the process used by Congress to apportion the 535 House of Representative districts among the fifty states following the decennial census. But the two terms have been used interchangeably so much over the last forty years that they are virtually synonymous. We choose to employ the term "reapportionment" because that's the term most frequently used in public discourse.

37. Parker, *Black Votes Count*, 106–110; Chapter 57, Laws of the State of Mississippi, 1962 Second Extraordinary Session; Chapter 41, Laws of the State of Mississippi, 1966–1967 First Extraordinary Session.

38. "Reapportionment Fight Scheduled Next Week," *Jackson Clarion-Ledger*, March 30, 1962.

39. Section 254, Mississippi Constitution of 1890, as printed in the Official and Statistical Register, State of Mississippi, 1908, Mississippi Department of Archives and History; population data taken from Mississippi Statistical Summary of Population, 1800–1980, Economic Research Department, Mississippi Power & Light Company, February 1983. This presentation does not account for the "floater" representative that was allocated to Harrison and Jackson counties and the "floater" representative that was allocated to Hinds and Yazoo counties.

40. *Colegrove v. Green*, 328 U.S. 549 (1946).

41. Thomas Vocino, John H. Morris, and D. Steve Gill, "The Population Apportionment Principle: Its Development and Application to Mississippi's State and Local Legislative Bodies," *Mississippi Law Review* 47 (November 1976): 946.

42. *Baker v. Carr*, 369 U.S. 186 (1962).

43. *Wesberry v. Sanders*, 376 U.S. 1 (1964).

44. *Reynolds v. Sims*, 377 U.S. 533 (1964).

45. "Seating of Legislature Challenged," *Biloxi Daily Herald*, October 18, 1960; Joel Blass, interview with the authors; Gerald Blessey, interview with the authors. The plaintiffs were Marvin Fortner, W. D. Alberts, J. K. Milner, Cleve Allen Jr., Carl Stanton, all of Gulfport, and Sam Maxwell, of Long Beach.

46. Edmund Noel, "State Group Will Push Reapportionment Suit," *Jackson Clarion-Ledger*, March 27, 1962.

47. "Sisson Is Thwarted by Horton," *Biloxi Daily Herald*, May 29, 1962.

48. "Ruling Is Made in Harrison County Case," *Biloxi Daily Herald*, June 7, 1962; Tom Cook, "Coast Jubilant Over Decision of Chancellor," *Biloxi Daily Herald*, June 7, 1962.

49. "Judge Horton Refuses to Halt Reshuffle Vote," *Jackson Clarion-Ledger*, October 21, 1962.

50. Vocino, Morris, and Gill, "Population Apportionment Principle," 952.

51. Parker, *Black Votes Count*.

52. Peggy Connor, interview with the authors; Guyot, interview; *Jackson Clarion-Ledger*, October 4, 1965; the other plaintiffs were Anne E. Taylor, Forrest County; Augusta Wheadon, Lowndes County; Raphis Hayes, Holmes County; Katherine Crowell, Lauderdale County; Henry Kirksey, Hinds County; Elijah Conwell, Bolivar County; and Alma Carnegie, Holmes County.

53. Connor, interview.

54. *Connor v. Johnson*, 256 F. Supp. 962 (1966).

55. *Connor v. Johnson*, 256 F. Supp. 962 (1966).

56. *Connor v. Johnson*, 265. F. Supp. 492 (1967); Al Bronstein, interview with the authors.

57. Chapter 391, Laws of the State of Mississippi, 1971 Regular Session.

58. *Connor v. Johnson*, 330 F.Supp. 506 (1971); James Saggus, "Federal Court Orders Own Reapportionment Plan," *Jackson Clarion-Ledger*, May 19, 1971.

59. Chapter 394, Laws of the State of Mississippi, 1971 Regular Session.

60. Parker, *Black Votes Count*, 110–113.

61. *Connor v. Johnson*, 402 U.S. 690 (1971); Parker, *Black Votes Count*, 113–115; "Court Overturns Hinds At-Large Election Plan," *Jackson Clarion-Ledger*, June 4, 1971.

62. Parker, *Black Votes Count*, 110.

63. *Connor v. Johnson*, 330 F. Supp. 521 (1971); Charles M. Hills Jr., "Hinds Redistricting Insurmountable Task," *Jackson Clarion-Ledger*, June 15, 1971; George Peach Taylor, interview with the authors.

64. James Saggus, "House Gives Redistricting Final OK," *Jackson Clarion-Ledger*, April 4, 1975.

65. *Connor v. Waller*, 396 F. Supp.1308 (1975); *Connor v. Waller*, 421 U.S. 656 (1975); Jack Elliott, "U.S. Ruling Demands One-Man Districts, Lawyer Says," *Jackson Clarion-Ledger*, June 6, 1975.

66. *Connor v. Waller*, No.3830(A), So. Dist. Miss., unreported case dated July 11, 1975.

67. Jack Elliott, "Districting Case Goes before Panel," *Jackson Clarion-Ledger*, June 20, 1975.

68. *Connor v. Coleman*, 425 U.S. 675 (1976), 679; Vocino, Morris, and Gill, "Population Apportionment Principle," 966–968.

69. Jack Elliott, "Reapportion Soon, Court Urges State," *Jackson Clarion-Ledger*, May 20, 1976.

70. Steve Cannizaro, "Panel Draws 1-Member Senate Lines," *Jackson Clarion-Ledger*, August 25, 1976; Steve Cannizaro, "Panel: Soon Will Draw Own Districting Plan," *Jackson Clarion-Ledger*, June 16, 1976; *Connor v. Finch*, 419 F.Supp.1072 (1976), 1074–1075; *Connor v. Finch*, 419 F. Supp.1089 (1976), 1090; *Connor v. Finch*, 422 F. Supp.1014 (1976).

71. *Connor v. Finch*, 431 U.S. 407 (1977), 425–426; Parker, *Black Votes Count*, 124–126; Hester, "Mississippi and the Voting Rights Act," 839–841.

72. Stephanie Saul, "Likelihood of Special Session Increases," *Jackson Clarion-Ledger*, August 9, 1977; Stephanie Saul, "Special Session to Meet for State Reapportionment," *Jackson Clarion-Ledger*, August 10, 1977; Stephanie Saul, "Reapportionment Panel Organizes, Begins Sessions," *Jackson Clarion-Ledger*, August 14, 1977; Hester, "Mississippi and the Voting Rights Act," 840–842; Parker, *Black Votes Count*, 125–127.

73. Steve Cannizaro, "Remap Baffles Judges," *Jackson Clarion-Ledger*, February 15, 1978.

74. Horace S. Scruggs, *Witness to Change: The Authorized Biography of Judge Dan M. Russell, Jr.* (Bay St. Louis, Miss.: Char Baby, 2004), 62.

75. David Bates, "Court Panel Upholds State Reapportionment," *Jackson Clarion-Ledger*, June 2, 1979; *State of Mississippi v. United States of America*, 490 F. Supp. 569 (1979), affirmed by U.S. Supreme Court at 444 U.S.1050 (1980).

76. Coleman, USM Oral History, 207.

77. Coleman, UNC Oral History, 4007, 1990, 12.

78. Coleman, USM Oral History, 208.

79. Charles M. Hills, "Legislators Close Out 1957 Special Session," *Jackson Clarion-Ledger*, December 12, 1957.

80. Scruggs, *Witness to Change*, 62. Russell confirmed this in an interview with the authors, but had little else in the way of memories from the Connor litigation.

81. Bill Simpson, "Neshoba Fair Has Candidates' Focus," *Jackson Clarion-Ledger*, August 1, 1963.

82. Henry Kirksey, interview with the authors; Johanna Newman, "If Henry Kirksey Has Any Record, It's Mississippi's Reapportionment," *Jackson Clarion-Ledger*, October 1, 1978.

83. Three of the lawyers for the Connor plaintiffs whom we interviewed—Al Bronstein, George Peach Taylor, and John Maxey—independently agreed that Coleman was in complete control of the lawsuit.

84. Bass, *Unlikely Heroes*, 164–168; oral history with Robert F. Kennedy conducted by Anthony Lewis in 1964, in *Robert Kennedy: In His Own Words*, ed. Edwin O. Guthman and Jeffrey Shulman (New York: Bantam Books, 1988), 109.

85. Mary Hannah Curzan, "A Case Study in the Selection of Federal Judges in the Fifth Circuit, 1953–1963" (Ph.D. diss., Yale University, 1968), 32.

86. "Judge Due to Rule on Suit to Speed Up Negro Registration," *New York Times*, March 9, 1964; Schlesinger, *Robert Kennedy*, 308–309; Branch, *Pillar of Fire*, 247.

87. Charles V. Hamilton, *The Bench and the Ballot: Southern Federal Judges and Black Voters* (New York: Oxford University Press, 1973), 133.

88. Victor S. Navasky, *Kennedy Justice* (New York: Antheneum, 1975), 284–286; copy of October 16, 1963, letter from Judge Cox to John Doar obtained from the John F. Kennedy Presidential Library in Boston.

89. Victor McTeer, interview with the authors. McTeer gives full credit to Allain for saving his legal career on that day.

90. Reuben Anderson, interview with the authors; see also Cole, interview; and Fred L. Banks Jr., "The United States Court of Appeals for the Fifth Circuit: A Personal Perspective," *Mississippi College Law Journal* 16 (Spring 1996): 275–288; Taylor, interview.

91. Taylor, interview.

92. Guyot, interview; see also Dittmer, *Local People*, 191–192.

93. McLemore, interview.

94. Bennie Thompson, interview with the authors.

CHAPTER 7. RONALD REAGAN AND JON HINSON, 1980–1981

For coverage of the 1980 presidential campaign, we relied on Jeff Greenfield, *The Real Campaign: How the Media Missed the Story of the 1980 Campaign* (New York: Summit Books, 1982); Elizabeth Drew, *Portrait of an Election: The 1980 Presidential Campaign* (New York: Simon and Schuster, 1981); and Jack W. Germond and Jules Witcover, *Blue Smoke and Mirrors: How Reagan Won and Why Carter Lost the Election of 1980* (New York: Viking Press, 1981). For background on Ronald Reagan, we used Lou Cannon, *President Reagan: The Role of a Lifetime* (New York: Simon and Schuster, 1991).

1. Carmichael, USM Oral History, 95.
2. Jeff Greenfield, *The Real Campaign: How the Media Missed the Story of the 1980 Campaign* (New York: Summit Books, 1982), 232; "The Carter Presidency," in *Congress and the Nation*, vol. 5, 1977–1980 (Washington, D.C.: Congressional Quarterly, 1981), 957–958.
3. Cupit, interview.
4. David W. Kubissa, "Chairmanship Tops Democrats' Agenda," *Jackson Clarion-Ledger*, April 18, 1980; Cupit, interview; Cole, interview; McLemore, interview.
5. David W. Kubissa and Jo Ann Klein, "They Come Out Swinging," *Jackson Clarion-Ledger*, April 20, 1980.
6. Danny Cupit, Ed Cole, Les McLemore, and Steve Patterson, interviews with the authors.
7. David W. Kubissa, "Democrats Tap One Chairman Amid Party Rift," *Jackson Clarion-Ledger*, May 11, 1980; David W. Kubissa, "Dems Test Reaction to Squabble," *Jackson Clarion-Ledger*, May 13, 1980.
8. Patterson, interview.
9. Patterson, interview.
10. Patterson, interview.
11. David W. Kubissa, "Ford Blasts Carter's Economic, Defense Programs," *Jackson Clarion-Ledger*, February 13, 1980; Jo Ann Klein, "Democratic Senator Tapped by Reagan Campaign," *Jackson Clarion-Ledger*, January 17, 1980; Mounger, interview.
12. Jo Ann Klein, "State GOP Leadership Remains Intact," *Jackson Clarion-Ledger*, May 11, 1980; Clarke Reed, interview; Mounger, interview.
13. Edsall and Edsall, *Chain Reaction*, 134.
14. Griffith, interview.
15. Jo Ann Klein, "Reagan Wows Crowd at the Neshoba Fair," *Jackson Clarion-Ledger*, August 4, 1980; "Ronald Reagan Speaks at Fair Sunday," *Neshoba Democrat*, August 7, 1980; Douglas E. Kneeland, "Reagan Campaigns at Mississippi Fair," *New York Times*, August 4, 1980.
16. Edsall and Edsall, *Chain Reaction*, 131.
17. "Legislature Ends Session Studded with Milestones," *Jackson Clarion-Ledger*, March 31, 1979.
18. Greenfield, *Real Campaign*, 236–237.
19. Edsall and Edsall, *Chain Reaction*, 131–133; *Green v. Kennedy*, 309 F. Supp.1127 (1970).

20. Griffith, interview.

21. Jack W. Germond and Jules Witcover, *Blue Smoke and Mirrors: How Reagan Won and Why Carter Lost the Election of* 1980 (New York: Viking Press, 1981), 21; Greenfield, *Real Campaign*, 241–242.

22. Gene Monteith, "Little Fanfare for First Lady in Columbus," *Jackson Clarion-Ledger*, October 31, 1980.

23. David W. Kubissa, "President Woos Southern Vote in State Speech," *Jackson Clarion-Ledger*, November 1, 1980.

24. See also, for example, Stephen D. Shaffer, "Changing Party Politics in Mississippi," in Robert H. Swansbrough and David M. Brodsky, eds., *The South's New Politics* (Columbia: University of South Carolina Press, 1988), 192–194.

25. "Politics and National Issues," in *Congress and the Nation*, 26–27.

26. McLemore, interview.

27. Stevens, interview.

28. David Bates, "Revelations from Jon Hinson Could Alter Congressional Race," *Jackson Clarion-Ledger*, August 9, 1980; "Rep. Hinson Bares Two Incidents from Past," *Tylertown Times*, August 14, 1980.

29. Mounger, interview; Yerger, interview; "GOP Leaders Vow to Back Rep. Hinson," *Jackson Daily News*, August 11, 1980.

30. David Bates, "Hinson: I Was Sick and Tired of Worrying," *Jackson Clarion-Ledger*, August 16, 1980.

31. Johanna Neuman, "Hinson Survived Fire at X-Rated Theater," *Jackson Clarion-Ledger*, August 9, 1980.

32. Johanna Neuman, "Hinson Was Regular Visitor at Theater, Deposition Reveals," *Jackson Clarion-Ledger*, August 28, 1980.

33. Tom Clifford and David Hampton, "Hinson Arrest Details Revealed," *Jackson Daily News*, October 9, 1980.

34. Tom Clifford and Dewey English, "Arresting Officer Confirms Details of Hinson Arrest," *Jackson Daily News*, October, 10, 1980; "Park Service Disavows Claims Made in Hinson Television Ads," *Jackson Daily News*, October 17, 1980.

35. Wendell Rawls Jr., "Mississippian Gains Despite Sex Issue," *Washington Post*, October 8, 1980; Mounger, interview.

36. David Hampton, "Racial Split Aids Hinson Victory in 4th District," *Jackson Daily News*, November 5, 1980.

37. Tom Clifford, "Prosecutor May Reduce Charges against Hinson," *Jackson Daily News*, February 5, 1981; Tom Sherwood, "Hill Police Arrest Congressman on Sodomy Charge," *Washington Post*, February 5, 1981; "Wednesday Arrest Rocks Hinson Staff," *Jackson Clarion-Ledger*, February 8, 1981.

38. Cliff Treyens, "Hinson Backers Demand Resignation," *Jackson Clarion-Ledger*, February 5, 1981; Lynn Watkins, "Retzer, Mounger, Yerger Say of Hinson: Resign," *Jackson Clarion-Ledger*, February 5, 1981.

39. "That's It, Jon," *Jackson Daily News*, February 5, 1981.

40. Transcript of February 5, 1981, ABC News report by Rebecca Chase.

41. Johanna Neuman, "Hinson Arrest Is the Talk of Washington," *Jackson Clarion-Ledger*, February 6, 1981.

42. Johanna Neuman, "Hinson Resigns Effective April 13," *Jackson Clarion-Ledger*, March 14, 1981.

43. Tom Clifford, "Hinson Faces Long Road, Minister Says," *Jackson Daily News*, March 18, 1981.

44. Johanna Neuman and Cliff Treyens, "Hinson Put on Probation in Sex Case," *Jackson Clarion-Ledger*, May 29, 1981.

45. John Flynn, "Community Reaction Runs from Shock to Humor," *Jackson Clarion-Ledger*, February 6, 1981.

46. Associated Press, "Singletary Denies Knowing of Hinson Arrest Before Aug.," *Jackson Daily News*, October 2, 1980; John Holloman, interview.

47. Johanna Neuman, "News to Him, Cochran Says of Hinson Disclosures," *Jackson Clarion-Ledger*, August 18, 1980; "Cochran Asks Support in Campaign Swing," *Tylertown Times*, October 28, 1976; Cochran, interview.

48. "Parents of Former Rep. Jon Hinson Die in Blaze," January 2, 1984; "Ex-Representative's Parents Killed by Blaze in Mississippi," *New York Times*, January 3, 1984; "Supervisor, Wife Lose Lives in Fire," *Tylertown Times*, January 5, 1984.

49. "Jon Hinson Dies at 53," Associated Press, July 25, 1995; obituary in *Tylertown Times*, July 27, 1995.

50. "Ex-Congressman Back for Gay Center Benefit," *New Orleans Times-Picayune*, March 13, 1994; Anita Lee, "Hinson to Help Raise Money for Gay Center," *Biloxi Sun-Herald*, March 12, 1994.

51. Cliff Treyens, "Winter Sets Date for Election to Replace Hinson," *Jackson Clarion-Ledger*, March 20, 1981.

52. David Hampton, "GOP Convention to Nominate Candidate," *Jackson Daily News*, February 17, 1981; Cliff Treyens, "GOP Votes for Convention to Pick Candidate," *Jackson Clarion-Ledger*, February 17, 1981.

53. David Hampton, "GOP Gives 4th District Nod to Liles Williams," *Jackson Clarion-Ledger*, April 5, 1981.

54. Cupit, interview.

55. Cliff Treyens, "Dowdy, Herring Back Extended Rights Act," *Jackson Clarion-Ledger*, May 21, 1981; see also James M. Glaser, *Race, Campaign Politics, and the Realignment in the South* (New Haven, Conn.: Yale University Press, 1996), 44–58.

56. Art Harris, "Hinson's Memory Haunts His Mississippi District," *Washington Post*, June 17, 1981.

57. Judy Putnam, "Dowdy Beats Williams by Paper-Thin Margin," *Jackson Clarion-Ledger*, July 8, 1981.

58. David S. Broder, "Party Chiefs Launch Post-Mortems of the Mississippi Election Upset," *Washington Post*, July 10, 1981.

59. David W. Kubissa, "Finch Takes Campaign to Atlanta, Dallas," *Jackson Clarion-Ledger*, January 17, 1980.

60. "Nothing to Hide," *Jackson Clarion-Ledger*, January 29, 1980.

CHAPTER 8. EDUCATION TRANSFORMS THE LEGISLATURE, 1982

For background on the 1982 education reform fight, we used as our reference Andrew P. Mullins Jr., *Building Consensus: A History of the Passage of the Mississippi Education Reform Act of 1982* (Mississippi Humanities Council and the Phil Hardin Foundation, 1992); for background on the Stennis election, we used Raymond D. Strother, *Falling Up: How a Redneck Helped Invent Political Consulting* (Baton Rouge: Louisiana State University Press, 2003).

1. House Journal, 1982 Regular Session, 61.
2. Simpson, USM Oral History, 12–13.
3. David B. Ogle, *Strengthening the Mississippi Legislature* (New Brunswick, N.J.: Rutgers University Press, 1971), 80–81.
4. In addition to the individual citations, the story that follows was informed by interviews the authors conducted with William Winter, Ray Mabus, Dick Molpus, David Crews, Tommy Walman, David Watkins, Tervell Stubbs, Sonny Merideth, Jack Gordon, Brad Dye, John Henegan, and Tim Ford.
5. Andrew P. Mullins Jr., *Building Consensus: A History of the Passage of the Mississippi Education Reform Act of 1982* (Mississippi Humanities Council and the Phil Hardin Foundation, 1992), 9–27. Ray Mabus pointed out in an interview for this book that he has since learned that in 1982, New Hampshire also did not require a mandatory public kindergarten system.
6. Mullins, *Building Consensus*, 29–62.
7. House Journal, 1982 Regular Session, 61.
8. Nancy Weaver, "Inaction on Education Reform a Tradition," *Jackson Clarion-Ledger*, December 6, 1982.
9. Winter, interview.
10. Judy Putnam, "Kindergarten Bill Clears Panel Vote, Goes to Full House," *Jackson Clarion-Ledger*, February 4, 1982; House Journal, 1982 Regular Session, 148.
11. Robert Clark, USM Oral History, 23; Walman, interview.
12. House Journal, 1982 Regular Session, 258; Mullins, *Building Consensus*, 75–77.
13. Robert Clark, USM Oral History, 22–23; Tom Walman, USM Oral History, 215; Judy Putnam, "Optional Bill Would Tax Sales; Speaker Slows Kindergartens," *Jackson Clarion-Ledger*, February 11, 1982.
14. Terrell Stubbs, interview with the authors; Dick Molpus, interview with the authors.
15. Sonny Merideth, interview with the authors.
16. Simpson, USM Oral History, 29.
17. Buddie Newman, USM Oral History, 34.
18. Judy Putnam, "Kindergarten Bill Dies without Vote in House," *Jackson Clarion-Ledger*, February 12, 1982; House Journal, 1982 Regular Session, 270.
19. Judy Putnam, "Kindergartens Die at Hand of Speaker," *Jackson Clarion-Ledger*, February 14, 1982.
20. Molpus, interview.

21. Gene Monteith, "Newman: ABC Kindergarten Report a 'Hatchet Job,'" *Jackson Clarion-Ledger*, August 28, 1982; Mullins, *Building Consensus*, 103; "Kindergartens Had No Chance," *Mississippi Press*, August 30, 1982.

22. "9 Papers in Mississippi Being Sold to Gannett," *New York Times*, April 2, 1982.

23. Charles Overby, MSU Oral History, 19–20; Charles Overby, USM Oral History, 171–172.

24. Mullins, *Building Consensus*, 170.

25. Mullins, *Building Consensus*, 164.

26. "Winter: Special Session on Education Possible," *Jackson Clarion-Ledger*, April 7, 1982.

27. Winter, interview.

28. Mullins, *Building Consensus*, 96; Crews, interview.

29. Mullins, *Building Consensus*, 94; Molpus, interview; Ray Mabus, interview with the authors.

30. Mullins, *Building Consensus*, 112; Molpus, interview.

31. Mullins, *Building Consensus*, 107–122; Molpus, interview. The legislator quoted by Mullins is Senator Ellis Bodron of Vicksburg.

32. Winter, interview.

33. Mullins, *Building Consensus*, 136.

34. Cliff Treyens, "Winter to Meet with 2 Key Opponents," *Jackson Clarion-Ledger*, December 2, 1982; Mullins, *Building Consensus*, 143; Winter, interview; Sonny Merideth, interview with the authors.

35. Cliff Treyens, "Lawmakers Plan Action on Session," *Jackson Clarion-Ledger*, December 3, 1982.

36. Fred Anklam Jr., "Winter Has Attention; Can He Get Action," *Jackson Clarion-Ledger*, December 5, 1982; Lucy Hovious, "Survey: Programs Likely to Pass but Not Funds," *Jackson Clarion-Ledger*, December 5, 1982.

37. Mullins, *Building Consensus*, 144–145.

38. Nancy Weaver, "Inaction on Education Reform a Tradition," *Jackson Clarion-Ledger*, December 6, 1982.

39. Cliff Treyens, "Kindergarten Funding Already on the Ropes," *Jackson Clarion-Ledger*, December 7, 1982.

40. House Journal, 1982 First Extraordinary Session, 7–12.

41. Fred Anklam Jr., "Senate to Be Site of Kindergarten Fight," *Jackson Clarion-Ledger*, December 8, 1982.

42. Meredith, interview.

43. Cliff Treyens, "Today's House Vote on Tax Bill May Decide Education Plan's Fate," *Jackson Clarion-Ledger*, December 11, 1982; House Journal, 1982 First Extraordinary Session, 18.

44. Cliff Treyens, "Kindergarten, Raises Included in Package," *Jackson Clarion-Ledger*, December 12, 1982.

45. Treyens, "Raises Included"; House Journal, 1982 First Extraordinary Session, 19–48.

46. Senate Journal, 1982 First Extraordinary Session, 34.

47. Fred Anklam Jr., "Education Bill Heads toward Finance Panel," *Jackson Clarion-Ledger*, December 14, 1982; Mullins, *Building Consensus*, 169.

48. Molpus, interview.
49. Fred Anklam Jr., "Education Reform Faces Tough Test in Senate Panel," *Jackson Clarion-Ledger*, December 15, 1982.
50. Dye, interview; Bob Montgomery, interview with the authors; Jack Gordon, interview with the authors; Mullins, *Building Consensus*, 167–168.
51. Mullins, *Building Consensus*, 171–173; John Henegan, USM Oral History, 101.
52. Fred Anklam Jr., "Senate Passes Education Bill with Sales Tax," *Jackson Clarion-Ledger*, December 17, 1982; Senate Journal, 1982 First Extraordinary Session, 40–103.
53. Cliff Treyens, "Panel May Produce Education Compromise Today," *Jackson Clarion-Ledger*, December 18, 1982.
54. Cliff Treyens, "Kindergartens Schedule Snags in Committee," *Jackson Clarion-Ledger*, December 19, 1982.
55. Mullins, *Building Consensus*, 179.
56. Merideth, interview.
57. Gordon, interview.
58. Fred Anklam Jr., "Winter Signs Education Reform," *Jackson Clarion-Ledger*, December 22, 1982.
59. Mullins, *Building Consensus*, 165.
60. Mullins, *Building Consensus*, 196.
61. Newman, USM Oral History, 29.
62. Dye, interview.
63. David W. Kubissa, "Winter Sworn In as 58th Governor," *Jackson Clarion-Ledger*, January 23, 1980; House Journal, 1980 Regular Session, 76.
64. Brian Williams, "Yazoo City Republican Lawyer Set to Campaign against Stennis," *Jackson Clarion-Ledger*, February 16, 1982.
65. Cliff Treyens, "Stennis Backs Extension of Voting Rights Act," *Jackson Clarion-Ledger*, May 26, 1982.
66. Johanna Neuman, "GOP Senate Candidate Barbour Won't Concede Black Vote to Stennis," *Jackson Clarion-Ledger*, July 16, 1982.
67. Johanna Neuman, "Barbour Leaves D.C. with Reagan Support," *Jackson Clarion-Ledger*, June 24, 1982.
68. Charles L. Overby, "Reagan Promises Stennis He'll Stay Out of Campaign," *Jackson Clarion-Ledger*, September 21, 1982.
69. Griffith, interview.
70. Raymond D. Strother, *Falling Up: How a Redneck Helped Invent Political Consulting* (Baton Rouge: Louisiana State University Press, 2003), 136–137; Brian Williams, "Stennis Touts Himself as Battling Lawyer," *Jackson Clarion-Ledger*, August 6, 1982.
71. Brian Williams, "I'm Man Enough for Senate Job, Barbour Retorts," *Jackson Clarion-Ledger*, September 21, 1982.
72. Stennis, interview; see also Barbour, MSU Oral History, 33–34, where he discussed his own poll results, which compare almost exactly with the one done for the Stennis campaign.
73. Election returns published in the 1980–1984 *Official and Statistical Register*; Stennis lost Rankin County by 143 votes and Yazoo County (Barbour's home county) by 400 votes.

74. Johanna Neuman, "Stennis Wins Election to 7th Term," *Jackson Clarion-Ledger*, November 3, 1982.

75. Barbour, MSU Oral History, 39–40; Congressional Record, Daily Digest of the 98th Congress, 1st Session, April 13, 1983; Johanna Newman, "Vacant Judgeship," *Jackson Clarion-Ledger*, November 4, 1982.

76. Joe Blount, MSU Oral History, 1; Barbour, MSU Oral History, 55–56; Andy Kanengiser, "Former Rep. Blount to Head Tax Commission," *Jackson Clarion-Ledger*, April 2, 2004.

77. Brian Williams, "Canton Schoolteacher Wins Chairmanship of GOP in Mississippi," *Jackson Clarion-Ledger*, April 30, 1982.

CHAPTER 9. THE ALLAIN/BRAMLETT CAMPAIGN AND WILLIAM WINTER'S LEGACY, 1983

The indispensable resource for the 1983 campaign is William Franklin West, "The Case of the Reluctant Story: the Allain Sex Scandal" (Master's thesis, University of Mississippi, 1995).

1. As quoted in William Franklin West, "The Case of the Reluctant Story: the Allain Sex Scandal" (Master's thesis, University of Mississippi, 1995), 235–236.

2. John Felton, "Foreign Policy," in *Congressional Quarterly Almanac*, 98th Congress, vol. 34 (Washington, D.C.: Congressional Quarterly, 1984), 109–112.

3. Mounger, interview.

4. Mounger, interview; see also West, "Case of the Reluctant Story," 16–17.

5. Mounger, interview.

6. West, "Case of the Reluctant Story," 18; Mounger, interview; Spell, interview.

7. Bill Minor, "GOP Appears Ready to Give Up on Bramlett, Try for Lesser Races," *Jackson Clarion-Ledger*, October 2, 1983; John Emmerich, "Bramlett Looks the Part, but Isn't Likely to Get It," *Jackson Clarion-Ledger*, October 2, 1983; Carpenter, interview.

8. West, "Case of the Reluctant Story," 22–24.

9. West, "Case of the Reluctant Story," 24–25; Spell, interview.

10. Cliff Treyens, "Family Issue Called GOP Desperation," *Jackson Clarion-Ledger*, October 13, 1983; Tom Oppel, "Divorce Issue Mudslinging, Evers Charges," *Jackson Clarion-Ledger*, October 15, 1983.

11. Mounger, interview.

12. West, "Case of the Reluctant Story," 30–31; Spell, interview.

13. Mounger, interview; Crymes Pittman, interview with the authors; Patterson, interview; West, "Case of the Reluctant Story," 44.

14. Jack Elliott, "Allain, Bramlett Poll Results Don't Match," *Jackson Clarion-Ledger*, October 16, 1983; Spell, interview; Mounger, interview; Patterson, interview.

15. Mounger, interview; West, "Case of the Reluctant Story," 41–42.

16. Mounger, interview; Patterson, interview.

17. Patterson, interview; Joe Zucarro, interview with the authors, Winter, interview; West, "Case of the Reluctant Story," 49–50.

18. Patterson, interview.

19. Mounger, interview; Spell, interview.

20. Wilkie, *Dixie*, 265.

21. Spell, interview.

22. Cliff Treyens, "Political Bull Could Buck Either Way," *Jackson Clarion-Ledger*, October 26, 1983; Cliff Treyens, "Party Officials React Differently to Allegations," *Jackson Clarion-Ledger*, October 26, 1983; West, "Case of the Reluctant Story," 61–65.

23. Patterson, interview; Cupit, interview; Pittman, interview.

24. Patterson, interview; Tom Oppel, "Crisis Puts Allain Advisers to the Test," *Jackson Clarion-Ledger*, October 30, 1983.

25. Tom Oppel and Cliff Treyens, "Allain Prepares to Sue; Bramlett Calls for Polygraph Test," *Jackson Clarion-Ledger*, October 27, 1983; Patterson, interview; West, "Case of the Reluctant Story," 70.

26. Mounger, interview; West, "Case of the Reluctant Story," 129–130.

27. Mounger, interview.

28. Tom Oppel, "Allain Says He Will Face Lie Detector," *Jackson Clarion-Ledger*, October 28, 1983; Wanda Cantrell, "Spell Wants Independent Test for Allain," *Jackson Clarion-Ledger*, October 29, 1983; West, "Case of the Reluctant Story," 98–100.

29. Wanda Cantrell, "Officers' Statements on Allain Released," *Jackson Clarion-Ledger*, November 2, 1983; West, "Case of the Reluctant Story," 167–168; Spell, interview.

30. Tom Oppel, "Bramlett Out if Allain Can Pass 3 Tests," *Jackson Clarion-Ledger*, November 3, 1983; West, "Case of the Reluctant Story," 137–140; Spell, interview.

31. Patterson, interview; Pittman, interview.

32. Tom Oppel, "Allain's Lie Test Doesn't Satisfy Republicans," *Jackson Clarion-Ledger*, November 4, 1983; West, "Case of the Reluctant Story," 143–145; Pittman, interview.

33. Patterson, interview.

34. Tom Oppel, "Democratic Leaders Rally around Allain," *Jackson Clarion-Ledger*, November 5, 1983.

35. As quoted in West, "Case of the Reluctant Story," 135–136.

36. Patterson, interview.

37. Mounger, interview.

38. West, "Case of the Reluctant Story," 178–180; Spell, interview; Pittman, interview.

39. West, "Case of the Reluctant Story," 186–236.

40. West, "Case of the Reluctant Story," 257.

41. Mounger, interview.

42. Quoted in West, "Case of the Reluctant Story," 173–174.

43. John Grisham, interview with the authors.

44. William Alexander Percy, *Lanterns on the Levee: Recollections of a Planter's Son* (New York: Alfred A. Knopf, 1972), 148.

45. Chester M. Morgan, *Redneck Liberal: Theodore G. Bilbo and the New Deal* (Baton Rouge: Louisiana State University Press, 1985), 247–250.

46. Robert Clark, UNC Oral History, 8; this story was captured by Jack Bass and Walter DeVries when they interviewed Clark as part of their research for their 1976 book, *Transformation of Southern Politics*, 186.

47. Winter, interview.

48. Winter, interview; Heber Ladner, "Memorial Address at the Acceptance and Unveiling of the Statue of Theodore Gilmore Bilbo, April 12, 1954," State Law Library, Jackson, Miss.; "Winter Explains Why He Had Bilbo Statue Moved," *Jackson Daily News*, November 19, 1982; LoLo Pendergrast, "Bilbo Both Adored, Ridiculed during Life," *Jackson Clarion-Ledger*, November 21, 1982.

CHAPTER 10. THE EROSION OF LEGISLATIVE POWER, 1984

For information on the 1984 campaigns, we relied on Elizabeth Drew, *Campaign Journal: The Political Events of* 1983–1984 (New York: MacMillan, 1985); Jack W. Germond and Jules Witcover, *Wake Us When It's Over: Presidential Politics of* 1984 (New York: MacMillan, 1985); and Robert P. Steed, Laurence W. Moreland, and Tod A. Baker, eds., *The* 1984 *Presidential Election in the South* (New York: Praeger, 1985).

Court Case

Alexander v. State of Mississippi, 441 So.2d 1329 (Miss. 1983)

1. Emily Wagster, "Allain Survived Shabby Era in Politics," *Jackson Clarion-Ledger*, October 14, 2001.
2. The nine agencies were: Commission on Budget and Accounting, Board of Economic Development, Board of Trustees of the Public Employees Retirement System, Central Data Processing Authority, State Personnel Board, Medicaid Commission, Capitol Commission, Wildlife Heritage Committee, and Board of Corrections.
3. Cliff Treyens, "Legislators Unduly Influence Boards, 2 Senators Testify," *Jackson Clarion-Ledger*, November 19, 1982.
4. Steve Kirchmayr, interview with the authors; Bill Allain, interview with the authors.
5. "Allain: Legislators Have 2 Weeks before Suit," *Jackson Clarion-Ledger*, April 6, 1982.
6. Dennis Camire, "Legislators May Be Sued Over Jobs by Weekend," *Jackson Clarion-Ledger*, April 7, 1982.
7. Maria Halkias, "36 Legislators Beat Allain to the Punch," *Jackson Clarion-Ledger*, April 8, 1982; Kirchmayr, interview.
8. Allain, interview.
9. Cliff Treyens, "Allain's Legislators Suit Is Heard," *Jackson Clarion-Ledger*, November 16, 1982.
10. *Alexander v. State of Mississippi*, 441 So.2d 1329 (Miss. 1983).
11. Tom Oppel, "Court Ruling Will Overhaul Legislature," *Jackson Clarion-Ledger*, November 24, 1983.
12. Tom Oppel, "War Predicted as Rift Widens," *Jackson Clarion-Ledger*, May 5, 1984.
13. Tom Oppel, "Plan for State Restructuring Is Questioned," *Jackson Clarion-Ledger*, May 2, 1984; Tom Oppel, "Reorganization Compromise OK'd by House, Senate," *Jackson Clarion-Ledger*, May 9, 1984.
14. House Journal, 1984 Regular Session, 1030–1032.

15. Allain, interview; Kirchmayr, interview.
16. Tom Oppel, "Allain Signs Government Shake-up Bill," *Jackson Clarion-Ledger*, May 10, 1984.
17. Tom Oppel, "Mondale Says Running Mate to Win South," *Jackson Clarion-Ledger*, August 1, 1984.
18. Edsall and Edsall, *Chain Reaction*, 180.
19. David O. Sears, Jack Citrin, and Rick Kosterman, "Jesse Jackson and the Southern White Electorate in 1984," in Laurence W. Moreland, Robert P. Steed, and Tod A. Baker, eds., *Blacks in Southern Politics* (New York: Praeger, 1987), 208–209; see also E. Lee Bernick and Charles L. Prysby, "Reactions to the Jackson Candidacy among Southern Black Democratic Party Activists," in Moreland, Steed, and Baker, *Blacks in Southern Politics*, 191.
20. Douglas D. Rose and Paul J. Stekler, "Win, Jesse, Win: A Test of Models of Race and Vote," in Moreland, Steed, and Baker, *Blacks in Southern Politics*, 166.
21. Black and Black, *Vital South*, 259–260.
22. Margaret Henry, "President Wins Cheers from Coast," *Biloxi Sun-Herald*, October 2, 1984; Cliff Treyens, "Reagan Speaks to Thousands on Gulf Coast," *Jackson Clarion-Ledger*, October 2, 1984.
23. Irene Page, "Fritz Talks Faith, Rips Reagan Cuts," *Northeast Mississippi Daily Journal*, September 14, 1984; Cliff Treyens, "Mondale Faces Tough Crowd on Tupelo Stop," *Jackson Clarion-Ledger*, September 14, 1984.
24. Edsall and Edsall, *Chain Reaction*, 178, 212–213; see also Linda F. Williams, "Blacks and the 1984 Elections in the South: Racial Polarization and Regional Congruence," in Moreland, Steed, and Baker, *Blacks in Southern Politics*, 91–92; and Black and Black, *Vital South*, 313–314.
25. Cliff Treyens, "Dem Leaders Meet with Winter about Senate Candidacy in '84," *Jackson Clarion-Ledger*, June 16, 1983; Winter, interview.
26. Coleman Warner, "Winter Wavers after Accepting Chancellorship," *Jackson Clarion-Ledger*, December 15, 1983; Coleman Warner, "Winter Accepts Ole Miss Chancellorship," *Jackson Clarion-Ledger*, December 16, 1983; Tom Oppel, "Winter Move Revives Dems' Senate Hopes," *Jackson Clarion-Ledger*, December 20, 1983.
27. Tom Oppel, "Key Financial Backers Would 'Sit Out' Winter Campaign," *Jackson Clarion-Ledger*, February 3, 1984; Tom Oppel, "Winter Says He's in Race for Senate," *Jackson Clarion-Ledger*, February 7, 1984; Cupit, interview; Winter, interview.
28. Robert Ourlian and Wanda Cantrell, "Black Group Wants to Field Own Senate Candidate," *Jackson Clarion-Ledger*, August 5, 1984; Tom Oppel, "Dem. Chairman, Black Dissidents Agree to Hold Reconciliation Talks," *Jackson Clarion-Ledger*, August 7, 1984; Tom Oppel, "Meeting Fails to Satisfy Black Dems," *Jackson Clarion-Ledger*, August 22, 1984; Tom Oppel, "State Dem Leaders Hedge on Blacks' 17 Demands," *Jackson Clarion-Ledger*, August 31, 1984; Steve Riley, "Walls Blasts Dems; Hinds at Candidacy," *Jackson Clarion-Ledger*, September 6, 1984; Johnnie Walls, interview with the authors.
29. Ourlian and Cantrell, "Black Group Wants to Field Own Senate Candidate."
30. Wayne Weidie, "John Stennis Can Endorse Two Democrats, but Not Robert Clark," *Jackson Clarion-Ledger*, October 28, 1984.

31. Walls, interview.
32. Walls, interview; Patterson, interview.
33. Steve Riley, "Walls Drops 2nd District Senate Plans," *Jackson Clarion-Ledger*, September 8, 1984; Walls, interview.
34. Quoted in Alexander P. Lamis, "Mississippi," in Robert P. Steed, Laurence W. Moreland, and Tod A. Baker, *The* 1984 *Presidential Election in the South: Patterns of Southern Party Politics* (New York: Praeger, 1985), 67.
35. See, for example, Alexander P. Lamis, *The Two-Party South*, 2nd ed. (New York: Oxford University Press, 1990), 254.
36. Minor, *Eyes on Mississippi*, 128.
37. Winter, MSU 1991 Oral History, 28; Winter, interview.
38. Taken from the *New York Times* account quoted in Lamis, *Two-Party South*, 235–236. The exchange even prompted the publication of a cookbook filled with recipes exclusively from men: Lindy Ross Aldy and Carol Taff, eds., *Down Here Men Don't Cook: A Cookbook by Mississippi Men* (Jackson, Miss.: Southern Images, 1984).

CHAPTER 11. THE RISE OF MIKE ESPY, 1985–1986

For background on Robert Clark and his 1982 and 1984 campaigns, we relied on Will D. Campbell, *Robert G. Clark's Journey to the House: A Black Politician's Story* (Jackson: University Press of Mississippi, 2003); Melany Neilson, *Even Mississippi* (Tuscaloosa: University of Alabama Press, 1989); and Michael B. Preston, Lenneal J. Henderson Jr., and Paul L. Puryear, *The New Black Politics: The Search for Political Power*, 2nd ed. (New York: Longman, 1987).

Journal articles we used for background on the reapportionment litigation include Frank R. Parker, "The Mississippi Congressional Redistricting Case: A Case Study in Minority Vote Dilution," *Howard Law Journal* 28 (1985); Byron D'Andra Orey, "Black Legislative Politics in Mississippi," *Journal of Black Studies* 30 (July 2000); Vagn K. Hansen, "Equal Electoral Opportunity: The Impact of the 1982 Amendments to the Voting Rights Act on Congressional Districting in Mississippi," paper prepared for the annual meeting of the Southern Political Science Association, November 6–9, 1985; David Collier Nagle, "The Results Test of Amended Section 2 of the Voting Rights Act: An Examination of the Senate Report Factors," *Mississippi Law Journal* 54 (June 1984); and Gary H. Brooks and William Claggett, "Black Electoral Power, White Resistance, and Legislative Behavior," *Political Behavior* 3, (1981).

Court Cases

Connor v. Johnson, 279 F.Supp. 619 (1966)
Connor v. Johnson, 386 U.S. 483 (1967)
Jordan v. Winter and *Brooks v. Winter*, 541 F. Supp. 1135 (Miss., 1982)
State of Mississippi v. Smith, 541 F. Supp. 1329 (DC, 1982)

Brooks v. Winter, 461 U.S. 921 (1983)

Jordan v. Winter and *Brooks v. Winter*, 604 F. Supp. 807 (Miss. 1984)

Mississippi Republican Executive Committee v. Brooks, 469 U.S. 1002 (1984)

American Civil Liberties Union of Mississippi v. Mississippi State General Services Administration, 652 F. Supp. 380 (Miss. 1987)

1. Mike Espy, interview with the authors.
2. Frank R. Parker, "The Mississippi Congressional Redistricting Case: A Case Study in Minority Vote Dilution," *Howard Law Journal* 28 (1985): 397–398; Rowland, *Official and Statistical Register*, and continuing with the *Official and Statistical Registers, State of Mississippi*, issued through 1972.
3. Secretary of State, *Mississippi Official and Statistical Register, 1964–1968*, 52.
4. Charles M. Hills, "House Approves Plan for Redistricting State," *Jackson Clarion-Ledger*, January 14, 1966. Former State Representative Sonny Merideth concurred in this observation in an interview with the authors.
5. *Connor v. Johnson*, 386 U.S. 438 (1967).
6. Cliff Treyens, "Most Favored Redistricting Plan Has Least Changes," *Jackson Clarion-Ledger*, August 6, 1981.
7. SB 2001, Senate Journal, 1981 Extraordinary Session, 18–20; House Journal, 1981 Extraordinary Session, 26–31.
8. Art Harris, "Blacks, Unlikely Allies Battle Miss. Redistricting," *Washington Post*, June 1, 1982; Scott Levanway, interview with the authors.
9. Brian Williams, "Black Concentration Was a Factor, Campbell Testifies," *Jackson Clarion-Ledger*, May 14, 1982; Levanway, interview; Jerris Leonard, interview with the authors.
10. Harris, "Blacks, Unlikely Allies."
11. Harris, "Blacks, Unlikely Allies."
12. Brian Williams, "Campbell Says Delta District Would Hurt Blacks Politically," *Jackson Clarion-Ledger*, May 15, 1982.
13. Parker, "Congressional Redistricting," 404.
14. Brian Williams and Cliff Treyens, "Congress Districts Rejected by U.S.," *Jackson Clarion-Ledger*, March 31, 1982.
15. "Retzer Lobbied U.S. to Reject Plan," *Jackson Clarion-Ledger*, April 29, 1982; Levanway, interview; Leonard, interview; Walls, interview.
16. Brian Williams and Cliff Treyens, "State Officials Dodge Defense of Redistricting Plan," *Jackson Clarion-Ledger*, April 2, 1982; Cliff Treyens, "Mississippi Sues U.S. Over Congressional Districts," *Jackson Clarion-Ledger*, April 8, 1982.
17. *Jordan v. Winter* and *Brooks v. Winter*, 541 F.Supp. 1135 (Miss. 1982); Brian Williams, "Court Restores Black-Majority Delta District," *Jackson Clarion-Ledger*, June 10, 1982.
18. Clark, interview.
19. Fred Anklam Jr., "Ex-President Ford Appears at Fundraiser for Franklin," *Jackson Clarion-Ledger*, August 29, 1982; Melany Neilson, *Even Mississippi* (Tuscaloosa: University of Alabama Press, 1989), 62–64; Will D. Campbell, *Robert G. Clark's Journey to the House* (Jackson: University Press of Mississippi, 2003), 120–125.

20. Karen Hinton, "2nd Congressional District: Robert Clark/Webb Franklin," *Jackson Clarion-Ledger*, October 17, 1982.

21. Neilson, *Even Mississippi*, 86.

22. Vagn K. Hansen, "Equal Electoral Opportunity: The Impact of the 1982 Amendments to the Voting Rights Act on Congressional Redistricting in Mississippi," paper presented at the annual meeting of the Southern Political Science Association, November 6–9, 1985, 14; Adam Clymer, "Race Raised as an Issue in Mississippi House Contest," *New York Times*, October 14, 1982; Neilson, *Even Mississippi*, 95; Lamis, *Two-Party South*, 56–57.

23. Neilson, *Even Mississippi*, 95–96.

24. David Collier Nagle, "The Results Test of Amended Section 2 of the Voting Rights Act: An Examination of the Senate Report Factors," *Mississippi Law Journal* 54 (June 1984): 289–318.

25. *Brooks v. Winter* and *Winter v. Brooks*, 461 U.S. 921 (1983).

26. *Jordan v. Winter* and *Brooks v. Winter*, 604 F.Supp. 807 (Miss. 1984). This decision was upheld by the U.S. Supreme Court at 469 U.S. 1002 (1984). See also Tony Tharp, "Congressional Remap Ordered," *Jackson Clarion-Ledger*, December 22, 1983.

27. *Mississippi Republican Executive Committee v. Brooks*, 469 U.S. 1002 (1984).

28. Tom Oppel, "State Remap Plans Upheld by High Court," *Jackson Clarion-Ledger*, November 14, 1984.

29. Espy, interview; Walls, interview.

30. Espy, interview.

31. The information and quotations in these paragraphs came from an interview with Mike Espy, along with observations of one of the authors, who was involved in Espy's campaign.

32. Dan Davis, "2nd District Runoff Appears Likely," *Jackson Clarion-Ledger*, June 5, 1986.

33. Dan Davis, "Espy Gains 243 Votes from Error," *Jackson Clarion-Ledger*, June 6, 1986; Espy, interview; Walls, interview.

34. Dan Davis, "Farm Bill to Regain Markets, Franklin Says," *Jackson Clarion-Ledger*, October 14, 1986; Carla Hall, "Espy's Mississippi Milestone," *Washington Post*, December 19, 1986.

35. Dan Davis, "Espy Panelists Discuss Issues Down on Farm," *Jackson Clarion-Ledger*, October 23, 1986; Marshall Ingwerson, "Espy's Mississippi Victory," *Christian Science Monitor*, December 22, 1986.

36. Dan Davis, "Espy Banking on Plea to Black, White Voters," *Jackson Clarion-Ledger*, October 28, 1986.

37. Sewell and Dwight, *Mississippi Black History Makers*, 26–37.

38. "Political Report," *Congressional Quarterly Almanac*, 99th Congress, 2nd Session (Washington, D.C.: Congressional Quarterly, 1987), 11-B.

39. John Lewis, with Michael D'Orso, *Walking with the Wind: A Memoir of the Movement* (New York: Simon and Schuster, 1998).

40. "Election '86," *Jackson Clarion-Ledger*, November 6, 1986; Carla Hall, "Espy's Mississippi Milestone," *Washington Post*, December 19, 1986.

41. Espy, interview; Jeff Copeskey, "Espy Takes House Oath, Makes History," *Jackson Clarion-Ledger*, January 7, 1987.

42. Anderson, interview; Banks, interview.

43. Marc DeFrancis and Mary K. Garber, "An Advocate's Struggle," *Focus* 25 (August 1997): 3–4.

44. Anne Q. Hoy, "Courthouse Mural Spurred Civil Rights Attorney," *Jackson Clarion-Ledger*, February 15, 1981; Bill Minor, "Pugnacious Frank Parker Opened Legislative Halls to Black Leaders," *Jackson Clarion-Ledger*, July 20, 1997; Harold Cox letter to Frank Parker, February 18, 1971, photocopy in the authors' possession; John Maxey, interview with the authors; Cupit, interview; one of the authors was granted access to the courtroom and viewed the mural.

45. "Civil Rights Attorney Frank Parker Dies at 57," *Jackson Clarion-Ledger*, July 12, 1997; Maxey, interview; Kirksey, interview; Walls, interview; Thompson, interview; David Lipman, interview with the authors.

46. John Brittain, E-mail to the authors, April 4, 2006.

47. Maxey, interview.

48. Parker, *Black Votes Count*, 127.

49. Newman, "If Henry Kirksey Has Any Record."

50. Allain, interview; Kirksey, interview.

51. *ACLU v. Mississippi State General Services Administration*, 652 F.Supp. 380 (Miss. 1987).

52. Mary Dixon, "Sillers Cross Flap Is Legal Tossup, Lawyers Say," *Jackson Clarion-Ledger*, December 4, 1986; "Rushing Pulled Off Radio Show Permanently," *Jackson Clarion-Ledger*, December 17, 1986.

CHAPTER 12. HIGHWAYS, BUDDIE NEWMAN, AND RAY MABUS, 1987

For a good amount of detail on the work of the citizens' group that lobbied on behalf of the highway program, we used: William M. Cash and R. Daryl Lewis, *AHEAD: From Grassroots Movement to Four-Lane Highway System in Mississippi* (Brandon, Miss.: Quail Ridge Press, 1998).

1. Dan Davis, "House Strips Newman's Powers 75–45," *Jackson Clarion-Ledger*, January 10, 1987.

2. See, for example, William Rabb, "Lawmakers May Add 2 Lanes to 2 Roads 15 Miles Apart," *Jackson Clarion-Ledger*, February 15, 1987; William M. Cash and R. Daryl Lewis, *AHEAD: From Grassroots Movement to Four-Lane Highway System in Mississippi* (Brandon, Miss.: Quail Ridge Press, 1998); John Pennebaker, interview with the authors; Gene Triggs, interview with the authors; Montgomery, interview.

3. "Gov. Allain Vetoes Highway Agency's Appropriation Bill," *Jackson Clarion-Ledger*, April 10, 1986.

4. Dan Davis and Shawn McIntosh, "Session Ends with Highway Flap Unsolved," *Jackson Clarion-Ledger*, April 12, 1986.

5. Cash and Lewis, *AHEAD*, 27–32; Sam Waggoner, interview with the authors; Triggs, interview.

6. Cash and Lewis, *AHEAD*, 34–35; Waggoner, interview; Montgomery, interview.

7. Cash and Lewis, *AHEAD*, 35–36; Waggoner, interview; Triggs, interview; Carmichael, interview. Carmichael would later help Representatives Pennebaker and McCoy draft the bill they introduced.

8. Cash and Lewis, *AHEAD*, 36–38; Waggoner, interview; Triggs, interview.

9. Cash and Lewis, *AHEAD*, 38; Waggoner, interview.

10. Cash and Lewis, *AHEAD*, 39–40.

11. Cash and Lewis, *AHEAD*, 40.

12. Waggoner, interview; Pennebaker, interview.

13. Pennebaker, interview.

14. Cash and Lewis, *AHEAD*, 43–54; Triggs, interview.

15. Dan Davis, "Allain Wants Referendum on Tax Issue," *Jackson Clarion-Ledger*, January 15, 1987.

16. Jeff Copeskey, "Legislators Disagree with Allain on Taxes, Highways," *Jackson Clarion-Ledger*, January 15, 1987.

17. Jeff Copeskey, "Senate Passes Highway Plan with 5 Cent Tax," *Jackson Clarion-Ledger*, January 21, 1987. Notably, Minor was elected to the Transportation Commission, successor to the Highway Commission, in 2003.

18. Jeff Copeskey, "House Committee Passes 2-Cent Gasoline Tax," *Jackson Clarion-Ledger*, January 28, 1987.

19. Jeff Copeskey, "House Defeats Highway Bill; 2nd Vote Likely," *Jackson Clarion-Ledger*, January 30, 1987; House Journal, 1987 Regular Session, 151–159.

20. Cash and Lewis, *AHEAD*, 59–60; Pennebaker, interview; Triggs, interview.

21. Jeff Copeskey, "House Passes Highway Bill by One Vote," *Jackson Clarion-Ledger*, January 31, 1987; House Journal, 1987 Regular Session, 161–163; Pennebaker, interview.

22. Jeff Copeskey, "2 Senate Panels Clear Highway Bill," *Jackson Clarion-Ledger*, February 25, 1987; Cash and Lewis, *AHEAD*, 66–68; Waggoner, interview; Triggs, interview.

23. Jeff Copeskey, "Senate Approves $1.6 Billion Bill for State Highways," *Jackson Clarion-Ledger*, February 27, 1987; Senate Journal, 1987 Regular Session, 682–718.

24. Jeff Copeskey, "House OKs $1.6 Billion Highway Bill," *Jackson Clarion-Ledger*, March 5, 1987; House Journal, 1987 Regular Session, 554–555.

25. Dan Davis, "Allain Vetoes Highway Bill, Cites Tax Hike," *Jackson Clarion-Ledger*, March 10, 1987.

26. Glenn Endris, interview with the authors; Pennebaker, interview. In Cash and Lewis, *AHEAD*, 72–73, Fredericks is portrayed as the Gulf Coast representative who approached Pennebaker and McCoy about switching his vote, followed by Gulf Coast Representative Glenn Endris. In an interview with Endris, he mentioned the *AHEAD* book and recounted the story told in this book. Endris's version was corroborated in an interview with John Pennebaker. Fredericks died several years ago, and the authors did not interview Representative McCoy for this book.

27. Jeff Copeskey, "House Overrides Allain's Veto of Highway Bill," *Jackson Clarion-Ledger*, March 12, 1987; House Journal, 1987 Regular Session, 655–656; Pennebaker, interview; Merideth, interview.
28. Cash and Lewis, *AHEAD*, 73; Triggs, interview.
29. Jeff Copeskey, "$1.6 Billion Highway Bill Becomes Law," *Jackson Clarion-Ledger*, March 13, 1987; Senate Journal, 1987 Regular Session, 1031–1032; Dye, interview; Montgomery, interview; Pennebaker, interview.
30. Dan Davis, "Buddie Newman to Quit Legislature," *Jackson Clarion-Ledger*, April 1, 1987; Newman, USM Oral History, 5; John Junkin, MDAH Oral History.
31. House Journal, 1974 Regular Session, 128–131; Merideth, interview; Newman, USM Oral History, 29–30; Stone Barefield, interview with the authors; Cliff Treyens, "House Rejects Rules Change on First Day," *Jackson Clarion-Ledger*, January 4, 1987; Mike Mills, interview with the authors; Grisham, interview.
32. Tommy Reynolds, interview with the authors; Norma Fields, "Twelve Members Seeking to Decrease House Speaker's Power," *Northeast Mississippi Daily Journal*, December 14, 1983.
33. Treyens, "House Rejects Rules Change"; Mills, interview; Grisham, interview; House Journal, 1984 Regular Session, 4–29.
34. Ed Perry, Cecil Simmons, Terrell Stubbs, Tommy Walman, Tommy Reynolds, John Grisham, Mike Mills, and Sonny Merideth, interviews with the authors; see also Newman, USM Oral History, 38–41.
35. Davis, "House Strips Newman's Powers"; see also Simpson, USM Oral History, 42.
36. Ed Perry, interview with the authors.
37. Cecil Simmons, interview with the authors.
38. House Journal, 1987 Regular Session, 43–46; Dan Davis, "House Rebels to Face Newman in Showdown," *Jackson Clarion-Ledger*, January 9, 1987; Davis, "House Strips Newman's Powers."
39. House Journal, 1987 Regular Session, 63–64; Dan Davis, "Rebel Leader Voted Speaker Pro Tempore," *Jackson Clarion-Ledger*, January 15, 1987.
40. Davis, "Newman to Quit Legislature"; Dan Davis, "Newman Won't Seek Speaker's Post," *Jackson Clarion-Ledger*, March 27, 1987.
41. Newman, USM Oral History, 38–41.
42. Tim Ford, interview with the authors; Tommy Walman, interview with the authors.
43. House Journal, 1988 Regular Session, 32; "Lumpkin to Support Sillers as Speaker," *Jackson Clarion-Ledger*, January 2, 1956.
44. Grisham, interview; Nancy Pate, "The Firm Waltzes to the Top," *Orlando Sentinel*, March 31, 1991.
45. Dan Davis, "Allain Passes Up Chance to Seek Re-Election," *Jackson Clarion-Ledger*, June 6, 1987.
46. Mabus, interview.
47. Mabus, interview.
48. James R. Crockett, *Operation Pretense: The FBI's Sting on County Corruption in Mississippi* (Jackson: University Press of Mississippi, 2003).

49. Dan Davis and Shawn McIntosh, "Mabus Wins Big," *Jackson Clarion-Ledger*, August 26, 1987.

50. Jack Reed, interview with the authors.

51. Jack Reed, interview.

52. Jerry O'Keefe Jr., UNC Oral History, 28–29; House Journal, 1972 Regular Session, 546–548.

CHAPTER 13. THE CAMPAIGN TO SUCCEED JOHN STENNIS, 1988

In contrast to the dearth of primary sources about Jim Eastland, Mississippi State University embarked on a project in the early 1970s of interviewing a relatively large number of people who had association with John Stennis. Transcripts of those interviews are available and provided a wealth of information for this book.

Other materials we used for Stennis include James A. Peden Jr., "A Matter of Honor: A Study of the Censure of United States Senator Joseph R. McCarthy" (University Scholars Program, University of Mississippi, 1966); Michael S. Downs, "Advise and Consent: John Stennis and the Vietnam War, 1954–1973," *Journal of Mississippi History* 55 (May 1993); William C. Allen, "Senators Poindexter, Davis, and Stennis: Three Mississippians in the History of the United States Capitol," *Journal of Mississippi History* 65 (Fall 2003); and Joseph Crespino, "Southern Roots of the New Right: John C. Stennis and Federal School Desegregation, 1954–1972," paper delivered at the Miller Center of Public Affairs' American Political Development Program, November 7, 2003.

For the 1988 campaigns, we used Elizabeth Drew, *Election Journal: Political Events of 1987–1988* (New York: William Morrow, 1989); Christine M. Black and Thomas Oliphant, *All by Myself: The Unmaking of a Presidential Campaign* (Chester, Conn.: Globe Pequot Press, 1989); and Jack W. Germond and Jules Witcover, *Whose Broad Stripes and Bright Stars: The Trivial Pursuit of the Presidency, 1988* (New York: Warner Books, 1989).

1. Patterson, interview, remembering a speech Jim Eastland gave at a function honoring both Stennis and Eastland.

2. See, for example, John Hailman, MSU Oral History, 43–44; Speakes, MSU Oral History, 2; and George Reedy, MSU Oral History, 4; see also Shawn McIntosh, "Senator Cites Health, Age, in Passing Up 8th Term," *Jackson Clarion-Ledger*, October 20, 1987; and Joe Atkins, "Stennis Returns to Senate Work," *Jackson Clarion-Ledger*, October 23, 1987.

3. John Hampton Stennis, MSU Oral History, 6.

4. Reedy, MSU Oral History, 4–5.

5. This accounting of the McCarthy era and Stennis's role in the special committee was summarized from James A. Peden Jr., "A Matter of Honor: A Study of the Censure of United States Senator Joseph R. McCarthy," paper submitted in fulfillment of the requirements of the University Scholars Program, University of Mississippi, June 1, 1966. Stennis's speech begins on page 15986 of the November 12, 1954, issue of the *Congressional Record* for the Senate; see also Caro, *Master of the Senate*, 554–557.

6. Ed Brunini, MSU Oral History, 26; see also Derian, MSU Oral History, 1.

7. In the books we used as references for the period 1954–1965, Stennis's name rarely turns up in the indexes, while Eastland always has several entries to account for his public and often unseemly statements about civil rights and African Americans. Eastland, in other words, made for good copy.

8. Bill Spell, MSU Oral History, 32–36; Spell, interview.

9. John Stennis, LBJ Oral History, 1972, obtained from MSU, 10.

10. James T. Wooten, "Carter Accepts Help of Stennis, Eastland," *New York Times*, September 18, 1976.

11. *Congressional Quarterly Almanac*, 97th Congress, 2nd Session, 1982 (Washington, D.C.: Congressional Quarterly, 1983), 373–379.

12. Neilson, *Even Mississippi*, 85–92.

13. Weidie, "Stennis Can Endorse Two Democrats"; Dan Davis, "Political Veteran Says State Needs a Democrat," *Jackson Clarion-Ledger*, October 26, 1988. The reporter in this last article mentions that Stennis's endorsement of Dowdy was "the first time Stennis has actively campaigned for another candidate," apparently unaware of Stennis's support of William Winter and Walter Mondale in 1984, his support for Robert Clark in 1982, and his "active" campaigning on behalf of Lyndon Johnson in 1964 and John Kennedy in 1960.

14. Reedy, MSU Oral History, 30–31.

15. Brunini, MSU Oral History, 40–44; Spell, MSU Oral History, 41; Speakes, MSU Oral History, 29–30; Spell, interview; Dye, interview.

16. Speakes, MSU Oral History, 27.

17. Spell, MSU Oral History, 30–31; Spell, interview.

18. Michael S. Downs, "Advise and Consent: John Stennis and the Vietnam War, 1954–1973," *Journal of Mississippi History* 55 (May 1993): 87–114.

19. Hailman, MSU Oral History, 20–23.

20. Bob Woodward and Carl Bernstein, *The Final Days* (New York: Simon and Schuster, 1976), 60–71; Stanley I. Kuter, *The Wars of Watergate: The Last Crisis of Richard Nixon* (New York: Alfred A. Knopf, 1990), 402–413.

21. Joe Atkins, "Stennis Votes with Majority against Bork," *Jackson Clarion-Ledger*, October 24, 1987.

22. Fred Slabach, MSU Oral History, 27–33.

23. Elizabeth Drew, *Election Journal: Political Events of 1987–1988* (New York: William Morrow, 1989), 258–261.

24. Jeff Copeskey, "Dukakis Vows 'Real War' against Drugs," *Jackson Clarion-Ledger*, June 18, 1988.

25. Dan Davis, "Bush's Son Blasts Dukakis as Too Liberal; Dem Nominee Speaks Today," *Jackson Clarion-Ledger*, August 4, 1988.

26. Jack W. Germond and Jules Witcover, *Whose Broad Stripes and Bright Stars? The Trivial Pursuit of the Presidency 1988* (New York: Warner Books, 1989), 4–6.

27. Griffith, interview; see also Edsall and Edsall, *Chain Reaction*, 215–230; and Lamis, *Two-Party South*, 310–314.

28. Dan Davis, "Dowdy, Lott Swap Punches in 1st Debate," *Jackson Clarion-Ledger*, April 9, 1988.

29. Jeff Copeskey, "Lott: Dowdy 'Very Similar' to Dukakis," *Jackson Clarion-Ledger*, October 4, 1988.

30. Carpenter, interview.

31. Dan Davis, "Dowdy Tells Lott: Dump Chauffeur," *Jackson Clarion-Ledger*, August 4, 1988.

32. Jeff Copeskey, "'I'm Nobody's Chauffeur,' Says Lott's Security Officer," *Jackson Clarion-Ledger*, September 13, 1988; Carpenter, interview.

33. According to Lott's campaign manager, Tim Carpenter, this was the strategy: "over perform in Lott's home district, and try and run about even in other parts of the state."

34. Marty Russell and Norma Fields, "Letters Reveal Lott Critical of NASA Site," *Northeast Mississippi Daily Journal*, October 26, 1988; Jane Hill, "Wayne Dowdy Is in Search of Trent Lott's Petard," *Northeast Mississippi Daily Journal*, October 29, 1988; "Lott Erred in Claiming Yellow Creek Credit," *Biloxi Sun-Herald* editorial reprinted in the *Northeast Mississippi Daily Journal*, November 6, 1988. Lanny Griffith, Bush's southern political director, offered this example in his interview with the authors.

35. Jeff Copeskey, "3 4th District Runoff Hopefuls File Campaign Finance Reports," *Jackson Clarion-Ledger*, March 17, 1988.

36. In the interest of full disclosure, the reader should be advised that Collins's primary run-off victory came at the expense of one of the authors.

37. House Journal, 1957 First Extraordinary Session, 1538–1543.

38. House Journal, 1988 Regular Session, 107–108.

39. Taken from Governor Coleman's address to a joint session of the legislature, November 5, 1957, reprinted in House Journal, 1957 First Extraordinary Session, 1483–1488; refer also to Coleman's September 16, 1957, televised address, reprinted in the House Journal, 1957 First Extraordinary Session, 1502–1503.

40. Refer to Coleman's November 18, 1957, address to the legislature, reprinted in the House Journal, 1957 First Extraordinary Session, 1518–1522.

41. Refer to the statement from Walter Sillers, reprinted in the House Journal, 1957 First Extraordinary Session, 1655–1660; Winter, interview.

42. William Rabb, "Opponents of Constitutional Convention Fear the Unknown," *Jackson Clarion-Ledger*, January 31, 1988; Reed Branson, "State Farmers Oppose Constitution Rewrite," *Jackson Clarion-Ledger*, February 16, 1988; Dan Davis, "Gun Owners' Ads Warn against Convention," *Jackson Clarion-Ledger*, April 19, 1988; Charles E. Menifield, Stephen Shaffer, and Charles E. Jones, "Voting Behavior among African-Americans in Southern State Legislatures," paper presented at the annual meeting of the American Political Science Association, 2000.

43. House Journal, 1988 Regular Session, 1317.

44. Spell, interview; see also Spell, MSU Oral History, 41–42; Larry Speakes tells essentially this same story in his MSU Oral History, 32–33, though he says that it is "probably not true," but "it sort of describes the difference between the two men."

CHAPTER 14. LIQUOR AND GAMBLING IN MISSISSIPPI, 1989–1990

1. Charlie Capps, USM Oral History, 24.
2. "The Impact of the Gaming Industry—10 Years Later," produced by the Harrison County Development Commission, August 2002; information from the Mississippi Gaming Association Web site, accessed on October 21, 2005, and in conversations with staff at the Mississippi Gaming Commission.
3. Norman Ritter, "A Tax on Lawbreakers Only," *Life*, May 11, 1962; Winter, interview.
4. James Saggus, "Johnson Shatters Liquor Precedent," *Jackson Clarion-Ledger*, February 3, 1966; Minor, *Eyes on Mississippi*, 157–158.
5. Senate Journal, 1966 Regular Session, 134; see also Saggus, "Johnson Shatters Liquor Precedent"; and Johnston, *Politics*, 167–173.
6. "Deputies Seize Booze before Ball Reception," *Jackson Clarion-Ledger*, February 5, 1966; Dye, interview; Merideth, interview.
7. James Bonney, "Local Group Seeks Proof Liquor Law Not Effective," *Jackson Clarion-Ledger*, March 18, 1966.
8. Charles M. Hills, "Legal Liquor Proposal Nears House Calendar," *Jackson Clarion-Ledger*, April 19, 1966; "Hinds County Seeks to Void State Law," *Jackson Clarion-Ledger*, April 9, 1966; "Liquor Ban Held Valid until High Court Rules," *Jackson Clarion-Ledger*, April 12, 1966.
9. Tommy Gollott, interview with the authors.
10. Quotes and information for these two paragraphs come from Dave Palermo, "The Day Gambling Died," *Biloxi Sun-Herald*, August 23, 1989.
11. Sources for this early period include interviews with Rick Carter, Gerald Blessey, Tommy Gollott, Glenn Endris, and Buddy Medlin, and the following newspaper articles: George Lammons, "State High Court Upholds *Europa's* 10-Day Reprieve," *Biloxi Sun-Herald*, December 22, 1987: Ron Grove, "Ship Hosts Blue-Chip List," *Biloxi Sun-Herald*, December 21, 1987; George Lammons, "Reprieve Lets Gambling Ship Cruise Sound," *Biloxi Sun-Herald*, December 19, 1987; Kim Bouchillon, "Casino Ship Owners Hope for Payoff on Gamble in Biloxi," *Jackson Clarion-Ledger*, December 19, 1987; "Gulf Ship Plans to Cast Off Due to Legal Ruling," *Biloxi Sun-Herald*, December 16, 1987; George Lammons, "Legal Issue Resurfaces," *Biloxi Sun-Herald*, December 15, 1987.
12. Blessey, interview; Blessey, USM Oral History, 14; speech delivered by Gerald Blessey on February 19, 2003, "Recent History of Legal Gambling on the Mississippi Gulf Coast," copy in authors' possession.
13. Lammons, "Reprieve Lets Gambling Ship Cruise Sound".
14. House Journal, 1988 Regular Session, 199–200; Terry R. Cassreino, "House OKs Gambling in Sound," *Biloxi Sun-Herald*, February 18, 1988; Dan Davis, "Gambling Ships Get House OK," *Jackson Clarion-Ledger*, February 18, 1988; Norma Fields, "Gambling Legalized on Ship Off Gulf Coast," *Northeast Mississippi Daily Journal*, February 18, 1988.
15. Terry R. Cassreino, "*Europa* Rejected Again as Council Members Lobby," *Biloxi Sun-Herald*, March 31, 1988; Blessey, interview.

16. George Lammons, "*Europa Star* Will Pull Out of Biloxi," *Biloxi Sun-Herald*, November 11, 1988.

17. Unless otherwise specifically cited, the narrative in this section of the chapter is based on interviews with Rick Carter, Tommy Gollott, Bob Montgomery, Scott Levanway, Sonny Merideth, Brad Dye, Glenn Endris, and Buddy Medlin.

18. Morgan Falkner, "Businessmen Plan Gulfport-Based Ship," *Biloxi Sun-Herald*, February 24, 1988; Molpus, interview.

19. "Mississippi Gaming Pioneer Dies," *Biloxi Sun-Herald*, October 16, 2003.

20. Stuart Down, "Pride of Mississippi Adds a Little Las Vegas to Waters Off Gulfport," *Biloxi Sun-Herald*, February 20, 1989.

21. Terry R. Cassreino, "Pride Bills Face Crucial Senate Vote," *Biloxi Sun-Herald*, March 23, 1989; Joe O'Keefe, "Senate to Vote on Legalizing Casino Gambling Aboard Cruise Ship," *Jackson Clarion-Ledger*, March 23, 1989.

22. Senate Journal, 1989 Regular Session, 1661–1662. In addition, one senator voted "present" and two senators "paired" on the vote, a quaint practice that allows an absent senator to allow a senator present on the floor to announce how the former "would have voted" if present. Only one of the nine senators was actually recorded as absent when the Senate opened for business that day and took the roll call.

23. Terry R. Cassreino and Sharon Stallworth, "Gambling Bill Gets OK in Senate," *Biloxi Sun-Herald*, March 24, 1989; Dan Davis, "Senate OKs Bill That Allows Gambling in Mississippi Sound," *Jackson Clarion-Ledger*, March 24, 1989.

24. House Journal, 1989 Regular Session, 850–852.

25. Terry R. Cassreino, "Gambling Tax Bills Look Safe," *Biloxi Sun-Herald*, March 25, 1989; Joe O'Keefe, "Gambling Bill Passes House, Goes to Mabus," *Jackson Clarion-Ledger*, March 25, 1989.

26. Robert Naylor Jr., "Legislator Says He'll Offer Bill to Allow Riverboat Gambling," *Biloxi Sun-Herald*, November 27, 1989.

27. Andy Kanengiser, "Senate Approves Bill That Would Legalize Gambling on Riverboats," *Jackson Clarion-Ledger*, February 3, 1990.

28. House Journal, 1990 Regular Session, 711–712; Andy Kanengiser, "Riverboat Gambling Still Afloat after House Fight; New Roll of the Dice Possible," *Jackson Clarion-Ledger*, March 8, 1990.

29. Senate Journal, 1990 Regular Session, 1431–1436. No senators were absent on the morning roll call.

30. Louise Taylor, "Record Vote Clears Berth for Harrison," *Biloxi Sun-Herald*, March 11, 1992.

31. Blessey, interview.

32. Louise Taylor, "Nevada Casino Owners Are Not Very Supportive," *Biloxi Sun-Herald*, August 1, 1992.

33. Sources for this section include an interview the authors had with Bobby Moak as well as Greg Lacour, "24 Hours of Wind, Water, and the Horror of Hurricane Katrina," *Biloxi Sun-Herald*, September 4, 2005; Jerry Hirsch, "Katrina's Aftermath," *Los Angeles Times*, September 5, 2005; Arnold Lindsay, "Hurricane Katrina," *Jackson Clarion-Ledger*,

September 3, 2005; Suzette Parmley, "Mississippi's Gaming Industry Devastated," *Philadelphia Inquirer*, September 1, 2005; Jill Zeman, "Scene on the Gulf Coast," *Lincoln (Neb.) Journal Star*, September 4, 2005.

34. These are excerpts from a letter Donald E. Wildmon, founder and chairman of the American Family Association, posted on his Web site during the special session.

35. Emily Wagster Pettus, "Barbour Woos Conservative Lawmakers Over Onshore Casinos," *New Orleans Times-Picayune*, September 26, 2005.

36. Geoff Pender, "House OKs Onshore Casinos," *Biloxi Sun-Herald*, October 1, 2005.

CHAPTER 15. REPUBLICANS GAIN THE GOVERNOR'S MANSION, 1991

1. The section is based on personal files and records maintained by the authors, experiences with the Mabus administration and the 1991 campaign, and subsequent discussions over the years with participants during the period 1988 to 1991, as well as on interviews the authors had with Verne Kennedy, Billy Powell, Lanny Griffith, Tim Carpenter, Steve Patterson, Pam Johnson, Clarke Reed, and Ray Mabus.

2. Jay Eubank, "Mabus Slashes $15M from State Budget," *Jackson Clarion-Ledger*, January 16, 1991.

3. Jay Eubank and Andy Kanengiser, "Mabus to Lawmakers: No Tax Hike for Education," *Jackson Clarion-Ledger*, January 4, 1990.

4. Eubank and Kanengiser, "No Tax Hike for Education."

5. Jay Eubank, "Mabus: Death of Education Funding Would Mean Death of State's Dreams," *Jackson Clarion-Ledger*, June 18, 1990.

6. Carpenter, interview.

7. Jay Eubank, "Republican Governor's Race Hotter," *Jackson Clarion-Ledger*, August 19, 1991.

8. Billy Powell, interview with the authors.

9. Adam Nossiter, *Of Long Memory: Mississippi and the Murder of Medgar Evers* (Reading, Mass.: Addison-Wesley, 1994), 226.

10. Jay Eubank, "Dowdy Vows to End 4 Years of Governor-Legislative Feuding," *Jackson Clarion-Ledger*, September 13, 1991; Andy Kanengiser, "Dowdy to Announce Candidacy for Governor," *Jackson Clarion-Ledger*, May 12, 1991.

11. Andy Kanengiser, "Lost or Last! Top Post and Past Spice Debate," *Jackson Clarion-Ledger*, July 13, 1991.

12. Jay Eubank, "Bitterness Fills Debate between Mabus, Fordice," *Jackson Clarion-Ledger*, October 20, 1991.

13. Andy Kanengiser, "Gubernatorial Candidates Offer Education to Retirees on Funding for Universities," *Jackson Clarion-Ledger*, November 2, 1991.

14. Reed Branson, "Miss. Lawmakers Override 1990 Veto on Regulation of Abortion Clinics," *Memphis Commercial Appeal*, January 18, 1991; Jay Eubank, "Abortion Bill Veto Overridden," *Jackson Clarion-Ledger*, March 29, 1991.

15. Stephen D. Shaffer and David Breaux, "Mississippi Politics in the 1990s: Ideology and Performance," paper presented to the American Political Science Association, 1997.
16. See, for example, Sarah C. Campbell, "Disenchanted Black Voters Hurt Mabus," *Jackson Clarion-Ledger*, November 6, 1991; and Nossiter, *Of Long Memory*, 227.
17. Verne Kennedy, interview with the authors.
18. Cathy Hayden, "More Money No Answer to Better Schools, Fordice Says," *Jackson Clarion-Ledger*, January 23, 1992.
19. House Journal, 1992 Regular Session, 1091; Senate Journal, 1992 Regular Session, 2215.
20. O'Keefe, UNC Oral History, 28.
21. Reed Branson, "Sonny Merideth Won't Seek Re-Election as Miss. Lawmaker," *Memphis Commercial Appeal*, August 8, 1991.
22. Richard Compere, "Public Sector Collective Bargaining in Mississippi: An Argument for Acceptance," *Mississippi Law Journal* 56 (August 1986); Lynn Watkins and Henrietta Buck, "Legislature Oks Teacher Pay Hike Plan," *Jackson Clarion-Ledger*, March 18, 1985.
23. Merideth, interview.
24. Sid Salter, interview with Wayne Dowdy, *Jackson Clarion-Ledger*, August 7, 2005.

CHAPTER 16. THE POLITICS OF REAPPORTIONMENT, 1992–1993

We found background information on Bennie Thompson and his campaign in James M. Glaser, *Race, Campaign Politics and the Realignment in the South* (New Haven, Conn.: Yale University Press, 1996), and Joe Klein, "The Emancipation of Bolton, Mississippi," *Esquire*, December 1985. For the 1992 election in general, we relied on Jack W. Germond and Jules Witcover, *Mad as Hell: Revolt at the Ballot Box,* 1992 (New York: Warner Books, 1993).

Court Cases

Watkins v. Mabus, 771 F.Supp. 789 (1991)
Watkins v. Fordice, 791 F.Supp. 646 (1992)

1. This was the opening sentence in the August 9, 1991, article filed by the *Washington Post* political reporter Thomas B. Edsall, who was covering the Mississippi legislative reapportionment fight: Thomas B. Edsall, "Redistricting on Hold for a Year; Court Defers Action after Legislature's Black-Liberal Coalition Disintegrates," *Washington Post*, August 9, 1991.
2. For the section of on the House leadership fight and legislative reapportionment, we relied on interviews with Tim Ford, Tommy Walman, Ayres Haxton, Bobby Moak, Cecil Simmons, Ed Perry, Danny Cupit, and Tommy Reynolds.
3. House Journal, 1990 Regular Session, 54–55.

4. Andy Kanengiser, "Efforts to Alter House Rules Fail by 1 Vote," *Jackson Clarion-Ledger*, January 6, 1990; Ford, interview.

5. Andy Kanengiser, "Ford Foes: House Speaker Trying to Purge Opponents," *Jackson Clarion-Ledger*, April 14, 1991; Reed Branson, "The Sound You Don't Hear Is Redistricting Wrangle," *Memphis Commercial Appeal*, March 22, 1991.

6. Bennie Thompson, MDAH Oral History, August 31, 1997, 16–17.

7. "Wrangling Over Redistricting: Two Views; A Fair Shake for Minorities," *Memphis Commercial Appeal*, May 10, 1992.

8. Reed Branson, "Decision Time: Rival Remap Plans Go to Floor," *Memphis Commercial Appeal*, April 27, 1991.

9. House Journal, 1991 Regular Session, 1246–1263; Jay Eubanks and Andy Kanengiser, "Voting Lines, Battle Lines Drawn," *Jackson Clarion-Ledger*, April 28, 1991.

10. Reed Branson, "Suit Seeks Court-Ordered Redistricting in Mississippi," *Memphis Commercial Appeal*, July 2, 1991; Jay Eubank, "Stop Elections, Say Opponents of District Lines," *Jackson Clarion-Ledger*, July 2, 1991.

11. Jay Eubank, "Justice Dept. Rejects State's District Lines," *Jackson Clarion-Ledger*, July 3, 1991.

12. Jay Eubank, "Racial Slurs Mar Work on Voting Lines," *Jackson Clarion-Ledger*, July 14, 1991; Ayres Haxton, interview with the authors.

13. Reed Branson, "Judges Open Redistrict Debate to More Voices," *Memphis Commercial Appeal*, July 16, 1991; Reed Branson, "Judges Warn Miss.: Settle Remap Fight or We Redraw Lines," *Memphis Commercial Appeal*, July 27, 1991.

14. Adam Nossiter, "Blacks, Whites Wheel and Deal Over Mississippi Reapportionment," *Atlanta Constitution*, July 27, 1991.

15. Jay Eubank, "As Many as 11 Redistricting Plans Offered," *Jackson Clarion-Ledger*, July 25, 1991; Andy Kanengiser, "Factions in Redistricting Flap Work against Clock," *Jackson Clarion-Ledger*, July 26, 1991.

16. Branson, "Decision Time."

17. Tom Baxter, "Politics, Redistricting Blurs the Lines in Mississippi," *Atlanta Constitution*, August 1, 1991.

18. Edsall, "Mississippi Redistricting on Hold."

19. See, for example, Jay Eubank, "Voting-Line Battle Remains Alive, Well with Judges' Rebuff," *Jackson Clarion-Ledger*, July 31, 1991; and Jay Eubank, "Schism Develops among Black Legislators Over House Deal," *Jackson Clarion-Ledger*, July 31, 1991.

20. Jay Eubank, "Lawmakers Will Run in Old Districts," *Jackson Clarion-Ledger*, August 3, 1991; *Watkins v. Mabus*, 771 F.Supp. 789 (August 1991). The *Watkins v. Mabus* decision was upheld by the U.S. Supreme Court on November 12, 1991, at 502 U.S. 954.

21. House Journal, 1992 Regular Session, 37–38.

22. House Journal, 1992 Regular Session, 189–191.

23. *Watkins v. Fordice*, 791 F. Supp. 646 (May, 1992); Paul Barton, "Justice OK's Miss. House Remap Plan; Hits Senate Plan," *Memphis Commercial Appeal*, March 31, 1992; Sarah C. Campbell, "House Debate Today on Remap," *Jackson Clarion-Ledger*, February 14, 1992.

24. House Journal, 1993 Regular Session, 152–154.
25. House Journal, 2000 Regular Session, 30–31; Ford, interview; Perry, interview.
26. Stephen D. Shaffer, "Mississippi 1992 Elections: Friends and Neighbors Fight the Liberal Label," in Steed, Moreland, and Baker, *1992 Presidential Campaigns*.
27. Griffith, interview.
28. Espy, interview.
29. Sarah C. Campbell and Jay Eubank, "Hesitant Mabus Calls Special Session to Consider Districts," *Jackson Clarion-Ledger*, December 12, 1991.
30. Jay Eubank, "Stronger Black Voting District Approved," *Jackson Clarion-Ledger*, December 21, 1991.
31. Thompson, interview; Joe Klein, "The Emancipation of Bolton, Mississippi," *Esquire*, December 1985, 258–262.
32. Andy Kanengiser, "GOP Selects Yazoo City Man House Candidate," *Jackson Clarion-Ledger*, February 14, 1993.
33. Steve Walton, "Will Espys Build Empire on Politics?" *Jackson Clarion-Ledger*, March 21, 1993.
34. Jimmie Gates, "Thompson Waging Grass-Roots Campaign for 2nd District Post," *Jackson Clarion-Ledger*, March 25, 1993.
35. Glaser, *Race*, 147–159.
36. Espy, interview.

CHAPTER 17. THE GOP CONSOLIDATES POWER, 1994–1996

1. Mac Gordon, "After 53 Years, Whitten Says Enough," *Jackson Clarion-Ledger*, April 6, 1994.
2. For this section, we relied on Ward Sinclair, "House Power Broker's Rise," *Washington Post*, December 26, 1978; Gordon, "After 53 Years"; Andy Kanengiser, "Bush Joins Mississippi in Recognizing Whitten's Service," *Jackson Clarion-Ledger*, January 26, 1991; Emily Wagster and Butch John, "The Chairman Lays Down the Gavel," *Jackson Clarion-Ledger*, September 10, 1995; Marty Russell, "Jamie Whitten: 1910–1995," *Northeast Mississippi Daily Journal*, September 10, 1995; Guyton, interview; and Neal R. Peirce, *The Deep South States of America* (New York: W. W. Norton, 1974), 201–203.
3. James W. Brosnam, "Whitten Ousted as Key House Chairman," *Memphis Commercial Appeal*, December 8, 1992; Craig Winneker, "Mississippi Chairs Face Ouster Tues. Trouble for Whitten, Montgomery," *Roll Call*, December 7, 1992.
4. *Congressional Quarterly Almanac*, 103rd Congress, 2nd Session, 1994 (Washington, D.C.: Congressional Quarterly, 1995), 14–18, 561–592.
5. Mac Gordon, "Republican Fighting Clinton Administration," *Jackson Clarion-Ledger*, October 24, 1994.
6. Bill Minor, "Mississippi Joins Nation in Political Mud-Slinging," *Jackson Clarion-Ledger*, November 6, 1994.
7. Bill Minor, "When 1st District Runoff Ends, Both Party Nominees Will Be Bloody," *Jackson Clarion-Ledger*, June 26, 1994.

8. Mac Gordon, "Wheeler, Wicker to Face Off," *Jackson Clarion-Ledger*, June 29, 1994.
9. Mac Gordon, "Democrat Refutes Ties to President's Policies," *Jackson Clarion-Ledger*, October 24, 1994.
10. *Jackson Clarion-Ledger* analysis of Roger Wicker's ad, October 30, 1994.
11. Mac Gordon, "Fordice: Don't Link Change to Re-Election Bid," *Jackson Clarion-Ledger*, January 2, 1994. This section is based on personal files and records maintained by the authors, experiences with the Fordice administration and involvement in the 1995 campaign, subsequent discussions over the years with participants during the period 1992 to 1996, and interviews the authors had with Verne Kennedy, Billy Powell, Lanny Griffith, Dick Molpus, Danny Cupit, and Clarke Reed.
12. Sarah C. Campbell and Reagan Walker, "Fordice Bristles at Federal Interference," *Jackson Clarion-Ledger*, January 18, 1992; "Governor Sorry about Guard Gaffe," *Jackson Clarion-Ledger*, January 24, 1992.
13. "Fordice Remarks on Religion Get Notice," *Jackson Clarion-Ledger*, November 18, 1992.
14. Sid Salter, "Fordice Admits Marital Trouble," *Jackson Clarion-Ledger*, April 9, 1993.
15. Andy Kanengiser, "Governor's Wife Says No Divorce," *Jackson Clarion-Ledger*, April 10, 1993.
16. Andy Kanengiser, "Fordices Vow to Work on Marriage—Privately," *Jackson Clarion-Ledger*, April 14, 1993.
17. Emily Wagster, "No Honeymoon in Fordice-Molpus Debate," *Jackson Clarion-Ledger*, April 14, 1995; Mark Leggett, "Fordice, Molpus Kick Off Campaign in Feisty Debate," *Northeast Mississippi Daily Journal*, April 14, 1995.
18. Emily Wagster, "Governor's PRIME Proposal Won't Be on Ballots in 1996," *Jackson Clarion-Ledger*, October 5, 1995.
19. Emily Wagster, "Fordice Urges Supporters to Push Tax Cut," *Jackson Clarion-Ledger*, January 15, 1995.
20. Emily Wagster, "Governor's Tax Cut Plan Looks Dead," *Jackson Clarion-Ledger*, February 23, 1995.
21. Emily Wagster, "Stubborn House Kills Tax Cuts," *Jackson Clarion-Ledger*, February 24, 1995.
22. Sid Salter, "Who Won Neshoba Fair Debate?" *Jackson Clarion-Ledger*, August 10, 1995; Bill Minor, "Raucous Debate Had Little Substance," *Jackson Clarion-Ledger*, August 10, 1995.
23. Bobby Harrison, "Fordice, Molpus Swap Barbs," *Northeast Mississippi Daily Journal*, August 4, 1995; "Fordice, Molpus Engage in Historic Gubernatorial Debate," *Neshoba Democrat*, August 9, 1995.
24. Mac Gordon, "Fordice, Molpus Squabble after Debate," *Jackson Clarion-Ledger*, October 25, 1995; Kennedy, interview; Molpus, interview.
25. Emily Wagster and Mac Gordon, "Veto Sends Lawmakers Back to Work," *Jackson Clarion-Ledger*, April 7, 1995.
26. Alexander P. Lamis, ed., *Southern Politics in the 1990s* (Baton Rouge: Louisiana State University Press, 1999), 263–265.

27. Reed Branson, "Rep. Parker Switches to GOP," *Memphis Commercial Appeal*, November 11, 1995.

28. John Dittmer introduction to Aaron Henry with Constance Curry, *Aaron Henry: The Fire Ever Burning* (Jackson: University Press of Mississippi, 2000), x.

29. B. Drummond Ayres Jr., "In the South of the '70's, Jackson Integrates Pools," *New York Times*, June 14, 1975.

30. Sonny Montgomery, MSU Oral History, 5–6.

31. Minor, *Eyes on Mississippi*, 317.

32. Bill McAllister, "Veterans' Champion on Hill Will Retire," *Washington Post*, October 3, 1995; *The Almanac of American Politics, 1996* (Washington, D.C.: National Journal, 1995), 756–757.

33. Stephen D. Shaffer and Randolph Burnside, "Mississippi: GOP Consolidates Its Gains," in Laurence W. Moreland and Robert P. Steed, eds., *The 1996 Presidential Election in the South* (Westport, Conn.: Praeger, 1997), 6, obtained from Shaffer's Mississippi State University Web site.

CHAPTER 18. TOBACCO, 1997–1998

Books that have been written about the tobacco settlement include Michael Orey, *Assuming the Risk: The Mavericks, the Lawyers, and the Whistle-Blowers Who Beat Big Tobacco* (Boston: Little Brown, 1999); Dan Zegart, *Civil Warriors: The Legal Siege on the Tobacco Industry* (New York: Delacorte Press, 2000); Carrick Mollenkamp, Adam Levy, Joseph Menn, and Jeffrey Rothfeder, *The People vs. Big Tobacco: How the States Took on the Cigarette Giants* (Princeton, N.J.: Bloomberg Press, 1998); Peter Pringle, *Cornered: Big Tobacco at the Bar of Justice* (New York: Henry Holt, 1998); and Michael Pertschuk, *Smoke in their Eyes: Lessons in Movement Leadership from the Tobacco Wars* (Nashville, Tenn.: Vanderbilt University Press, 2001).

1. The value of the settlement was ultimately raised to $4.1 billion as Mississippi gained additional money from the settlements of other states with tobacco companies.

2. The following sections are based on personal files and records maintained by the authors, experiences with the principals, subsequent discussions over the years with participants during the period 1995 to 1998, as well as with interviews the authors had with Richard Scruggs and Mike Moore; Paul Brodeur, *Outrageous Misconduct: The Asbestos Industry on Trial* (New York: Pantheon Books, 1985); Michael Orey, *Assuming the Risk: The Mavericks, the Lawyers, and the Whistle-Blowers Who Beat Big Tobacco* (Boston: Little Brown, 1999); Michael Pertschuk, *Smoke in Their Eyes: Lessons in Movement Leadership from the Tobacco Wars* (Nashville, Tenn.: Vanderbilt University Press, 2001); "The Tobacco Settlement: Practical Implications and the Future of Tort Law," *Mississippi Law Journal* 67 (Spring 1998): 847–881; Myron Lewis and Henry Weinstein, "Dramatic Events Helped Corner Elusive Industry," *Los Angeles Times*, June 21, 1997; Carrick Mollenkamp, "Drama Had Huge Cast, Folksy Star," *Richmond Times*

Dispatch, June 22, 1997; Kevin Sack, "Tobacco Industry's Dogged Nemesis," *New York Times*, April 6, 1997; Alix M. Freedman and Suein L. Hwang, "Seven Men with a Common Goal," a *Wall Street Journal* story that ran in the *Seattle Times*, July 16, 1997; "Michael C. Moore: He Smoked Out Tobacco," *National Law Journal*, December 29, 1997; transcript of the interview Jeffrey Wigand had with *60 Minutes* at www.jeffreywigand.com; and transcript of ABC News Special Report, "The Tobacco Files," September 8, 2004.

3. Orey, *Assuming the Risk*, 241.
4. Orey, *Assuming the Risk*, 239.
5. Philip J. Hilts, "Tobacco Company Was Silent on Hazards," *New York Times*, May 7, 1994; see also Myron Levin, "Tobacco Firm Lawyers Try to Smoke Out Possible Mole," *Los Angeles Times*, May 17, 1994.
6. Orey, *Assuming the Risk*, 197–198.
7. Mike Moore, interview with the authors.
8. Jack Elliott Jr., "Tobacco Industry Asks Court to Dismiss Medicaid Claims," Associated Press, February 20, 1996.
9. Sarah C. Campbell, "Fordice Critical of Lawsuit Mentality," *Memphis Commercial Appeal*, May 25, 1994.
10. Orey, *Assuming the Risk*, 304–305.
11. Richard Scruggs, interview with the authors.
12. Emily Wagster, "Governor Sues Attorney General," *Jackson Clarion-Ledger*, February 17, 1996; Jack Elliott Jr., "Governor Sues Attorney General to Block Tobacco Lawsuit," Associated Press, February 16, 1996; Reed Branson, "Snuff Tobacco Lawsuit, Fordice Asks Court," *Memphis Commercial Appeal*, February 17, 1996.
13. *In re Kirk Fordice*, 691 So.2d 429.
14. Myron Levin and Henry Weinstein, "Mississippi High Court Allows Suit against Tobacco Firms," *Los Angeles Times*, March 14, 1997.
15. Reed Branson, "Tobacco—The Green Light Is On for Miss. to Sue for Reparation," *Memphis Commercial Appeal*, March 14, 1997.
16. Henry Weinstein and Myron Levin, "$368 Billion Tobacco Accord," *Los Angeles Times*, June 21, 1997.
17. Pertschuk, *Smoke in Their Eyes*, 283; Scruggs, interview; Moore, interview; Lott, interview. See also Bob Hohler, Michael Kranish, Brian McGrory, and Estella Duran, "How the Tobacco Deal Went Up in Smoke," *Boston Globe*, June 19, 1998.
18. Transcript of ABC News Special Report, "The Tobacco Files," September 8, 2004.

CHAPTER 19. THE LEGACY OF KIRK FORDICE, 1999

1. Senate Journal, 1996 Regular Session, January 9, 1996, 28–29.
2. Jay Eubank, "Odds Favor Fordice to Table All Gambling," *Jackson Clarion-Ledger*, January 24, 1992. This section is based on personal files and records maintained by the authors, experiences with the Fordice administration, subsequent discussions over the

years with participants during the period 1995 to 1999, and interviews the authors had with Verne Kennedy, Billy Powell, and Clarke Reed.

3. Lee Ragland, "Governor Appoints 3 to Gaming Commission," *Jackson Clarion-Ledger*, August 14, 1993.

4. Lynne Jeter, "Mississippi Mourns a Legend, Builder, Businessman, Governor," *Mississippi Business Journal*, September 13–19, 2004.

5. Lee Ragland, "Panel May Require Land-Based Ventures for Casinos," *Jackson Clarion-Ledger*, August 13, 1994; Lee Ragland, "Gaming's House of Cards Rests on Hotel Foundation, Panel Says," *Jackson Clarion-Ledger*, August 24, 1994.

6. Denise von Herrman, Robert Ingram, and William C. Smith, "Gaming in the Mississippi Economy," a report produced by the University of Southern Mississippi, June 30, 2000.

7. Joseph Ammerman, "Governor Lashes Out at Lawmakers," *Jackson Clarion-Ledger*, March 19, 1998.

8. Senate Journal, 1999 Regular Session, 131–133.

9. Butch John and Emily Wagster, "Fordice, Traveling Alone, Injured in Wreck," *Jackson Clarion-Ledger*, November 6, 1996.

10. Emily Wagster, "Fordice, Woman Vacation," *Jackson Clarion-Ledger*, June 9, 1999.

11. Emily Wagster, "Fordice to Seek Divorce," *Jackson Clarion-Ledger*, June 11, 1999.

12. Emily Wagster, "Other Woman Hurt Marriage," *Jackson Clarion-Ledger*, June 24, 1999.

13. This section is based on personal files and records maintained by the authors, experiences with the Fordice administration and the 1999 campaign, subsequent discussions over the years with participants during the period 1995 to 1999, and interviews the authors had with Verne Kennedy, Billy Powell, Clarke Reed, Ed Cole, and Billy Mounger.

14. Mark Leggett, "Fordice First to Punch Time Clock," *Northeast Mississippi Daily Journal*, as appeared in the *New Orleans Times-Picayune*, July 24, 1994; "Prisons, Welfare Still Focus, Says Gov.," *Memphis Commercial Appeal*, August 4, 1994.

15. Powell, interview; Gina Holland, "Fordice, Briggs Unite in Preparation for '95," *Memphis Commercial Appeal*, December 3, 1994.

16. Sandra Nettles, "Parker Explains Why He Switched to GOP," *McComb Enterprise-Journal*," November 12, 1995.

17. Cole, interview.

18. Joseph Ammerman, "Musgrove Combative, Parker Irritated in Columbus Debate," *Jackson Clarion-Ledger*, October 21, 1999; Emily Wagster, "Musgrove, Parker Spar Over Education, TV Ads," *Jackson Clarion-Ledger*, October 19, 1999; Emily Wagster, "Gubernatorial Candidates Making Final Push," *Jackson Clarion-Ledger*, October 25, 1999.

19. Emily Wagster, "Musgrove's Road Work Intensifies," *Jackson Clarion-Ledger*, October 31, 1999; Joseph Ammerman, "Parker Drives Hard to Stay on Course," *Jackson Clarion-Ledger*, October 31, 1999.

20. Emily Wagster, "Musgrove Cut Parker's Lead in Final Days," *Jackson Clarion-Ledger*, November 6, 1999.

21. Mounger, interview.

22. Eric C. Clark, "The Mississippi Constitutional Convention of 1890: A Political Analysis" (Master's thesis, University of Mississippi, 1975), 82–83; Sallis, "Color Line in Mississippi Politics," 299–300; Kirwan, *Revolt of the Rednecks*, 79–81.
23. Emily Wagster, "Fordice: Accept Popular Vote," *Jackson Clarion-Ledger*, November 12, 1999.
24. House Journal, 2000 Regular Session, 31–33; Emily Wagster, "House to Choose Governor," *Jackson Clarion-Ledger*, November 20, 1999.
25. Emily Wagster, "Musgrove Wins," *Jackson Clarion-Ledger*, January 5, 2000; Orley Hood, "Historic Race Runs Final Lap," *Jackson Clarion-Ledger*, January 5, 2000; House Journal, 2000 Regular Session, 32–33.

CHAPTER 20. THE STATE FLAG AND CONGRESSIONAL REAPPORTIONMENT, 2000–2001

For background on the flag issue, we read Robert E. Bonner, "Flag Culture and the Consolidation of Confederate Nationalism" *Journal of Southern History* 68 (May 2002); David G. Sansing, "A Brief History of the Confederate Flags," published on the Web at Mississippi History Now, an online publication of the Mississippi Historical Society, and accessed on September 6, 2004; and Judge Leslie Southwick, "Separation of Powers at the State Level: Interpretations and Challenges in Mississippi," *Mississippi Law Journal* 72 (Spring 2003).

Court Cases

Mississippi Division of the United Sons of Confederate Veterans v. Mississippi State Conference of NAACP Branches, 774 So.2d 388 (2000)
Smith v. Clark, 189 F.Supp.2d 502 (2001)
Smith v. Clark, 189 F.Supp.2d 503 (2002)
Smith v. Clark, 189 F.Supp.2d 529 (2002)
Branch v. Smith, 538 U.S. 254 (2003)
Mauldin v. Branch, 866 So.2d 429 (2003)

1. Reprinted in Robert E. Bonner, "Flag Culture and the Consolidation of Confederate Nationalism," *Journal of Southern History*, 67 (May 2002): 314.
2. David G. Sansing, "A Brief History of the Confederate Flags," published on the Web at Mississippi History Now, an online publication of the Mississippi Historical Society, accessed September 6, 2004.
3. Jimmie Gates, "Lawsuit Targets Confederate Emblem," *Jackson Clarion-Ledger*, April 20, 1993.
4. *Mississippi Division of the United Sons of Confederate Veterans v. Mississippi State Conference of NAACP Branches*, 774 So.2d 388 (2000); see also Judge Leslie Southwick, "Separation of Powers at the State Level: Interpretations and Challenges in Mississippi," *Mississippi Law Journal* 72 (Spring 2003): 927–1027; and Andy Kanengiser and Emily Wagster, "Flag Rights Issue Rejected," *Jackson Clarion-Ledger*, May 5, 2000.

5. Emily Wagster, "Battle Lines Clear at Hearing on Flag," *Jackson Clarion-Ledger*, October 27, 2000.

6. Emily Wagster, "Jeers, Shouts, Hecklers, Mar Turbulent State Flag Meeting," *Jackson Clarion-Ledger*, November 3, 2000.

7. Emily Wagster, "Debate on Flag Helping?" *Jackson Clarion-Ledger*, November 13, 2000.

8. Emily Wagster, "Whites Appeal for Changing Flag at Final Hearing," *Jackson Clarion-Ledger*, November 14, 2000.

9. Robert Schoenberger, "Is State's Image at Stake?" *Jackson Clarion-Ledger*, February 5, 2001.

10. Bradley G. Bond, *Mississippi: A Documentary History* (Jackson: University Press of Mississippi, 2003), 301.

11. House Journal, 2001 Regular Session, 59–60; Senate Journal, 2001 Regular Session, 105–107; Chapter 301, Laws of 2001.

12. Jerry Mitchell, "Memories of Brave Men Should Live on with Flag," *Jackson Clarion-Ledger*, April 15, 2001.

13. An earlier version of these statistics was included in the *2002 Handbook of the Mississippi Legislature*, distributed by Capitol Resources, LLC and Butler, Snow, O'Mara, Stevens, and Cannada, PLLC. The statistics in this section were updated using the revised precinct returns, courtesy of Capitol Resources, LLC.

14. Emily Wagster, "Flag Vote Date High Priority," *Jackson Clarion-Ledger*, January 1, 2001.

15. Wagster, "Battle Lines Clear."

16. The section is based on personal files and records maintained by the authors; experiences with the reapportionment litigation; subsequent discussions over the years with participants during the period 2001 to 2002; interviews the authors had with Billy Powell, Billy Mounger, Grant Fox, Rob McDuff, Tim Ford, and Hob Bryan; the numerous state and federal court decisions resulting from the reapportionment litigation, which are itemized in the bibliographical essay; and the interviews that David F. Maron and J. William Manuel conducted with Rob McDuff, Carlton Reeves, and Mike Wallace in the December 2002–January 2003 issue of the *Mississippi Lawyer*.

17. Merideth, interview.

18. Emily Wagster, "Lawmakers Look at Redistricting Options," *Jackson Clarion-Ledger*, August 10, 2001; Emily Wagster, "Tuck: Redraw Lines Objectively," *Jackson Clarion-Ledger*, August 21, 2001; Patrice Sawyer, "House Speaker Says Two Big Hurdles Remain for Lawmakers," *Jackson Clarion-Ledger*, October 18, 2001; Gordon, interview.

19. Patrice Sawyer, "Tuck: Redistricting at Impasse," *Jackson Clarion-Ledger*, October 20, 2001.

20. Patrice Sawyer, "Ford Predicts Court Fight Over Redistricting," *Jackson Clarion-Ledger*, November 4, 2001.

21. Patrice Sawyer, "Judge OKs Democrats' Map," *Jackson Clarion-Ledger*, December 22, 2001.

22. Patrice Sawyer and Gregg Meyer, "Judges Go with Own Map Specs," *Jackson Clarion-Ledger*, February 5, 2002.

23. *Smith v. Clark*, 189 F.Supp. 2d 512 (2002).

24. Patrice Sawyer, "GOP Accused of Remap Sabotage," *Jackson Clarion-Ledger*, February 9, 2002.
25. *Smith v. Clark*, 189 F.Supp. 509.
26. Ana Radelat, "Info Request May Snag Remap Plan," *Jackson Clarion-Ledger*, February 15, 2002.
27. *Smith v. Clark*, F.Supp. 548; *Branch v. Smith*, 538 U.S. 254 (2003).
28. J. William Manuel, "Interview with Rob McDuff and Carlton Reeves about Mississippi Congressional Redistricting Appeal to the Supreme Court of the United States," *Mississippi Lawyer* (December 2002–January 2003): 12.
29. David F. Maron, "Interview with Mike Wallace about the Mississippi Congressional Redistricting Appeal to the United States Supreme Court," *Mississippi Lawyer* (December 2002–January 2003): 15.

CHAPTER 21. THE CONSEQUENCES OF TORT REFORM, 2002

Two books written about the litigation against the asbestos industry that we referred to are Paul Brodeur, *Outrageous Misconduct: The Asbestos Industry on Trial* (New York: Pantheon Books, 1985), and Michael Bowker, *Fatal Deception: The Untold Story of Asbestos* (Emmaus, Pa.: Rodale, 2003).

We found very helpful a report that was compiled for the National Center for State Courts by Beverly Pettigrew Kraft, dated November 22, 2002, and entitled "2002 Appellate Court Races in Mississippi: the Candidates, the Issues and the Backdrop." We also found useful the transcript of a November 2001 symposium on Mississippi's civil justice system that was sponsored by the University of Mississippi Law School and that was reprinted in the *Mississippi Law Journal* 71 (Winter 2001).

Court Cases

Jackson v. Johns-Manville Sales Corporation, 750 F.2d 1314 (1985)
Jackson v. Johns-Manville Sales Corporation, 757 F.2d 614 (1985)
Coca Cola Bottling Company, Inc. of Vicksburg v. Reeves, 486 So.2d 374 (1986).

1. Perry, interview.
2. Danny Cupit, Lance Stevens, David Baria, and Bill Liston interviews with the authors; Julie Goodman, "Gov. Calls Special Session with Twist," *Jackson Clarion-Ledger*, August 24, 2002. The election results were calculated by the authors starting with 1971, when Republicans began seriously to contest statewide and legislative elections.
3. This section is based on personal files and records maintained by the authors; experiences with the effort to pass tort reform for the period 1993 to 2006; subsequent discussions over the years with participants during this period; interviews the authors had with Verne Kennedy, Steve Dickson, Bob Montgomery, Danny Cupit, Mike Mills, Tim Ford, Richard Scruggs, Paul Benton, and John Maxey; and a confidential interview with the authors. We also found useful a report compiled for the National Center for

State Courts by Beverly Pettigrew Kraft. The report was dated November 22, 2002, and entitled "2002 Appellate Court Races in Mississippi: The Candidates, the Issues and the Backdrop," as well as the transcript of a November 2001 symposium on Mississippi's civil justice system that was sponsored by the University of Mississippi Law School and that was reprinted in the *Mississippi Law Journal* 71 (Winter 2001): 847–883.

4. Orey, *Assuming the Risk*, 231–233; Robert F. Couch, "The Ingalls Story in Mississippi," *Journal of Mississippi History* 26 (August 1964): 192–206.

5. *Jackson v. Johns-Manville Sales Corporation*, 750 F.2d 1314 (1985); Orey, *Assuming the Risk*, 97–121; Michael Bowker, *Fatal Deception: The Untold Story of Asbestos* (Emmaus, Pa.: Rodale, 2003), 165–182.

6. Bowker, *Fatal Deception*, 99–102; Orey, *Assuming the Risk*, 29–31.

7. Orey, *Assuming the Risk*, 31–65.

8. *Jackson v. Johns-Manville Sales Corporation*, 750 F.2d 1314 (1985); *Jackson v. Johns-Manville Sales Corporation*, 757 F.2d 614 (1985); Jon Frank, "Alabaman Wins Asbestosis Damages, *Biloxi Sun*, June 4, 1982; Orey, *Assuming the Risk*, 240–245.

9. Scruggs, interview.

10. Scruggs, interview. The "Coca Cola Bottling case" is *Coca Cola Bottling Company, Inc. of Vicksburg v. Reeves*, 486 So.2d 374 (1986).

11. Jim Hannaford, "Asbestos Firms Offer Settlement," *Biloxi Sun-Herald*, June 14, 1991; Emily Wagster, "Asbestos Lawsuit Jury Awards $9.26M to 6 Ingalls Workers," *Jackson Clarion-Ledger*, August 6, 1993; Tom Donnelly, "Jury Awards $2.76 Million," *Mississippi Press*, August 11, 1993.

12. House Journal, 1992 Regular Session, 426.

13. Jane Fritsch, "Sometimes, Lobbyists Strive to Keep Public in the Dark," *New York Times*, March 19, 1996. This and other revelations about the 1988–1993 M-FAIR lobbying campaign were uncovered, ironically, as part of the examination of tobacco company documents in connection with the Mississippi-led lawsuit against the tobacco industry (see, for example, Carl Deal and Joanne Doroshow, "The CALA Files," a report released in 2000 by the Center for Justice and Democracy and Public Citizen). The Fritsch article was inspired by a secret tape recording of a 1994 speech given by Neal Cohen, a consultant who worked in the Mississippi campaign on behalf of M-FAIR.

14. Jay Eubank, "Tort Reform Fight Splits Legislature," *Jackson Clarion-Ledger*, January 19, 1993.

15. Mills, interview.

16. The exact language in Section 2(c) of Chapter 302, Laws of 1993, is: "The provisions of [this law] should not apply to . . . causes of action for persons and property arising out of asbestos."

17. House Journal, 1993 Regular Session, 309.

18. Senate Journal, 1993 Regular Session, 606–607; Sarah C. Campbell, "House Bill Limits Awards for Lawsuits," *Jackson Clarion-Ledger*, February 10, 1993; Jay Eubank, "Tort Reform Bill Headed to Fordice," *Jackson Clarion-Ledger*, February 18, 1993.

19. "Record Jury Awards in '98 Include One from Miss.," *Jackson Clarion-Ledger*, January 8, 1999.

20. "Mississippi Jury Awards Five People $150 Million in Fen-Phen Trial," Associated Press, December 21, 1999. In 2004 and 2005, the U.S. Attorney for the Southern District of Mississippi successfully prosecuted several recipients of fen-phen awards for falsifying their claims.

21. See, for example, Beverly Pettigrew Kraft, "Judges Fall Behind Foes in Cash Race," *Jackson Clarion-Ledger*, October 12, 2000; "U.S. Chamber Meddling in Judicial Race Is Ill-Informed," *DeSoto Times Today*, October 19, 2000; "Supreme Court Politics: U.S. Chamber of Commerce Soaks Races with Its Cash," *Northeast Mississippi Daily Journal*, October 25, 2000; William Glaberson, "U.S. Chamber Will Promote Business Views in Court Races," *New York Times*, October 22, 2000; and Robert Lenzner and Matthew Miller, "Buying Justice," *Forbes*, July 21, 2003.

22. Peter H. Stone, "Jousting Over Judges," *National Journal*, June 24, 2000.

23. Jerry Mitchell, "Hitting the Jackpot," *Jackson Clarion-Ledger*, June 17, 2001.

24. "Mississippi Town Becomes Lawsuit Central," Fox News, June 6, 2001; "The Poor Southern County That's Big on Lawsuits," *Financial Times*, August 17, 2001; "Jury Awards Put Miss. County on Map," *Charleston Daily Mail*, July 2, 2001; Robert Pear, "Mississippi Gaining as Lawsuit Mecca," *New York Times*, August 20, 2001.

25. Lynne Wilbanks Jeter, "Doctors Rethinking Practices," *Mississippi Business Journal*, November 12–18, 2001.

26. John Porretto, "Insurer to Exit Malpractice Business," *Jackson Clarion-Ledger*, December 13, 2001.

27. Reed Branson, "Tort Reform Faces Tough Miss. Fight," *Memphis Commercial Appeal*, January 22, 2002.

28. Emily Wagster, "Adventures Put Judge in Spotlight," *Jackson Clarion-Ledger*, June 26, 2001.

29. Taken from a mailer from the Mississippi State Medical Association in authors' possession.

30. Jerry Mitchell, "U.S. Chamber Targeting Mississippi," *Jackson Clarion-Ledger*, May 4, 2002; "Doctor Warns Economic Council of Medical Crisis," Associated Press, May 21, 2002.

31. Lott, *Herding Cats*, 243–277. The *Jackson Clarion-Ledger* devoted a special section to Lott's resignation on December 21, 2002, called "Lott's Fall from Power."

CHAPTER 22. THE HALEY BARBOUR YEARS, 2003–2006

1. Henry Barbour, interview with the authors.

2. "President, Wife Receive Rousing Coast Welcome," *Jackson Clarion-Ledger*, September 9, 1969.

3. Barbour, USM oral history, 18.

4. Barbour, USM oral history, 15–23.

5. This section is based in part on interviews the authors had with Haley Barbour, Henry Barbour, Merle Flowers, John Grisham, Stuart Stevens, T. Clovis Williams, and a confidential interview.

6. Nicholas Dawidoff, "Mr. Washington Goes to Mississippi," *New York Times*, October 19, 2003.

7. Carpenter, interview.

8. Campaign finance data obtained from reports on file with the secretary of state's office. The $13.5 million includes $11.3 million reported by the Barbour campaign and $2.2 million reported by the state Republican Party, most of which came from the Republican Governors Association and which was spent on behalf of the Barbour campaign.

9. Henry Barbour, interview; copy of Musgrove's letter in authors' possession; Kyle Wingfield, "Ten Commandments Monument Removed from Alabama Courthouse Rotunda Despite Protests," August 27, 2003; Emily Wagster Pettus, "Musgrove, Barbour Say Mississippi Should Take Alabama's Ten Commandments Monument," August 27, 2003.

10. Henry Barbour, interview; "National Right to Life Endorses Tuck, Barbour," Associated Press, September 8, 2003; Shelia Hardwell Byrd, "Tuck Criticizes Blackmon for Making Abortion Challenge," Associated Press, October 1, 2003; Shelia Hardwell Byrd, "Tuck Signs Affidavit Swearing She Hasn't Had an Abortion," Associated Press, October 29, 2003.

11. Dawidoff, "Mr. Washington Goes to Mississippi."

12. In the House, Republicans started the 2000 term with thirty-three members. There were eighty-six Democrats and three independents. After the 2003 elections, Republicans had forty-six members in the House, while Democrats had seventy-six. During the course of the four-year term, five Democratic incumbents switched parties, and the elections resulted in Republicans picking up a net of eight additional seats. In the Senate, there were thirty-four Democrats and eighteen Republicans after the 1999 elections. At the end of the 2003 elections, that ratio had changed to twenty-nine Democrats and twenty-three Republicans—three incumbent Democratic senators switched parties during the four-year term, and Republican candidates took two Democratic open seats. Since the 2003 elections, Senator Ralph Doxey has switched from a Democrat to a Republican, Senator Billy Harvey has died, and there have been seven special elections to fill one vacancy in the Senate and six in the House. The Republicans won the Senate race and picked up a House seat, leaving the Senate with a twenty-seven to twenty-four Democratic majority and the House with a seventy-five to forty-seven majority. One vacancy remains in the Senate.

13. Text of Haley Barbour's speech to the legislature, in *Jackson Clarion-Ledger*, September 27, 2005.

CONCLUSION

1. Haley Barbour, interview with the authors.

2. These figures are courtesy of Capitol Resources, LLC, publishers of the 2006 *Legislative Handbook*.

3. Swan Yerger, USM oral history, 21.

4. Sid Salter, "National, State Democratic Platforms Reflect Differences," *Jackson Clarion-Ledger*, July 25, 2004.
5. Lamis, *Two-Party South*, 54.
6. The abortion legislation (SB 2922) was approved by the House on March 2, 2006, by a vote of 94–25. Of the twenty-five "no" votes, twenty-four were by African Americans. The legislation died later in the session when a conference committee could not agree on compromise language. The gay marriage legislation (HCR 56) was approved in the House on March 1, 2004, by a vote of 97–17 and was approved in the Senate on April 7, 2004, by a vote of 51–0. All seventeen "no" votes in the House were by African Americans.

INDEX